DATE DUE

AP 29 '94			
DE 22 '95			
MR 18 '97			
DE 6 '01			
DE 19 '01			
JA 29 02			
DE 17 '02			
DE 15 03			
DE 17 '04			
AP 27 '06			
MY 12 '08			
FE 12 '09			
JE 9 '10			

Democracy, Peace, and the Israeli-Palestinian Conflict

Democracy, Peace, and the Israeli-Palestinian Conflict

edited by
Edy Kaufman
Shukri B. Abed
Robert L. Rothstein

Lynne Rienner Publishers • Boulder & London

Published in the United States of America in 1993 by
Lynne Rienner Publishers, Inc.
1800 30th Street, Boulder, Colorado 80301

and in the United Kingdom by
Lynne Rienner Publishers, Inc.
3 Henrietta Street, Covent Garden, London WC2E 8LU

Library of Congress Cataloging-in-Publication Data
Democracy, peace, and the Israeli-Palestinian conflict / edited by Edy
  Kaufman, Shukri B. Abed, and Robert L. Rothstein.
    p. cm.
  Includes bibliographical references and index.
  ISBN 1-55587-342-1
    1. Jewish-Arab relations—1973- 2. Democracy—Israel. 3. Israel—
  Politics and government. 4. West Bank—Politics and government.
  5. Palestinian Arabs—Politics and government. I. Kaufman, Edy.
  II. Abed, Shukri. III. Rothstein, Robert L.
  DS119.7.D398 1993
  327.5694017'4927—dc20   92-39883
                                                              CIP

British Cataloguing in Publication Data
A Cataloguing in Publication record for this book
is available from the British Library.

Printed and bound in the United States of America

The paper used in this publication meets the requirements
of the American National Standard for Permanence of
Paper for Printed Library Materials Z39.48-1984.

Contents

CONCLUSION

Acknowledgments

This book is the collaborative product of a community that has explored the relationship between democracy and peace across national borders and continents over the last four years. In addition to the ten Arab and Jewish Israeli, Palestinian, and U.S. contributors for whom this was a matter of academic and personal concern, we would like to thank the staff of the Harry S Truman Research Institute for the Advancement of Peace at the Hebrew University of Jerusalem who were involved in the preparation of the workshops and other related activities. Particular mention should be made of Chaia Beckerman, the institute's director of publications, who with great patience and commitment supervised the preparation of the manuscript for submission to the publisher. Our gratitude also goes to the staff of the Center of International Development and Conflict Management of the University of Maryland at College Park, and in particular to its past director, Dr. Murray Polakoff, who put together the final workshop of the project, lining up the best talents and the leading authorities of the university to share their time and wisdom with the research team.

This enterprise was made possible by a generous grant from the United States Institute of Peace, which enthusiastically followed our work and hosted a session for the discussion of the preliminary findings in Washington, D.C.

And last but not least, our profound appreciation for the work of Lynne Rienner and the staff of Lynne Rienner Publishers in bringing our manuscript to print, with special mention of Project Editor Gia Hamilton, as well as copyeditor Larry Borowsky, whose efforts improved the manuscript immeasurably.

The relevance of peace and democracy to the resolution of the Israeli/Palestinian conflict has been highlighted even more since the beginning of the Middle East peace talks. We hope that the academic community that has worked so intensively on developing a concept—to the stage where such a volume of evidence and findings could be prepared—will continue to work together in this important endeavor until the shared values of peace and democracy are achieved.

Edy Kaufman
Shukri B. Abed
Robert L. Rothstein

INTRODUCTION

1

Coauthoring in a Conflict Situation

Edy Kaufman

The idea for a book that examines the connection between democracy and peace evolved gradually in the late 1980s through the observation of two parallel processes, both topical on the political science agenda at the time. The first is the extraordinary process of democratization worldwide and the growing tendency to resolve international conflict by means other than war. Although this process is not irreversible, its rapid expansion and the near failure of attempts to halt it make for a strong "sense of history"[1] in what has been referred to by Rosenau as our "turbulent world."[2] Within this context, as democratic regimes become more universal, the assumption that democracies do not wage wars against each other is put more to the test.[3] As George Quester recalled at a workshop where some chapters of this book were presented, according to the Marxist vision, socialist countries would also supposedly refrain from war among themselves. Reality has shattered such idealistic images. Even though minimal expressions of liberal democracy coincide with the absence of war, its triumph is not necessarily inevitable. Nonetheless, with both extreme left- and right-wing ideologies disappearing from the globe, democracy's development in the Middle East may increasingly become a question of *when* rather than *if*.

The second process we noticed is the slow pace of movement toward peace in the Israeli-Arab conflict, despite considerable opportunities for its resolution. We became intrigued by this question: If it is true that democratic states are not prone to fight wars between or among themselves, what conditions may accelerate and foster trends toward democratization in a region where less progress can thus far be detected than anywhere else? And, more specifically, *can the Israelis remain democratic* facing continuous wars and exercising control over a large population that has no civil and political rights? *Can the Palestinians become democratic* when their Arab brethren are lagging far behind? If these two questions can be answered positively, *how would this strengthen the prospects for peace?*

Shukri Abed and I had an early opportunity to speculate publicly on

3

these issues in 1988.[4] They continued to brew on the Mount Scopus campus as part of the Israeli-Palestinian academic dialogue at the Harry S Truman Research Institute for the Advancement of Peace. We were aware that in situations of ethnic, national, religious, linguistic, or cultural conflict, members of the confronting societies tend not to cooperate across their respective societal lines. The Israeli-Palestinian conflict has cut virtual chasms between the two peoples and persisted for over a century, rendering its resolution extremely difficult. With generous sponsorship by the United States Institute of Peace, we were able to form a joint team to conduct systematic research on the topic. In the face of serious obstacles, our strong adherence to democratic principles has been a powerful common denominator throughout, a perhaps expected bond among the members of the research team. But within this broad consensus, no claim of affective neutrality can be made. We share a clear commitment to principles such as majority rule, pluralism, and human rights. Armed with the predisposition to care and express concern for our own peoples, we applied these principles to raise delicate and often painful questions while critically studying our respective institutions or societies.

At a certain juncture, it became essential to involve a leading theorist with general expertise in the issue, and Robert Rothstein, a leading U.S. scholar, agreed to join our team at a moment when he was himself linking his general observations about democratization to political reality in the Middle East.[5] He is the only participant in the project without direct personal involvement in the Israeli-Palestinian conflict. His participation does not reflect a broader need for a third party in our conflict-resolution exercise. To be sure, third-party intervention can be of vital importance at certain stages of negotiation. Yet the fact that most of our work was conducted amidst the real conditions of asymmetry between occupier and occupied on the contested land did not affect the determination of the Israeli and Arab participants to deal with each other as equals, with shared mutual respect. We called upon Dr. Rothstein to contribute to the project for the added value of his personal expertise.

It is, however, no simple matter for Israeli and Palestinian academics to bring a joint enterprise to fruition. One of the most dramatic moments in the course of the project came a week before the outbreak of the Gulf War—when cleavages between Palestinians and Israelis were very deep—in the joint decision to proceed with rather than cancel the planned project workshop.[6] The nature of research conducted by the protagonists in real time and inside the area of conflict may differ to a certain extent from that conducted mostly by third parties in laboratory or pastoral conditions elsewhere. We hope our book provides readers with an extra measure of insight into both points of view.

The Middle East may serve as a modest example of the dynamic nature of historical processes, showing that progress in the world community is the result of long-term structural changes as well as the comprehension of realities by "epistemic communities,"[7] individuals who share a common interpretation of these processes. The small group of Jewish and Arab participants in the project differ in their views on many political events. Nevertheless, all feel that in the last decade of the twentieth century, the swelling number of democratic regimes[8] taking power in whole regions of the world (Latin America, Eastern Europe) and in individual, scattered countries is a distinctive and extraordinary phenomenon.

Together, we have also examined the premise of the correlation between democracy and peace with an eye to refining it. In doing so, we became increasingly aware of the danger of generalizing, given the expansion of democracies that are new and fragile. Still, the premise has held true so far.

In supporting the idea of democracy, the research team works within the formal consensus of both the Israeli and Palestinian body politics. From general statements of adherence to democratic principles expressed in both sides' declarations of independence to the rhetoric of leaders such as Yassir Arafat and Ariel Sharon, forms of commitment to democracy are abundant. We concur that the claim of some Israeli political leaders that Israel is the only democracy in the Middle East need not be interpreted as a unilateral wish to perpetuate this situation. Rather than making a self-fulfilling prophecy of the statement that the Jewish state is to remain forever the only democracy and hence the preferred partner of the Western world, the sensible complementary question could be phrased as follows: What measures can be undertaken to ensure that Israel will not remain the only democracy in the region?

Even if one assumes a positive attitude among Israeli leaders toward the advancement of democracy in the region, it may not be within their power to affect processes throughout the Middle East. However, history shows that when democratic states have gained control of the destiny of another people as a result of war, they have made conscious choices affecting the democratization process among that population. Palestinian trends in the Occupied Territories can definitely be influenced by Israeli policies. At different stages, Israeli defense ministers have supported more or less democratic expressions of Palestinian leadership and have opened and closed electoral options. Such interaction between the two parties is a central preoccupation of this book. Rather than doubting the true intention of Israeli policymakers in advancing democracy in the territories, the challenge is to focus the discussion on implementation.

Israel's status as the only democracy in the Middle East is often cited with the corollary that as long as its Arab neighbors are not democratic, real peace is not feasible. Setting aside the ambiguity of the term "real," history does not bear out such an assumption. Consider, among other examples, the improving relations between the superpowers, from the Cold War period to the eventual rapprochement of increasingly similar domestic regimes, as well as the "cold peace" between Egypt and Israel that has endured more than a decade in spite of the high level of hostilities in which both parties have been embroiled with third states. Hence, our project does not consider democracy to be a precondition for peace between Israel and its neighbors, but it maintains that there is an interrelationship between both domestic and external political processes, so that the development of democratic values and institutions could be an added facilitating factor.

*   *   *

The first part of the book deals with the problems of the correlation between peace and democracy as well as with its relevance to the Israeli-Palestinian conflict. Robert Rothstein's first chapter deals with the problematic nature—despite its current universal validity—of the proposition that democratic states do not conduct war between and among themselves. He stresses the increasing threat to the generalization, particularly given the social and economic problems of many of the poor and developing countries. Clearly, the failure of many nondemocratic regimes is not necessarily equivalent to the success of democracy.

Rothstein provided many of the participants in this project with a conceptual organizing framework. Definitions of the key terms "peace" and "democracy" are required to give researchers and readers of this study a conceptual common denominator. Peace, the first concept, can be taken as "the absence of war," though domestic strife, influenced by external actors, is an increasingly prevalent form of conflict. Although clear evidence of the decrease in the likelihood of international wars between democracies exists, so far, only pioneering work has been conducted on the degree and scope of protracted domestic conflict.[9]

In the case of Israel, it is important to address not only conventional wars but also the consequences of the massive uprising within the borders under its control, as well as the use of sporadic violence across its frontiers. For the Palestinians under occupation, this situation has meant continuous suffering, not only as a result of confrontation with Israel but also because they have become targets of violence perpetrated by the Arab states. The increase in hostilities between Palestinians and Israelis, together with the depolarization of world politics and the increasing tendency of major powers to turn to domestic priorities, emphasizes the basic characteristics of what Azar called "protracted social conflict."[10] The Gulf War brought back awareness of the international dimension of the Israeli-Arab conflict, but the subsequent regional peace negotiations highlighted once again the priority and salience of the Israeli-Palestinian dimension in the conflict-resolution process.

Defining "democracy" is more problematic. There seems to be a consensus that universal, free, and pluralistic suffrage is a necessary but not sufficient condition. The freedom to elect representatives is exercised only once every few years, but the basic conditions for maintaining such freedoms must be kept intact all the time. History shows how electoral democracies have brought into power regimes that made a point of cancelling basic freedoms, crushing opposition, and eventually ending the electoral process altogether. While there is consensus that the meaning of democracy must encompass more than just electoral politics, defining the scope of individual rights that are implied is more difficult. The Universal Declaration of Human Rights is often seen as a standard to aim for rather than an immediate imperative. For the purpose of this study, we can begin with the premise that "a society is . . . a full democracy if it has a political system that guarantees both the civil and political liberties of its people."[11]

If we were to confine our study to the political rather than the socio-economic expressions of democracy, the scope of our definition would include not only the nature of political institutions but also "civil competence"—the encouragement of high levels of political participation. By focusing on the type of society instead of on all-inclusive standards based on checks and balances between executive, legal, and judiciary powers, we can see democratization as a process with many stages. These include the buildup of participatory local institutions, a civil society, an independent judiciary, and political competition. Such stages have the effect of moving regimes toward respect for fundamental human rights, tolerance of opposing views, and adherence to principles of accountability, fair elections, and effective governance.

In Chapter 3, Abed and I discuss at length some of the ideas already expressed in this introduction, narrowing the applicability of the universal proposition to the Israel-Palestinian conflict. This Arab-Jewish coauthored article represents a trend among scholars and adherents on both sides to present to the public a shared vision and analysis of conflict-related issues.[12]

The second and third parts of the volume examine the situation of the parties to the conflict. Although it may be difficult to establish that strengthening democracy on both sides of the conflict will absolutely advance the cause of peace, an analysis of current trends is of central importance. The focal research question is: To what extent does the absence of peace between Israelis and Palestinians affect the nature of their politics and societies? Preventing Israel from becoming less democratic and aiding the Palestinians in becoming more democratic are, as mentioned, values shared by the contributors to this volume, as well as potentially important components of the conflict's resolution. In our project workshops, pragmatic issues often emerged in terms of addressing democratization as a dynamic, human-made process. We asked ourselves what might speed up this process among the Palestinians and what might slow down or set back the accomplishments of Israel's democracy.

When national security considerations prevail over the rule of law for prolonged periods of time, as has been the case in Israel since its creation, what is the norm and what is the exception to the legitimation of restrictions on its democratic practices? The task of maintaining Israel's democratic standards despite an unremitting state of war was exacerbated when the Palestinian uprising (intifada) began in 1987. The perceived need for even higher levels of repression to curb the civilian rebellion brought sharply into focus the effects of the occupation on Jewish society within Israel. Even if there has been a significant level of agreement about the importance of "democracy for the Jews," to what extent are such values maintained when deep schisms affect political tolerance in Israel?[13] Minister of Education Shulamit Aloni reminds us that "any jurist knows that there can be no rule of law and no justice without restraints upon the capricious will of the majority and without the subordination of the ruler to a supreme normative system." She continues, "The faith in Israeli democracy, just because we are a pluralistic society with many parties and hold elections from time to time, is exaggerated."[14]

Three chapters in the book discuss the existence of trends away from democratization among Israeli Jews. Alon Pinkas deals with the impact of the occupation at the level of Israeli political institutions. He shows how the association between national and individual security considerations has affected the civil and political rights of Israelis, in the context of denial of such rights to the neighboring Palestinians. My chapter introduces arguments about the impact of wars in democracies and other colonial situations, in an attempt to assess the degree of erosion of pluralistic values and the acceptance of dissent among the public at large and among key segments of Israeli society. Charles Liebman looks at antidemocratic values in the Jewish religious leadership and the religious community in general.

The chapter on the Arabs in Israel provides a bridge between these chapters and those on democratization in the Arab world and among the Palestinians. Nadim Rouhana and As'ad Ghanem study the development of democratic values and strategies among this group, a most relevant investigation in terms of the potential for democratization in the adjacent territories.[15]

In the Arab world, the issue of democracy came to the fore even more saliently in the aftermath of the Gulf War. On one hand, a relationship was seen ex post facto between the repressive nature of Saddam Hussein's domestic regime in Iraq and his intense hostility toward both immediate and more remote neighboring countries. The "liberation" of Kuwait highlighted the double standard applied by some Western powers in endorsing democratization. The Palestinians seem to have been once again the great losers, at least in the short run, and serious doubts about the wisdom of the policies of their leadership began to percolate within broad political circles. The need for the Palestine Liberation Organization to establish its representative nature and legitimacy through electoral procedures has become widely recognized within the organization; the arguments against are more in terms of timing than principle.

How expedient is it for a national liberation movement to postpone democratic practices until "the day after" it becomes a sovereign authority? Examples of ruthless regimes resulting from legitimate struggles for self-determination are, unfortunately, abundant. The ambivalence of the demand for self-determination has been discussed by Raymond D. Gastil, who points out that on the one hand it is a demand for freedom, while on the other "it is a demand for independence unrelated to the maintenance of those freedoms basic to liberal democracy."[16] In more positive terms, is it not in the best interest of the Palestinians to press now for democratic practices within their own political community? To what extent is implementation possible under occupation? While theoretical material about transitions to democracy in societies under foreign control is not abundant,[17] cases of democratic regimes that played the role of military occupiers offer exceptionally fertile ground for comparative analysis.

Four chapters focus on the issue of democracy for the Palestinians. Shukri Abed deals with the historical, cultural, and religious background of the Arab Middle East, assessing the obstacles and opportunities for the development of democracy and the constraints that the Palestinians face. Moshe Ma'oz analyzes the development of institutions and leadership in the West Bank and Gaza, going back to the formative stages but stressing the post-1967 period, to establish the changes that have occurred in relation to the issue of internal democracy. Ziad Abu-Amr describes the prevailing views on democracy among Islamic fundamentalists in the Occupied Territories, presenting in an unequivocal manner the limited chances of its coexistence with current normative religious interpretations. Manuel Hassassian discusses the trends toward democratization within PLO ranks and the Palestinian diaspora at large. In light of Dr. Liebman's findings on Jewish religious attitudes toward democracy, the reader may care to speculate about the hostile relationship likely to emerge between Palestinians and Israelis if antidemocratic trends do prevail within both societies, or even if fundamentalism becomes a strong force in one of them.

Finally, Rothstein looks critically at the entire product of our joint enterprise. Stressing its shortcoming and the missing analytic links puts our conclusions in a realistic albeit fragile perspective. His "restrained pessimism" in the short run and "moderate" optimism in the long run sum up fairly and accurately the prevailing feeling in the research team.

* * *

This project has encouraged both Israelis and Palestinians to take a critical look inward and trace the obstacles and opportunities for the development of democracy within their respective societies. (In a few chapters, notably those by Ma'oz and Rouhana and Ghanem, the policies of the opposite society are also addressed.) Thus, in the workshops in Jerusalem and College Park, we were able to experience an atmosphere more conducive to in-depth analysis than that surrounding prevailing forms of debate on the conflict, where comments are mostly confined to accusations against the other side and protagonists often talk at cross-purposes before a concerned public.

A few cautionary remarks: First, while we attempted to devote an equal amount of resources and space to the analysis of the two societies, the chapters are not absolutely symmetrical. The studies of institutionalization and erosion of democracies do not necessarily use the same conceptual frameworks, nor can the obstacles and advantages for each society be determined by reversing negative signs to positive ones. Furthermore, the salience of the role of one side for the other is not symmetrical: Resolution of the conflict with Israel is the absolute primary determinant for Palestinian nation building, while factors not directly related to the conflict can play central or secondary roles at different times for the established Israeli society and state. From this perspective, it is difficult to isolate the variables of war and occupation and single them out as the main explanation for the presence of "undemocratic" values and practices. The centrality of occupation to Palestinian lives notwithstanding, events in the Arab world and general trends toward modernization may have affected aspects of democratization to no less an extent than the Israeli occupation. Furthermore, while we have tried to examine the interrelationship between peace and democracy in light of global trends, with specific analysis of democracy in Israel and democratization among Palestinians, there is no systematic comparison herein with states and nations that underwent similar processes. Analysis of other democratic states at war or keeping a civilian population under occupation and analysis of democratization issues within national liberation movements have the potential to provide a better understanding of what in the nature of the conflict is shared by the two sides and what is specific to one or the other. Unfortunately, limited resources precluded the possibility of addressing such wider issues during the first stage of research. An offshoot of this project will focus on democratic states that have functioned as military occupiers in a postwar situation and try to ascertain patterns of democratization for civilian populations under temporary foreign control.

Needless to say, in this kind of intellectual exercise more than in others, the contributors are totally free to express their own points of view. The editors and other colleagues have presented the authors with critical comments, but ultimately all have been totally free to incorporate or disregard them. The expectation of the project participants is that Arab and Jewish policymakers will find the idea behind the book and the specific argument, instrumental to the peace process, which was launched in Madrid since the inception of our work. By presenting converging aspects of peace and democracy, the findings of the book can provide food for thought to leaders on both sides. Perhaps the shared understanding of historic processes by a small group of Palestinian and Israeli academics can reach wider circles that take in those who are in control of political power in both societies. The presence of numerous academics within the Palestinian delegations at the recent peace talks shows at least a partial connection between intellectual dialogue and concrete proposals. The path from Palestinian universities to the negotiating table may be shorter than that between academic life and political power among their Israeli counterparts, however. In expanding the level of interest outside the academic circles into wider sectors of the civil society, there are probably few shortcuts.

It is extremely important to flag the dangers of moving away from analytic to prescriptive discourse and crossing the thin divide between being policy-relevant and being political. For an integrated team, moving from diagnosis to prognosis carries with it the risk of fragmentation and polarization, of moving from consensus back to separate advocacy of partisan points of view.

Then again, the real challenge is indeed to translate the general principles established in this study to the agenda of the Israeli-Palestinian peace process. At the workshop in College Park that preceded the completion of this book, several concrete questions were raised in an attempt to deal in real time with issues that have emerged as relevant in bilateral and multilateral regional talks. A few examples of these questions indicate the potential application of the issues raised in this study. Relevant questions for Israeli policymakers range from the general ("To what extent do you feel that democratic values and practices within Israel are being strengthened, are stable, or are deteriorating, and what are the effects of a state of war or a military government?") to the specific ("In the Israeli-Palestinian dimension of the bilateral talks, should democratization and concrete human-rights improvement be among the confidence-building measures in the first steps of moving away from confrontational proposals?"). Some questions relevant to Palestinian policymakers are related to the broader scope ("Taking into account the armed forces' curbing of the fundamentalist Islamic victory in the elections in Algiers, to what extent and at what stage can incipient democracies rule out the participation of forces that do not express commitment to respect for individual civil and political rights?"), and others are narrower ("Is the Palestinian delegation to the peace conference likely to arrive at substantial results without legitimation through some form of democratic endorsement? Can such legitimation come after some concrete achievement or is it preferable to empower the current delegates as formal representatives in some measure sooner rather than later"?).

Other questions can be addressed to both parties. Some of these are speculative ("To what extent can shared democratic values be a common denominator for Israelis and Palestinians, and could this be strong enough to prevail over the existing national, ethnic, religious, cultural, and other cleavages? Could some common democratic institutions be shared by Israelis and Palestinians, and at what level?"). A more concrete question is, "Given the insignificant level of progress in the multilateral regional negotiations, and learning from the European experience, should the introduction of a "basket" (a set of guiding principles) dealing with the democratization and human rights dimension be seen as a delaying or as a confidence-building factor?"

We hope that by the time this book is published, some of these questions will have found answers among the leaders of both nations and the arguments will have become obsolete. Even if questions such as these do not emerge in the substantive debates of the peace process, we hope this study will at least make the public more aware of the cost to democracy of a collapse in the negotiating process and the cost of the long-term consequences of continuous absence of peace. Most Israeli and Palestinian leaders have pledged their commitment to democracy, making this a point of convergence. Within each community, the need to preserve or develop democracy may cut across the lines that fragment political parties and movements. Rather than translating the findings of this study on the issue of democracy and peace into concrete answers, the participant researchers have ventured to pursue the question of its relevance to conflict resolution in dialogue with the leaders of both communities. The richness of the subject needs to be explored further by an epistemic community of those who are concerned with finding a compromise solution to one of the most longstanding unresolved problems of our era.

Notes

1. The term "sense of history" is used in a more restricted sense than the deterministic one attached to the work of Francis Fukuyama, *The End of History and the Last Man* (New York: Free Press, 1992) and to the article in the *International Herald Tribune*, "States Can Break Up, Democracies Can Grow Up" (February 10, 1992, p. 4).

2. James Rosenau, *The United Nations in a Turbulent World* (Boulder: Lynne Rienner Publishers, 1992).

3. This proposition is discussed in more depth in Rothstein's contribution, and its application within the Israeli-Palestinian context is studied by Kaufman and Abed. A summary of the relevant studies concludes that "virtually all have noted that, at the dyadic level, democracies simply do not fight one another." T. Clifton Morgan and Sally Howard Campbell, "Domestic Structure, Decisional Constraints,

and War," *Journal of Conflict Resolution,* Vol. 35, No. 2 (June 1981), p. 187. In the same volume, see also D. Marc Kilgour, "Domestic Political Structure and War Behavior," pp. 266–284, and Randolph M. Siverson and Julian Emmons, "Birds of a Feather: Democratic Political Systems and Alliance Choices in the Twentieth Century," pp. 285–306.

4. E. Kaufman, S. Abed, and A. Ikeda, *Intifada and Peace Process,* Joint Research Programme Series No. 74 (Tokyo: Institute of Developing Economies, 1989), pp. 11–80.

5. Robert Rothstein, "Democracy, Conflict and Development in the Third World," *Washington Quarterly,* Vol. 14, No. 2 (Spring 1991), pp. 43–66, and "Change and Continuity in the Middle East," *Washington Quarterly,* Vol. 14, No. 3 (Summer 1991), pp. 139–160.

6. See coverage of proceedings in *Truman Institute News* (February 1991).

7. "Epistemic communities are defined loosely as a group of intellectuals sharing a common causal understanding on a particular subject and who organize to turn this understanding into action strategies." Emanuel Adler, *Cognitive Evolution: A Dynamic Approach for the Study of International Relations and Their Progress,* book manuscript, pp. 43–77. See also Peter M. Haas, "Do Regimes Matter? Epistemic Communities and Mediterranean Pollution Control," *International Organizations,* Vol. 43 (Summer 1989), pp. 377–403.

8. Samuel Huntington, "Democracy's Third Wave," *Democracy* (Spring 1991), pp. 12–34.

9. According to this leading expert, minorities' grievances in Western democracies and Japan "usually are expressed in protest, rarely in rebellion, and the most common responses by governments in the late twentieth century are to accommodate their interests rather than forcibly subordinate or incorporate them." Ted R. Gurr, "Minorities in the Advanced Industrial Democracies," in *Minorities at Risk* (forthcoming).

10. Edward Azar, *The Management of Protracted Social Conflict: Theory and Cases* (Aldershot, UK: Darmouth Publishing, 1990).

11. Raymond D. Gastil, "What Kind of Democracy?" *The Atlantic Monthly* (June 1990), p. 92.

12. This trend, initiated years ago by Elias H. Tuma and Haim Darin-Drabkin in *The Economic Case for Palestine* (New York: St. Martin's Press, 1977), is seen most recently in Mark A. Heller and Sari Nusseibeh's *No Trumpets, No Drums: A Two-State Settlement of the Israeli-Palestinian Conflict* (New York: Hill and Wang, 1991). Moshe Amirav and Hanna Siniora coauthored an interesting paper entitled "Jerusalem: Resolving the Unresolvable," Israeli-Palestinian Peace Research Project, Working Paper Series, No. 16, Arab Studies Society and the Harry S Truman Research Institute (Winter 1991/1992). The issue of Jerusalem has also been addressed by Naomi Chazan, with commentary by Fouad Moughrabi and Rashid I. Khalidi, in "Negotiating the Non-Negotiable: Jerusalem in the Framework of an Israeli-Palestinian Settlement," Occasional Paper No. 7, American Academy for the Advancement of Science (March 1991).

13. According to Sprinzak, "Given the post-1967 conditions, the erosion of Israel's democracy and the emergence of Jewish violence were probable; contrary to many unfounded beliefs and theories, no one is immune to violence, not even Israeli Jews." Ehud Sprinzak, "Fundamentalism, Terrorism and Democracy: The Case of Gush Emunim," *New Outlook* (September–October 1989), p. 16.

14. Shulamit Aloni, "Defending Human Rights," *Jerusalem Post,* May 5, 1986.

15. Interestingly, Defense Minister Arens extrapolates that the

"Westernization" and "Israelization" of Israeli Arabs who are "for all purposes Palestinians" and who have coexisted with Jewish Israelis for forty-three years, means that the same can happen with the Palestinian population in the territories "who lived side by side with us for 24 years and are gradually adopting our political life-style." See "Patience and Determination," *Ha'aretz,* December 11, 1991.

16. Gastil, "What Kind of Democracy?" p. 96.

17. See discussion of the three classic models, none dealing with the transition to democracy of societies under foreign occupations, in Giuseppe Di Palma, *To Craft Democracies—An Essay on Democratic Transitions* (Berkeley: University of California Press, 1990), pp. 5–76. Di Palma mentions that international factors operate on democratization processes in various ways, ranging from outside imposition by military occupation to statements of support and sympathy, but occupation is not discussed among the four ways of exercising international influence.

THE THEORETICAL FRAMEWORK

2

Democracy and Conflict

Robert L. Rothstein

Conflict has been endemic in the Third World. Most of the wars that have taken place since 1945 have been fought between Third World countries, and much of the internal conflict has also been in the Third (and "Fourth") Worlds. Given unsettled boundaries (especially in Africa and the Middle East), declining economic performance, ethnic and communal divisions, and the widespread availability of arms, the level of conflict is hardly surprising. Indeed, it may well rise as global interdependence and changes in the international division of labor increase inequalities within and between regions, as awareness of disparities in standards of living (and quality of governance) are spread by international communications, and as the decline of the Cold War and escalating demands for a sharply limited pool of international financial resources increase fears of being left behind. In the past, an elite focus on internal survival and the lack of a capacity to project power effectively (except against one's own citizens) may have kept the amount of external warfare relatively limited. But systemic turbulence, the widespread availability of ever-more destructive arms, and the fears induced by weakness may diminish reluctance to engage in war.

Will increased democratization, if it continues, reduce the likelihood of international conflict? Will this trend be powerful enough to overcome or diminish the trends that may generate increased conflict? Until recently, most analysts argued that the likelihood of war did not vary greatly with regime type: Democracies were as likely to be involved in wars as non-democracies.[1] However, Rudolph Rummel has instigated a scholarly debate by arguing that democratic (or relatively free) states do not fight each other, that more free states mean less war in the system, and that these propositions hold whether the definition of "more free" is strictly political or also includes economic freedom (in effect, a relatively open economy). He also contends they apply whether one is discussing the frequency or the intensity of war.[2]

This is an immensely important debate. In practical terms, if having more democracies clearly implies we will have less conflict, we see foreshadowed the possibility of an entirely different international system, a system in which the paradoxes of the "security dilemma" become progressively less powerful influences on state behavior and war as a means of dispute settlement is gradually displaced by the technique of peaceful resolution. We also see the emergence of a general principle of guidance for policymakers: Support for transitions to democracy and the consolidation of new democracies would or could replace the Soviet menace as a framework for thinking about policy.[3]

The debate is equally important in scholarly terms. If democracies exhibit unique and consequential patterns of conflict behavior, the argument that regime type is not usually a powerful explanatory variable needs to be substantially revised. Such a conclusion would also refute the contention by neorealists that on crucial decisions of war and peace it is the structure of the international system, especially the distribution of capabilities and the balance of power, that is determinative. Rather, in some important cases the crucial factor would be the nature of the states involved, not the structural environment.[4] Finally, there may be an important point at stake in this debate about systemic change itself. Transformations of international systems have usually followed major wars. Now, however, we may see the possibility of systemic change not only from shifts in the nature of the actors in the system but also from shifts in attitudes and norms (about war, or acceptable forms of governance, or the environment, or human rights) among leaders and the public at large.[5] What we may be seeing is a partial redefinition of security in a post–Cold War environment. Concern for security is still prominent, but the composition of security— what needs to be defended by what means—is rapidly changing. A proliferation of democratic states in the system presumably also would imply that the conventional distinction between domestic and external politics would continue to erode, with attendant effects on the style and substance of international diplomacy. Taken together, these points necessarily suggest a need to reorient—perhaps to reinvent (partially)—the theoretical debate in international relations.[6]

Many of the justifications for supporting democracy by the United States constitute essentially "milieu" goals that seek to affect the "shape of the environment in which the nation operates."[7] Such goals, which are always problematic when they conflict with more immediate and practical goals, are also not likely to be very persuasive to citizens of Third World countries obsessed by the need to quickly improve their standard of living. Moreover, the romance of violence, the satisfaction of inflicting pain on actual or presumed enemies, and the hope of achieving change by the use of violence still seem powerful motivations in many parts of the Third World. I note this here only to emphasize that, while the developed countries have an obvious interest in maintaining peace among themselves and an "environmental" interest in maintaining peace in the Third World, the Third World itself may be much more ambivalent about the reduction of conflict. Tensions between the developed countries may be seen as a means of leverage for the Third World—as in the Cold War—and violence within the Third World may be seen as a necessary means of social change. I do not mean to suggest an absolute distinction between the two worlds; there are always important differences in degree that must be taken into account. Nor do I mean to imply a moral distinction between the two worlds, as material and other conditions are vastly different. What I do mean to suggest here is that simple extrapolations from what happened among one group of countries to what will happen among another group of countries, even if they come to be described as democracies, may not be appropriate.[8]

We shall in the next section discuss the issue of who fights whom and where democracies fit into the pattern of conflict. We shall also discuss why democracies do not appear to fight each other and whether the reasons are likely to hold for the kind of democracies now emerging in the Third World. Some comment is also necessary about the relationship between democracy and ethnic conflict; it would hardly make much sense to support democratization if it increased the likelihood or intensity of ethnic unrest. Finally, the prospects for conflict must also be assessed in the context of other changes that are occurring within the international system, not least of which are the end of the Cold War and the consequent shifts in attitudes toward the Third World.

Who Fights Whom?

What sort of empirical support is there for Rummel's arguments about the peaceableness of democratic states? Findings on the relationship between democracy and conflict have tended to be mixed and inconclusive. There is also substantial disagreement with some of Rummel's key points. The disagreements are not surprising, not only because of significant differences in defining and using key concepts (democracy and conflict) but also because of important differences in the kinds of conflict being studied and the time period under examination. And it is worth emphasizing that relatively small shifts in how concepts are defined or measured can have relatively large effects on the results obtained. These empirical and conceptual disagreements among highly intelligent and methodologically sophisticated analysts are something of a warning against coming to any simple conclusions about the impact of democracy on conflict.

One study by Steve Chan has concluded that "contrary to the view that freedom discourages war, the evidence points in the direction that it is associated with more war."[9] He does not find convincing evidence that freer countries are less likely to start wars but does find empirical support for the

proposition that democracies fight nondemocracies as much as nondemocracies fight each other. Chan finds some partial support for Rummel in the
years since 1973, with freer countries apparently less war-prone recently
than in the more distant past.[10] Weede also concludes that democratic states
were as frequently involved in war as other states in the 1960s and 1970s
but confirms Rummel's finding that the democratic states were less
involved in war in the very narrow period that Rummel studied
(1975–1980).[11] A more recent study by Maoz and Abdolali finds that free
states are neither more nor less conflict-prone than nonfree states, that
democracies are disproportionately likely to initiate disputes against autoc-
racies, and that the proportion of democracies in the international system
positively affects the number of disputes.[12] Thus, Rummel's argument that
a system with more free or democratic states will also be more peaceful has
not received much support from other researchers; perhaps we can rest with
that well-known Scottish verdict, "not proven."[13]

The one argument all the analysts agree on is that democracies do not
fight other democracies. This argument, which has a long intellectual history, has attracted a great deal of attention.[14] There has been much rummag-
ing through history and much definitional jousting in the search for cases
where democracies have fought each other. Quibbling aside, the absence of
direct conflict is impressive and intriguing.[15] Surely, one would presume,
conflicts of interest or miscalculations would have produced a war between
democracies at some point. But we can only seem to find close calls.

The fact that democracies do not fight other democracies raises a number of important questions. The first is obvious but extraordinarily difficult
to resolve: Why should democracies be inherently more peaceful than other
states? An attempt to answer this question is important because, unless we
can relate the peaceableness of democracies toward each other to specific
characteristics of democracy, the argument itself will be inconclusive: The
pacific qualities might be related to other characteristics (level of development, geography, the nature of the international environment, etc.) that
have little to do with democracy itself.

The analysts who have attempted to answer this question have focused
on two sets of characteristics normally associated with democracy.[16] One
set relates to the familiar constraints on leadership in a democracy—the
division of powers, the difficulties of achieving consensus amid great
diversity of values and interest, the existence of crosscutting pressures, the
weakness of coalition governments, and perhaps also the difficulty of generating enough hatred against an enemy if the government does not control
the media or the legislature. Secrecy and the suppression of dissent are
inevitably harder to achieve when the procedures of democracy are operating effectively. It may also be harder to conceal the development of especially dangerous weapons in a democracy, which reduces the fear of surprise attack or unanticipated technological breakthroughs. Democracies

also tend to spend relatively less than nondemocracies on the military, perhaps because of popular demands for increased expenditures on welfare, which might suggest that the initial inclinations of leaders (and the public) are not likely to be toward military solutions to a conflict.

The second set of characteristics relates to the attitudes and behavior of citizens in a democracy. People who perceive themselves as autonomous and self-governing are likely to respect others who have the same rights and share the same norms.[17] Citizens of a democracy also do not want to risk death or pay the costs of war, especially when they are enjoying the fruits of prosperity.[18] Perhaps also, if we accept the argument that democracy should be valued as an end in itself because (in part) it generates greater self-fulfillment, one might postulate that such citizens would be less frustrated and less needful of lashing out in resentment against real or presumed enemies. Finally, perhaps citizens of a democracy read their own press clippings; that is, the self-image of peaceableness, of willingness to seek and accept reasonable compromises, may generate its own momentum, its own drive—so to speak—to "keep the streak alive."

If we think about the problem of explaining the absence of war between democratic states in terms of different levels of analysis, we can see that most of the preceding arguments fall either at the individual or state level. However, these levels of analysis seem to me necessary but not sufficient to prove the hypothesis. Despite structural and perceptual similarities, there are many important differences between democracies—in historical experiences, degree of prosperity, institutional arrangements, the power and skills of different governments, the vagaries of personality, and so on. Under the circumstances, one would expect to find some cases over a period of two centuries in which the differences were more consequential than the similarities—in effect, a few cases in which the war option seemed a reasonable or necessary response to serious conflicts of interest with other democracies. The difficulty of finding counterexamples suggests the existence of powerful forces encouraging peaceful behavior, forces that encompass the internal characteristics of democracy but also include certain patterns of behavior that gradually seemed to stand to reason in the international arena. Without the latter, one can at least hazard the guess that the internal differences would in some cases have led to deviant (i.e., warlike) behavior externally.

Perhaps one can gain additional insight by reversing the question. Suppose we ask not why democracies do not fight other democracies but rather why they fight nondemocracies as frequently as they do? A supposedly peaceful populace and a supposedly constrained leadership have been able to intervene consistently against nondemocratic states, to use violence (legally and illegally) against them, and to maintain sufficiently high levels of military spending. The obvious point is that the exact same internal characteristics that presumably foster peacefulness toward one group of states foster a very different pattern of behavior toward another group of states.[19] The critical question seems to be why one set of rules applies to democracies and another set applies to nondemocracies—even nondemocracies that have supported the West against the former Soviet Union.

The answer must be sought in different patterns of thought or different norms of action and perspective in the international arena itself. These norms are, of course, in some sense a reflection of generally shared experiences, values, and institutions, but it is the way in which they are extrapolated and not extrapolated to the relations between states that is crucial. What has happened in regard to relations between democratic states, as Michael Doyle has argued, is that "conventions of mutual respect have formed a cooperative foundation for relations among liberal democracies of a remarkably effective kind." These have created a "liberal zone of peace, a pacific union."[20]

Trying to understand how the creation of this zone of peace has occurred may give us some insight about how to expedite or facilitate the process in current circumstances. On the one hand, we have a set of domestic characteristics that has generated peace and prosperity internally; on the other hand, we have a set of international norms that has guaranteed peace and prosperity in parts of the international system. We want to try to understand how the first was transformed into the second. One way of doing this, I believe, is by looking very briefly at how norms develop and what role they play in establishing expectations and principles of order in the international system.[21]

Norms in the international order have usually been incorporated in treaties and formal law, if only because the absence of shared values and cultures necessitates rather more precise and clearly articulated standards of behavior. And many of the norms about democracy and the protection of human rights have been incorporated in a variety of international covenants. But they have been applied selectively and they have exerted influence on actions only in one set of relationships.[22] Here norms have performed crucial functions: They have guided the process of reasoning, they have drawn attention to important factors, and in simplifying and directing the choice of alternatives they have been useful problem-solving mechanisms.[23] They facilitate consistent patterns of cooperation, which would not be possible if only shifting patterns of interest were consequential, and they help also to establish rules of the game for conflict. However, in regard to the nondemocratic world, the norms have frequently been ignored, dismissed as inappropriate, or used cynically.

In civil society one assumes that the values of community (of *gemeinschaft*) are inevitably, and perhaps unfortunately, superseded by the values of society (of *gesellschaft*). Community ties are displaced or diluted by urbanization, industrialization, and secularization. In effect, shared history, values, and interests, the basis of community, facilitate the creation and maintenance of informal, almost intuitive norms of justice, tolerance, and the peaceful settlement of disputes. Conversely, in a society that operates like a market, in which trust is limited, relations are contractual, and my gain is perceived as your loss, norms must be formally enacted, and there is widespread awareness that they may not be applied effectively or consistently to particular cases.[24] The society of states, while hardly without order, has at best been perceived as an even more instrumental and distrustful version of domestic society. Within that larger society, however, democratic states have managed thus far to carve out among themselves a separate normative order, an order that does not necessarily require formal laws to function and in which doing what stands to reason leads to peaceful settlement of disputes.

There is no simple explanation for how two systems of international relations emerged, but some speculations may be appropriate. As Axelrod has noted, "It is easier to get a norm started if it serves the interests of the powerful few."[25] The norm obviously will also be easier to maintain if it is supported by the powerful. The rich and powerful can seek to impose their norms, which are largely extrapolations from their own society, not only because they believe in the superiority of their own norms but also because the norms themselves ensure the continuation of a system that benefits the powerful. Commitment to this normative order is likely to be particularly strong if adherence to the norms is associated with material success and if the issues in conflict between the supporters of the norm are more easily settled by accommodation than by conflict. Among themselves, rich, stable, status quo powers are not likely to find many issues worth fighting about; success in peaceful settlement, in turn, is likely to create or to buttress a culture of compromise and conciliation.

The rich and powerful democracies also tend to seek different goals in the international system. They do not want or require extensive intervention or governance by international institutions. They want only rules that make the international order stable and predictable, a framework for voluntary cooperation, and some capacity for troubleshooting when serious problems occur. Indeed, when problems do arise that seem to require an unusual degree of cooperation, the tendency is to create small groups of the like-minded to work out a compromise solution—the Group of Five, the Group of Seven, the summits of "those who really count." All of these factors make it easier for a group of stable, rich countries to seek a particular set of milieu goals, goals that can be achieved largely by national actions and do not seek from others gains that would generate war-threatening conflicts. The democracies have been trading states imbued with the confidence (until recently) that they can compete effectively in a milieu of openness and fairness. A "level playing field" and observance of existing rules presumably suffice. Observance of the norms within the community of like-minded nations is neither demanding nor difficult.

This perspective on the external order helps explain why two different normative systems have developed. Opposition to the norms and practices of the democratic order has always been present. In the Third World itself, liberal democracy has been denounced as a Western intrusion and its procedures (competition, participation, a free press, etc.) interpreted as luxuries for poor and divided countries. A market economy until recently has been rejected in favor of a closed system with a great deal of government involvement, purportedly because such a system is more efficient at extracting savings from a poor society and in ensuring that resources are properly allocated—"properly" frequently meaning for the benefit of the rulers. In addition, war and violence as a means of social change, survival, or aggrandizement have never completely lost their allure. Finally, the international order has not only been seen as exploitative and in need of fundamental reform but also as a source of necessary resources for development.

These two normative orders existed in uneasy tension for decades, the one successful on its own terms, the other at least seeming to hold out the prospect of success for very differently situated countries. The normative dominance of the first was formally institutionalized at the international level, but effective implementation of the norms was largely limited to one small group of states. But the success of the democratic states in governance and the achievement of widespread prosperity, however flawed, and the manifest failures of the socialist states and much of the Third World in achieving either, have seemed in the past decade to offer an extraordinary (and unanticipated) opportunity: the triumph beyond rhetoric of liberal democracy and a liberal economic order, and the prospect of a unified normative order, more widespread prosperity, and a reduction of international conflict. But one needs also to emphasize strongly that it is much too early to proclaim a definitive, normative victory, because norms are in flux. The democratic countries are themselves in danger of violating some of their norms (especially in the economic order), and it is far from clear that acceptance of liberal norms in the Third World is very profound or that such acceptance will necessarily produce the anticipated benefits of prosperity and stability in the current international environment.

In sum, the democratic states seem to have established a zone of peace among themselves because of a particular set of internal characteristics, because they were able to establish a separate normative order, and because the prosperity and stability generated within this zone made its continuation and its defense against opposition imperative. Strong support by the United States, its willingness to pay the collective goods cost of leadership, and its ability to institutionalize its values in the UN and other organizations were catalysts in the process. But, as just noted, skepticism about extrapolating these patterns of behavior to the Third World may be warranted.

In the first place, the more limited and restricted forms of democracy that are likely to prevail in the Third World, with greater restrictions on individual freedoms and greater power for ruling elites, imply that the factors that inhibit an "easy" choice of war are likely to be less powerful than in the First World: The diversity of interests and values may not be expressed, and the aversion to risk may not be as high. The last point reflects the fact that many in the Third World feel they have little to lose in using violence; they are not getting richer, and they are certainly getting more dissatisfied with the status quo. Attitudes that foster a willingness to compromise and to share power will be difficult to establish if growth rates decline, the distribution of income becomes more unequal, and ethnic and other groups fight over declining shares of scarce resources. The economic problems will be exacerbated if the international economic order remains unstable and if the new democracies must compete with each other for market access, foreign investment, and foreign aid. Actual or potential instability may increase spending on arms, which undermines development and makes the military a more dangerous threat to democracy.[26] Moreover, in areas such as the Middle East, decades of hatred and mistrust and the continued depiction of enemies in horrific terms will not be easily or quickly overcome by installation of a new form of government. All these factors are likely to make the extension of the democratic zone of peace to the Third World problematic.[27] One ought also note that, while more democracies seem to be emerging, many of the states in the system are not democratic and are likely to resist efforts at democratization. Because democracies seem to fight nondemocracies with great frequency, and because some new democracies may slip back into authoritarianism, the likely outcome is an international system with a mixed and shifting composition and with many potential conflicts as regimes change and as conflicts over land (within and between countries) develop. In short, the trend toward new democracies is not likely to threaten the need for conflict theorists.

Two other reasons for caution must be noted. The first concerns the fact that the basis of a great deal of conflict may be shifting increasingly to economic and resource issues. There is no inherent reason why these conflicts should end in war; in the abstract, they seem more easily resolved by compromise.[28] Nevertheless, international (and some domestic) economic conflicts are coming increasingly to resemble classic "security dilemma" conflicts, in that the stakes have risen greatly, defensive actions to protect national interests can have negative external effects and lead to spiraling retaliatory efforts (as with efforts to cut imports and increase exports), and the perception of zero-sum outcomes seems more prevalent. It is reasonable to ask whether democratic regimes, to the extent that leaders must compete for the popular vote or are dependent on support from powerful interest groups, are more likely to exacerbate conflict by making nationalistic short-run policy responses. The question is whether democratic regimes in a period of economic crises might increase the amount of economic conflict in potentially dangerous ways.[29]

The second reason for caution concerns the possibility that democracy in deeply divided societies may actually increase the likelihood of internal conflict. We shall discuss this issue in the next section.

Democracy and Internal Conflict

In the twentieth century, 36 million people have been killed in wars, 119 million have been killed by governments in brutal campaigns of genocide, massacre, and "retaliation."[30] The vast majority of the latter deaths have been perpetrated by totalitarian governments or, more recently, by unsavory autocrats such as Pol Pot, Idi Amin, and Hafez el Assad. By itself, this kind of murderousness is a strong reason for supporting democracies, which have no such record of barbarism, not only because of the basic human rights at stake but also because the fear of governmental terrorism can undermine progress toward economic development and political stability.[31]

The more difficult question concerns the relationship between democracy and the management or exacerbation of ethnic conflict. There have not been many democracies in deeply divided societies (India, Sri Lanka, and Israel are exceptions), but then again there have not in the past been many democracies in any circumstances in the Third World. In any case, a number of analysts of ethnic conflict have taken it for granted that democracy is inappropriate for divided societies and that majority rule, competitive parties, and an open political system are a recipe for chaos. The central point in this indictment has been that democratic procedures may actually generate or exacerbate ethnic conflict. Democracy often encourages politicians to manipulate ethnic and communal conflicts for their own benefit, the argument goes, increasing the likelihood that ethnic or other groups will organize to pursue their own interests; therefore, the democratic process itself can undermine national unity, complicate the allocation of resources, and make effective government more difficult.[32] The underlying assumption here seems much like the familiar argument that economic development in its initial stages requires authoritarian government to impose sacrifices and to maintain public order. And in both cases it can at least be said that authoritarian regimes have usually been as ineffective in dealing with these problems as democratic regimes.

Consociational democracy and other forms of power sharing were one response to fears about the potentially destructive consequences of unrestrained democratic competition in divided societies. Advocates of consociational democracy assumed that ethnic conflicts were not a transitory problem that would disappear in the process of economic and political development.[33] Rather, a stable democracy would emerge via a "grand coalition" of the most powerful groups, a mutual veto, proportionality in the allocation of opportunities and offices, and an important degree of ethnic autonomy.[34] Horowitz has argued: "Underlying virtually every severe case of ethnic conflict is a fear of competition. . . . All have a sense that their antagonists . . . are . . . better equipped to deal with the world they confront. They are often better educated and are seen to be more energetic or well-organized or more hardworking or clever."[35] Insofar as this argument is true, consociational democracy is also an antidote to the competitiveness of liberal democracy: It promises stability, predictability, and guaranteed shares of available resources.

If consociational democracy could guarantee ethnic peace or had done so effectively in the Third World, some of its manifest deficiencies would be more bearable. But it has not done so, as the case of Lebanon indicates. In the circumstances, its deficiencies in terms of democracy (elite dominance, secrecy) and its inflexibility and limited capacity to innovate may generate more costs than benefits.[36] The problem is that the initial agreement may be increasingly undermined by patterns of change (population growth rates, differential economic performance, educational changes, etc.) that the agreement ignores and that it has no means of responding to. Thus, short-run success can be bought at the price of greater long-run conflict. These criticisms are not meant to imply that consociational democracy is bound to fail or that there are no cases in which it might be a preferable alternative. Rather, as Horowitz emphasizes, there are a variety of forms of conflict management in divided societies, and some of them may be more effective in particular cases and more likely to protect and even enhance the benefits of democracy.[37]

There are some analysts who believe democracies have a better record than authoritarian regimes in dealing with ethnic conflict, largely because democracy presumably makes it possible to articulate grievances and to work to get them addressed. Gurr, for example, argues: "The ultimate resolution of ethnic conflicts depends most fundamentally on the implementation of democratic norms of equal political rights and opportunities and pluralistic accommodation of the demands of contending groups."[38] While one hopes Gurr is correct, the "ultimate resolution" has not occurred in India, Sri Lanka, Eastern Europe, or Northern Ireland. Perhaps one reason for ongoing discord, although we cannot pursue the point here, is that the critical variable is not democracy per se but rather the role of the state in any regime. If ethnic conflict is politicized by competition to control a biased state, then movement toward a neutral state may be needed to help resolve some ethnic conflicts.

The ambiguities and uncertainties, it seems to me, reflect the fact that there are many different kinds of ethnic conflict, a variety of forms of democratic governance, and constant changes in the external environment.

Before making any simple generalization about the relationship between democracy and ethnic conflict, we need to know, among other things, what goals the different ethnic groups seek; how perceptions of ethnicity have changed over time; whether the conflict has a religious component; what rates of economic growth have been achieved; what relationship there is between economic performance and ethnic demands; whether the democratic system is centralized or decentralized and what electoral system has been adopted; and whether the world economy is growing or not growing. There are many possible answers and many possible relationships among the answers to these questions. The democracy variable is only one factor among many, and it does not seem prudent to suggest that it can or will resolve all major ethnic conflicts. Nevertheless, it is important to understand that the assumption that democracy is incompatible with the resolution of ethnic conflict is also misleading. Democracy may be helpful, even necessary, in some ethnic conflicts, harmful in others, and of little relevance in yet other cases. As the economists say, it all depends.

Presumably, rapid rates of economic growth would make the management of ethnic problems easier. But again the uncertainties are vast. On one level, the economic issue may not be very important because of "the willingness of ethnic groups to sacrifice economic interest for the sake of other kinds of gain."[39] But by the same token, good economic performance cannot be overlooked in many cases, not only because it can provide some gains but also because it gives the government the power and the confidence to try to deal with ethnic problems without repression.

The relationship between economic growth and ethnic conflict cannot be separated from the role of the state in Third World development. The dominant role of the state in most Third World countries has meant that the struggle to control and influence resource allocations has seemed to necessitate the mobilization and countermobilization of ethnic groups.[40] The polarization of ethnicity has thus been almost inevitable, not only because resources have been very scarce but also because the state has seldom been fair and unbiased. Even if rapid growth does occur, it may increase expectations and generate bitter conflicts over the distribution of shares. Adoption of market reforms, which may initially increase distributional inequities, may be thwarted by the protest of groups that are left behind. The hope that the state will help or compensate the losers will not be fulfilled if growth is stagnant, if the state is corrupt or inefficient, or if it is compelled by external pressure to diminish its activities and reduce welfare spending.[41]

The question of whether democracy reduces ethnic conflict does not have a single answer. Nevertheless, on balance, one might predict that democracies have a better record at conflict reduction than most authoritarian governments. The fact that democracies do not tend to massacre their populations, tend to spend less on the military, and give groups a means to articulate their grievances may mean that ethnic conflicts will be resolved in less violent channels. Democracies may also gradually change popular perceptions of how to deal with grievances—although there are counterexamples in Northern Ireland, India, and Sri Lanka. Much will depend on how well new democratic states establish the legitimacy of an unfamiliar form of government and how well they meet the material needs of their citizens. External aid could be of profound significance in the transitional period, but getting it may be difficult with the end of the Cold War and the continuation of global economic turbulence. Still, the new democracies may have an advantage here because the need to give aid only for strategic purposes has declined and the moral argument to give aid to countries that have adopted democratic norms and principles is (or should be) strong.

There is another source of internal (and external) conflict that requires a brief comment. The continuing deterioration of the resource base in many Third World countries and regions may be undermining the possibility that *any* form of government can effectively meet the needs of its citizens. The linked and escalating problems of excessive population growth, declining agricultural productivity, deforestation, desertification, and increasing water shortages are familiar, but the questions of how to deal with them and whether democratic or authoritarian regimes are more likely to handle these issues are unresolved. One should also note that resource constraints can generate internal and external conflicts and that, for the poor countries, simply divising an effective strategy to begin dealing with these issues will require substantial external aid and a great deal of regional cooperation. With economic conditions deteriorating everywhere and with the familiar tendency of political systems to focus on the short run in full swing, the prospects for either aid or cooperation are not very high.

Fears about resource shortages have already had negative effects on growth rates and quality-of-life indices. They have also had some negative effects on military spending. For example, sharply increased military expenditures in Asia have been attributed not only to internal strife but also to fears about future disputes over oil and fishing rights in the ocean.[42] And there has been much talk in the Middle East about future "water wars," which will probably diminish the possibilities of significant reductions in military spending. Fears that the West Bank and Gaza will not be economically viable because of population pressures, agricultural decline, and water shortages have also played some part in raising Israeli doubts about the stability of a Palestinian state.

As Brown indicates, all the policies that might begin to diminish these problems create serious internal threats: Cutting subsidies, changing agricultural practices, enforcing pollution controls, conserving water, and preserving the forest all threaten the livelihood of some groups.[43] It is unclear, however, whether democratic or authoritarian governments will be relatively more effective in imposing necessary but painful policies. For example, high population-growth rates, which increase the number of young and low-income people, may be the most important link in the syndrome of deterioration, but there is disagreement about which form of government is more effective on this issue—indeed, whether forms of government make much difference at all.[44] Conversely, there is some evidence that the democracies that have given their citizens some socioeconomic rights (such as Costa Rica and Sri Lanka) also have better food-grain output and lower birthrates.[45] In any case, whether, how, or when the deterioration of the resource base is likely to lead to increased conflict is unclear. Many different patterns of response are possible, in part because factors other than resource shortages affect the decision to use violence, but it does seem plausible to suggest that elite perceptions of rising demands and diminishing means to meet them will lead, sooner or later, to new justifications for authoritarianism and war against neighbors.[46] One doubts that these responses will diminish the problem, not least because there is little evidence to suggest that authoritarian regimes (barring the "good," or paternalistic, East Asian regimes) will make the right policy choices or elicit sufficient support for necessary sacrifices by the citizenry. On the margin, perhaps democratic regimes, if they receive enough external support, will be more effective because greater legitimacy may give them somewhat more time to deal with the issues. There is some evidence that citizens of a democracy may be more willing (up to a point) to sacrifice immediate material benefits for a greater say in choosing their rulers and having more protected rights, and there is also some evidence that democratic policy-making can be more flexible and more able to correct mistakes quickly. But it is also clear that unless necessary policies are adopted quickly and unless the international response to what is a shared problem is rapid and generous, resource deterioration could become irreversible.

The Decline of the Cold War

What impact will the decline of the Cold War have on Third World conflicts? There is no simple answer to this question because changes in the Cold War intersect with a variety of other factors, any or all of which will be perceived or interpreted differently by different actors. Moreover, the effects, whatever they are, are likely to shift over time, and response patterns are likely to reflect a prolonged learning process that may produce some surprising or unanticipated results. After all, patterns of thought, interpretations of roles and interests, and rules of engagement (and disengagement) are all in flux.

One ought also note that the decline of the Cold War and the process of democratization are only partially linked. The process of democratization, at least outside what used to be called the "Soviet bloc," is a response to a variety of autonomous factors, although the process might be energized by a double "demonstration effect": the failure of the socialist model of development, and the experiences of democratization and the adoption of market economics in Eastern Europe. Conversely, democratization might be partially derailed by a shift of limited aid and investment funds to Eastern Europe and the former Soviet Union or by a manifest failure of the transformation process in these areas. The Cold War, whether in decline or resurgence, has also followed its own imperatives. Support for the Third World and debates about whether we should support one or another country have traditionally reflected Cold War calculations. How these relationships will change now is a broader question that we cannot discuss here. We shall examine only the narrower question of whether Cold War developments are likely to affect conflict in the Third World—which will, in turn, affect some aspects of Third World democratization.

Most wars in the Third World have begun from largely local causes, and the superpowers have been dragged in to protect their own goals. The local causes for conflict are hardly diminishing and may even accelerate if economic and resource problems lead to conflict and ethnic groups increase their demands for autonomy or independence. Obviously, then, the amount of Third World conflict is unlikely to diminish—in fact, the number of violent conflicts in the world does not appear to have diminished since 1985, despite the decline of the Cold War and continued democratization. The constancy of the level of conflict also seems to imply that the major effect of the decline of the Cold War is likely to be on the character (intensity, scope, duration) and the consequences (in terms of military expenditures and development) of war rather than on its frequency.[47]

There is one important qualification to this argument. The decline of the Cold War might increase the frequency of war by removing the restraining effect of the superpowers and the implicit rules of conduct that developed within the Cold War. As the United States sees less need to intervene in local conflicts and as the former Soviet Union loses the ability and inclination to do so, restraint may disappear as the aggressor sees a diminished threat of intervention from its opponent's patron. The absence of superpower patrons, or at least their unreliability as future supporters, may also generate greater pressures to build local arms industries—a process already well underway—and to import even more foreign arms, whatever the development costs.[48] The calculus of choice for Third World decisionmakers may also change with less patron involvement; they will have to make their own decisions on the likelihood of winning or losing a conflict, presumably with less information about the intentions and capabilities of the potential opponent. The number of miscalculated wars may go up sharply. In short, there is some chance that the decline of the Cold War will affect both the character and frequency of Third World wars, although the decision to go to war will continue to reflect many factors only partly related to the Cold War itself.

As the Cold War antagonists cut military spending, there is an almost inverse reaction in the Third World. Not knowing what to expect, leaders are increasing military expenditures, constrained only by the availability of financial resources and growing pressure from international institutions to reduce the defense budget.[49] Insofar as this effort to maintain control also means a decline in spending on other needs, it may only generate the very discontent it is designed to avoid. As foreign aid dwindles and as the relative cost of using force increases, there may also be a rising tendency to strike "out of the blue" or to use the most horrific weapons in order to win quickly. This tendency may be especially pronounced if leaders in the Third World, mindful of what happened in the Gulf War against Saddam Hussein, invest heavily in their own chemical, biological, and nuclear arsenals. In a region like the Middle East, the reciprocal fear of surprise attack may generate preventive or preemptive wars.

The crumbling of the ideological battle lines will probably make both the United States and Russia much more indifferent to domestic transformations in the Third World. In the Third World democracies, this might mean less U.S. opposition to leftist or rightist radical parties, who will be energized by economic decline and protected by democratic procedures.[50] Thus, perversely, the survival of some weak democracies in the Third World might be undermined by the protection granted to radical left or right groups—fundamentally antidemocratic—and the complacency of the strongest external supporter of democracy. The fact that the stakes for the United States in most Third World conflicts may be lower and may not seem to necessitate a rapid or generous response may also undermine the very regimes we seek to establish.

One final point may be worth making in the present context. It concerns the role of the military in new democracies. In some cases, especially in Latin America, the lessening of the presumed threat from the former Soviet Union and Cuba, as well as the manifest failures of military regimes in dealing with economic problems, have generated the need to define a new role for the military. In other places, there are either internal or external threats that seem to justify a continuing and relatively large share of the budget for the military. But the loss of cheap arms from abroad, the costliness of keeping up in ever more expensive arms races, and rising demands from other sectors of the economy imply a long period of instability in the relationship between the military and democratic governments. The military's hostility to the "messiness" of democratic politics and its desire to retain its share of the economic pie will undoubtedly lead, sooner or later, to the revival of the military coup.[51] The point here is simply that the decline of the Cold War has set many Third World militaries adrift, with as yet uncertain consequences.

The effects of the decline in the Cold War are indeterminate, if largely because the drama has not yet come to an end and it is only one factor— albeit a very important one—among many that are changing the nature of the international environment. We can at least say that the need to provide for security in a deteriorating domestic and international environment without the strong support of a rich patron implies continuing problems for new democracies in terms of rising military expenditures (to keep up with neighbors, to pacify the military, or to defend against real threats), declining foreign aid levels, and escalating domestic turmoil. It seems likely that the effort to involve regional or international agencies in the process of conflict resolution will continue, but whether these institutions can be effectively reformed and whether they will be given the power and resources to act remain open questions.

The argument in this chapter has been that, apart from saying that democracies don't fight other democracies, making strong conclusions about the relationship between democracy and conflict are premature. What we can say is that the democracy variable may be important in some cases but that it is likely to have very different effects in different contexts. Having more democratic regimes does not guarantee less international conflict as long as there are still a reasonably large number of nondemocratic regimes in existence and as long as we are uncertain about whether poor and weak Third World democracies will behave much like developed and stable democracies. At an aggregate level, democratic countries seem to spend relatively less than nondemocratic ones on the military, but there is much variation. In addition, with Cold War patronage on the decline, potential enemies arming rapidly, and economic conditions worsening, even peaceful democracies may have no choice but to increase arms spending. It is difficult to generalize about democracy and ethnic conflict, although, as I have argued, democracies may be better at ethnic conflict resolution than many analysts have assumed. On other issues, such as economic or resource conflicts, all judgments about the effects of democracy on particular outcomes are very tentative until more detailed case studies are available. Given the uncertainties and ambiguities, it might be prudent to conclude with a simple reminder: The record of authoritarian regimes in regard to these matters is seldom better, frequently worse, and in the long run strikingly less promising, than that of democracies.

Implications for the Middle East

On one level, the arguments in this chapter have very little to do with the Middle East or the conflict between Israel and the Palestinians. Whether democracies do not fight other democracies and whether they are more likely to resolve or exacerbate internal conflicts are interesting and important issues. But there is only one democracy in the Middle East, so there is as yet no possibility of conflict between democracies. Moreover, even if the Palestinians were to be granted a state or an autonomous political entity, and even if that state or entity turned out to be genuinely democratic, it is not clear how much difference it would make if the rest of the Middle East remained under the control of heavily militarized authoritarian regimes.[52] Even if these regimes were apparently less hostile to Israel because of (at least) an interim agreement with the Palestinians, Israel would still have a significant security problem. The Palestinian state or entity could fail or become radicalized and blame its problems on the failure to recover all of Palestine, and the other regimes might still find it useful to blame the "alien" Israeli presence for their problems. In effect, the security situation would remain unstable because the regional threat would still be present and because the Palestinians, democratic or not, would have to be considered potential allies of their Arab neighbors in any conflict.[53]

Conclusions about the effects of democracy on internal conflict are equally problematic and unclear. One of the major virtues of democracy, of course, is that it provides a set of rules to resolve conflicts peacefully. But this perceived advantage presumes that the conflict is resolvable, that the parties are willing to compromise and to live by the rules of the game. Ethnic or other conflicts do not always fulfill this requirement. In any case, Israeli treatment of its own Arab citizens has been about what could be expected given the security situation and the shortage of resources. Would the Palestinians treat their own minority groups (perhaps even Israeli settlers who chose to stay behind) as well or better? We do not really know, but a likely shortage of resources does not bode well. Nor does the apparent tendency to silence dissent within the Palestinian community itself by assassination provide much ground for optimism. Still, no firm conclusion is possible: Living with and learning about democracy might generate tolerance and a willingness to compromise, but an authoritarian regime might be more effective at containing internal conflicts. Factors other than democracy, especially the strength and fairness of socioeconomic performance, are likely to tip the balance in one direction or the other.

In Latin America and parts of Africa, democracy—or at least some forms of political liberalization—has emerged virtually by default. The dismal record of so many authoritarian regimes and closed economic systems was so apparent and the leadership so inept that the forces of change won relatively easy victories—which is not to say that they could easily consolidate their victory. However, the transition from authoritarianism in the Middle East is likely to be far more difficult and perhaps far bloodier. Entrenched national security states, frequently dominated by small groups that know they are fighting for their own survival, may put up prolonged resistance to regime change. Massive arms spending, fundamental conflicts between ethnic and religious groups with their own version of the "truth," and the absence of a culture of tolerance and compromise suggest very dangerous and perhaps regionally destabilizing transitional conflicts. It is not clear that the forces of democracy will win; indeed, in some cases support for democracy by opposition forces may merely be a disguise to reimpose a different authoritarian regime, as some fear is the case with Islamic fundamentalists. In short, even if we take it on faith that democracies will not fight democracies, the "wars to end wars" could be extraordinarily costly.

Finally, suppose we assume that the Palestinians and perhaps other Arab states do in fact become democratic. Can we safely assume that there will be no conflict between Israel and these states or between the Arab states themselves? It would be possible to do so only if we could prudently assume that the factors responsible for the peaceableness of democracies toward each other exist in the new democracies and that they will operate in the same fashion. (Of course, we must also assume that we know what these factors are; I will assume that they correspond to the factors discussed earlier in this chapter.) In any case, whether the factors relate to the internal characteristics of democracy, the belief systems of the officials who make decisions about conflict, or the creation of a particular normative system between democracies, singly or in combination, it is highly unlikely that such factors will exist to the same degree or operate in the same manner in new democracies. The democratic systems themselves will be far more imperfect—democratic forms will exist well before democratic values and norms have been established—and the belief system and normative structures are, at best, likely to reflect a mixture of the new and the old. In addition, the new democracies will be much poorer; they are likely to continue to see some value in fighting for territory and resources, and the culture of violence will still be very strong. In fact, given the apparently profound hatred of the Arab and Palestinian masses for Israel, any political change that gives greater power to the masses and less power to the more cautious ruling elites might generate greater and more intense conflict in the Middle East.

In sum, the fact that democracies do not fight democracies is both irrelevant in the short run and of very uncertain and problematic significance in the long run as regards the Middle East. This conclusion is in no way meant to be an argument against the emergence of democratic government in the Middle East. The Middle East desperately needs movement away from the brutal and repressive governments that dominate some countries and the reactionary, almost theocratic governments that dominate others. But the arguments for democratization, some of which may gradually also affect the likelihood of conflict, must rest on arguments other than the presumed peaceableness of democracies.

We shall briefly consider some of these arguments in the concluding chapter. But I do want to emphasize one crucial point about the democratization process. While short-run pessimism is surely justified, if largely because of massive state power, internal discontent that can take antidemocratic forms, and sociocultural obstacles, the long-run prognosis may not be quite so grim. Even imperfect democracy achieved at great cost may be preferable to the continuation of the status quo. And one must emphasize that friendship between, say, Israel and Syria, while certainly preferable, may not be necessary. It will be enough if democracy generates some willingness to settle disputes peaceably and eliminates the need for governments to seek legitimacy by threatening unending war against Israel. Moreover, while democracy in the near term might actually impede the peace process as leaders rush to satisfy an aroused constituency, over time it is the only basis for stable peace both internally and externally. Whatever agreements are negotiated will have the support of both leaders and the public. The quest for scapegoats to justify authoritarianism will have disappeared, arms spending may have diminished, and citizens will have alternative means to express their disenchantment with existing governments.

Notes

1. Erich Weede, "Democracy and War Involvement," *Journal of Conflict Resolution*, Vol. 28, No. 4 (December 1984), p. 649.

2. R. J. Rummel, "Libertarianism and International Violence," *Journal of Conflict Resolution*, Vol. 27, No. 1 (March 1983), pp. 27–71. Note that there is a potential ambiguity in using "relatively more free" as a defining characteristic, as such states, whatever their comparative status at the time, may also not meet current standards of procedural democracy. Thus in the early cases some other characteristics (say level of development) might be more significant.

3. Carried to the extreme, the argument might suggest the need to intervene forcibly to impose democracy on nondemocratic states. But the use of violence to end violence is morally and practically unacceptable, at least as a general rule. It also takes for granted what needs to be proved: that the new democracies will behave as peaceably as the old.

4. On the neorealist debate, see Robert O. Keohane, ed., *Neorealism and Its Critics* (New York: Columbia University Press, 1986).

5. Shifts in the nature of the actors need not be toward democracy to be important: the failure of the Soviet Union, for example, would be profoundly important irrespective of the new political arrangements that emerge. And on normative shifts, movement need not only be toward new norms but also could be toward increasing influence for old or older norms.

6. For an argument about the need to move toward a postrealist theoretical synthesis, see my introduction in Robert Rothstein, ed., *The Evolution of the Theoretical Debate in International Relations* (Columbia: University of South Carolina Press, 1991).

7. Arnold Wolfers, *Discord and Collaboration* (Baltimore: John Hopkins University Press, 1962), p. 73.

8. We shall return to this issue shortly.

9. Steve Chan, "Mirror, Mirror on the Wall—Are the Freer Countries More Pacific?" *Journal of Conflict Resolution*, Vol. 28, No. 4 (December 1984), p. 632.

Chan also notes that the four countries with highest war-per-years scores are democracies: Israel, India, France, and Great Britain (pp. 626–627).

10. *Ibid.*, pp. 632–633.

11. Weede, "Democracy and War Involvement," p. 657. Jack Vincent, "Freedom and International Conflict: Another Look," *International Studies Quarterly*, Vol. 31, No. 1 (March 1987), pp. 103–112, also disagrees with Rummel's findings.

12. Zeev Maoz and Nasrin Abdolali, "Regime Types and International Conflict, 1816–1976," *Journal of Conflict Resolution*, Vol. 33 No. 1 (March 1989), pp. 3–35 (my italics).

13. Note that the uncertainty about democracy and conflict involvement in no way implies a better record for authoritarian regimes. Note also that there are so few Third World states that can legitimately be called democracies and that of those that are democracies, there is so much disparity in size or distance that findings about the effects of democracy on Third World conflict must be taken as very tentative.

14. An excellent article by Michael W. Doyle, "Kant, Liberal Legacies, and Foreign Affairs," *Philosophy and Public Affairs*, Vol. 12, No. 3 (Summer 1983), pp. 205–235, has been influential. Also very useful is Zeev Maoz and Bruce Russett, "Alliances, Contiguity, Wealth, and Political Stability: Is the Lack of Conflict Among Democracies a Statistical Artifact?" paper prepared for delivery at the American Political Science Association meeting, San Francisco, 1990. Their answer to the question is that they cannot reject the notion that the political systems of democracies "inherently causes them to refrain from fighting one another" (p. 21).

15. Perhaps the case of Israel and Lebanon in the 1948 war is a partial exception, but there is some ambiguity about how democratic Lebanon was and how much it actually fought.

16. Doyle, "Kant, Liberal Legacies," and Maoz and Russett, "Alliances, Contiguity, Wealth," are especially useful on this issue.

17. See especially Maoz and Russett, "Alliances, Contiguity, Wealth," p. 3.

18. John Mueller, *Retreat From Doomsday: The Obsolescence of Major War* (New York: Basic Books, 1989), discusses the aversion to war as citizens become richer and have more to lose. See especially p. 252. One should note that it is not clear that citizens of authoritarian states are any more willing to risk death or the loss of prosperity (when they have it).

19. One analyst suggests that democratic governments usually require complex coalitions to make policy and that these coalitions, which are risk averse, won't voluntarily start conflicts that carry big risks. This implies that the democracies are more likely to pick on weak opponents rather than strong opponents: for the United States, Grenada and Nicaragua but not the Soviet Union. There are, however, problems with this argument, not only in regard to particular wars and the strengths of particular internal coalitions but also in regard to the fact that it fails to explain why democracies never fight other democracies and do fight nondemocracies—irrespective of internal coalitions. See Allan Lamborn, *The Price of Power: Risk and Foreign Policy in Britain, France and Germany* (Boston: Unwin Hyman, 1990), pp. 347–348.

20. Doyle, "Kant, Liberal Legacies," p. 213.

21. Norms can be defined in different ways, but I shall here accept Axelrod's argument that a norm—or standard of behavior—exists to the extent that individuals (or states in our context) usually act in certain ways and are usually punished when seen not to be acting in this way. See Robert Axelrod, "An Evolutionary Approach to Norms," *American Political Science Review*, Vol. 80, No. 4 (December 1986), p. 1097. Norms, when not formally transformed into law, are

usually complied with voluntarily or even instinctively; consequently support for them is in the form "more or less," not "either/or."

22. It is, no doubt, the tribute vice pays to virtue that nondemocracies feel the need to use the language of universal norms even when they behave abominably. Perhaps in some small way rhetorical support for norms can eventually have a degree of practical influence. But it usually takes more profound changes to increase the power or salience of particular norms—as we shall see.

23. On these functions, see Friedrich V. Kratochwill, *Rules, Norms, and Decisions* (Cambridge: Cambridge University Press, 1989), pp. 14, 67.

24. The distinctions between community and society are in the form of ideal types. In practice, there is a great deal of intermingling. There is a useful discussion in Horace M. Miner, "Community Society Continua," in *International Encyclopedia of Social Sciences* (London: Collier Macmillan Publishers, 1968), pp. 174–180.

25. Axelrod, "An Evolutionary Approach to Norms," p. 1108. Support by the powerful is of course not the only means of establishing a norm, but it is particularly important in the international system.

26. For a discussion of the relationship between arms spending, threat perception, and legitimacy, see Robert Rothstein, "The Security Dilemma and the 'Poverty Trap' in the Third World," *Jerusalem Journal of International Relations,* Vol. 8, No. 4 (1986), pp. 1–38.

27. As noted earlier, the test for the peaceableness of Third World democracies is yet to come—perhaps in the Middle East someday and in Central America in the next decade.

28. This was at least true in the past, when most economic conflicts were not emotional, only affected small groups of citizens, and seemed more easy to compromise by a division of shares. But this may be changing, as noted below.

29. Of course, even if this were true, one could argue that the disputes are more likely to be settled peacefully. In any case, there may be other reasons to prefer democratic regimes, however they behave in economic conflicts.

30. The numbers are from a lecture by R. J. Rummel, excerpted in the *United States Institute of Peace Journal,* Vol. 1, No. 4 (September 1988), p. 6.

31. It is important to note that democracies are not without blemishes in their treatment of their own citizens. There has been a great deal of internal violence in Jamaica, India, Sri Lanka, Israel, and Columbia. But the amounts have been relatively limited, given the circumstances, and none of these governments have approached the level of barbarism of the Amins et al.

32. See, for example, Dov Ronen, "The Challenges of Democracy in Africa: Some Introductory Observations," in Dov Ronen, ed., *Democracy and Pluralism in Africa* (Boulder: Lynne Rienner Publishers, 1986), pp. 1–4. It is interesting that many indigenous African scholars until very recently seemed to share these negative views. However, perhaps following fashion, there has been a sea change in views and a deluge of works about the emergence of democracy in Africa.

33. On consociational democracy, see Arend Lijphart, *Democracy in Plural Societies* (New Haven: Yale University Press, 1977). For some astute critical comments, see Donald L. Horowitz, *Ethnic Groups in Conflict* (Berkeley: University of California Press, 1985) pp. 569–576.

34. Lijphart, *Democracy in Plural Societies.* It has seemed to me, given the characteristics noted, that consociational democracy might be more accurately called "consociational oligarchy."

35. Donald L. Horowitz, "Making Moderation Pay: The Comparative Politics of Ethnic Conflict Management," in Joseph V. Montville, ed., *Conflict and*

Peacemaking in Multi-ethnic Societies (Lexington, MA: Lexington Books, 1991), p. 454.

36. There are other criticisms of consociational democracy that I shall not discuss. For more extended comment, see Horowitz, *Ethnic Groups in Conflict*, and Kenneth D. McRae, "Theories of Power-Sharing and Conflict Management," in Montville, ed., *Conflict and Peacemaking*, pp. 93–106.

37. Horowitz, *Ethnic Groups in Conflict*, pp. 598ff.

38. See his comments in "Speaking About Democracy and Peace," *United States Institute of Peace Journal*, Vol. 3, No. 2 (June 1990), p. 3.

39. Horowitz, *Ethnic Groups in Conflict*, p. 131.

40. See Milton J. Esman, "Economic Performance and Ethnic Conflict," in Montville, ed., *Conflict and Peacemaking*, p. 480.

41. *Ibid.*, for good general comments on all these matters.

42. See the *New York Times*, May 2, 1990, for some of the details on rising arms spending.

43. Janet Welsh Brown, "Why Should We Care?" in Janet Welsh Brown, ed., *In the U.S. Interest* (Boulder: Westview Press, 1990), pp. 1–18, has interesting comments on these matters. The pattern of response to resource deterioration could vary greatly from irrational acts of violence (terrorism, assassination) to desperate attempts to emigrate to wars against neighbors—or perhaps just to despair and resignation.

44. For example, Vaman Rao, "Democracy and Economic Development," *Studies in Comparative International Development* (Winter 1984–1985), p. 76, insists that only nondemocratic states have succeeded in controlling population growth rates. But I have examined recent World Bank figures and have found a much more mixed record on this issue.

45. Edgar Owens, *The Future of Freedom in the Developing World* (New York: Pergamon Press, 1987), pp. 52–63.

46. Bruce Russett, "Prosperity and Peace," *International Studies Quarterly*, Vol. 27, No. 4 (December 1983), pp. 381–387, has made some very interesting and suggestive comments on the issue of when war is likely to be chosen.

47. This is also the position of Mueller, *Retreat From Doomsday*, p. 254.

48. On patterns of Third World military spending, see two articles by Daniel P. Hewitt: "Military Expenditures in the Developing World," *Finance and Development*, Volume 28, No. 3 (September 1991), pp. 22–25; and "What Determines Military Expenditures?" *Finance and Development*, Vol. 28, No. 4 (December 1991), pp. 22–25.

49. For evidence showing restraint in response to financial pressures, see Hewitt, "What Determines Military Expenditures?" p. 22.

50. The indifference may not extend to takeovers by Islamic fundamentalists, given the potential threat to other Arab governments, possible turbulence in oil markets, and a renewed possibility of terrorism (and the acquisitions of nuclear weapons). Note the restrained response of the U.S. government to the recent military takeover in Algeria.

51. How soon before the military begins to intervene again may depend on "disaster myopia." As time passes and the military begins to forget how badly it dealt with economic problems, tolerance of civilian ineptitude is likely to erode quickly.

52. How would democratization affect the character of war rather than its frequency? There is no clear answer, but one might speculate that in the short run the distrust and hatred of the past would persist and that, consequently, the intensity and severity of any conflict might increase. This might also be true because of the

nature of the latest generation of arms. Whether the destructiveness of the latter might also shorten the duration of war or make a pre-emptive war more likely (because of the need to "use them or lose them," etc.) is also unclear. Fear of not having enough such weapons or of being surprised by a breakthrough of some sort may also increase military expenditures (to buy or build weapons), which will decrease development spending. Finally, would the structure of deterrence be affected by democratization and the dangers of massive amounts of dangerous weapons? Again, if it is, the short-run effects are likely to be negative.

53. While there has been some movement in both the Arab and Israeli camps toward compromise, if largely because of a certain fatigue with conflict and a rising concern with socioeconomic problems, it seems to me that a majority of Israelis (even some in the peace camp) see the Arab and Palestinian shifts as pragmatic rather than principled. That is, these Israelis assume that the Arab states and the Palestinians would still like to destroy Israel and that Israel remains a symbol of defeat and a stand-in for decades of frustration and discontent. In this view, the peace process reflects only the absence of an Arab military option, and massive arms expenditures suggest that the "preferable" option will be adopted if it can be. Even if these judgments are untrue, prudent Israeli decisionmakers must assume it might be true—which is why the Israeli security situation might not improve greatly because of the peace process or a prolonged process of democratization.

3

The Relevance of Democracy to Israeli-Palestinian Peace

Edy Kaufman
Shukri B. Abed

Machiavellian realists have often said that there are no eternal enemies, although such protracted struggles as that between the Palestinians and the Israelis seem to belie this assertion. Yet history has seen far more virulent and long-lived enmities eventually transformed into productive and mutually beneficial relationships. Turning conflict into cooperation and moving from enmity to friendship requires concerted effort and constant attention to common interests, needs, and characteristics. Israelis and Palestinians, though they often seem not to realize it, do have a common interest in ending their century-old conflict. This chapter shows that pursuit of democracy and the adherence to democratic values may provide a means for effecting significant and positive change in the relationship between the Semitic cousins. Drawing on the discussion of the relationship between democratic regimes and peace developed in the previous chapter, we consider the prospects for such a proposition in the Israeli-Palestinian conflict, with democracy seen as a converging interest of the two parties.

Setting the Frame of Mind

It seems at times as if every idea about peace between Palestinians and Israelis has already been formulated. So wide has been the gap between them that few new avenues are perceived as open for the resolution of a conflict that has persisted, with more or less vehemence, for close to a century. The stakes are astronomically high and the penalty for failure extremely grave, as this local conflict continually threatens to spill over into broader disputes among the nations of the region and of the world. Because of the strategic importance of the Middle East and its oil reserves, regional confrontations such as the Gulf War escalate rapidly and loom as formidable obstacles to moderate thinking on the Palestinian question.

Five years after the intifada (Palestinian uprising) against the Israeli occupation began, two years after the Gulf War, and with the opening of the Middle East Peace Regional Conference, it seems that prospects for a resolution are improving, although obstacles remain visible. On the one hand, no future accords between Israel and surrounding Arab states can lead to a lasting peace unless the demands and aspirations of the Palestinians as well as those of Israelis are minimally addressed. On the other hand, reducing the level of expectations, at least on the part of one party, may allow the limited conditions of both to be met halfway in an interim, staged agreement.[1] Partial solutions can provoke serious upheavals among the maximalist groups and their followers, and implementing such agreements will most likely produce serious cleavages in both societies. However, lack of progress in the peace process will also have negative domestic effects (discussed in Chapter 5) as well as regressive outcomes in the region. The "cold peace" with Egypt may be jeopardized if there persists a lack of visible progress in the peace process.

In situations of conflict, each side tends to fixate on the negative and to assume that concessions to the opponent are detrimental to its own interests. Palestinians and Israelis are no exception. Statements by leaders of both communities often express mutual frustration, suspicion, and even apathy, only serving to further protract the political stalemate. What are the basic parameters of the Israeli-Palestinian conflict? For Palestinians, the foremost concern appears to be the pursuit of statehood; for Israelis, the maintenance of their security. Given that most Israelis view an autonomous Palestinian state as antithetical to Israeli security, we must proceed to ask how these two seemingly contradictory concerns can be reconciled. In other words, how can we achieve a solution that simultaneously satisfies the fundamental needs of both communities? What type of future solution can best guarantee Israel a lasting peace and secure borders while addressing the basic Palestinian aspirations for an independent governmental entity?

Current discussions about moving one step at a time through a period of Palestinian self-rule under Israeli control encounter many technical concerns. Some resistance can be overcome by not disclosing the light at the end of the tunnel—independent statehood for the Palestinians—to either side. Even if such constructive ambiguity has the merit of postponing the wider areas of disagreement for a future discussion, it may be best accompanied by examination of the lessons of history as well as assessments of the current progress toward reconciliation in other regions among national, ethnic, religious, linguistic, and cultural communities. This exercise requires huge leaps of imagination and continual re-examination of the problem from ever new and different angles. Until recently, the political leaders of both nations have explored a limited number of creative avenues in their search for resolution, stressing the uniqueness of the protracted state of conflict. Oversimplified, one-dimensional solutions are usually premised on the popularly accepted principle that one side's concession may signal to the other one side's defeat. For example, an Israeli withdrawal from the territories occupied after the 1967 war could likely have mutually beneficial consequences, but the concept is often dismissed without closer examination because it is broadly perceived as a security threat to Israel. This perception holds despite Israel's qualitative military strength (superior to that of the surrounding belligerent Arab states combined), the strong prospects for demilitarization of the West Bank, and even the feasibility of expanding Israel's security zone by guaranteeing the inviolability of Jordanian borders to Iraqi and Syrian incursion.[2]

What is needed today is a move beyond the boundaries of our present grim, patently unacceptable reality. Transcendence of the current paradigms of inquiry necessitates what Edward de Bono refers to as "lateral thinking." De Bono explains: "Instead of proceeding step by step in the usual vertical manner, you take up a new and quite arbitrary position. You then work backwards and try to construct a logical path between this new position and the starting point. Should such a path prove possible, it may eventually be tested with the full rigors of logic. If the path is sound, you are then in a useful position which may never have been reached by ordinary vertical thinking."[3]

In the case of the Israeli-Palestinian conflict, are there future options, points of convergence, once we reject the zero-sum premise? Thinking laterally, for example, we can ask ourselves: Are there possible safeguards against war other than the occupation of the territories in the West Bank and the Gaza Strip? Let us assume that for most citizens of the Jewish state there is no single issue more important than security. No country faced with the actual and potential threats of both conventional and guerrilla warfare to which Israel feels itself vulnerable could deny the importance of geopolitical considerations. Yet, in light of the meteoric proliferation of deadly arms in the region, there can be no doubt about the decreasing importance of conventional topographic obstacles, so often mentioned as a justification for retaining the territories. Powerful missiles can be launched from Syria, Saudi Arabia, or, as we saw, Iraq and reach Tel Aviv in a matter of minutes.

Lateral thinking encourages consideration of nonmilitary "soft" aspects of security, new dimensions of foreign policy that should be considered in the region's search for formulas promoting peace. In addition to formal treaties and agreements offering guarantees such as demilitarization, the presence of international peace forces, early-warning stations, and satellite monitoring, emphasis should be placed on de facto common interests that could strongly motivate both sides to seek and maintain peace.

The Relationship of Democracy to Peace

Following De Bono's lead, we can return to the study's basic assumption and a basic tenet in world politics: In general, democratic states tend to avoid war as a tool for settling disputes among themselves. An important security priority for Israel, then, is to ensure that the Palestinian entity develops democratic institutions. By the same token, the Palestinians have a legitimate interest in seeing their neighbor Israel remain democratic.[4]

Since the creation of nation-states and the establishment of Western-style, liberal, democratic regimes the tendency has been to resort to means other than formally declared warfare to solve their conflicts. From Kantian theories to meticulous checks of data banks that tabulate the correlates of war, this proposition seems to hold firm. It is confirmed in a pioneering study entitled *Resort to Arms* (1982), wherein Small and Singer provide a chronological table of international wars over the past 200 years.[5] Other scholars and statesmen have added their support. In the appendices of his article "Liberalism and World Politics," Michael Doyle provides a table of "liberal regimes" based on Kant's four characteristics: market and private economies, polities that are externally sovereign, citizens who possess juridical rights, and republican representative government. These have grown in number from only three in the eighteenth century to fifty during the period between 1945 and 1982.[6]

Using the data of a most comprehensive work by Brecher and Wilkenfeld entitled the International Crisis Behavior (ICB) Project,[7] we can analyze the few cases showing a positive correlation between wars and democracies. These two scholars studied international conflicts fought between 1929 and 1985; within this span, so rare and so marginal are those instances of warring democratic regimes that they are worth enumerating:

1) Israel-Lebanon, 1948–1949. Lebanon's involvement in the war against the newly independent state of Israel consisted essentially of a declaratory position in solidarity with other nondemocratic Arab states. No significant acts of combat took place between the two democracies.

2) Guatemala–United States, 1954. In this confrontation, an expeditionary force, armed by the United Fruit Company and trained by the Central Intelligence Agency but mostly composed of and led by Guatemalan exiles, invaded from Honduran territory and took control of Guatemala a few days later. The United States's high level of involvement still falls short of the many other direct military interventions in the region.

3) Turkey-Cyprus, 1974. The Cypriot National Guard, led by officers of the Greek army, seized the government on July 15, 1974, committed to the union of the island and Greece. They deposed elected President Makarios, who fled the country, and on July 20 Turkey sent the army and effectively took control of part of the island. A few days separated a democratic regime and an act of aggression.

4) Israel-Lebanon, 1982. Israel's invasion of Lebanon in 1982 was originally aimed at the "semiautonomous" Palestinian zone in the south of Lebanon. It was coordinated, to a certain extent, with the tacit understanding of the late Lebanese president, Bashir Gemayl. Some have questioned if this torn country could be considered a democracy at that time.

The relative weakness of the handful of exceptions is self-evident. It is nonetheless a significant finding that half of the borderline cases involve Israel. Since the early 1980s many countries have provided further illustrations of democratization. In his 1986 acceptance speech in Oslo, Nobel Peace Prize laureate Oscar Arias, president of Costa Rica, expressly linked the formal solution of the conflicts in Central America to parallel efforts to democratize the regimes in the area. In Central America policymakers are not seeking peace alone, "nor only the peace that will follow some day from political progress, but rather peace and democracy together, indivisible elements." Bloodshed among the contending guerrilla and armed forces, declared Arias, is inseparable from the end of the repression of human rights. While every nation has the right to freely choose its political or ideological system, the Costa Rican leader insisted that every government respect universal human rights, and he stressed that a nation that mistreats its own citizens is more likely to maltreat its neighbors.

In Chapter 2, Robert Rothstein points to the fragility of generalization, noting that in developing countries the scarcity of resources, the unequal income distribution, and the vast sectors of the population below the poverty line generate a highly unstable situation. The impact of economic constraints on an Israeli-Palestinian peace may be of lesser significance given relatively high standards of living, the foreign aid that can be anticipated as a built-in dimension of the conflict's resolution, and prospects resulting from regional cooperation. Nonetheless, the lessons of history call upon the parties to capture in their imagination the meaning of such developments elsewhere. Caution is surely in order given the profound roots and existential characteristics of the Arab-Jewish dispute.

Democracy and the Israeli-Palestinian Conflict

The theory of peaceful coexistence between democratic neighbors remains to be tested in the Israeli-Palestinian conflict. Perhaps the most significant stumbling block to peace is mutual doubt regarding the wavering commitment to such ideals by the involved parties. Criticism notwithstanding, Israel continues to be a vibrant democracy internally. While not a few Israelis might be willing to concede that a democratic Palestinian state could be a desirable future neighbor, many disbelieve absolutely that the Palestinians (or any Arab nation, for that matter) are capable of establishing and maintaining a democracy. The fact that there has never been an Arab democracy (with the exception of Lebanon—hardly an encouraging example) is considered proof that there never will be one. The Arab people are often viewed by Israelis and other Westerners as inherently incapable of self-government through democratic means.

To be sure, an analysis of the surrounding Arab regimes does not provide much encouragement, with authoritarianism and human rights violations a regular feature of the region's political landscape.[8] The political traditions in the Arab world certainly do not support or provide role models for any fledgling efforts at democratization. Such negativism, however, can be countered by the following observations.

First, nothing in world politics is etched in stone. It has been widely documented that the commitment to developing democratic forms of government—once an exclusive province of the West—has spread in the past two decades into southern Europe, Latin America, and Asia. In Africa, too, the strengthening of democratic institutions at a grassroots level seems to be an emerging, consistent pattern.[9] Even as latecomers to the democratization processes, Middle Eastern nations are beginning to initiate small-scale yet significant democratic reforms. And the dizzying pace at which certain Eastern European states have plunged into democratization in recent years, as well as the more plodding efforts of the former Soviet republics, demonstrate how quickly a political landscape can change once a commitment to change exists.

In the second place, the Palestinians do not equal the Arabs. Their experiences are unique in the Arab world and, in fact, render them likely candidates to spearhead democratization reforms in the Middle East. Certain developments in the Palestinian community—within Israel, in the Occupied Territories, and at large—definitely justify a cautious optimism regarding the prospects for a future democratic Palestinian state, as the following points suggest:

1. The language of the Palestinian Declaration of Independence reflects a philosophical commitment to the development of democratic institutions.[10]

2. Within the PLO the importance of democratic procedures for leadership succession or in relation to majority-supported resolutions, replacing consensual decisionmaking, is gradually being recognized. Even the more radical groups, such as the Popular Front for the Liberation of Palestine (PFLP), stated in 1988 their willingness to play the role of loyal opposition during the exploration of political avenues.

3. In the Occupied Territories, Palestinians have become acquainted with the election process, beginning with the 1972 and 1976 municipal elections and continuing today, for example, in the election of representa-

tives to a large number of trade, professional, and other civil-society organizations.

4. The high percentage of educated Palestinians, including an impressive number of university graduates, has contributed to a considerable loosening of the traditional structure. An educated and well-informed population is certainly a prerequisite for building and maintaining democratic societies.

5. For many years now, the Palestinians have engaged in dialogues and heated debates among themselves concerning their future. The debates have led to a wider acceptance of the principles of *negotiation* and *compromise,* two cornerstones of democratic development. Indeed, these are the essence of democracy in its truest sense.

6. The issue of freedom is fundamental to the outlook of many in the present Palestinian professional and political elites in the West Bank and Gaza Strip. Almost exclusively Western-educated, the elite strata of the Occupied Territories is Western-oriented and will most likely play a major role in formulating the nature of the regime in the future Palestinian state. In fact, should the Palestinian entity *not* be a democratic one, many of the social, political, and cultural leaders of the community today would be censured, replaced, and possibly exiled, something they would certainly choose to forestall.

7. The dispersion of the Palestinians around the world can be seen as a further guarantee for decentralized decisionmaking. The diffusion of power is an important precondition for pluralism. Only democracy can encompass the cultural diversity and the varying points of view that are a result of the conditions of exile suffered by the Palestinians over the past forty years.

8. Paradoxically, military control in the Occupied Territories has promoted the stirrings of democratization among people who are ruled *undemocratically.* Repression of Palestinian leaders during the intifada, for example, has accelerated the dispersion of decisionmaking power to the grassroots level and to the younger generations.

9. The Palestinian uprising represents a landmark in terms of Palestinian *self-assertion.* Under the conditions of the intifada, the Palestinians in the Occupied Territories have taken the initiative and established *new patterns of collective behavior,* including different forms of grassroots organization. Taking one's destiny into one's own hands and collective behavior are two characteristics of democratic behavior.

10. The intifada has also enhanced the role of women in the Palestinian community. Many women are considered community leaders, and some of them have become internationally recognized as spokeswomen for the Palestinian cause. The centrality of women in the Palestinian community undermines the *traditional* view of women in the Arab world and brings the Palestinian society one step closer to social equality.

11. A Palestinian state will most likely be dependent to some degree on

the economic and even political support of Western countries (including the United States and the Western European countries, particularly those of the Common Market), as Palestinians have recognized that they cannot afford to alienate Western countries by creating a nondemocratic state.

Although the intifada has certainly been a decisive factor in the development of democratic behavior among Palestinians living within the Occupied Territories, it has also created certain stumbling blocks to such development, the most important being the large number of political assassinations of "alleged collaborators," which only contributes to a climate of insecurity for expression of dissent from leadership decisions.

Yet Palestinian political elites seem increasingly to realize that their best chance for an independent state lies in their genuine espousal of democratic principles, an expedient position to adopt in an increasingly Western-led world community. For their part, Israelis must realize that they have good reason to support the gradual and eventual establishment of a democratic Palestinian governmental entity that would not only guarantee the rights of its own citizens but also preserve cooperative and productive relationships with its neighbors, as democratic states are wont to do. Achieving such shared values in an admittedly polarized situation may contribute to shifting alliances in the region by stressing acquired commonalities between the two regimes and their constituencies.

Contradiction and Convergence

De facto arrangements based on common norms and values have been implicitly adopted by the two warring parties since before the Six Day War. Armistice lines, "red lines" restricting military presence, and the often limited nature of wars have frequently been based on tacit understandings by both sides. The reciprocal treatment of prisoners of war serves as a graphic illustration of this phenomenon: Both sides usually refrain from executing prisoners of war and are willing to exchange prisoners. Other areas of convergence include the "open bridges" policy by which Jordan, Israel, and the Palestinians benefit from the passage of merchandise and people over the Jordan River. The use of water from the Jordan and Yarmuk rivers, once seen as a source of friction, is now understood to work to the mutual benefit of Israel and certain Arab countries. President Anwar Sadat and Prime Minister Menachem Begin altered the course of history with a peace treaty and emerging forms of cooperation, leaving unresolved aspects of the conflict to be addressed in an incremental and gradual fashion in the future.

The most perceptive leaders on both sides understand that war and continued civil strife exact their toll on both sides and are of no lasting benefit to either. The late Israeli defense minister Moshe Dayan, for example, stressed the importance of rebuilding the cities on the Suez Canal, thus increasing the economic costs of a new war with Egypt. In a similar vein, one retired Israeli general emphasized the damaging psychological consequences of repression. He argued that Israel's abstention from excessive harshness and repressive behavior should reduce the intensity of Palestinian hostility, thereby mitigating (even if only mildly) the motivation of individual Palestinians to seek revenge against their oppressors.[11] Pursuing this logic implies that avoiding forms of collective punishment in the West Bank and the Gaza Strip, where retaliatory antagonism is manifold, should be considered a high priority for promoting Israel's security concerns.

Questions once considered unnegotiable are now becoming the subject of political discussions, increasing the possibility that pragmatism will win out over dogmatic, ideological positions. For example, a prominent member of the PLO has admitted the possibility of Jewish settlers remaining in the West Bank and Gaza Strip after an Israeli withdrawal: "The right of Israelis to live in the state of Palestine and the right of Palestinians to live in the state of Israel should be subject of negotiations."[12] The presence of settlers in a Palestinian state, even as a result of a unilateral decision, may further legitimate the status of the Palestinians born and living as citizens within the Jewish state. Other discussions revolve around the unilateral preference of many Palestinians to restrict their security forces in a future state to a well-trained police guard rather than a full-scale army. Military balance with Israel cannot be realistically achieved given the lack of sufficient air space for the effective operationalizing of combat planes. Forgoing an army would save the new state the high expenditure of a full defense budget and complement the widely shared Israeli aspiration for demilitarization in a future Palestinian state. Even if it coincides with Israeli security concerns, not forming a military cast may be in the best interest of Palestinian civil society. Without a praetorian guard and without any Palestinians with inherited royal claims, chances for democracy may be better there than elsewhere in the Arab world.

The aforementioned examples illustrate that the Israelis, the Palestinians, and their Arab supporters have already adopted certain informal, mutually beneficial rules of the game despite the unresolved, indeed conflict-riddled, political situation. All of these examples demonstrate some of the existing areas of convergence and offer insight into other possible areas of mutual benefit, such as the development of democratic norms in the region.

The strengthening of democratic institutions and practices among both the occupier and the occupied can represent an important priority for promoting a peaceful relationship between Palestinians and the Jewish state. If the Israeli government were to acknowledge and pursue multidimensional aspects of security maintenance (for example, economic, political, and cultural areas of convergence) rather than propagate historical or mythical commitments to promote purely military security, a rational strategy could be developed to encourage democratization in both communities. However, if such options are unavailable, it may be important for pragmatic Palestinians to agree to the short-term measures proposed by the Israeli establishment that by design or default will encourage future democratic reforms. Arguments about immediate resolution of questions related to the jurisdiction over territories (land, natural resources, water, the subsoil, the territorial sea, and air space) may take longer to resolve than agreement between the military occupier and the occupied on the democratic transfer of authority from one people to another.

Furthermore, many favor the idea of holding elections in the West Bank and the Gaza Strip for an interim self-governing authority or an administrative council as an integral part of the Palestinian autonomy scheme, as suggested in the Camp David agreement. The idea of the interim authority appeared initially to be the preference of the PLO, while the administrative council plan came to be embraced by Israeli Prime Ministers Yitzhak Shamir and Yitzhak Rabin, as well as by Egyptian President Hosni Mubarak in his "Ten Point" document. What was seen until 1991 as a unilateral Israeli preference can now be argued to benefit both sides. A solution involving a key mechanism of democratization may be preferable to one that comes mostly as an imposition from outside. As it happened, the Madrid peace conference paved the way in October 1991 for a combination of both Israeli and Arab strategies.

As an illustration of how matters of confrontation can become issues of convergence, we may elaborate this idea in more detail. At the early stages of the peace talks that took place in 1992 in Washington, focus on an interim period of autonomous self-rule as part of a staged solution appeared as a potential area of agreement by both sides, to which the main world actors also assented. Within it, the question of voting is of crucial importance.[13] Although the Israeli government only promised municipal elections within the framework of the Camp David agreement, even such limited steps could further democratic processes. Israeli authorities moved in the direction of dialogue with traditional or elected Palestinian leadership during the first decade after occupation after 1967, but then switched to a preference for deals with the traditional, authoritarian, uneducated, and sometimes corrupt elites (the Village Leagues) on the assumption that such elements of the occupied population would more readily acquiesce to Israeli rule. This tactic was clearly not designed to encourage future cooperation on an equal footing between the two nations. Unfortunately, a tendency to support indigenous democratic leadership among the Palestinians—as a reflection of enlightened self-interest—does not prevail within the Israeli establishment. Judging from the experience of elections held by nonrepresentative regimes in other areas of the world (including the Philippines, Chile, and

Nicaragua), problems of control by the authorities have been bypassed by the strong presence of an international observer. Representatives of international organizations—parliamentarians, journalists, and other formal or informal observers—play a crucial role in ensuring that political campaigns and elections are conducted such that the state authorities cannot control the results. The international community could encourage Israeli authorities to see that elections in the West Bank and Gaza adhere to similar standards for voting as within Israel. Active foreign monitoring could provide the Palestinian leadership with the necessary and reasonable protection of their interests in the elections without unduly infringing on Israel's safety. Cooperation among Israeli authorities and Palestinian leaders regarding electoral procedures and perhaps even the formation of mixed Israeli/Palestinian bodies might serve as yet another incremental step toward addressing each other's needs and interests, thus forming an additional area of political convergence.

The results of such elections will most likely leave Israel in the position of having to recognize and interact with individuals who have unequivocally identified themselves with the Palestine Liberation Organization. However, the past stands, advocacy, and behavior of the PLO in exile have left many Israelis without trust in its present leadership. Hence, the more specific question to be considered is: What type of leadership can answer Israel's concern for lasting peace and security while meeting the basic aspirations of the Palestinians?

Once municipal leadership is elected, there should be no reason the mayors could not constitute the temporary representative body and serve as a partner for negotiations regarding the subsequent steps in the peace process. In fact, it would not be the first time the elected mayors played a major role in the political life of the Occupied Territories. Following the sweeping 1976 victory of the nationalist candidates in most towns and cities of the West Bank, the mayors "within the first few months in office . . . performed impressively in municipal affairs, and demonstrated a remarkable cooperation and coordination among themselves in political issues. . . . Despite . . . different approaches and personal-regional rivalries, most, if not all, West Bank mayors endeavored to sustain a united front toward the Israeli government and other external forces."[14]

In other words, there is a historical precedent for the elected mayors becoming the temporary representative body for the Palestinian population of the West Bank and Gaza. To be sure, according to Moshe Ma'oz, this earlier elected body was subjected to measures undertaken by the Israelis "to counter . . . independent tendencies of the mayors. While upholding its own financial allocations and supervising the registration of external monies, [the military government] tried to confine the activities of the mayors to merely municipal issues, and, accordingly, reduce their powers and hold them on a short leash."[15] However, the military government's efforts to curb the political activities of the mayors were not successful at the time, and today, given the intifada and the emergence of a new post–Cold War world, it would be even more difficult, if not impossible, to implement such a repressive strategy. Increasingly, leading Israeli politicians have advocated the principle of Palestinian elections.[16]

It is interesting to consider in this connection what processes have occurred in the past when occupying powers have withdrawn from territories where democracy eventually prevailed (Austria, West Germany, Italy, Japan). Where the occupying power perceived its presence to be the result of an unprovoked attack by a nondemocratic regime, it has not felt obliged to evacuate the conquered lands until a democratically elected government is in place. Moreover, restrictions have been enforced on the vanquished, such as the outlawing of irredentist parties advocating revanche or territorial expansion. In most cases, interim periods of self-government last a good number of years. When the defeated countries became independent, some elements within them originally perceived such stipulations as limiting their freedom, but in retrospect they may not be unhappy with the outcome. A key example is post–World War II Japan.

Following this line of reasoning (i.e., turning disadvantages into advantages), we see that the Israeli government, consciously or unconsciously, can facilitate the development of a Palestinian leadership compatible with both minimum PLO aims and the implementation of democratic processes. These first steps are most likely to endure and evolve if begun from below rather than from above. In a well-known article on developmental democracy, Richard Sklar has advocated the formation of local government or an autonomous judiciary as a stage in bottom-up democracy building in developing countries.[17] From this point of view, and given the fact that the Palestinians have no previous experience in independent statehood and truly representative institutions, beginning from the grassroots and working upward may be a more prudent and systematic way of establishing permanent pluralistic institutions. Interim periods of transition to democracy are not necessarily a disadvantage for the Palestinians; at the same time, they can provide an increased sense of security and familiarity to the Israelis.

The above discussion has attempted to illustrate means by which the Israeli government might facilitate the development of a Palestinian leadership that is compatible with PLO-declared aims *and* committed to strengthening democratic norms, with a clear endorsement of the principles of coexistence within both communities.

There is a broad preference among those politically active on both sides for a democratic form of government in any type of future solution.[18] Without defining the specific terms of which existing democratic model would be selected, many analysts now believe that the Palestinians' political agenda is grounded in a Western-style democracy and that they seek respect for civil and political rights within a state providing for the basic needs and promoting the welfare of the entire population.

The Effect of the Situation on the Standards of Democracy

It is also sensible to speculate on the future effect of prolonging the current state of belligerence. If democracies contribute to peace, is it reasonable to make the inverse inference? Subsequent chapters discuss the present trends in Israel, an established regime, in a systematic manner. Briefly, it may be necessary to recall that the democratic nature of Israel, or of any state, is not axiomatic. In fact, some of the democratic standards of the Jewish state have significantly deteriorated since 1967. As Pinkas and Kaufman show in Chapters 4 and 5, respectively, striking examples of institutional problems can be found in the rulings of the Supreme Court of Justice relating to the population of the Occupied Territories and in the rulings of lower courts concerning Arabs in Israel.[19] No less troublesome is the lack of popular support for basic principles of civil and political rights, particularly among the youngest age groups. In one recent public opinion poll, 40 percent of Israeli youth indicated that they "hate all Arabs."[20]

Prior to the Palestinian uprising, many analysts contended that Israeli control of the West Bank and Gaza Strip was a model of "benign occupation." Proponents claimed that even if rule in the territories did not attain the democratic standards within Israel proper, Palestinians there nevertheless enjoyed relatively greater freedom than those living under Arab occupation or in Arab countries. Freedom of the press, academic freedom, and other civil liberties were relatively greater under Israeli occupation than under Arab authoritarian regimes in the region. However, the concept of benign occupation and its alleged relative benefits have been sharply repudiated since the uprising began in earnest.

The intifada represents a landmark in terms of Palestinian self-assertion in the process of political development in the West Bank and Gaza. For the first time since the 1967 war and the beginning of the Israeli occupation, the Palestinians have taken the initiative and established new patterns of collective behavior, including different forms of grassroots organizing. For twenty years, from 1968 to 1987, the local population reacted to the directives of the Israeli authorities. Since then the trend has been reversed: Most of the time the local population has gained the initiative, and its dominant strategy has forced the military and civilian administration into primarily reactive measures. The focused striving for empowerment, coupled with increasingly pragmatic views (such as the acceptance of territorial compromise with Israel), has been persuasive in advancing the Palestinian point of view. Yet frustration with the dearth of political achievements has strengthened the hand of extremist factions, intensifying the number of executions as a form of struggle, for example. Similarly, there exists a clear and present danger that democracy within Israel proper will begin to disintegrate as extreme chauvinist, militarist, and fundamentalist forces seek to silence those with opinions that differ from their own.

Both Palestinians and Israelis may fail to recognize this dangerous trend, which threatens to blight their chances for a political life without intimidation. And both sides need recognize that the surest way to guard against such dangers is to proceed with haste to resolve their mutual differences. For the Palestinians, democratization should not necessarily be made contingent upon the outcome of either the cessation of intifada or progress in the peace talks. For the Israelis, the setbacks in democratic practices require immediate institutional and educational remedies, regardless of the outcome of the peace negotiations. The long-term commitment to Israeli and Palestinian democratization should prove a powerful impetus toward a future peaceful resolution of the conflict.

Discussions of things that can be done to improve the human rights situation have been a confidence-building factor in the peace talks. Some measures, such as the release of Palestinian minors, the elderly and sick, and peaceful dissenters from Israeli prisons, could be seen as unilateral humanitarian gestures that would, it is hoped, meet with some relaxation in the intifada resistance. Other measures could be advanced multilaterally: such as granting that Jews in Syria be allowed to exit the country, and similar number of Palestinians be allowed back in the West Bank and Gaza.

Conclusions

For the Jewish people, the highest priority has been and continues to be assuring security in a complex Middle East landscape that is perceived as hostile. With powerful missiles that can now be launched from neighboring and remote Arab countries, the traditional approach to Israeli security—focusing on the maintenance of a qualitatively strong military force, diplomatic cease-fires, and unwritten understandings—is no longer adequate. More creative approaches are called for in addressing security questions. Rephrasing the question often allows for broader insight into the problem than traditional modes. The symbolic presence of limited military forces to assert claims of sovereignty without posing an offensive threat, disbanding and disarming irregular forces, a commitment to refrain from preemptive strikes or surprise attacks, notification of military maneuvers, regular meetings of military officials of all sides, the mutual acceptance of early-warning systems and international observers, interim nonbelligerency statements—all these measures can build confidence in the realm of security. Beyond military de-escalation and conventional diplomacy, can emphasis be placed on de facto common political interests that will strongly impel both sides to promote their respective security and identity needs?

The Palestinians have been coming to terms with the irreversibility of Israel's existence as an established state and adjusting their demands; they now seek the end of occupation in the remaining areas of Palestine occupied by the Jewish army after 1967. In a spacial sense, accommodation to two states, side by side, seems a viable long-term proposition.

There was a trend that suggested that in order to avoid an imposed solution from outside the region, the Israelis and Palestinians should come to a gradual agreement via concrete incremental actions, such as holding elections among the Palestinian population in the West Bank and Gaza. If perceived to be expedient, elections moving gradually from local to central bodies in itself could be justified by the top leadership of both sides. Granted, serious differences exist between the Israeli proposal for an administrative council[21] and the model of the Palestinian Interim Self-government Authority (PISGA).[22]

The ascendancy of a Labor/left-of-center coalition in June 1992 substantially changed the degree of concessions and the willingness to compromise by the Israeli partner. Still, asymmetry in the level of power of both sides may predetermine that the concessions the Israelis are willing to undertake will fall short of the Arabs' minimum expectations. Replacing the leadership of one of the parties with a more internationally accepted figure could be a great incentive for peace.

Nonetheless, the Palestinians may come to a moment of truth in which they must decide whether to consent to those restricted choices proposed by the occupation government. If such conditions would be considered negligible, the door remains open for unusual challenges, such as the formula of "unilateral elections"; namely, if the peace talks fail to lead anywhere, the Palestinians can declare their intention to proceed with the election plans on their own.[23] At the same time, can Palestinians visualize even the replacement of Chairman Yassir Arafat by democratic procedures? (As a rule, leadership changes in the Arab world occur "by accident"—natural or purposeful.) Can a new leader with a different, peace-loving image strike more international support and inspire more confidence among Israelis?[24] These questions have begun to be addressed publicly.[25]

With respect to the PLO leadership in Tunis, it could be argued that it is not in the Palestinians' overall interest to elect alternative representatives from the West Bank and Gaza at the national level because of the possible antagonism—whether real or merely perceived—between leaders in the territories and leaders in exile. Alternatively, the PLO can make very clear that any legitimately elected authorities in the territories will automatically be accepted as *their* representatives, thereby co-opting them into its structure. As previously mentioned, it is highly likely that the local elected representatives will identify themselves with the majority groups within the PLO organizations, particularly with its mainstream.

In short, there do seem to be areas of potential agreement based on interests shared by the Israelis and the Palestinians. Not a few people on the two sides have expressed their conviction of the need to end an increasingly senseless confrontation in emotional terms.[26] In the words of Bassam Abu Sharif, a noted Palestinian leader who has stressed the urgency of moving from points of conflict to issues of convergence, "No one can understand the Jewish people's centuries of suffering more than the Palestinians. We know what it is to be stateless and the object of fear and prejudice of the nations."[27] Tom Segev forecasts the long-term implications of the Holocaust to be a more humanistic and universal interpretation of suffering[28] that may also encompass the tragic lot of the Palestinian people.

The search for democracy in the Middle East at this moment in history is increasingly seen to be in the best interests of both peoples. The Gulf War may have served as a catalyst by accelerating processes already in motion. Yet it is simply too soon to tell whether the ultimate outcome of the crisis will be further bloodshed or a move toward peace and democratization in the region, or perhaps some of both.[29] Harkabi has coined the idea that the parties have to choose "between bad and worse," an outcome only feasible with the Israelis gaining back their own and with the growing capability of the Palestinians to separate grand designs from realistic possibilities.[30] While concurring with those who are pessimistic that there is room for doubt, we can but append the lesson learned from bloody enemies in Europe and elsewhere: The correlates of peace and democracy provide a most fertile ground for prosperity and growth.

Notes

1. For a more detailed analysis see Edy Kaufman, *Israelis and Palestinians in the Peace Process* (Tokyo: Institute of Developing Economies, 1992).

2. For a detailed exploration of this option see Joseph Alpher, "Palestinian Settlement: The Security Issues," Israeli-Palestinian Peace Research Project, Working Paper Series, No 14, Harry S Truman Research Institute (Winter 1991/1992).

3. Edward de Bono, *The Use of Lateral Thinking* (Harmondsworth, Middlesex, England: Penguin Books, 1975).

4. General reference to the idea is made in Jerome Segal, *Creating the Palestinian State* (Chicago: Lawrence Hill, 1989), pp. 129–130. ("This perception [lasting peace] will be strengthened by an additional consideration: it is almost unknown for two democracies to wage war on each other. Thus, given Israeli democracy, Palestinian democracy will mean increased security for both sides.")

5. Melvin Small and David Singer, *Resort to Arms: International and Civil Wars, 1816–1980* (Beverly Hills: Sage Publications, 1982).

6. Michael W. Doyle, "Liberalism and World Politics," *American Political*

Science Review, Vol. 80, No. 4 (Dec. 1986), pp. 1151–1169. An analysis of the argument that democracies do not fight other democracies is offered by Robert Rothstein in an unpublished speech, "Weak Democracy and the Prospects for Peace and Prosperity in the Third World," delivered at the United States Institute for Peace conference, Conflict Resolution in the Post–Cold War Third World, October 3–5, 1990, in Washington, D.C.

7. Michael Brecher, Jonathan Wilkenfeld, and Sheila Moser, *Crises in the Twentieth Century* (Oxford and New York: Pergamon Press, 1988.)

8. Interestingly enough, Egypt, the only Arab country to have thus far concluded a peace treaty with Israel, has a regime that appears to be more open and free than those of its Arab neighbors. But even there, much remains to be desired.

9. See Richard L. Sklar, "Developmental Democracy," *Comparative Studies in Society and History,* Vol. 29, No. 4 (October 1987), pp. 686–714.

10. Sari Nusseibeh, *Ha'aretz,* September 7, 1989. See also Jonathan Kuttab, *Jerusalem Post,* September 10, 1989.

11. Reuven Gal, ed., *The Seventh War: The Effects of the Intifada on Israeli Society* (Tel Aviv: Hakibbutz Hameuchad, 1990), in Hebrew.

12. Nabil Sha'th, speech at Columbia University, in *Davar,* magazine supplement, March 13, 1989, in Hebrew.

13. Advocacy has been increasing within the civil society in the West Bank and Gaza for the principle of free and democratic elections. See Talal As-Safi, "Peace Plan to Solve the Palestinian Question" (Jerusalem, May 1991).

14. Moshe Ma'oz, *Palestinian Leadership on the West Bank* (London: Frank Cass, 1984), p. 140.

15. *Ibid,* p. 143.

16. For former Minister of Defense Moshe Arens the issues of elections in chambers of commerce or municipalities were "positive steps in a chain of democratic processes." *Yediot Hachronot,* September 17, 1991.

17. Richard Sklar, "Developmental Democracy," *Comparative Studies in Society and History,* Vol. 29, No. 4, October 1987, pp. 686–714.

18. Mark Heller, *A Palestinian State: The Implications for Israel* (Cambridge: Harvard University Press, 1983).

19. *Ha'aretz,* March 9, 1988.

20. *Ha'aretz,* August 8, 1989.

21. "A Pocket of Autonomy in a Sea of Security," *Ha'aretz,* March 3, 1992.

22. The draft text of "The Joint Jordanian-Palestinian Delegation—The Palestinian Track," circulated in Washington on January 14, 1992, called for a freely elected 180-member legislative assembly in which Palestinians from the West Bank, including Jerusalem and Gaza, should participate fully, and in which freed political detainees should be included.

23. One scheme calls for elections among Palestinian constituencies worldwide, including the Occupied Territories. The plan includes four sequential components: 1) education and training in democratic procedures; 2) voter registration; 3) establishment of a reliable, computerized system for tallying ballots; and 4) establishment of an internal and international monitoring system of the election process. See Mubarak Awad, "Draft Proposal: Democratic Development and Internal Elections in the West Bank and Gaza," *Nonviolence International,* Washington, D.C., 1991).

24. According to Segal, "It is almost inconceivable that any Israeli government could refuse to sit down with the elected leadership of the Palestinian population. . . . Even without elections, the PLO has won something close to this exclusive right [as representative of the Palestinian people], though its hold on this right is periodi-

cally tested. But it is one thing to be viewed in the Arab world as the legitimate representative of the Palestinian people; it is very different when that is how a Palestinian leadership is perceived in Israel and the United States." Jerome Segal, *Creating the Palestinian State* (Chicago: Lawrence Hill, 1989), pp 128–129.

25. See article by Mubarak Awad and Edy Kaufman, "Side by Side: Two Paths to Change," *Los Angeles Times*, April 1, 1992.

26. "1) Are the Palestinians and Israelis satisfied with the ongoing conflict and the bloodletting, as well as the displacement of thousands of families and the destruction? 2) Do both people deny the fact that they are the sons of Adam and Eve? 3) Have the Israelis and Palestinians pledged to pursue their enmity? 4) Is it true that the Palestinians and Israelis cannot ever live together? 5) Do the Israelis and the Palestinians see any difference between the God of Moses, Jesus and Muhammad?" Talal As-Safi, *Peace Plan*, p. 3. The author of the pamphlet has been arrested five times since 1980.

27. *New York Times*, June 22, 1988.

28. Tom Segev, *The Seventh Million—The Israelis and the Holocaust* (Jerusalem: Keter Publishing House and Domino Press Ltd., 1991), in Hebrew.

29. Paradoxically, democratization has begun to seem possible in Kuwait and even in Saudi Arabia as a direct result of the conflict in the Gulf. See the analysis by Thomas Friedman in "Curiously a Dictator Forces the Middle East to Ponder Democracy," *New York Times*, September 2, 1990.

30. Yosheafat Harkabi, *Israel's Fateful Hour* (New York: Harper-Collins Publishers, 1988). See also Edy Kaufman, "Co-authoring in the Israeli-Palestinian Conflict," in *Journal of Palestine Studies* (forthcoming, Spring 1993). In a review essay of *No Trumpet, No Drums: A Two-State Settlement of the Israeli-Palestinian Conflict* (New York: Hill and Wang, 1991), Mark Heller and Sari Nusseibeh say that the authors are searching for what Heller calls 'the least undesirable choice'."

THE ISRAELIS:
SAFEGUARDING DEMOCRACY

4

Garrison Democracy: The Impact of the 1967 Occupation of Territories on Institutional Democracy in Israel

Alon Pinkas

Self-criticism is the secret weapon of democracy, and candor and confession are good for the political soul.—Adlai Stevenson

The greatest peril to Israeli democracy is the constant and protracted tension between the rule of the law and security considerations. This inherent tension is a characteristic of most modern democracies, but the case of Israel evinces it in its extreme form. Israel has been under a real and perceived external threat since its establishment in 1948. Maintaining the principles and procedures of democracy under a permanent state of war is a difficult task, one that is unprecedented in political history and one with which Israel has been coping since its inception.

In the center of this broad aspect of the Israeli democratic experience lies the core problem: the conflict between the supremacy of the law and security considerations. This tension conspicuously lacks a solid center of gravity. The result is a disequilibrium in the equation, incessantly influenced by security and internal political developments. In capsule form, it can be argued that although the relative weight of the rule of law factor is generally increasing inside the Green Line, in the territories occupied following the 1967 war it is regressing at the expense of security considerations. This differential and inverse development is the key to defining the relations between Israel and the territories through democratic parameters and criteria.

Hence, when the effects of the occupation on Israeli democracy are examined, the cardinal question is: To what extent and in what form is the occupation a part of security? Any possible influence the occupation has on institutional democracy in Israel stems entirely from that question.

In the wake of the Six Day War of 1967, Israeli society and the Israeli polity underwent a drastic transformation, precipitated by the demographic and political implications of territorial expansion. Prior to 1967 Israel was a

Jewish state in the early consolidation phase of a nation-building process, with jurisdiction over a small Arab minority. Hence, democracy developed independently and at a pace set by a national and political agenda capable of sustaining the burdening questions of sovereignty, identity, equality, and rights and equality before the law. The conquest and ensuing occupation of territories, and more significantly of 1.7 million indigenous inhabitants, threw Israel back to the preindependence state of affairs. During preindependence the conflict comprised two mutually exclusive communities and national liberation movements with incompatible and apparently irreconcilable national interests and aspirations. The profound transformation was the reversal of the process by which Israel was establishing itself, slowly but steadily, as a nation-state. It was not a homogeneous nation-state in the sense that, for example, Sweden is, but the discernible trend was toward a considerable Jewish majority, especially with the mass exodus of Arabs— through voluntary flight and expulsions—after the 1948–1949 war.

This study attempts to identify the problems and dangers that Israeli democratic institutions have been confronting since the occupation of territories following the 1967 war. The basic premise is that the twenty-five-year-long occupation has exacted a heavy price from Israeli democracy, impairing its development.

The impact of the occupation is greatest on the democratic values of Israeli society and the overall regard to democracy on the grassroots level. Conventional wisdom, supported by studies, has it that the occupation adversely influenced public perceptions of democracy; it has been widely perceived as "corrupting the soul of Israeli society." Rarely, however, have the occupation and its side effects been depicted as having a negative influence on Israel's democratic institutions. That lends credence to the presumption that the Green Line, delineating Israel's prewar borders, is also the dividing line between democracy and a nondemocratic military government. These issues and impacts are discussed elsewhere in this book.

There has indeed been a profound impact on the institutional level of democracy in Israel. This impact emanates primarily from the historical fact that the Israeli democracy is uniquely and fundamentally an institutional, "formal" democracy rather than a liberal democracy. The impact and ramifications are evident in three main areas: the legal system and the rule of law, the political system and its shifts of alignments and emphasis, and the issue of security. Accordingly, this study is structured in a way that attempts to incorporate these realms of interaction into one harmonious theme. Other areas of institutional democracy that have affected and been affected by the occupation, such as the economy or the government bureaucracy, are derivatives of the three main areas mentioned above and will be dealt with when appropriate.

This study contends that the centrality of security in Israeli social and political life, as well as the supremacy of all things considered security in the Israeli body politic and ethos, render security, in its broad and encompassing sense, one of democracy's institutions. This is a particular rather than universal concept, true perhaps only in the case of Israel, where security has institutional expressions far beyond other democracies. In Israel national security is not merely a concept integral to economic and political life, as in other countries. Rather, it is a central sphere of activity, crucial to the polity's very existence. This sphere consists of the institutions related to security and the "security situation." It is therefore an institutional entity no less than a set of military-political policies and defined interests.

All possible domains of influence on democracy are exclusive categories, and each deserves independent research. Put together in this study they only shed light on the interrelationship between occupation and institutional democracy.

The study is divided into five subsections, dealing, respectively, with the special nature of the Israeli democracy; the security issue and the idea of "protracted temporariness" defining Israel's undecided relations with the Occupied Territories; the justice and legal systems; the transformation of the political system resulting from the occupation; and several explicitly unprescriptive conclusions.

The time frames used in this study correspond to the sections. The year 1967 is the natural point of departure for any discussion on the occupation and its implications and ramifications. However, Israeli democracy preceded the occupation, and in order to understand its characteristics and intrinsic problems it is necessary to go back to the "Yishuv" (the pre-1948 Jewish community in Palestine) days before political independence in 1948. The impact of the occupation on the Israeli political system was in essence manifested only after 1977, when the right-wing Likud Party assumed power and ascended to political dominance in Israel. Even so, 1967 remains the watershed year of Israeli politics.

The Formal Democracy

The Israeli democracy is a unique democracy. None of the Zionist activists and leaders who managed political, economic, and social affairs in the formative years of the preindependence Yishuv community came from a liberal background or from a democratic political tradition. The vast majority of them came from Russia in three waves—in the years following the failed 1905 revolution, in 1917–1920 following the Bolshevik Revolution and Russian civil war, and between 1923–1926, when the revolution turned into a party dictatorship. Most of these leaders were ideological supporters and sympathizers of various left-wing parties, and if they shared one common characteristic, it was a basic belief in collectivism as a principle of political and social life.

Collectivism eventually became a defining attribute of Israeli culture, from the Kibbutz movement to fundamental social perceptions and codes of behavior. Collectivism transcended the societal domain and gradually became a version of nationalism that lacked the individual-rights component indigenous to Western democratic systems.[1] In the West, beginning in the mid- to late nineteenth century, democracy was widely perceived as consisting of two components: formal procedural democracy, expressed through universal suffrage and free and open competition between parties, and the liberal component that safeguards the rights of individuals and political and ethnic minorities. Western, or "liberal," democracy contains a checks-and-balances system that restrains power and prevents abuse and usurpation. Eastern Europe, which produced the Zionist leadership, did not go through the liberal phase of democracy and did not adopt democracy as a normative ideology. Rather, the procedural stage was introduced immediately as a substitute to tyranny and dictatorship.

Starting in 1933, when it became the ruling party in the World Zionist Organization (WZO), and throughout the Yishuv days, Mapai (the Land of Israel Workers Party, Labor's precursor) was the dominant political party. Yet it never attempted to exercise a tyranny of the majority. It formed arrangements, using methods similar to coalition-building processes, that were based on low ad hoc common denominators. It also relied on an implicit understanding by other parties that integration into the power structure amounted to recognition of Mapai's leading role. For example, the arrangement reached between Mapai and the religious parties in the 1933 WZO elections constituted a model for later arrangements in the Israeli system after independence was attained in 1948. The democratic element in those arrangements was purely procedural and formal.[2] Adherence to democracy and a real commitment to its ideological tenets was never unconditional in the Yishuv days. A consensus on democratic norms and institutions, freedom of association, a parliamentary regime, plurality of political parties, a free press, and an independent judiciary was always ostensibly declared. But consensus has not always prevailed concerning the specifics of the broad concept of democracy.[3] An illustrative example is the emergency-time regulations governing the press in Israel.[4] The political culture that developed after the 1977 elections exposed this lingering defect in the Israeli democracy.

Hence, most of the problems of Israeli democracy can be traced to the circumstances in which the Yishuv emerged and the formative years of the Israeli political system. Before independence, Mapai, as well as other political parties, tended to attribute absolute validity to its values and political and social agendas.[5] Competing ideologies were depicted as misleading, false, contemptible, and destructive. However, in the absence of means of coercion or a definitive political arbitration process, such as elections, available to a sovereign state, the only way to maintain a form of orderly political life was to concentrate on the institutional arena. Although they had never embraced democracy as an ideology, these groups based political life on a pluralistic system if only out of necessity or convenience.

Eventually, the institutions established by the Yishuv led to the institutions of the Israeli democracy. In contrast to the development of liberal democracies in Western Europe and the United States, democratic institutions antedated ideology in Israel. It can therefore be argued that the Yishuv's experience with democracy illustrates a reversal of the traditional causal relationship between the development of democratic ideology and the development of democratic institutions.[6] Instead of democratic ideology shaping the structures and contours of a democratic system, formal institutions preceded the substantive elements of democracy and shaped the Israeli polity for many years to come. The inevitable result was a democracy that focused on the various aspects of representation—a multiparty system, free elections, and coalition politics. Less emphasis was put during the early years on political tolerance, the role and importance of the opposition as a restraining balance to the government, freedom of information, and individual rights.[7]

The ambivalent attitudes toward some elements and components of democratic culture affected the responses of the Israeli body politic on issues relating to perceptions of democracy. Horowitz and Lissak discern several major conflictual dilemmas underlining the Israeli democratic culture: 1) representative versus participatory democracy; 2) rule of law and individual rights versus considerations of *raison d'état*; 3) application of freedom of political organization versus the imposition of restrictions and limitations; 4) collectivism versus individualism in relation to the confrontation between social mobilization for collective goals and the protection of individual rights (this conflict also relates to the tension between mission orientation and pragmatism); and 5) universalism based on normative principles versus particularism based on ad hoc decisions.[8]

These dilemmas are by no means abstractions. They are part and parcel of all major political debates in Israel and most cleavages crosscutting Israeli society. The Palestinian issue and Arab-Jewish relations are to some degree manifestations of these dilemmas. If Israel completed a de-facto integration of the territories without incorporating their inhabitants into the Israeli system, and continued to deprive those inhabitants of political rights, the question would become: What exactly are the boundaries of national collectivity if the governmental system is one but rights and the legal system have a different meaning and substance on different sides of the Green Line? Sovereignty without accountability, needless to stress, is undemocratic.

Yet underlying these predicaments is an even greater dilemma—the identity question, or the perception of Israel as a Jewish nation-state as opposed to a civil political entity. To a large extent, democratic institutions and democratic attitudes in Israel are defined along these lines of controversy. Commensurately, attitudes toward the occupation correspond to a party's or an individual's stand on the identity issue—in short, the difference between the "Land of Israel" and the *state* of Israel as two competing frames of reference.

Ideology thus had a dual role in the development of Israeli democracy, acting as both a unifying and dividing factor. Until 1967 Israeli democracy was on its way to formulating a democratic ideology that would complement the establishment of institutions. Israeli society had a well-defined external threat against which it developed a clear consensus, supported by a degree of social cohesion and general acceptance of democracy. That trend was reversed with the occupation, when ideological disputes eroded social cohesion and national consensus and consequently the effectiveness of the democratic system. The development of a democratic ideology and its institutional expressions was primarily threatened by the fundamental perception of the territories as a security issue.

Nation in Arms and Society in Uniform

The be-all and end-all of the Israeli polity is security and ensuring its physical existence. Since its inception, Israel has been facing an external military threat and has been in a permanent state of war with the Arab world. Israel is unique among twentieth-century democracies in that it has fought more wars than any other and has been in some kind of state of emergency for the majority of its existence.

The strategic balance and geopolitical relations between Israel and the Arab world are characterized by their perpetual asymmetry. The Arab world has at its disposal immensely and disproportionately greater resources than Israel. Any Israeli military victory, therefore, convincing as it may be, will forever be local and tactical. Strategically, Israel cannot defeat the Arab world; conversely, an Arab victory will by definition be strategic because it would probably mean the destruction of Israel. Another asymmetry is the fact that the minority under Israeli control, whether the Arab minority in Israel proper or the Palestinians in the Occupied Territories, is actually an outer majority encircling Israel. That ratio also influences perceptions toward the Arabs as a minority and the institutional procedures pertaining to the treatment of that minority. The uniqueness of the Israeli case is further complicated by the fact that the territories it is holding are adjacent to its borders. In this respect, the French experience in Algeria as an analogy has but limited value.

Thus, Israel was forced to strengthen its military might and formulate a

viable and effective deterrent capability in order to compensate for its infe-
riority in staying power, i.e., the combination of demographic, geographic,
and economic resources and the willingness and ability to sustain heavy
civilian casualty rates. The balance between the two components, supplemented by external outside support, constitute overall national strength.[9]

The Israeli Defense Forces (IDF), perceived to be one of the original
creations of Zionism and Israel (the renaissance of the Hebrew language
and the kibbutz are others), became a central institution in society, and
security and the security situation evolved into pivotal tenets of Israeli culture and ethos. The security ethos emanated from a reaction to military
threats, wars, and a continual state of subconventional war marked by terrorism and border skirmishes. Subsequently, this ethos transcended reality
and assumed almost religious dimensions with a theology of its own, a language, cultlike codes, myths, and epochs. One need only listen to two
Israeli reservists, neither of whom is a decorated general, talking about
their experiences from the last exercise to fully comprehend the phenomenon. Security is also a creed in Israel in that it offers a general outlook of
the world and offers explanations and a point of ideological reference with
which to interpret reality. It is not uncommon to see both Knesset members
and laymen referring to Israel's international relations or economic hard-
ships, the quality of customer service, or the quality of soccer through a
security perspective—how security affects it and how security is affected
by it.

Security gradually evolved into a separate sphere of public and state
affairs, quite distinct from other domains of life. It became set apart to the
extent that it constituted an entity of activities and references, that it gained
dominance and supremacy in the political culture. By no means was it independent of other areas of national life. On the contrary, security encompasses economic and social domains that in other countries are only
remotely connected to national security. The water issue, irrigation, and
agricultural policy are inextricably linked to security. The Employment
Service sometimes deals with Arab residents from a security perspective,
and many industries are involved primarily or as a second production line
in defense-related products. The list of sectors affected by security is end-
lessly long.

The permanent state of war with the Arab world conditioned the Israeli
public to voluntarily mobilize in the name of collective effort and national
security. Furthermore, by and large the public willingly accepts compart-
mentalization from the security sphere concerning decisionmaking processes, the formulation of national security doctrine, and the applicability of the
rule of law to the security sphere.[10] The Israeli public will accept in the
name of security afflictions that, had they been applied in other domains—
say, car registration or municipal taxes—would cause a revolt to erupt. The
Israeli public and body politic comfortably assume that having certain

democratic rights suspended or civil rights infringed upon is perfectly permissible and justifiable if done in the name of security. This assumption applies equally to military censorship of the press, as well as to policies in the territories. All that need be done is to portray that act or policy as pertaining to security, and the public intuitively tends to support it. (What did change, in the wake of the 1984 General Security Service [GSS, or Shabac] affair [also known as the "Number 300 bus line affair"] was the impunity with which violation of rights were carried out.)[11]

The Israeli concept of national security is not a product of a cognitive and rational process alone; it is also the cumulative collection of national experience, fears, and ideologies.[12] This conception stems from a real threat and sense of national emergency, but the magnitude of the phenomenon clearly exceeds the real requirements for "securitizing" society. Like any other religion, the church of security ultimately subordinated the adherents, who turned willingly into a fighting society rather than a civil society.

Protracted Temporariness

Nineteen-sixty-seven was a watershed year not only because Israel acquired territories three times its prewar size but also because it reverted the Arab-Israeli conflict to its core circle—a conflict between Jews and Palestinians. After the 1948 war, the intercommunal feud between two mutually exclusive communities with incompatible aspirations for control of the same territory became an interstate war between sovereign political units. That war signalled the internationalization of the Arab-Israeli conflict.[13]

Immediately following the 1967 war, the impact of occupation was felt through the reopening of the identity question—the Land of Israel versus the state of Israel, which corresponds to the definition of Israel as a national as opposed to civil society.[14] But the occupation produced an ideological schism that dominates Israeli politics and defines value systems to this very day—annexation versus partition, or, in the terminology commonly used, territorial compromise versus the idea of no return of lands occupied in a war of aggression. Successive Israeli governments have decided not to decide and have preserved the status quo. Likud critics, especially since 1986, when Yitzhak Shamir became prime minister, charge that the status quo was immortalized, if not glorified. The justifications were that there is no credible or serious partner to talk with and that as long as the occupation was depicted as benign, it did not exact a price that Israeli society was unable or unwilling to pay.

Until 1977 Israeli leaders deferred any decision on the final status of the territories by defining the situation as temporary pending a political solution acceptable to Israel, i.e., a solution that would satisfy its minimum security requirements. Since then, transience has become the status quo, and the new reality is that of a protracted temporariness.[15]

The strategic justifications for this shift were ample. First and foremost was the concept that the Palestinians were part of the Arab-Israeli conflict. The intercommunal dimension was ignored or, worse yet, never understood, and Israeli policies in the territories were construed as being integral to national security. The Palestinians and the Arab states, as one unit, were threatening Israel's existence. Therefore, all attitudes and perceptions concerning the territories and their inhabitants were viewed through the security lens.

Security Rules

The security sphere is a combination of institutions and organs dealing directly and indirectly with security and security perceptions, promulgated based on the common, almost slangy term "the security situation" (*h'matsav ha'bithoni*). Occupation broadened the term and the concept, which now included the territories and incorporated them into the threat-security equation. The process by which security considerations were generally subject to the rule of the law within the Green Line was halted and in fact reversed outside of it. The occupation allowed Israel to restrict individual freedom and deprive people of democratic rights in the name of security considerations.[16] It was the sacred-cow factor incarnate. Israeli legal norms did not apply, and civil rights were never implemented in the territories. The security establishment, an Israeli institution, prevailed and ruled the land. Expenditures in the territories were conveniently defined as investments in security, and Jewish settlements, some of whose legality was only retroactively approved, were sugarcoated as "security requirements."

The dominance of security is perhaps the greatest impact the occupation has had on institutional democracy in Israel. The feedback between security and other institutions is extensive. It relates to income-tax collection in the territories, road infrastructures built by government-owned firms or private contractors, employment qualifications and labor demand (to serve in security related jobs), censorship, economic policies and investments, mortgages, government incentives to live in the territories, and political realignments. The intercommunal conflict also nudged patterns of economic integration between the territories and Israel toward more cooperation. But above all, the occupation has precipitated a collective effort to enhance security through the establishment of an irreversible Israeli presence in the territories. This mobilization has been evident emphatically since 1977, when Likud rose to power and an ideological dimension was added to security considerations and rationales in justifying Israeli policies in the territories. This aspect will be discussed later.

In conclusion, the centrality of security in Israeli society and the development of the creed of security are unequivocal attributes of the Israeli polity. Stemming as they do from a real threat and permanent state of war, they are understandable, even somewhat justified. However, the incorporation of the territories into the security sphere both psychologically and policywise has had a profound impact on institutional democracy, its procedures, the rule of law, and political realignments, in that it broadened the confines and boundaries of the collective's perceptions of security and threats. This broadening influenced the role of the IDF, the nature of relations it has with its civilian authorities, and the extent to which patently undemocratic means are employed, and accepted, under the aegis of security.

The Green Line of Justice

The occupation's most visible impact on Israeli democracy is evident in the legal system, or more precisely, in the erosion of the "rule of law" concept. The occupation resulted in the creation of more than one legal system in the same territorial unit. This duality is by definition and nature political and is inherently discriminatory and biased. As Mordechai Bareket, director of the Israeli Customs Department, said, "If I had tried to implement within the Green Line just some of the means I employed in the territories in order to increase tax collection, I would have been hanged in Zion Square."[17]

The origins of the problem are the reality of protracted temporariness and prolonged indecision on the status of the territories. The legal complexities stem from security legislation and its offshoots.

The establishment of the state of Israel marked a shift from communal norms to statehood concepts. The rule of law and its universal application have consequently become a cherished principle. Before 1967 the implementation of this fundamental and indispensible democratic principle was a desired goal. Transforming it from an abstract concept to a prevailing practice was a healthy indication of the Israeli democracy's maturation.[18] The occupation reversed this trend. Israel was now controlling heavily populated areas to which her legal norms did not apply, which entailed ramifications for the rule of law in Israel itself.[19]

The Rule of Law or the Law of the Rulers

The rule of the law is one of the basic Western democratic values. It is tied to the concepts of equality before the law and civil and human rights. In most democracies the rule of law is used interchangeably with democracy itself, attesting to the value's centrality. Yet the rule of law is not a neutral term with a priori validity detached from political ideologies and realities. The acceptance of the rule of law as a principle governing social and political rights constitutes a political decision in and of itself.[20]

Itzhak Zamir, the former legal counselor to the government, predicates the rule of law on three basic principles: 1) Formal—Citizens have a duty to abide by the law as it was interpreted by the court; 2) Institutional—The duty to abide by the law is not only legal but involves conscience. Because the law stems from a representative power and thus enjoys legitimacy, the rule of law is in the institutional sense the rule of democratic law as opposed to the rule of tyranny; 3) Essence—The rule of law should mean the rule of the just law. Democratic law does not necessarily mean the rule of justice.[21]

In short, the law obliges the general public to express values considered vital to the fair and equitable life of free men. Therefore, one must aspire to attain and practice the institutional and essential elements of the rule of law, not just the formal. But, as discussed previously, Israeli democracy is indigenously a formal democracy that has been extraordinarily slow in adopting democratic values—which, along with political reasons and security considerations, is why the rule of law does not prevail in the territories.

The legal system that developed and was applied in the territories is part of a combination of four parameters defining Israeli policy. They are 1) an outer legal system—the Israeli system supplemented by international law applicable to the Occupied Territories (the legal foundations of the system in the territories rest on both sources); 2) the Israeli system, as interpreted with respect to the territories, where security considerations are the prime and determining factor; 3) policy formulated in the upper echelons of the Israeli political system; and 4) an ideological attitude and political approach according to which the territories are not occupied land. Underlining these parameters is the Israeli system's ambivalent attitude to the Occupied Territories. On the one hand, the territories are considered a separate entity governed by the military. On the other hand, there is no Israeli government authority that is not involved to some degree in managing life in the territories. Government organs charged with performing services inside the Green Line meddle in West Bank and Gaza Strip affairs as if they were integral parts of Israel.

The sources of legitimacy for these activities are emergency-time regulations and security legislation. The source of authority is the political echelon. Decrees issued by military commanders and statutes published by the government require the approval of the civilian echelons, despite the fact that the military governor or commander is legally the chief legislator.[22] Emergency arrangements and regulations are not a rare phenomenon in political history. The United States employed them in occupied Germany and Japan, and the Philippines made extensive use in the 1970s, as did India during its war with Pakistan in 1971. More relevant, it was the law of the land in Mandatory Palestine under British rule. In fact, emergency regulations in Israel and the territories emanate from the 1945 emergency-time regulations formulated by the British authorities.

The most prominent feature of emergency legislation in Israel is that it is the ordinary and permanent state of affairs. This is a strange characteristic containing a built-in contradiction. "Emergency" is prima facie a term specifically denoting times of crisis.[23] This peculiarity is a direct derivative of Israel's security environment since 1948, and the best the Israeli democracy did was to mitigate some of its patently undemocratic practices.

Emergency legislation in both Israel proper and the Occupied Territories can be enacted through three channels: 1) mandatory legislation—the Defense Regulations (also known as Emergency Legislation) of 1945; 2) administrative legislation—emergency regulations issued by the appropriate government minister under Section 9 of the Law and Administration Ordinance (1948); and 3) Emergency Legislation through primary legislation by the Knesset. Arrangements for executing and enforcing each of these legislation alternatives is entrusted to a separate authority such as the military or the police.[24]

The Defense (Emergency) Regulations, 1945, allow for the use of the method of martial law in Israel and in the Occupied Territories.[25] Under the defense regulations, a military commander, authorized through his position, may exercise legislative, judicial, and executive powers over a broad segment of public life. The key issue is that he may do so at his own discretion, as long as he acts on the basis of military considerations and calculations. His actions are evaluated by his superiors, who are accountable to the government through the minister of defense.[26] Ultimately, any action gets the prior approval of the political level. This pattern was reinforced following confusion during the first year of the Palestinian intifada.

The second course for enacting emergency legislation, authorizing a minister to make emergency regulations under Section 9 of the Law and Administration Ordinance, delegates to the government—the executive branch in functioning democracies—legislative authority. The justification for this provision is that in times of war Section 9 enables legislation to pass quickly, unimpeded by procedural delays.[27] This form of enactment was widely used in labor disputes in the 1970s, another example of security-designated mechanisms used by democratic institutions in Israel.

The third option for enacting emergency legislation, the Knesset, is the link between the two other methods. However, certain emergency legislation repealed by the Knesset may be revived, according to the power conferred by Section 9, by a minister. Thus, the will of the executive may prevail over that of the legislature, in dangerous opposition to proper democratic practice. When emergency legislation is imposed in the territories, it becomes categorically self-evident how the occupation can impact democratic institutions.

Yet it is not just on those occasions when emergency legislation is repealed and revived that democratic institutions are damaged. Any attempt to decide an explicitly political debate and struggle by means of enforcing security legislation, which is disputable at best, undermines the legitimacy of the law. Like security, the law is confiscated and crudely mobilized by politicians determined to promote their agenda, even at the high price of impairing and abusing democracy.

Following the occupation, the legislative trend was to remove formal obstacles in the way of activities in the territories. This politically motivated course of action used emergency regulations through primary legislation—the Knesset—and secondary legislation—the military—to achieve its objective. The next phase was to enact laws and issue regulations applicable directly and specifically to the territories. In the first month after the 1967 war, the defense minister issued the emergency-time regulations, which empowered Israeli courts to try individuals who had violated the law in the territories.[28] This decree expanded the authority of Israeli courts and simultaneously deprived local courts of the authority to try Israeli citizens.

The issue at stake was another basic tenet of democracy—equality before the law. The ambivalence of the legal system was such that if an Arab from Hebron murdered an Israeli citizen in Tel Aviv, he would be tried by a military court in Hebron. Yet if an Israeli citizen murdered an Arab in Jenin, he would be brought to justice in Israel proper. Arabs from the territories were thus subject to "territorial" law, while Israelis were subject to "personal" law and could be tried only by Israeli judges. This arrangement is a flagrant violation of the "equality before the law" principle.

The 1967 emergency regulations decree created a new legal reality shaped by the Emergency Regulations—Jurisdiction and Legal Assistance law that amended existing regulations concerning Israeli citizens.[29] In 1984 the justice minister was authorized to amend by decree—with the consent of the Knesset Constitution, Law and Trial Committee—any additions to emergency regulations. This provision affected freedom of movement, association, taxation, and other issues. As a result, Israeli law now applied to the territories, although not in full, lest it be construed as de jure annexation. The definition of "Israeli citizen" was phrased in such a way that only Israeli citizens and non-Israeli Jews were included in it. The outcome was preferential status for Israeli citizens in the territories.[30]

Security Legislation

The striking fact of life concerning the interplay between security and the law in the Occupied Territories is that there is no exact legal definition of state security or security considerations. This omission would not be remarkable were it not for the reason for it. After all, even the military, political scientists, strategists, and journalists covering the issue cannot agree on a clear-cut definition. But the reason given for the absence of a legal definition is that it avoids impeding the military commander's "absolute discretion."[31] Not only is the commander's discretion unimpeded, the general body of security legislation is being created with little if any parliamentary supervision. The executive branch enjoys total freedom of activity.[32]

The vast majority of daily legislation in the territories is enacted through decrees issued by regional military commanders, authorized by international law to perform these practices according to the Fourth Geneva Convention.[33] Constitutional law professor and Knesset member Amnon Rubinstein argues that the longer Israeli control of the territories lasted, the deeper security legislation permeated into broader domains of daily life. That prompted a de facto change in the status of the territories, manifested in two ways: The imprint of the Israeli legal system was enhanced, and the two sides of the Green Line became more similar. As a result of the increase in Jewish settlements in the territories, special legislation applicable only to Jews was drafted.[34] It enforced political and civil rights and duties used in Israel on Israeli citizens, leading to a distinction between two systems of law—in essence, legal dualism marred by discriminatory characteristics.

The High Court of Justice

The Israeli Supreme Court of Justice (in its capacity as High Court of Justice) is frequently referred to as both the last resort of legal assistance and hope for the Palestinians in the territories and the only effective supervision mechanism balancing the executive's policies. In short, the court is perceived as the last bastion of democracy and gatekeeper against deprivation and abuse of rights. Insofar as the territories are concerned, the court's record is ambiguous.

The High Court of Justice (hereafter HCJ) is only a partial remedy to problems arising from security and emergency regulations and legislation, primarily because it does not constitute an appeals court before which an individual or an organization can challenge judicial decisions. Furthermore, the US concept of judicial review does not exist fully in the Israeli system, and the constitutionality of laws is not subject to review by the court. The HCJ involves itself in random issues, confined to defined grounds of reasoning and contingent upon the absence of alternative means of remedy and assistance.[35]

The HCJ is thus active only when the plaintiff can prove excess of authority, partiality, or unreasonableness. A glance at the HJC's record on appeals submitted by territories Palestinians, as compared to other plaintiffs, indicates a grim picture. To begin with, the HCJ's authority to intervene in the territories is under debate. Supreme judges have said on occasion that they deliberate appeals from the territories because the state implicitly assents and does not challenge the court's authority. In this sense the occupation expanded the High Court's activities and role. Moshe Negbi, a legal scholar and legal affairs commentator for *Hadashot* daily, said that the idea was pure naiveté. Israel thought that it would teach the Palestinians the meaning of democracy. A form of enlightened occupation.[36]

The statistics seem discouraging. Dr. Avishai Erlich of Tel Aviv University quantified the pleas submitted to the HCJ between 1967 and 1986 by Jews, Israeli Arabs, residents of the territories, and corporations and companies. The results clearly show that if one wanted to win an appeal he or she would preferably be a corporation but would certainly refrain from being a Palestinian. Of the 716 pleas submitted by Palestinian residents of the territories, 9 were accepted and 707 rejected. Israeli Jews submitted 70 percent of the pleas and accounted for 65.2 percent of the pleas accepted. Palestinians from the territories submitted 6 percent of the pleas and constituted 1.4 percent of those accepted.[37]

But Negbi argues that the statistics are misleading. The issue is not how many pleas were submitted by Palestinians, he says, but how many arbitrary deeds and abusive actions were prevented and averted simply because the military fears the HCJ.[38] The significance of this factor is unclear. It could be construed as a positive effect on Israeli democratic institutions in that the occupation inadvertently and indirectly strengthened the HCJ to the benefit of society at large and put government agencies on a constant defensive. However, there is credence to the argument that the HCJ was merely the government's fig leaf, providing it with the humane and benign facade conducive to advancing political goals.

In recent years the trend has been toward an increased HCJ role in deciding legal issues pertaining to the territories. The cardinal issue remains, however, the outcome of a head-on collision between security considerations and the HCJ. Traditionally the court, in decisions within the Green Line, tended to accept the military's explanations and justifications. In recent years the HCJ is less inclined to accept the security establishment's version of things. In a series of decisions relating to military censorship, the GSS (Shabac), and the closure of *Hadashot* daily, it supported the rule of law and basic rights over security considerations. Those rulings can also be attributed to the occupation that exposed Israeli society to wrongdoings and abuses of power by the security organs.

The transformation in the HCJ's position and attitude was the 1979 landmark decision on the Elon-Moreh settlement in Samaria. On October 22, 1979, the HCJ ordered the evacuation of the settlement. For the first time, the court ruled that Jewish settlement in the territories is illegal and rejected the state's argument that the settlement was established for "security reasons."[39] The court found out that Chief of Staff Lt. Gen. Rafael Eitan gave sworn testimony that the settlement is vital to security. Yet the defense minister, Ezer Weizman, objected to the settlement in the midst of the Camp David negotiations, and a former chief of general staff, Haim Bar-Lev, testified that the settlement is of no military value. The court then asked Eitan to provide written answers to questions it presented to him, and when it determined that they were inconsistent with the original testimony, the court reached its verdict.[40]

The significance of the Elon-Moreh decision (HCJ case 390/79, *Duykat vs. the State of Israel*) was that it strengthened the rule of law in the territories despite political attempts to circumvent and ignore the law. In the decision, the judges stressed that even if Israeli law does not apply in the territories, government authorities cannot go about making policies without respecting Israeli law and legal norms that also contain international law.[41] The Elon-Moreh affair also exposed the cynical use the government made of security requirements in order to promote political and ideological goals.

The mechanisms adopted by Israeli society to determine priorities when the rule of law and security considerations clash are clear: When danger to national security is determined, expanded authority and expeditious procedures are given to functionaries. But within the Green Line, this power is checked and at times even balanced by courts, the HCJ, the press, and other independent observers. For example, in the 1989 HCJ ruling on *Ha'ir* weekly versus the chief military censor (the issue was a story the paper printed on the head of the Mossad), the judges said, "There are no special limitations on the scope of Judicial review over administrative considerations pertaining to state security."[42] These checks and balances do not exist in the territories, but the occupation has proved to be conducive, albeit indirectly, to the maturation of democratic institutions.

From the legal system perspective, the occupation has had an adverse impact on Israeli democracy. Despite the strengthening of the HCJ, the general balance sheet shows the formation of two distinct legal systems in the territories, a reality incongruous with democratic procedures or norms. The cumulative result of Israeli policies in the territories was the creation of one administrative system whose units are closely linked but which allows for inequalities in political and civil rights, income, and public services. The sole basis for distinction is the individual's citizenship. This political creation the legal system cannot and is unable to rectify.

The cardinal question, thoroughly exposed by the occupation, is whether the law, in a democracy under permanent security threats, serves as an instrument in the political struggle for control of the territory in dispute. Are there red lines delineating legal thresholds, the crossing of which would render the system inherently undemocratic? The issue, by nature political, is at the overheated core of Israeli politics. The instrumental approach to the law is prevalent on both sides in the territories. The Palestinians use it against Israeli occupation, and the Jews use it in the name of self-defense, supported by the conviction—undemocratic, needless to repeat—that the law is an impediment to Israeli control and eventual annexation of the territories. In this sense, the occupation also has had a deep impact on the Israeli political system.

Democracy Attenuated

The Six Day War and the ensuing occupation induced a major change in the Israeli national and political agenda. After 1967 most points of reference in Israeli politics and the substance matter of national debate and political discourse were to some degree related to the issue of the territories.

Before 1967 the political agenda in Israel was by and large dominated by social and economic affairs and issues. The concentrated national and political effort was focused on the intricate task of nation building, and the political system was characterized by a one-party dominance structure. All political controversies and disputes were decided by coalition-opposition parameters. The left-right artery was ideological, and its political manifestations were negligible due to the hegemonic powers of Mapai and its affiliate parties. The political cleavage between left and right was but a historical and academic, if not trivial, issue.

The rule of law collided occasionally with security considerations, but democracy was consolidating, and the law-security conflict applied only to an external threat. The emphasis on economic structuring, immigration absorption, and nation building gave the social-democratic Labor movement a clear edge over its right-wing opponents. Its almost undisputed central role in the establishment of the state awarded it a political advantage over any competing party or ideology.[43]

All that changed, at first incrementally, then drastically in 1967. Israel's political agenda was transformed in what can be seen with hindsight to be an irreversible way. The focus of the national and political agenda shifted from internal politics to the Arab-Israeli conflict. Within the political system, the shift was from civil politics to the politics of nationalism. The occupation precipitated the reintroduction of the "Jewish state" versus "state of the Jews" debate and redefined the political left and right in a way that corresponded to parties' attitudes toward the Palestinian question and the future of the territories.[44]

The shift of interests and priorities in the political arena was not merely a temporary diversion of attention. In fact, the dominance of the territorial issue was such that it practically paralyzed all other spheres of social, economic, and political life. The Israeli economy, its structural ills, the politicized civil service, substandard maintenance of road infrastructure, rampant labor disputes, the dysfunctional electoral system (in the eyes of some critics), the faltering health system, the highly politicized education system, and above all the conspicuous absence of sufficient legislation and action on civil rights issues—all these factors attest to the preeminence of the territories and occupation as the main focal point of the Israeli polity.

The rise of political ideologies concerning the territories brought about a realignment in Israeli politics. Parties were shifting their ideological platforms and emphasis in the direction of formulating comprehensive postures regarding the territories, peace and war, national security, the Palestinian issue, the settlements, and the specter of occupation. Eventually and inevitably, single-issue parties such as Tehiya, Moledet, and Morasha on the right and Citizens Rights Movement (CRM) on the left based their platforms on issues directly or indirectly linked to the occupation. Extrapolitical and nonparty movements such as Peace Now were formed to influence policy on the territories. Gush Emunim, the political arm of the Jewish settlers' movement, was formed in the wake of messianic sentiments emanating from the occupation, or "liberation of lands." The political system was consequently realigning along lines demarcated by attitudes toward the territories and preferred policies on the Arab-Israeli and Palestinian issue.

Party positions on law and security also underwent change. Between 1948 and 1967 the dominant factor predicting a party's position and stand on an issue was most likely the opposition-coalition line. The role of the opposition was consistent with democratic values, but its political weakness rendered it ineffective. During that period, the coalition usually supported the "security considerations" position, while the opposition (Herut, and later Gahal—the Herut-Liberals block) frequently invoked the rule of law principle, for lack of better and more effective political arguments.

Between 1967 and 1977 the territories became the political demarcation line, and the left-right artery became a good indicator of party stances. That indicator, however, was limited to attitudes concerning the occupation. Within the Green Line, divisions were still based on opposition-coalition, the former representing the longtime establishment, the latter a frustrated alternative.[45] Within this period of time there is a subperiod between 1967 and 1970. On the eve of the Six Day War, Gahal was introduced into the national unity government and gained considerable and unprecedented legitimacy in the electorate. For many years Herut, Gahal's precursor, was ostracized and derided by Ben-Gurion and his successors. Now Menachem Begin was in the limelight. Significantly, during its tenure in the government, Gahal became the dominant security legislation advocate, reversing its precoalition attitude. The reasons for this reversal were the occupation and Gahal's nationalistic view concerning Arab-Israeli relations. Seven years later, in 1977, after Likud (Gahal's new version) won the elections, security legislation was passed easily. In retrospect, Likud's key role in security legislation between 1967 and 1970 was conducive to its eventual self-portrayal as the national party and perhaps signalled its rise to dominance.

The third time frame lasts from the controversial 1982 war in Lebanon until today. When Labor realized that its 1977 electoral defeat was not a singular historical accident and that Likud mobilized the Oriental (Sephardi) middle class with fervent antiestablishment sentiments aggravated by the 1973 war, the political alignment changed, and with it traditional approaches to law and security. Since the war in Lebanon, the clear indicator of a party's position on the territories is its location on the left-right spectrum. This trend proved durable even throughout the 1984–1988 and 1988–1990 national unity governments. The left and the political center were identified with territorial compromise, alleviation of the occupation, and civil rights, while the right, both moderate and extreme, favored annexation or the status quo and depicted Palestinians as terrorists locked in a zero-sum conflict with Israel who therefore did not deserve civil rights as long as there was war. The law, according to the political right, could be periodically violated with relative leniency and even impunity as long as the breach was ideologically justified. Although this perspective has never been official Likud policy, very little has been done to arrest the trend and to politically punish leaders who outrightly advocate selective violations of the law.[46] The political controversies stemming from the intifada have only exacerbated this trend.

The occupation has therefore been responsible for a major shift in the focus of the agenda and a realignment of the political map, the first structural change of its kind in the Israeli political system. The emphasis a formal democracy places on forms of representation makes the impact even more visible. But the long-term effects of the occupation are in reviving ideological disputes and linking social and Arab-Israeli cleavages that cut society politically, as manifested in the Knesset and the election results.

It is important to note and stress that the intensive and extensive ideologization of the Israeli political agenda is tightly linked to developments in the security sphere and its policy expressions. These, in turn, affect and are affected by the rule of law in both practice and perception.

The Maturing Republic

The news pertaining to Israeli democracy is both bad and good. Israel is a precarious republic and a fragile democracy. Yet Israel is the only country in the world that has succeeded in maintaining democratic institutions and an acceptable level of civil rights despite a permanent and existential military threat, which has led to a nearly perpetual emergency-time atmosphere. The record is not unblemished, nor is it perfect even taking these adverse conditions into account. Yet if a condition of permanent war naturally encourages the creation of a garrison state, as Harold Lasswell predicted, then is it presumable that the damage could have been far greater?[47]

The truth may be quite the opposite. Despite obstructive and counterproductive conditions interfering in its development, the accomplishments of the Israeli democracy are impressive. But this success does not imply that it can sustain the burden of a protracted conflict or withstand the cancerous effects of occupying 1.7 million Palestinians who reject Israeli presence and practices altogether. The inability, or perhaps unwillingness, to determine the final status of the territories exacts a high price from Israeli democracy. Protracted temporariness confuses the Israeli democracy, and its legal miseries are compounded by a cynical political alignment that abuses its institutions. The greatest impact the occupation has on democratic institutions is the intensification and aggravation of the inherent tension between security considerations and the rule of law. Changing the legal status of the territories or implementing political and civil rights similar to those in Israel threaten to alter the nation's political balance and are likely to encounter fierce, some say violent, opposition.

The problem is that the modus vivendi reached is far from being conducive to democratic development on either the institutional or the ideological and value-system levels. The Israeli government and its security apparatus in the territories exercise broad authority without sufficient means of supervision and without being accountable to the population they control. Any way the issue is examined, the lingering problem remains the trade-off between security and law. Whatever compromises are reached, democracy ultimately pays a price. Thus, the Israeli case could prove to be of relevance to other democratic regimes facing a domestic threat—terrorism, subversion, organized crime on a large scale, or irredentist groups.

If some country wishes to draw lessons from the Israeli case, it will see with crystal-clarity that a protracted emergency regime is a high price to pay. The fact that the price is subject to a real threat index does not make things any better. It is easy to resort to emergency legislation whether it is necessary or not, but it is extremely difficult to jettison this course of action once adopted, for it appears to be effective and is eventually assimilated into public notions of vital security. An external threat is considerably easier to cope with and prepare for, because it is defined in precise and almost invariable terms, and its framework is visible and comprehensible. In the case of Israel, the internal threat was merged with an external threat. To some extent this assessment was justified strategically and politically; unfortunately the political and cognitive unification of the Arab-Israeli interstate conflict with the Jewish-Palestinian intercommunal feud blurred, rather than clarified, the threat.

The institutions developed by the Israeli democracy seem ill-suited to confront, mitigate, and neutralize the effects of an internal threat, which the occupation essentially is. This became evident in December 1992, when the newly elected (since June) Labor-led government decided to expel, or "temporarily remove," as it was phrased, 415 Hamas activists. Hamas, an Islamic fundamentalist group, represented an extreme case of an internal threat, merged with the regionwide ascent of fundamentalism. Following an unprecedented terror wave, Prime Minister Rabin's government hastily rounded up over 400 prospective deportees and sent them into Lebanese territory, or, as the Lebanese government defined it, "discharged them in a dumping ground."

The government attempted unsuccessfully to circumvent the High Court by presenting it with a political fait accompli. Again, Israeli institutions proved incapable of determining what comes first—security considerations or the rule of law.

The occupation affects the legal system, security policy, and the security sphere of government actions and public perceptions; it adversely affects the freedom of the press and enforces a single-issue realignment in the political system.[48]

Ultimately, Israeli democratic institutions have proven resilient enough to deflect life-threatening dangers to democracy. But the price has been an erosion of the rule of law principle and a trend of reversing the development of a democratic political culture. Despite the uniqueness of the Israeli model, institutions are essentially empty frames without solid ideological foundations or cultural contents. Those have been corrupted by a twenty-five-year-long occupation that seems to have put on a prolonged hold the development of a civil society, both a prerequisite and a cultural outcome of democracy.[49]

Notes

1. See Yonathan Shapiro, "The Historical Origins of Israeli Democracy," in Ehud Sprinzak and Larry Diamond, eds., *Israeli Democracy Under Stress* (Boulder: Lynne Rienner, 1993). For a detailed analysis and introduction see also Dan Horowitz and Moshe Lissak, *From Yishuv to State* (Tel Aviv: Am-Oved, 1977), chapters 1–3, in Hebrew, and Itzhak Galnoor, *Steering the Polity* (Beverly Hills: Sage Publications, 1982).

2. Shapiro, "Israeli Democracy," pp. 138–139.

3. See Dan Horowitz and Moshe Lissak, *Trouble in Utopia* (Albany: State University of New York Press, 1989), p. 144.

4. See Menachem Hofnung, *Israel—Security Needs vs. the Rule of Law* (Jerusalem: Nevo Publishing, 1991), pp. 176–195 (in Hebrew) for an in-depth analysis of the freedom of speech and of the press.

5. Horowitz and Lissak, *Utopia*, pp. 144–146.

6. *Ibid.*

7. *Ibid.* First signs of a shift were the Supreme Court decisions of 1953 in the appeal of the communist newspapers *Kol-Ha'Am* and *Al-Ittihad* against the interior minister's decision to close the latter for publishing information seen and perceived as "threatening to public security." See also Hofnung, *Security Needs,* pp. 176–182.

8. Horowitz and Lissak, *Utopia,* pp. 252–257.

9. Israel Tal, "On National Security," *Maarachot,* No. 286 (February 1983), p. 4, in Hebrew.

10. Dan Horowitz, "Israel and Occupation," *Jerusalem Quarterly,* No. 47 (Summer 1987), pp. 28–29.

11. Yoram Peri, "The Arab-Israeli Conflict and Israeli Democracy," in *Israeli Democracy Under Stress* (Stanford: Hoover Institution, 1990), p. 112.

12. See, Hofnung, *Security Needs,* pp. 271–277.

13. This interpretation of the development of the conflict has been for some time astutely discussed by Meron Benvenisti in numerous books and articles. He contends that the real conflict is the communal conflict, which is insoluble until the ripeness stage is reached. Israeli military, political, economic, and population presence in the territories, he argues, is "irreversible," and the conflict is therefore far from a solution. See also Horowitz, "Israel and Occupation," p. 24.

14. Horowitz, "Israel and Occupation," p. 25.

15. See Horowitz and Lissak, *Utopia,* pp. 45–47.

16. Horowitz, "Israel and Occupation," pp. 28–30.

17. B'Tselem report, "The Taxation System in the West Bank and Gaza," Israeli Information Center for Human Rights in the Occupied Territories, 1989, p. 3.

18. Horowitz, "Israel and Occupation," p. 29.

19. *Ibid.*

20. See Yitzhak Zamir, "The Rule of Law in the State of Israel," *Ha'Praklit,* special issue (Spring 1987), pp. 61–74, in Hebrew.

21. *Ibid.,* p. 61.

22. For a lengthy legal and political analysis of the military as legislator, see Amnon Rubinstein, *The Constitutional Law of Israel,* 2nd edition (Tel Aviv: Schoken, 1991), pp. 93–131, in Hebrew.

23. See Hofnung, *Security Needs,* p. 33.

24. *Ibid.,* pp. 33–49.

25. *Ibid.*

26. See "Basic Law: The Army, 1976," in Zeev Segal, *Israeli Democracy* (Tel Aviv: Ministry of Defense Publishing House, 1988), pp. 307–308, in Hebrew.

27. Hofnung, *Security Needs,* pp. 33–49.

28. *Ibid.,* p. 294.

29. *Ibid.*

30. See Amnon Rubinstein, "The Changing Status of the Territories—From a Held Deposit to a Legal Hybrid," *Iyunei Mishpat,* Vol. 11, No. 3 (October 1986), pp. 448–450, in Hebrew.

31. *Ibid.* p. 450.

32. See Hofnung, *Security Needs,* pp. 296–297.

33. Rubinstein, "Changing Status," p. 451.

34. *Ibid.*

35. See Segal, *Israeli Democracy,* pp. 238–261.

36. Roni Talmor, "We Therefore Reject the Plea—The High Court of Justice as the Occupation's Fig Leaf," *Ha'ir,* July 27, 1991, p. 51.

37. *Ibid.,* p. 52.

38. *Ibid.*

39. *Ibid.,* p. 51. See also Hofnung, *Security Needs,* pp. 98–99, 304–307.

40. Talmor, "We Therefore Reject," p. 52, and Hofnung, *Security Needs*, pp. 306–307.

41. Hofnung, *Security Needs*, p. 307.

42. *Ibid.*, p. 338.

43. Shlomo Avinieri, "1967—The Watershed of Israeli Politics," in *Israeli Democracy Under Stress*, p. 18.

44. This in no way suggests that the traditional and clear distinction between right and left, in the European sense, is applicable to the Israeli model. "Left" denotes a more moderate approach to the territorial issue and a willingness to compromise in exchange for peace. "Right" means a tougher stance and reluctance to compromise, as well as nationalistic tendencies. Thus, the left-right socioeconopolitical distinction is blurred and somewhat irrelevant to Israeli politics. Liberal capitalists are to be found on the left, while populists and semisocialists who get their votes primarily from the working classes are in many cases the right.

45. Hofnung, *Security Needs*, pp. 340–345.

46. *Ibid.*

47. See Peri, "The Arab-Israeli Conflict," p. 124.

48. Although major advances were achieved in the democratic role of the "Seventh Kingdom," they were more a result of indigenous reasons than the occupation. The deterioration of automatic trust in the government's monopoly over defining national security and security objectives began with the 1973 war and culminated in the days immediately preceding the 1982 invasion of Lebanon.

49. For a lengthy discussion of the lack of a "civil society" concept in Israeli political culture, see Gad Barzilai, *A Democracy in Wartime: Conflict and Consensus in Israel* (Tel Aviv: Sifriyat Poalim, 1992), Part 4, Chapter 2 in Hebrew.

5

War, Occupation, and the Effects on Israeli Society

Edy Kaufman

Living in Jerusalem, the meeting point of two nations at odds with each other, creates an awareness from which it is most difficult to detach oneself. When so much knowledge has been acquired through personal experience, there is no point in hiding behind expert opinions and footnotes in an attempt to redress some of the weaknesses of Israel's democracy.[1] Achieving a sober and balanced analysis of the effects of war and occupation on Israeli society is made even more problematic by the fact that most of the writings on the subject are the product of the similar, legitimate preoccupation of other concerned Jewish researchers and analysts. Turning our study's dependent variable into an independent variable, they raise the question of the effect of war on the democratic values of the Israeli people. Others assume that the policies that result from the perceived need to keep control over a foreign population will effect the value system of the ruling nation.

It is extremely important to examine generalizations that have emerged from analysis of other cases of war and occupation in contemporary history. We choose to be guided in our introspection by the perspectives of both continuity and change. An analysis of continuity and change over the years places Israel, in the last quarter of this century, between a colonial situation[2] (representing continuity) and war[3] (representing change). A unique combination in our times, it comprises intermittent short crisis periods of extreme hostility and prolonged in-between periods of a population's subjugation (perhaps the highest remaining case of dependency today). The two features have been closely intertwined since their incipient stages in the aftermath of the 1967 war.

The Six Day War was overwhelmingly perceived by Israeli Jews to be a case of an imposed military confrontation that threatened Israel's very survival. The resulting control over the territories was deemed necessary for security reasons rather than the result of premeditated annexationist policy. For this reason, Israeli Jews overwhelmingly have not seen the occupation as a colonial one but rather as an unforeseen outcome of an unwanted conflagration. Because they believe the territories were taken in a just war, one launched by Arab states that wished to destroy Israel, the mental disposition of many Israelis does not allow them to see themselves as occupiers. A considerable portion of the Israeli public has the outlook of a beleaguered nation facing the danger of annihilation. Often they regard the actions of Palestinian rebels as the continuation of the anti-Jewish pogroms in Eretz Israel (the Land of Israel) prior to the establishment of the state.[4]

In this context, placing Israel in the early stage of a decolonization crisis since the outbreak of the intifada, Sivan defines the colonial situation as one in which "one ethnic group rules over another, ethnically different, group within the same territory. The ruling group holds a monopoly of power as well as a disproportionately large share of the territory's economic resources."[5] Decisions to change such a situation are usually made because the metropol assesses the costs of the status quo as being too high and thus no longer in its best interests rather than because of a crisis in the metropol's value system. Even in the latter cases, a "guilty colonial conscience," to use Sivan's term, does not easily evolve into a majority view. Justifications for the behavior of colonial powers have often been easy to find, from the "white man's burden" of the British empire to the "civilizing mission" characteristic of France to Russian nationalism in the Soviet Union. In the particular case of Israel, Jews have found justification in nationalist tendencies and an attachment to the "Promised Land" of the covenant with their god and ancestors. Coupled with their sense of vulnerability to the threat of extermination and the verbal threats and actual behavior of their neighbors, these justifications have left many Israelis reluctant to accept a territorial compromise. Therefore, any change in the colonial situation here seems more likely when perceived interests, rather than values, are at stake.

To what extent does a colonial situation affect the democratic values of a people in the metropol? The historical precedent of countries such as Great Britain, France, Belgium, and the Netherlands indicates that in a largely consensual society, domestic democratic practices do not significantly deteriorate. Can we predict a similar outcome for Israeli democracy? Several dimensions that may have an impact on such an hypothesis are worth examining:

1. The Occupied Territories are adjacent to the pre-1967 Israel; they are not separate or remote as were the historical European colonies. Such geographic proximity introduces associations with the Darwinist-type of determinism in ensuring "vital space" (or *lebensraum*). An updated version of the argument is offered by Julian L. Simon: a) Rhetoric about resource scarcity induced by population growth has often contributed to international conflict, even if economics have not been the main motive in making

war; b) in the premodern era, war to obtain land and other natural resources sometimes may have been an economically sound policy; and c) politicians and others in industrially developed nations believe resources may still be a *casus belli*.[6] According to Simon, land and other resources are no longer worth acquiring at the cost of war. Nevertheless, clear economic rationales for some nations are not the only operative factors; continuous occupation, if its cost is perceived as low, may very well be acceptable, particularly when security is felt to be at stake. Thus, making exception in his concluding chapter, Simon notes, "This trend [that it is no longer worth acquiring land at the cost of war] does nothing to reduce the desire of many Arabs to make successful war on Israel, because that desire is motivated by hate and sentimental attachment to the land. Nor would this trend reduce the desire of many Israelis to hold on to the West Bank of what was Jordan before 1967 because of religious-historical-sentimental attachment to many places there, as well as because of military advantages and aesthetic appreciation of that area."[7]

2. The consolidation of a Jewish nation-state may still be at a premature stage. Israel's boundaries are not yet historically defined, and its political culture is still evolving. Israel is a new state, where melting-pot ideas are considered necessary for the formation of a strong national spirit. In such cases nationalism is a powerful magnet, and leaders often manipulate the populace for the sake of national unity and to promote their own hold on political power. This nineteenth-century nation-building process contrasts with the well-established regimes and national identities of the Western European colonial powers, whose deep-rooted values of democracy and equal rights resulted from centuries of often violent struggles. Furthermore, the majority of nonnative-born Israeli citizens was born in countries without a democratic tradition. Even if one could argue that within Jewish *kehillas* (communities) there were some basic democratic traits contained in the religious impact on daily life,[8] the overall context of the societies they inhabited clearly did not favor a democratic political culture.

3. The European examples have by and large involved homogenous populations.[9] Israel, by comparison, with its large Arab minority, is often subject to some confusion over the internal and external nature of its conflict with the Palestinians. That such a division is seen by many Israelis (and Palestinians) as artificial underscores the difficulty of separating the domestic from the international elements of the conflict; this difficulty may in turn subsequently affect Israel's democratic values. The conception of Israel as a Jewish state does have some exclusivist connotations,[10] which puts the remaining 14 percent of non-Jews in a position of unequal access to the same opportunities—a policy rationalized by many of Israel's Jews because of their Arab co-citizens' shared traits with their enemies in the rest of the Middle East.

4. The Israeli-Palestinian conflict can be described in terms of the

struggle for the self-determination of both nations. This description encompasses both the relatively newly independent Israel's demand for acceptance in the area and the Palestinians' appeal for world recognition of its state declared (on paper) forty years after Israel's creation. However, this is only one dimension of the problem. According to Benvenisti, an international conflict is conducted between groups separated by a demographic or political delimitation, whereas the Israeli-Palestinian conflict is internal in nature, and the enemy is perceived to be in a territory considered the homeland or motherland, even in the same city or region.[11] Theoretically, a separation of the two entities is possible, although it would require a difficult surgical operation, intertwined as the situation is with intracommunal strife between Arab and Jew. This characteristic is similar in many respects to the communal conflicts in Northern Ireland, the former Yugoslavia, and South Africa. However, Israel's case is perhaps the most complex and intrinsic, as the dimensions of the intracommunal conflict are reflected in a synthesis of different ethnic, religious, linguistic, cultural, and national traits, rather than any one or two elements alone.

5. The Palestinian struggle against Israel comes to the fore at a time when the processes of decolonization are at an advanced stage all around the globe. The conquest of territories and the expulsion, extermination, or subjugation of populations was a common albeit declining practice until World War II, when it virtually ceased. Self-determination for large and small nations alike is by now the name of the game in world politics, to the point that nationalism has factionalized existing states and threatens to become one of the most serious sources of instability in the depolarized world. At this late stage of history, then, with colonization nearing its end, what are the likely consequences of Israel's colonial behavior as it tries to maintain control over a population that rejects such unilateral Jewish domination?

These five issues are examined in the context of their relationship to the deterioration of democratic principles in Israel.

The second area of generalizations relates to the effects of war on democratic regimes, in light of the bearing of the past on the Jewish-Israeli frame of mind. This past includes a collective memory of centuries of persecution, intensified by the traumatic experience of the Holocaust; a war in each decade since Israel's independence (1948, 1956, 1967, 1973, 1982, 1991) and, in between, minor sporadic wars of attrition; continuous terrorism; and, since 1987, the latest (and most severe) civil rebellion, the intifada. With an earlier history of bloody confrontation between Arabs and Jews prior to statehood (1919, 1929, 1936), Israel has undoubtedly been the democratic country that has confronted war over the longest period of its autonomous existence. This situation has aptly been described by Prime Minister Yitzhak Rabin as one continuous "dormant war" that erupts every

few years into active conflict.[12] Additionally, since the 1967 war, the
Jewish state has undertaken control over a disenfranchised population
equivalent to about a third the size of its own—the Palestinians in the West
Bank and Gaza. The cumulative effect of these events could lead Israel to
become a garrison state.[13] According to Lasswell's pioneering work, a
democracy in a prolonged period of war is likely to become more authoritarian and will often have consensual support for its strong rule in the face
of threats to its security. Even if this scenario in Israel has so far not
evolved to such an advanced stage, the question arises: Is the Jewish state
particularly immune to a social disease of this kind?

   Barzilai argues that the influences of wars on democracies are varied
and complex, depending to a large extent on the preventive nature of a war,
its duration, and whether it is waged for national or partisan purposes or in
highly or sparsely populated areas. Whereas distinctions among types may
lead to different levels of consensus or dissent, "In most cases since the end
of World War II (1945), wars have actually tended to elicit serious domestic controversies, social and attitudinal rifts, much public protest, military
and civil disobedience, acts of violence, the delegitimation of regimes, fundamental difficulties in governability and the overthrowing of established
governments."[14] Barzilai goes on to claim that "these negative developments result from the existence of contradictions between the phenomenon
of democracy, on the one hand, and that of war, on the other." The main
difference is rooted "in the fact that while democracy offers human freedom and the conditions for pluralism and individualism, warfare demands
mobilization, considerable centralism and the imposition of a range of
restrictions on the scope of individual freedom."[15] In other words, we can
expect civil rights to be impinged upon and circumscribed when national
security considerations are prevalent, according to the perceived necessities
of those security requirements. In the case of Israel, Barzilai maintains that
until the 1982 war in Lebanon, all wars (except the 1973–1974 War of
Attrition) were perceived by the Israelis as preventive in nature. However,
since that war, contradictions between war and democracy have become
more apparent in Israeli society. Policies implemented to crush the intifada
since its outbreak in 1987 have furthered sharpened these contradictions.[16]

Threats to Democracy in Israeli Society

In looking into trends in Israeli society, this chapter excludes discussion of
how democratic institutionalized regime mechanisms, forms, and procedures have been affected—aspects Alon Pinkas addresses in Chapter 4. The
importance of the authorities' attitudes toward basic freedoms needs to be
stressed, however, because in the absence of a constitution or fundamental
law to guarantee civil liberties, the maintenance of such principles has in

effect devolved into the hands of the politicians and the courts. The latter use the very short but nonetheless remarkable document issued at Israel's independence as a basis for defending individual freedoms.[17]

Comparison of both institutional and leadership levels with a cross-section of Israel's Jewish population indicates that standards of democracy are more strongly affected at the grassroots level.[18] In this respect, Israel is not unique. As Michal Shamir points out, "Much research on political tolerance in democratic societies has shown the general public to be generally intolerant of political out-groups, and always much less tolerant than the political elites."[19] The general population appears to be more volatile and more susceptible to emotional reactions to an Arab threat. In comparison to social trends, institutional transformation and change are slower to occur; additionally, the influences that affect the country's elites may be different from those bearing on the public. Although both the public and elites may be strongly affected by ideological positions, among politicians, political, partisan, and electoral calculations may constrain the available range of choices. Such considerations are conspicuously lacking in the public's decisionmaking process.[20] One could still argue, however, that even at the leadership level there has been a significant erosion of democratic values over the years.

As mentioned in the introduction to this volume, adherence to democratic values needs to be measured above and beyond the primary prerequisite of participation in multiparty elections. Societal aspects will be analyzed here by looking at civil and political rights, as well as practices of political tolerance, which stand as basic premises of the pluralistic nature of democracy. The paradigm presented is set up to connect Israeli society with democratic values as follows. On the one side, we describe the prevailing values in Israeli society and among those seemingly most susceptible to undemocratic views: youth, Orthodox Jews, and Jews from Arab countries and their descendants (commonly and henceforth referred to as "Oriental Jews"). The latter group is also correlated to socioeconomic and education indicators. On the other side, we refer to Israeli attitudes toward general principles of pluralistic democracy, focusing specifically on the most frequent targets of hostility of these undemocratic attitudes. The most disliked and least tolerated groups are defined on the Arab-Israeli dimension of the four main cleavages that polarize Israeli society (socioeconomic, religion and state, ethnicity, and peace and security);[21] these groups are the left-wing Jews or the Israeli Arabs.[22] This dislike relates to the fact that matters of security have come to play a decisive role in the Israeli collective consciousness,[23] even more since the start of the intifada, when security and peace were singled out as the most important issues in the 1988 electoral campaign.[24] Finally, we relate specifically to those professional groups in society that, by the very nature of their role in fulfilling some basic function of a dynamic democracy, tend to be seen as controversial. These groups—including journalists, academics, the judiciary, and law enforcement agents—have become the target of criticism not only by the more extreme right-wing groups, but by some on the left of the political spectrum as well.[25]

Graphically the paradigm may be presented as follows:

**Democratic Values of Israeli
Society at Large**

Intolerant Attitudes Toward

Groups Within Israeli Society
Youth (age factor)
Orthodox (religious factor)

Orientals (ethnic, socioeconomic
  factor)

Pluralistic Democracy in General

*Greater Degree of Intolerance
  Toward*
Left Wing

Israeli-Arabs

Lesser Degree of Intolerance Toward
Journalists
Academics
Judiciary
Law Enforcement Agents

The deterioration in Israel's democratic situation has been aptly identified by Hofnung. In the past, he writes, "Israel has managed to deal successfully with security threats posed by neighboring enemy states, and during the years a principle of the 'rule of law' prevailed increasingly over security considerations within the 'green line.' However, the inability of the Israeli society to solve or to reduce the internal security pressure, in spite of the reduction in the external threat, is a source of continuous danger to Israeli democracy and the maintenance of the rule of law."[26]

An Introduction to the Public Response

Public opinion polls provide insight into the traits of contemporary Israeli society and highlight the emergence of a seemingly paradox. Ninety-two percent of citizens surveyed express overwhelming support for democracy as "the best form of government" while maintaining a preference for "strong leaders" who "would help the country more than all discussions and laws."[27] Arian also stresses the high level of support that Israelis accord abstract principles of democracy while simultaneously retaining their dislike for minority rights.[28] According to Dowty, "Public opinion polls continued to show that, despite a general support for democratic values, support for democracy has its weak points in popular feelings of support for the idea of a strong leader, in willingness to limit minority rights, and in the tendency to subordinate political rights to security considerations."[29]

Such basic and prevailing values of Israeli society have evolved over the years. This development may be attributed to the maturing of the founding fathers' pioneer mentality. However, in the formative years of the Israeli socialist ethos, liberal ideas were not as salient as such values as patriotism, voluntarism, and the priority of the collective will. Hence, changes over time did not take place from a departure point strongly rooted in pluralistic democratic values and political tolerance.[30] This tendency can be seen in light of the developments of the last decade, though as Sprinzak describes, it was soon after the 1967 war, with the seizure of the new territories, that there emerged "a newly born ultra-nationalist creature that brought together strange bed fellows: religious fundamentalism, military hard-liners, and labor settlement fanatics."[31] Two characteristics developed from this new political force: The radical right found an increasingly important role in party politics, and it fed an extraparliamentary movement with cycles of terrorist violence.

What was described as a growing force at the fringe of the political spectrum had by the early 1990s reached a majority position within the Israeli government. The radical right increased in electoral strength and political power and became incorporated into the governing coalition, achieving societal legitimacy. An example is the most militant and extremist force, the late Meir Kahane's Kach movement, characterized by "a fascist-like rejection of equality, human rights, parliamentary politics, and bourgeois mentality . . . combined with a very violent character and unrestrained ambitions."[32] This movement lacked legitimacy among political leaders and was a minority, but nevertheless made its voice heard. However, after Kahane's murder, Moledet (Homeland), with a platform that similarly highlighted the *transfer* of Arabs out of Israel and the territories, doubled its number of votes and further increased its strength in the 1992 elections. Its incorporation into the coalition government in 1990 paved the way not only for the tint of racist views in government decisions but also for increasing legitimacy among the populace. The same is true for other militant parties, although one of these, Tehiya (Renaissance), lost its seats in the Knesset in 1992.[33]

Within the previous Likud-led cabinet, there were a sizable number of ministers who did not emphasize democratic values in their political discourse. Instead, they promoted the ultraorthodox fundamentalist current represented by such groups as Shas (Sephardi Torah Guardians), Agudat Israel (Congregation of Israel), and Degel Hatorah (Flag of the Torah), which ask for the rulings of elderly rabbis regarding political matters. Additionally, a chauvinist grouping, labeled "secular neo-fundamentalists" by Sprinzak in his examination of the Israeli radical political right,[34] includes segments of Likud and the party Tehiya. A militarist group also stressed its belief that Israeli battlefield superiority permits the country to dictate the terms of peace according to its interests alone. They were represented by the strengthened Tzomet (Crossroad) party led by former Chief-of-Staff Rafael Eitan and prominent Likud Housing Minister Ariel Sharon, who has always stood for political and military maximalism.[35] Finally, a smaller number of ministers were ready to opportunistically switch loyalties from a Labor- to a Likud-led coalition for personal career gains. This lack of firm convictions weakens the adherence to sustained policies. Of the remaining ministers, only a minority advocated democracy as defined in this study. Insofar as they share such values, they do not seem to have made a priority of calling upon their followers to give primacy to equal rights and tolerance.

Some movements have used means unacceptable to democratic practice and manifesting a lack of tolerance to contending groups acting within the confines of legitimate practices. These tactics include extraparliamentary acts of civil disobedience, such as the establishment of unapproved settlements by Gush Emunim; intimidation by civilian paramilitary groups; the authoritarian control exercised by military rule over a population without many basic rights; the lack of accountability in elections; and coercive practices and clandestine monitoring. All may have prejudiced Israeli citizens toward an excessive use of regime intervention in individual freedom. This legitimation of the curbing of dissent sometimes appears with a violent expression. The monopoly of the extreme right has often been lethally expressed toward Arabs and only mildly physically toward Jews. The most extreme reaction to the Camp David accords that sanctioned the principle of land for peace has been the formation of a Jewish underground within the ranks of Gush Emunim. Some of their most extreme ideas have not been implemented as of yet—for example, the carefully planned destruction of the Muslim Dome of the Rock. Other instances of what was elsewhere described by Sprinzak as the "violentization" of Israeli democracy developed originally as retaliatory acts against scattered Palestinian murders of Jewish settlers. Certain massive plans, such as the blowing up of five Arab buses, were stopped by the Israeli security service.

It is furthermore worthwhile to examine the degree of impact that territorial occupation has had on governmental corruption. Sectors of the military and civilian administrations in charge of the territories may have found in the abuse of power a type of mechanism that spills over in the handling of public affairs in Israel. Concurrently, a severe blow to the standards of individual integrity of the leadership occurred recently when a number of Knesset members were charged with embezzlement and illegal appropriation of public funds.

No symmetry in terms of the acceptance of democratic values and actions can be found between the attitudes and behavior of the right and of the left. While this imbalance stands in contrast to the general tendency toward similar traits at political extremes, there is no significant organized radical left. Rightist activists take to demonstrations of violence or establish unauthorized West Bank settlements. However, the left makes a banner out of the rule of law, with strategies including mass demonstrations, lobbying and picketing, and the exposure of illegal acts in reports and appeals to the Supreme Court of Justice. Approaches placing conditions on, and even rejecting, democracy exist in both the radical right and left. However, in the state of Israel such left-wing groups are weak and lack public support, so there has been no real threat to the decisionmaking capability of the political system.[36] A strict adherence to the rule of law is fundamentally important to the philosophy of the pragmatic left. These groups feel such an approach increases their legitimacy and popularity. Exceptionally, regarding the issue of selective conscientious objection to military service in the territories (not directed at service in the IDF altogether), the left has been deeply divided. A majority of the politically moderate are objecting even to the legitimacy of refusing the call to duty.

Fifty percent of Israeli citizens find the intifada to have polarized their views. For example. opinion polls show that 57 percent of the populace believe the government needs to censor the media, while 54 percent express a lesser degree of trust in the IDF and other leaders of Israel.[37] Such dissonance between the moral values of the society and actual occurrences in the territories has been described by many as denial, facilitated by the process of routinization of nondemocratic behavior by Israelis.[38]

Youth

Much of the work conducted among youth has tended to focus on the researchers' own concerns, flagging the problems ahead. Yet the serious nature of such reliable studies deserves our undivided attention. At first glance, the trends among youth appear similar to those among the general population, with a high degree of support for the democratic form of government—more than 80 percent declare their support.[39] However, opposition to specific, concrete democratic rights such as freedom of the press, the right of Orthodox Jews to demonstrate, and public expression of advocacy of a Palestinian state was normally higher than half. One explanation of this gap may be that democracy is understood as a multiparty system with fair elections. However, some other studies, even at this formal level, show advocacy for restricting those parties perceived as "soft" toward the Arabs and/or composed mostly of Arab members. In such cases, an added explanation would connect the erosion of democratic values to the sense of patriotic and national identification, which rules out those supporting the Palestinian, defined as the enemy. Interestingly enough, and similar to prejudice in the perception of Jews in Diaspora countries by many of their conationals, Israeli youth tend to overestimate the percentage of Arabs among the country's inhabitants both within and beyond the Green Line.[40] When many Israeli youth define the enemy, their differentiation between Arabs in Israel and the Palestinians in the West Bank and Gaza is minimal. The same study showed that for areas within the Green Line, approximately 80 percent of youth thought Jews have more rights than Arabs to this country, as compared with two-thirds who claimed that Jews have more rights than Arabs in Judea, Samaria, and Gaza.

Such is the answer when put as a zero-sum question of either Arab or Jewish rights. However, studies that confront youth with a different set of questions aimed at testing their democratic stands provide a more mixed picture. In one instance, respondents of fifteen to eighteen years of age were asked if it is permissible to restrict the democratic rights of Arab citizens; 33 percent agreed, while 60 percent opposed. When asked if they would join or support Jewish organizations aimed at taking revenge upon Arabs for strikes against Jews, 39 percent responded in favor, with 60 percent opposed. On the other hand, 49 percent believed the Arabs in Israel have too many rights and that these need to be restricted.[41] Thirty-eight percent considered Arab rights to be sufficient, and only 9 percent thought the Arabs do not enjoy sufficient rights.

As a whole, only 40 percent of the youth supported full equality of rights for Israeli Arabs, and about 50 percent wanted to reduce these rights.[42] It seems clear that many of the Jewish youth would like to find ways of keeping a democratic self-image without exposing their country to the enemy. Hence, the salient preference for democracy is for Jews only. In this light, the willingness to curtail democracy in the aforementioned illustrations is directly connected to the point whereby the weakness of the system may play into the hands of the enemy. Once you accept the restriction of your enemies' rights, hatred toward other groups—perhaps the ultra-Orthodox Jews, for example—may also crop up and cause their rights to be restricted as well.

The above-cited statistics lead us to ponder the high level of positive responses to the question, "Do you hate Arabs?" A survey with upper-level high school students shows an average of about 40 percent expressing strong hatred of Arabs. The students responded that they hate "all" or "most" Arabs, and 60 percent declared possession of strong feelings of vengeance. This longitudinal study shows that over the last fifteen years there has been an increase in the level of expressed hatred toward Arabs.[43] In this study as well, no differentiation was made between Arabs who are Israeli citizens and those under military occupation.

In general, a trend toward a more pronounced polarization of political views among the youth as compared with the society at large can be detected. There is a tilt toward anti-Arab extremism. Various studies undertaken by the Jerusalem Van Leer Foundation may prove enlightening. Since 1984 the research institution has observed the attitudes toward the Arab-Israeli conflict among high schoolers of fifteen to eighteen years of age. In the September 1984 study, 60 percent of the respondents thought Arabs did not deserve full equality, and 42 percent were in favor of restricting the political rights of non-Jews. After a strong campaign for democratic values, a poll conducted in 1986 still showed 50 percent favorable to the idea of restricting Arab rights and 56 percent opposed to equal rights for non-Jews. One of the most troubling results emerged from a study commissioned by the Ministry of Education, with 60 percent preferring the "integrity of Eretz Israel" over "human rights." Sixty-seven percent would like to see Palestinians from the Occupied Territories encouraged to emigrate, and 69 percent are against granting them equal rights. These attitudes spill over to interpretations of democracy. The majority of participants in the survey favor it, yet three-quarters subordinate it to national security considerations.[44]

Within the same age group, 33 percent agreed to some degree or completely with the views of Rabbi Kahane and his Kach movement. The awareness of the erosion of democratic values was particularly addressed by the Ministry of Education in the mid-1980s in reaction to the racist predicament generated by Rabbi Kahane (who was eventually assassinated). The movement was barred from participating in the 1988 election, but with time educational efforts became weaker and routinized, and their lack of effectiveness was criticized.[45]

While the most troubling findings regarding youthful attitudes relate to the Arabs, Aryeh Na'or categorically stresses that they are not separate from findings toward the overall issue of dissent and intolerance. "The lesson for us is no different from that taught by recent history: there is no such thing as selective or partial democracy," he writes. "Curtailment of human rights—and it makes no difference what justification is cited for forsaking a step—will sap our democracy, and those who seek to curtail Arabs will end by curtailing the rights of Jews as well."[46]

Orthodox Jews

Salient antidemocratic attitudes among the religious orthodox community in Israel can be clearly identified. Eisenstadt considers a growing inward-looking orientation among religious groups to have contributed to "a legitimation for xenophobic behavior, based on biblical injunctions against Amalek, going against the recognition of the tensions between the particularistic and universalistic orientations which was characteristic of the older religious Zionist movements."[47] In Chapter 6 Liebman analyzes how attitudes of the religious Jewish leadership toward democracy relate to the influence of rabbinical law on legislative action. Pressure for the imposition of religious laws on the majority of nonobservant population shows how complex the picture is in terms of the religious establishment. Here I focus on one of the three aspects of ultranationalism as described elsewhere by Liebman as "ethnicnationalism."[48] A poll covering religiosity and attitudes to rights of Jews and Arabs in Eretz Israel finds 56 percent of Orthodox and 76 percent of ultra-Orthodox Jews (10 percent each of the total Israeli Jewish population) claim that "Eretz Israel belongs to the Jewish people and only Jews have rights in it," as compared to an average of 38 percent and 28 percent among traditional and secular Jews. Conversely, only 8 percent of ultra-Orthodox and 13 percent of Orthodox Jews considered both Arabs and Jews to have both national and personal rights in Eretz Israel, as compared with an average of 26 percent and 36 percent among traditional and secular Jews.[49]

Hatred toward the Arabs is particularly strong among Jewish religious youth, often twice that of the secular population.[50] Add in the high support for acts of revenge, and the road to racist predicaments becomes wide open. Therefore, it is not surprising that there were higher levels of support among the religious constituency than elsewhere for Rabbi Kahane, whose anti-Arab expressions were the strongest ever expressed from the Knesset podium.[51]

Sprinzak appropriately quoted a survey illustrative of the exceptional popularity of Kahane's ideas among 59 percent of religious youth.[52] The worrisome feature was not only the type of political discourse that now became an open avenue in which to compete for votes but also the legitimation of these ideas, mostly by tacit acceptance, but occasionally by open endorsement, on the part of prominent religious figures. For instance, the Ministry of Education, which established a special unit to advance democratic values among pupils, had at the head of its religious education branch a number of officers who stated that there was no necessary correspondence between democracy and Judaism.[53]

Some of the extremist voices in the religious camp use interpretations or quotes from authoritative Jewish sources in order to defend antidemocratic ideas, such as the right to expel non-Jews from the land or relegate them to an inferior position as tolerated individuals rather than equal citizens.[54] The growth of anti-Arab prejudice spawned the already mentioned violent underground manned by religious young people, with exemplary killings of Palestinian Arabs as its goal. Some Arabs were individually targeted, and others were picked in retaliation for Arab acts of violence against Jews. When brought to trial, many of these violent activists such as Yehuda Etzion (accused of taking part in an armed attack on West Bank mayors and an attempt to blow up the Temple Mount) testified that their acts were inspired by "loyalty to the entire history beginning with God's election of Abraham and ending with final redemption."[55] Once again, the most worrisome feature is not the violent behavior itself but the lack of intense and clear condemnation by prominent figures of the religious establishment, such as the chief rabbis. Kahane and other rabbis with close connection to the religious authorities came up with mitigating explanations for such behavior and eventually lobbied successfully for presidential pardons for the offenders. These apologists weakened the impact of the voices among the religious establishment that called, above all, for respect for the rule of law and denounced taking justice in one's hands.[56]

Other expressions of the erosion of democratic values among the religious Jewish population in Israel can be found in relation to issues such as the freedom of the press. When asked if there is too much freedom of the press in Israel and/or if freedom of the press endangers national security, the ultra-Orthodox or religious agreement is around 70 percent, as compared with 55 percent for the traditional public and 36 percent for the secular population.[57]

Oriental Jews

Research within the last two decades has suggested a relationship between ethnic origin and anti-Arab attitudes. Such sentiments are more pronounced among Israeli Jews originally from Arab countries and their descendants. Yochanan Peres, for instance, showed in 1971 that 78 percent of Oriental Jews were opposed to having Arab neighbors, as compared with 53 percent of the Ashkenazi Jews originating from Europe.[58] Such trends seem to be particularly salient when youth and ethnicity are correlated: In the same 1984 Van Leer study quoted by Sprinzak, 50 percent of Oriental high schoolers sympathized with Kahane's racist views.[59] Such a high figure is comparable to the large percentage of those claiming hatred of Arabs. Figures for young Oriental Jews tend to be approximately twice as high as those for Ashkenazi youth. In development towns, 76 percent of Oriental Jews who live in areas densely populated by their own ethnic group declare having "strong hatred" toward Arabs. This figure may be compared with 51 percent of Ashkenazi Jews expressing a similar viewpoint. On a kibbutz, Ashkenazis who live in similarly high concentrations of their own ethnic groups express a lesser degree of hatred; only 34 percent respond in this way, as against 48 percent of the Oriental Jews.[60]

While there seems to be little disagreement about the correlation between ethnicity and degrees of anti-Arab sentiment, there are strong discrepancies between explanations about the origins of such hatred. Yonah refers to a long-cited view that "repeated persecutions throughout the Arab world over the centuries instilled in Oriental Jews deep resentment and distrust of Arabs. . . . Oriental Jews' long sojourn in the Arab world has left its cultural impression on them . . . the hallmark of Arab fanaticism and intolerance."[61] Anti-Arab sentiment on the part of Oriental Jews lies also in their reaction to societal stereotyping of Arabs. "Being aware of the contempt with which their culture and values are generally viewed by the Israeli establishment, Oriental Jews came to perceive their affinity with

Arab culture as a liability and obstacle thwarting their desire to assimilate into Israeli society." Their adoption of anti-Arab views is intended "to minimize, first, their affinity toward Arabs and second, the significance of this affinity for Oriental Jews' collective self-identity," obtained through a reinterpretation of past experience in the Arab world.[62]

A more general assumption is often made that Jews originally from Arab countries and their descendants are more prone to political intolerance. However, that assumption also interplays with lower levels of income and education. Even homogenous and developed countries have segments of their populations for whom nationalism amounts to an emotional and irrational attachment to national symbols. This "my country right or wrong" mentality is found among groups located on the periphery of society because of low education, low income, low status, and advanced age. Such symbolic commitment is found to be stronger in less-developed countries within traditional segments of society. In the case of Israel, Peri and Goldberg reviewed contending explanations of the relationship between the factors of ethnicity and anti-Arab attitudes, and found not enough empirical evidence to corroborate them.[63] There is a strong correlation between one's level of education and one's position regarding territorial compromise and the PLO: The more hawkish Oriental Jews tend to have less education, whereas those with university degrees tend to be significantly more open to compromise.[64] Here, too, conservative tendencies among Oriental Jews stem from their desire to change their social status, which they perceive as being inferior to the veteran Labor Ashkenazi elite. They have long endorsed the viewpoints of the Likud Party as an alternative. According to Yonah, the tilt toward the right is the result of neither the distorted reinterpretation of past experiences in the Arab world nor a culturally inherent hostility toward the Arabs. Rather, this so-called "radicalization" of Orientals registers a protest in disguise against Ashkenazi cultural and economic hegemony, which has been identified mainly with the Labor Party. Upholding such a stand for a long number of years may have left anti-Arab sentiment increasingly entrenched.

In the microcosm of the development town populated primarily by those of Oriental descent, it is the socioeconomic factor that prompts support for the radical right. The insecure development town workers face high levels of unemployment and fear being displaced from their jobs by lower-paid Arab workers. Thus, class position, more than simple "hawkishness" regarding security issues, underlies the inordinate support in development towns for parties such as Kahane's. Peled emphasizes the development town inhabitant's relative deprivation and thoughts in accordance with the Split Labor Market Theory.[65]

At the same time, it is plausible that many insecure workers fear an arrangement in which they will be left to perform the jobs that Arabs do now.

Targets of Intolerance

The following portion of this study highlights societal hostility and criticism directed at fellow Jews and Arabs. Palestinians in the territories, who are formally deprived of full civil and political rights and living under temporary military government, are outside the scope of this study. Yet as a group subject to hostility, they merit at least a paragraph. When public opinion polls in Israel ask, "As long as no solution is achieved in Judea, Samaria and Gaza, are you in favor of increasing the civil rights of the Arabs in the territories, decreasing them, or leaving them as they are today?" only 6 percent agree to increase rights to include such liberties as the right to vote. Sixty percent suggest that rights should be left as they are today, and 17 percent suggest a decrease in these rights. The rest had no opinion.[66] A dual legal system that presently clearly favors the approximately 100,000 Jews in the territories who live side by side with 1.7 million Arabs raises the question of a double standard.

The main thrust of this chapter is to examine the area within the Green Line, where the civilian rule of law is supposed to guarantee equal rights. In moving from an examination of one type of territory to the other, we should mention the fragility of democratic principles in East Jerusalem, a part of the city that has been officially annexed and incorporated into Israeli civilian rule. Clear double standards exist in terms of human rights violations such as political imprisonment, procedures of detention, freedom of expression, freedom of the press, and freedom of movement. It is easier to have a debate about the intifada's violence at the Hebrew University than at a Palestinian research institute a mile away. A press conference at the Israeli press club in West Jerusalem would normally never be obstructed, but military authorities can declare a curfew to impede the same press conference in East Jerusalem.[67]

A clear difference occurs when special law enforcement corps deal only with the Arab population of the city. A most striking example is the state proceedings against ten members of the police force working in the "minorities unit." The ten have been charged with applying torture, obtaining false confessions, and lying in court to cover up the use of such methods.[68]

The "Belfastization" of Jerusalem, a term coined by Benvenisti, highlights the fact that finding a separate solution for the city seems to be an insurmountable obstacle. Meanwhile, the spectrum ranging from the lack of rights for Palestinians in Judea and Samaria to the more limited rights of their brethren in East Jerusalem to the larger enjoyment of rights of the Israeli Arabs in the rest of the country shows how the problem is not merely one of the Occupied Territories and sovereign Israel, but rather one between Arab and Jew.

Arabs in Israel

In evaluating standards of democracy within Israel proper, it should be made clear that Jewish attitudes toward Arabs are not clearly demarcated by the Green Line. Hatred of another ethnic group does not differentiate between who has citizenship and who does not.[69] According to Peri, it is necessary to look into long-term effects: "Not only has there been a process of legitimation of the use of supposedly legal violence, but a distinction has been taking root between those against whom violence is permissible and those against whom it is prohibited. This distinction is ethnonational, between Arabs and Jews, but makes no distinction between Arabs within or outside the Green Line."[70] Cries such as "Death to the Arabs!" are often heard in reaction to individual acts of Palestinian fanatics or terrorists, and the lingering sentiments of violence are applied to Israeli Arab citizens as well.

Israel's Arabs, who until 1966 lived under the tight control of a military government, saw with its abolition an opening toward greater equality. However, this process may have been slowed down after the 1967 war with the incorporation of the disenfranchised Palestinian Arabs under Israeli military rule over the West Bank and Gaza. Jews' mistrust of autonomous Arab expression in Israel leads, on the one hand, to barriers to Arab integration (if measured in terms of positions acquired in the upper echelons of society, let alone the security-oriented establishments obviously barred from Arab participation because of the continuous warlike situation). On the other hand, attempts to organize Palestinian universities, political parties, and other expressions of empowerment are massively rejected by the Jewish population.[71] Most researchers have stressed the aspects of inequality, dominance, and control, as discussed by Rouhana and Ghanem in Chapter 7.[72]

The scattered Jewish minorities, in their 2,000 years of exile, had no experience in controlling the destiny of another group. Dowty summarizes the Israeli policy:

> Had it been decided, for example, to counter discontent through a concerted policy of assimilation and material well-being, then the unequal distribution of benefits would have been corrected. Had it been decided, on the other hand, to maintain the peace by working with, and even reinforcing, the traditional social structure of Arab village life, then the boundaries between the two communities would have been maintained as strongly as possible. As it happened, a mixed and inconsistent policy followed.[73]

Problems of discrimination emerge already at the constitutional level and are thoroughly described by Kretzmer.[74] It is not the purpose of this chapter to investigate legal inequalities, yet it must be stressed that such an inconsistent policy has profound implications for the societal attitudes of the majority toward the Arab minority. Some popular ideas, such as the need to "Judaize" the western Galilee (which translates into an official redressing of the current minority proportions of Jews living there), reflect society's desire to dominate the Arab minority.

According to Cohen, Israeli Arabs are "separate and unequal."[75] In terms of civil rights, there has been an increasing lack of tolerance toward the Arabs' right to express their political opinion. A poll shows that 36 percent of the Israeli public would deny the right of Arab citizens in Israel to hold demonstrations, and another 37 percent have reservations on the subject.[76] More ambiguous is the strong support for excluding from the Knesset political parties that recognize the PLO as the legitimate representative of the Palestinian people, including parties such as the Communists or the Progressive List for Peace.[77] The delegitimation of Arabs in Israeli politics includes those who are elected to the Knesset within the Zionist parties. The general reluctance to allow Arabs to serve in the cabinet may clearly be influenced by the confidentiality of the security issues in a war-type situation, but it may also be identified as a result of the explicit and declared bond between nationality and Israel's definition as the state of the Jewish people.[78]

Sometimes harsh sentences are meted out to Arabs in Israel—sentences that possibly would not be applied to their Jewish countrymen—for peaceful expressions of solidarity with the Palestinians' right to self-determination. An illustration is the four-month term of imprisonment without bail of an Arab teacher in the Galilee, whose only crime was to show his pupils how to draw a Palestinian flag on the blackboard.[79]

Discrimination is not only visible on the socioeconomic level. There is clear evidence of inequality in occupational status and earnings between Jews and Arabs, particularly for Arabs who work in Jewish-dominated markets.[80] Many industrial plants, and not only those related to the military-industrial complex, have had a hidden policy of not hiring Arabs. By 1990 certain Jerusalem shopkeepers displayed signs reading "No Arab employed here" as a reaction to cases of Palestinians stabbing their Jewish employers. The signs were eventually removed, but hidden pressures and threats made temporarily more difficult the hiring of Arabs from both sides of the Green Line. Mistrust has evolved in Jewish-Arab relations, and each side is prone to perceive the worst in the other.[81] Sporadic Palestinian terrorist acts against Jewish civilians provoke increasingly massive violent reactions that may end in the beating of Arab bystanders and occasionally in lynch-mob-type situations that have caused the death of one Arab in Jerusalem.[82] Of late there have been isolated cases of vandalism and hooliganism, such as the beating of an Arab by high school students on a city bus. The other passengers did nothing to intervene.[83]

As long as Israel is in a war situation with Arab states while controlling the destiny of a large number of rebellious Palestinians, it will be objectively difficult to bridge the gap between the Arab and Jewish citizens of Israel. As one of the few Arabs who reached the position of deputy minister in the sixties, the late Abdul Aziz Zu'abi coined the phrase, "I cannot take my country fighting my people," a statement that speaks for itself. In principle, there should be a tolerance toward the Israeli Arabs' identification with the Palestinian people in particular and the Arab world in general, because there is a fully legitimated acceptance of Israeli Jewish identification with the communities in the Diaspora. However, "despite the fact that this sense of belonging is mentioned in Israel's Declaration of Independence, the Israeli government sees it as a betrayal of the loyalty of the Israeli Arabs as citizens of the state."[84] A situation of continuous occupation next door plus lack of full rights for Arabs in Israel resulted in the primacy of "Palestinian identity," which may eventually bring them to embark in the future upon a type of intifada within the Green Line.[85] Already during the first years of the intifada, political violence among Arabs in Israel began slowly to rise in tandem with the increasingly vociferous racist attacks against them.[86]

Peace Groups

No less dangerous than a situation of unequal access to rights are signs of the deterioration of the center in the societal spectrum (to be discussed in the next section) and symptoms of growing polarization resulting in hostile attitudes toward *Jewish* components in civil society. Adherents to the peace movement are seen as potentially assisting foreign interests, perhaps spying for the United States but more often working for the enemy. It appears not to matter if, for example, one of the most prominent advocates of peace, Shalom Achshav (Peace Now), grew out of an appeal by reserve officers in support of Prime Minister Begin's peace efforts.[87] Neither the adherence of most doves to the Zionist inspiration of the country nor attempts to operate the peace movement on a Jewish basis without Arabs seem to dissipate the general condemnation of membership in such an organization.

In 1990 Peace Now decided that tactically it may be worth creating an umbrella organization called Time for Peace affiliated with other peace-oriented Zionist political parties and the dovish wing of the Labor Party. The group's perceived need to change its image speaks volumes about its lack of appeal to large sectors of Israeli society. What must be stressed in the context of this chapter is the worrisome increase in verbal and even physical abuse toward such "peacenik" positions. Often such verbal negativism is espoused by the top leadership of the state. In a recent meeting of the Likud's Central Committee, former Prime Minister Shamir fell into what may be termed very poisonous political discourse. He expounded against "parties and groups advocating peace at any price, ready to give up the last piece of our national interest, those working under the services of foreign and hostile elements, terrorist organizations, and collaborating with Arabs, the most extreme of our enemies, who advocate armed struggle against Israel." At the same gathering, former Housing Minister Sharon used similar terms against the peace groups' (including the Labor Party's) "threat to democracy" and said, "The Jewish people are a great nation. But a part of it, it has something sick. We suffer from the left's effort to hit the government and that is how, naturally, they hit Israel."[88] The next day the spokesman of Peace Now reported to the police that several active members of the movement had received threatening telephone calls using the terms "Traitors, your end is coming." Left-wing MKs (Knesset members) also reported that they were subjected to a new wave of death threats following the prime minister's remarks.[89] Hebrew University political scientist Itzhak Galnoor puts it this way: "Delegitimation is recurring due to the peace process, as leaders charge the opposition camp with joining the enemy. If you don't adhere to the rules of the game, deterioration sets in. For the prime minister to start calling people traitors is very bad."[90]

Violent oral expressions calling the peace movement "a knife in the back of the nation" are harbingers of physical violence. Jewish peace activists traveling to a gathering with moderate Palestinians in Hebron were stopped on the way by roadblocks put up by a rioting settler, who shouted, "The Jews we don't like should be killed even before the Arabs."[91] In 1983 a grenade thrown at peace demonstrators killed Emil Grunsweig and injured several others, including the present Labor MK Avraham Burg. Peace activists take threats on their life seriously, and for good reason.[92] A leader of Peace Now and his family were recently exposed to consistent harassment. Noises around the house would keep the family continuously worried, and one morning they awoke to find their car tires punctured. However, the majority of the harassment was by mail or by telephone. The callers made sexual insinuations regarding the wife's relationships with Arabs and wrote letters charging that "the well-respected leader of Peace Now has collaborated with the criminals who applaud the killing of six million Jews." He was also termed a "squealer," one who provides information to the enemies of Israel. Repeated death threats, particularly against the ten-year-old daughter, brought the police to regularly patrol the immediate area around the house and to lay in wait for an assault to occur.[93] However, they were soon forced to leave because of a lack of manpower, and the patrols were taken up at times by members of Peace Now.[94] In the aftermath of the October 1990 Temple Mount incident, in which seventeen Arabs were killed, a Palestinian knifed three persons in the immediate proximity of the activist's home. An angry mob surrounded the house, verbally threatening the family and shouting that they were hiding the assassin, who was meanwhile wounded and apprehended elsewhere. The police presence prevented the building up of a lynch-mob atmosphere, yet the situation resulted in attacks upon journalists in the crowd. When the family's neighbor, who was a relative of one of the murder victims, asked people to let go of their hatred and invited the Peace Now neighbors to mourn together as a gesture of peace, flyers were dispersed by anti–peace movement activists. They read: "Peace Now people are happy with the murder." Another common accusation is that Peace Now will be responsible for future bloodshed and "a civil war which will jeopardize Israel's existence."[95] In one instance of combatting such viewpoints, Peace Now decided to sue a member of Knesset who accused the movement of supporting the murder of a Jew in a terrorist act in the West Bank. Another MK has called for outlawing Peace Now, citing the movement's "antinational activities in favor of the PLO which threaten the country's security as well as incite the U.S. to put pressure on Israel."[96]

Peace movements often feel that their right of assembly, particularly in Jerusalem and the West Bank, has been less tolerated by the authorities than acts conducted, often unilaterally and without official permits, by the annexationists.[97] The sensation of being antagonized and ostracized by large segments of the public under the incitement of irresponsible politicians and with the complacent attitude of the governmental agencies makes some among the peace camp feel increasingly alienated. Some have considered options such as emigration or a self-imposed type of internal exile.

It may be worth sharing with the reader a personal experience. In trying to prevent the expulsion from Jerusalem of Mubarak Awad, a Palestinian peaceful dissenter, I followed his prison-bound hunger strike with a similar hunger strike outside the walls. The expressions of passersby toward the group that accompanied me were frightful and included a fellow Jew shouting, "A pity that the Nazis did not finish you all."[98]

Law Enforcement Agencies

Law enforcement agencies, and particularly the Israeli Defence Forces, have increasingly become the target of criticism from contending parties. On the one hand, militant groups have charged that the army has not used sufficiently decisive and severe methods to protect Jews in the territories and prevent violence committed by Palestinians within the Green Line. The criticism from the settlers was supported by a wide margin in public opinion polls. When asked if more repressive measures should be used to curb the uprising "as long as there is no political solution," 74 percent responded in the affirmative. Eighteen percent replied that the present policy is the most appropriate, and only 8 percent felt the policy should be more lenient.[99]

Peri maintains that built into the nature of antisubversive warfare— when the target enemy is a civilian population—is a combination of military and nonmilitary measures. This equation increases the possibility of mutual recriminations between the political and military upper echelons, particularly in cases of failure or excess, when the level of operations becomes the subject of public debate.[100] The need to defend and explain the relative level of violence used in repressing the civil population affects the perceived neutrality of the army. The damage to internal cohesiveness, coming on the heels of internal debate about the justice of the war and the use of various tactics, is "liable to lead to a crisis in legitimacy for the army, something every professional officer dreads."[101]

Often decisionmakers at the political level decide on strategy, but segments of the public blame the army for carrying out a "dirty job" or, conversely, for the "lack of action." International opinion holds the Israeli army responsible for policies that contribute to the killing of innocent civilians, and are "excessively permissive." The military is also chastised for conducting investigations that are not "thorough and impartial."[102] One of the clearest examples was the debate generated around then–Minister of Defense Rabin's call to "break bones." The policy of using clubs indiscriminately was understood by a few officers and soldiers as a green light to include punishment of peaceful bystanders. The ex post facto explanations provided by Rabin that beatings in self-defense were a softer response than the use of live ammunition were received with some suspicion.[103] The families of soldiers brought to court and found guilty for such exceptional behavior insisted that they were only following orders from above. Similarly, the December 1992 decision to collectively punish by deporting to the Lebanese border a group of 418 Islamic fundamentalists was supported initially by nine of ten Israeli Jews.

B'Tselem, the Israeli Information Center on Human Rights in the Occupied Territories, has issued several reports regarding interrogation procedures that amount to the use of torture.[104] In reaction, retired general Shlomo Gazit argued that the problem is not the symptom (the alleged use of torture) but the disease (a coerced and continuous occupation). Gazit expressed appreciation of the fact that the charges were investigated by an official commission of inquiry under retired general Raphael Vardi, which led to the opening of judicial procedures against the perpetrators. However, the justification of the use of "moderate physical violence," as recommended by a previous commission of inquiry under Justice Moshe Landau in a secret appendix available only to the security service,[105] is given as a *raison d'état* resulting from security threats the country is facing. An admission of the worst excesses, considered to be exceptions, can be attributed to the "slippery slope" syndrome: The recurrent use of such practices was precipitated by an official endorsement of a secret set of norms legitimizing the use of an unspecified level of violence during interrogation.

The army often has to act against rebellious Palestinian children, women, and the civil population at large, raising the heated question of compartmentalized violence in the exercise of military duty. Do the conscripts and the reserve-duty soldiers bring this violent behavior back home? Peri affirms that there has been a considerable increase in the possession of arms in Israel. It has grown by 50 percent in 1988 to a total number of 200,000 gun owners for a population of 4.5 million. A correlation may exist between gun ownership and the use of violence.[106] The extent to which the overall increase in violence in the confrontation between Arabs and Jews affects crime in general is still open to debate, although several researchers have claimed to detect such an effect, including the former Minister of Police, retired general Haim Bar-Lev.[107] According to criminologist Simha Landau, the period of the intifada has been accompanied by a rise in violent crime within both the Israeli and Palestinian societies, possibly attributable to security-related stress.[108] Another psychologist has correlated the intifada's violence to an increase in sexual assaults.[109]

Another deteriorating aspect of the IDF's image is that, given the cover-ups and lack of reporting concerning government brutalities and excesses, IDF spokesmen are prevented from fulfilling their function. Traditionally considered by Israelis and their neighbors to be highly accurate,[110] the spokesmen are in fact, according to MK Amnon Rubinstein, doubly handicapped. "First he is lied to and then he has to bear the brunt of the retraction. . . . I am afraid that there are commanders in the IDF who are speaking to the soldiers in a double tone. The most important thing is for you not to get caught, even if the price is a false report."[111]

In the case of the border police, operating mostly in the Occupied Territories under the authority of the minister of police, there have been repeated stories involving excessive use of force, the indiscriminate use of live ammunition, lack of accountability, and nonreporting of grave incidents.[112] The police, albeit to a lesser extent, have been accused of excessive use of force not only against Arabs but also against Jews. A notorious case was the use of rubber bullets in dispersing an internationally cosponsored Peace Now demonstration surrounding the walls of Jerusalem's Old City.[113] A year later, Kach militants charged the regular police with having a biased attitude, and violence erupted at the funeral of Kach leader Meir Kahane. The militants attacked and wounded the policeman in custody of the Israel television building in Jerusalem. According to one study, two-thirds of the population believes that the police engage in illegal methods of obtaining information and use more physical force than is necessary. Forty-three percent respond that the police take bribes, and 60 percent suggest that they engage to one extent or another in illegal cover-ups.[114]

A nonviolent repercussion of this security situation has been the opposition of the police authorities to the elimination of national affiliation on Israeli identity cards. Originally conceived by the Orthodox rabbinate as a way to monitor the question of Jewish identity, it is now seen as an asset enhancing police efforts against terrorist actions, as "Arab" is a category.

Its removal could cause Jewish citizens some embarrassment at roadblocks, border checkpoints, and routine police checks.[115]

Strong criticism emanating from the two sides of the political spectrum and allegations and counterallegations from the law enforcement agencies about standards of behavior have come to the forefront during the period of the intifada. Tighter control over the Arab population has been accompanied by allegations of increased security service monitoring of peace-oriented groups, including the tapping of telephone lines.[116] Labor MK Avraham Burg claims it to be the highest ratio of telephone taps per capita among the Western democracies, and he cites the tapping of his own line as well.[117] Sporadically, and particularly since the beginnings of the regional peace conference in October 1991, the settlers have been expressing their lack of confidence in the IDF by conducting illegal patrols, perpetrating acts of intimidation in Arab villages, blocking roads, and retaliating with vandalism against terrorist killings of individual Jews. Often such acts have been stimulated or endorsed by the Council of Rabbis of Judea, Samaria, and Gaza.[118] All of these factors have caused serious damage to the reputation of the armed force once well known for its slogan, "the purity or arms," implying high standards of human behavior.

The Judiciary

The Supreme Court of Justice and the judiciary are among the institutions most respected by Israeli Jews.[119] The threats of the impact of security considerations have been recognized by members of the Supreme Court themselves. According to Justice Aharon Barak:

> Obviously, democracy is allowed and obliged to protect itself. Without security the democratic state could not be established. Nevertheless, it should not be forgotten that security is not only the army; democracy is also security. Our strength is in our moral force and in our cohesion to democratic principles, more so when great danger surrounds us. Indeed, security is not a goal in itself. Security is a means. The goal is the democratic rule which aids the government of the people to realize civil rights.[120]

Some of the perceived bias is explained by a lack of Arab participation within the judiciary. Never in the Supreme Court of Justice's close to half a century of independent history has an Arab been selected to serve, and in 1988 only 5 out of the 150 judges were Arab. Such a disproportionate figure is striking given that the system of appointment for judges in Israel is based on professional criteria. Furthermore, in the name of diversity, there is always a Sephardic and a Jewish Orthodox judge on the Supreme Court. A study shows that 56 percent of Israelis do not believe an Arab judge should sit on the Supreme Court.[121]

To the extent that ethnic bias may play a role in judicial decisions, the infrastructural lack of representation may signify a double standard at all levels. Many assume that Arabs may not provide the truth in their testimony, as indicated by a short-term minister of justice, Avraham Sharir, who commented that "Arabs are liars from birth."[122] The gravity of such inferences is exacerbated by the use of excessive force in extracting confessions, which often results in false admissions of guilt leading to conviction. While widely denounced in the treatment of Palestinian prisoners, the interrogation procedures of the security services met a full investigation in the case of an Israeli Arab officer of Circassian origin. The commission was headed by the venerable former president of the Supreme Court, Justice Landau. Although it denounced existing practices, the commission endorsed the use of "moderate physical pressure." Landau argued that the necessity to protect the lives of innocent citizens and the rule of law while preventing the use of illegal methods of torture make imperative a pragmatic and practical definition of appropriate levels of force.[123]

There is discrimination regarding the circumstances for the release on bail and suspended sentences.[124] Criticism becomes more salient when one notes the relative leniency of sentences for Jews accused of killing Arabs, who often end up charged with manslaughter, or "automatism"—simple reflex response. Various mitigating circumstances are cited to explain reduced charges.[125] The sporadic mention of the implementation of the death penalty against acts of terror raised the question of whether such a heavy sentence could be objectively carried out against both Arab and Jewish terrorists. Public opinion trends clearly exhibit a predisposition to use such a tool unilaterally. In 1984 more than half of the Israeli population disagreed with the view that "Jews who commit crimes against Arabs should be punished less harshly than Arabs who commit similar crimes against Jews."[126] The score was 58 percent opposed, 13 percent uncertain, and 11 percent in agreement. However, when the Jewish underground was exposed a year later and given heavy sentencing because of its assassination of Arabs, a strong movement for its amnesty evolved. A number of political manipulations and political party pressures led to an early release for the prisoners as a result of a presidential pardon and other administrative measure. Shulamit Har-Even has observed:

> If a man who commits murder is given a merciful and forgiving suspended sentence, or a lighter charge, or a commutation not in keeping with the law, because he is a Jew . . . and if another man tried for the same crime is sentenced to life imprisonment, or a long prison term, because he is an Arab . . . if a murderer goes free, and a man who talked with a PLO representative receives a prison sentence, and the trial of a suspected murderer is postponed from month to month without clear justification, there is no avoiding the conclusion that the terror and the Intifada have achieved at least one of their goals: the weakening of the people's faith in the judicia-

ry, and the loss of the judiciary's confidence in its own long-standing norms, in the wake of hysterical or deliberate pressure from the public or the political system.[127]

Finally, the willingness of the Supreme Court of Justice to implement in Israeli law the humanitarian clauses of the Fourth Geneva Convention makes this most honorable part of the Israeli judicial system vulnerable to the prevalence of security considerations above all. For example, nearly no remedy was found for Palestinians who appealed for the rescission of a military decision to demolish their homes. Kretzmer argues, "The Israeli legal system has been forced to accept the reality of the territories and, as it aspires by nature to avoid divorcing itself from social and political rituals, it resigns itself to and is taken in tow by the annexation and the violation of human rights."[128] On the other hand, some of the decisions of the Supreme Court have been seen as lifesavers for the rule of law, as in the case of a decision requiring Col. Yehuda Meir, accused of giving the command to break the arms and legs of twelve Arabs as exemplary punishment, to stand trial. The military prosecution had been satisfied to prescribe early retirement.[129] Retrial by a military tribunal in April 1992 resulted in the additional demotion of Meir's rank to private.

Media

According to Horowitz and Lissak, "Official means of communication acted until the sixties as a mouthpiece of the government, and the independence of the nonpartisan press was often perceived as impertinent by the political establishment."[130] There followed a trend toward greater respect for the freedom of the press, sustained by judicial rulings and the creation of a public broadcasting authority. This expansion of media autonomy was gradually reversed parallel to the deterioration of the situation in the territories. Given the continuous threats to Israel's security, the media has accepted to a large extent the imposition of censorship regarding sensitive military matters, as well as clandestine immigration and oil shipments. Mediating mechanisms for borderline cases have been established, resolved overwhelmingly with the consensus of the members of the Editors' Committee.[131] However, Arab newspapers published in Jerusalem, a city officially under Israeli sovereignty, are arbitrarily closed down and censored.[132] News of legitimate nonviolent activities and even the reproduction of articles previously published in the Hebrew press have been censored.[133]

The banning of the use of certain words and the circulation of certain books has been denounced as stupid and cruel, especially the denial of access to classic books for Arab political detainees in prisons and detention camps within the state of Israel.[134] The far-reaching 1933 Press Ordinance inherited from the British Mandate was described by a member of Israel's Supreme Court of Justice as "a draconian provision passed by a colonial regime and incompatible with the values of a democratic state."[135] However, large segments of the general public and groups at the extreme right have complained against the exposure of incriminating news, even news not necessarily connected to secrets of state. The high level of such public dependency upon information in Israel makes reactions more intense. As Frucht observes, "The attacks on the local press were indicative of the deep sense of frustration felt by the army as well as by many of the country's leaders and citizens. . . . [the media's] perceived offense was not so much that they distorted the news, but that they reported the news at all."[136]

At the same time, some liberal sectors asserted that freedom of expression has already been affected by policies such as the restriction on the usage of the term "Occupied Territories" within the Public Broadcasting Corporation monopolies over TV and radio. The official preference was for the terms "Judea, Samaria, and Gaza." It is also prohibited to interview PLO leaders. However, a wide range of opinions is expressed in the independent written press. A survey conducted by Rivka and Haim Gordon in 1989 found that the National Religious Party's newspaper *Hatsofeh* often used racist argumentation to describe the motives for an Arab violent act against a Jew. Other newspapers included in their analysis of news expressions that could indirectly encourage racism.[137]

Regarding the media, the public expresses contradictory values. On the one hand, in a 1984 survey 75 percent of Israelis maintained that "freedom of speech should be granted to all regardless of their opinion."[138] Conversely, a majority of the public has supported the government and agreed that there is a need for more censorship on military matters. In 1988, 68 percent of those surveyed expressed such a belief, but only 39 percent found the television news to possess a high level of credibility.[139] A study by E. Ya'ar based on a series of public opinion surveys reveals, first, that nearly half of the public believes that the press has too much freedom of expression. Only 7 percent believe freedom is too limited. Second, 61 percent accept the argument that freedom of the press endangers national security.[140] Already during the 1982 Lebanon War, then–Minister of Defense Sharon accused the press of "helping the enemy." Later, the intifada further exacerbated popular attitudes. The growing intolerance toward the media was manifested in the attacks on journalists and photographers by Israeli civilians and even by soldiers on active duty, as well as in the formation of a special group calling itself Citizens Against the Hostile Media. Expressions such as "leftist mafia" and "fifth column" are often thrown at the media by politicians and echoed by the public.[141] According to a foreign journalist, "Non-Jewish correspondents have had to deal with accusations of anti-Semitism, while Jewish journalists (myself included) are censured for self-hatred."[142] The media is criticized for the intensity of the coverage and for "providing evidence to the enemies of Israel" by reporting accurately on some violent incidents.[143] The existence of such pressure has a self-censoring effect on the journalists of Israel's television and print medias.[144]

A common criticism of the media is that intifada protagonists are triggered by the presence of television cameras into confrontational acts in the territories.[145] According to Kirshenbaum, such a presence may have an effect, but when the media is prevented access, the form of Palestinian popular revolt simply takes other shapes.[146] Under such pressures, Israeli journalist Dan Shilon complains about a "vicious circle": "The poor coverage, in terms of both quantity and quality, is responsible for the public's growing apathy about the Palestinian uprising, and also is responsible for the Israeli public's increasing hostility towards the West's criticism of Israel's policies in the territories."[147] In order to overcome the dissonance between values and reality, the public blames the carrier of bad news rather than the originators of such unpleasant pictures.

Intellectuals and Academics

Militant annexationist circles often consider the universities to be infected by the "PLO virus," allegedly spread by the large number of Israeli Arab students who have been supporting the "enemies of Israel." Criticism of an opposite tone has also surfaced against the lack of deeds and argumentation on the part of knowledgeable professors, who some charge should have been the first to stand up and severely criticize governmental politics. Cohen explains the passivity in terms of a denial mechanism that blocks out disturbing information. Regarding cases of atrocious behavior as "exceptional" fosters a sense of helplessness, diffusion of responsibility, and avoidance of identification with the victim.[148] Harkabi depicts the intellectuals as weaklings who have "abdicated their tasks as teachers and preachers to the public. They were disheartened by the difficulties of competing with demagogues, and by the calumny that they are defeatists and constitute the enemy's fifth column."[149]

When questions related to the intifada were posed to sixty-six professors at Tel Aviv University, only 18 percent expressed concern about the erosion of democracy in Israel. Eight professors were preoccupied because of the way principles of justice have been affected, and six agreed that intellectuals must use their skills and knowledge to analyze and expose the situation created by the intifada. Thirty-seven professors opted for abstract answers that did not require any specific commitment to concrete action, and thirty-three preferred to deal with the problem without relating to the issue of the intifada's resolution.[150]

An article under the subtitle "Survival of the liberal tradition among people long identified with it is questioned" posits reasons as to why liberal ideas are not reaching a sometimes scornful Israeli public. This failure is attributed, among other reasons, to the academics' being too identified with the Palestinian cause, too elitist, and too dismissive of Jewish religious tradition.[151] Still, not a few academics have strong opinions on the subject. Jonathan Shapira clearly stated that "the end of Israel's rule in the territories is essential for the solution to the crisis of democracy in Israel."[152] Sammy Smooha stirred a vociferous debate with his announcement that "the state of Israel is not a distinct Western democracy."[153] Zeev Sternhall predicts that "as long as the struggle with the Arabs goes on, anti-liberal trends will grow stronger and stronger. In a country without a constitution . . . liberal democracy is a kind of luxury. It is a heritage of the past that is easily destroyed."[154]

However, the large number of silent members of the academic community is noticeable. Because most of the funding for Israeli universities comes from the state, there has undoubtedly been an indirect desire not to overantagonize the establishment for fear of retaliation at the budgetary level. The invitation of Palestinians to speak at academic events has become increasingly resented by members of the Knesset who adhere to the extreme anti-Arab parties, as well as by several Likud Knesset members, who have made their views clear in telegrams to university authorities. Additionally, student groups and extremists from outside the universities have threatened to "blow up" the Israeli-Palestinian academic dialogue. This atmosphere of intimidation has affected to some extent academia's feelings of self-censorship, of being perceived as "outside the prevailing consensus," and of alienating the establishment.

The academic community's fear of appearing divided has led many professors to not address institutionally human rights violations and attempts to curtail freedom of expression. However, when the doors of a literature professor and the rector of the Hebrew University were set on fire, a condemnatory statement by twenty-six deans and rectors from universities all over the country was issued. A more incriminating criticism is made by Galili: "The government controls the tabs of a dwindling budget, so who would dare annoy a Knesset member on account of elusive values? One has to think about potential donors that are not of one political opinion. In a state where a moral position is interpreted as a political statement, silence is worth gold, or at least some thousands of dollars."[155] Galili contends that such a convenient silence is also reflected in the individual behavior of professors who think in terms of appointments.

One of the clearest illustrations of this trend has been the relative lack of action by Israeli universities in relation to the closure of Palestinian educational institutions soon after the outbreak of the intifada. This closure has been seen as a measure of collective punishment and is a highly unusual situation in the later part of this century. Even after more than three years of uninterrupted closure, the matter was not viewed as one of academic freedom. An attempt to get the Tel Aviv University Senate to call for the reopening of the Palestinian universities failed.[156] At the time of the writing of this chapter, Palestinian universities have been allowed to reopen.

Criticism has been voiced against educators, lawyers, and journalists contending that such professions demand sensitivity toward the victims of human rights violations and that too few strong advocates of human rights are found among the practitioners in these fields. In spite of this critique, it may still be held that intellectuals have been at the forefront of the struggle for democracy in Israel. While disparaging these groups for their lack of sufficient commitment to human rights, many Israelis with a prevailing attitude of intolerance toward Arabs and the left look upon intellectuals with what Sprinzak terms a "conspiracy paranoia." In this view, such groups constitute "the Jewish *Ashafists* (PLOers) who collaborate willingly with the enemy, and the leftists who care about the sentiments of the international left more than they do about their homeland."[157]

Conclusions

Often, an agreement reached in peace negotiations with the Palestinians raises the specter of civil war among Israelis, or at least of widespread violence instigated by the West Bank settlers. Perceived in the short term to be a worse calamity than the breakdown of talks and continuous status quo, this alternative (avoidance of a potential civil war among Jews) is in the long run not less costly for Israel. This chapter has highlighted the threats, both real and potential, to democracy in the Jewish state. There are no clear ways to assess the measurement of the decay or strengthening of a democratic system. Any attempt to examine values is fraught with the danger of injecting the personal biases of the researcher into the analysis as the standard for judgment, which may prejudice the ultimate interpretation. For instance, in Israel's case, how should we view the status quo for its democracy—as a step backward or a step forward? One could argue that a lack of development and progress, the mere stagnation or delay in terms of norms formation, is itself a step backward for a system whose nature is to continually aspire to a better form of government. At the same time, one could maintain that, given the external threat and young age of the country, simply aspiring to preserve the basic structures and ethos of a democracy is a worthy goal. It is also important to note that democratic values have not eroded at the same rate at different levels of Israeli society. Different characteristics are observable at the institutional and societal levels; we may also differentiate between the elite and grassroots levels. As a result, formidable barriers that tend to make a collapse of democracy in Israel unlikely may have been given insufficient weight or consideration. Indeed, in examining this issue we expressed concern about the erosion of democratic values and practices that has already taken place. However, another equally valid way to debate the question is to ask: Given all the hostility surrounding the Jewish state, the unceasing acts of terror against innocent civilians, and the still unresolved situation of a disenfranchised Palestinian population under its control for over half the state's independent life, why has the erosion of democracy within Israel been so insignificant to date? Could signs of acceptance and reconciliation by the Arabs toward Israel's existence bring about a reversal of the erosion of Israel's democratic standards? Would it be illogical to anticipate some mitigating effect on the extreme levels of hatred that characterize the emotional climate of the conflict to emerge from the bilateral talks? The Israeli-Egyptian example may provide some clues. Many Israelis developed a significant empathy for their former enemies when they encountered Egyptians while visiting Egypt. Some resolved the resulting cognitive dissonance by asserting that the Egyptians are not really Arabs; others maintained that the "cold" peace is not a "real" peace.

In some ways, the security dilemma contributes to the continuing strength of Israel's democracy. The acute controversy over the peace-war issue has indirectly helped in shaping Israel's civil society into a highly participatory community. This tendency for mobilization—some would say even hypermobilization—is demonstrated not only in the consistently high turnout for elections but also in the continuous engagement of a significant segment of the Israeli public in demonstrations, picketing, and other extraparliamentary activities that are the lifeblood of any democracy.

Furthermore, it should be noted that many of the following conclusions, as worrisome as they may appear at first, have not been considered within a comparative perspective, which would analyze the erosion of democracy among nations facing similar dilemmas. For instance, stressing the high levels of hatred among Jewish youth toward the Arabs does not take into account whether the rate is higher or lower among their Arab counterparts' attitudes toward them. To the best of my knowledge, there has as yet been no such research conducted among Palestinians on this question, which in itself may be a severe handicap in the normalization of relations between the two nations. However, even if one chose to compare Israel's case to the processes that occurred in some Western countries, it may well be argued that in the continuous state of war facing Israel, the erosion of democracy has not been as dramatic as in similar cases of people facing war and terror.

A related argument is often expounded on this theme. According to the "protected democracy" theory, Israel's actions are justified in the face of the enormous threats to its security. That is, a state's primary obligation, even in a democracy, is to ensure the survival of the state and safeguard its citizens. Proponents of this theory reason: "How can Israel work toward democratic ideals if the very existence of this state is threatened? Let us secure ourselves first. We are a new nation and should not be judged by the same criteria applicable to a two-hundred-year-old established democracy such as the United States. The implementation of democratic institutions took several years there as well." Nonetheless, the assumption that such a prolonged situation may produce long-term effects on individuals and the norms of society seem unavoidable. Gorni considers a prolonged war situation to be fertile ground for the growth of racism.[158] The seeds of hatred and fear feed the "kill or get killed" survival instinct and leave little room for accommodation or tolerance of challengers to one's security.

There will remain a portion of Israeli society that believes simplistically that a freely elected ruling majority should have no limits imposed on its collective will. Indeed, a few Israeli scholars feel that, under the circumstances, Israeli democratic institutions have survived fairly well, at least up until the major challenges of the last few years.[159] But a democracy demands that the majority respect the basic civil rights of all, including individuals in the minority. What is striking about observers of Israel's democracy is that even the optimists cannot completely ignore the troubling warning signs that may be on Israel's horizon or that may already have arrived. Michael Bar Zohar, a Labor parliamentarian, writes, "Israel's democratic foundations were not affected by the uprising [the intifada]. Democratic nations often curtail their freedoms when fighting for survival. We remained a free and open society in spite of being engaged in combat on several fronts, each vital to our existence. . . . Used to fighting a perpetual war of survival, Israel carried on as normally as possible. Our cultural and scientific life went on unperturbed."[160] Joining such an optimistic assessment, Bernstein points out, "The Jewish state has demonstrated again and again its capacity to nourish and maintain a democratic society under turbulent, and at times tempestuous, conditions."[161] At the same time, though, he warns of the heavy costs to Israel since the 1987 Palestinian uprising in the territories. Likewise, Bar Zohar recognizes that "we could not ignore the drama unfolding around us. The Palestinian insurrection had created a new reality."[162]

A forewarning was spelled out by Asher Arian in his assessment in 1984 that the persistence of Israel's democracy against heavy odds is as impressive as any of the state's more renowned accomplishments.[163] But, he continues:

> As in any other democracy, the experiment might fail. There can be no guarantee that the formula worked out in the past will be successful in the future. Israel's population is severely divided along political, ethnic, class and religious lines, and these cleavages tend to follow the pattern of distribution of opinion regarding the territories. The unfinished business of how two people share one geographical territory will continue to press for solution. Keeping the military open, loyal, and cooperative will remain a

top priority. All these pose serious—but not insurmountable—challenges to Israel's democracy.[164]

Meanwhile, the less optimistic observers of Israel's democracy have already detected several symptoms of decline, described in part in this article. Even if the rules of the game and structures of democracy are maintained and respected, certain trends might legitimately be viewed with concern. A democracy in form only will be a fragile democracy; if the formal institutions are not supported by a meaningful commitment to its substance—equal rights, pluralism, and tolerance—our findings second S. N. Eisenstadt's assessment that "the commitment to democratic values was being eroded."[165] After the 1982 Lebanon War, according to Sprinzak, the post-1967 era proved "that the belief that the Israeli society, or some segment of it, could remain uncontaminated by the bloody and tortuous Palestinian question was wishful thinking. Especially naive was the conviction in certain Israeli circles that the settlement of Judea and Samaria could take place at no extra cost to Israel's democracy, and that terrorism and violence were un-Jewish."[166] Frankel, while admitting that Israel remains a democratic state, cautioned long before the outbreak of the intifada that having a quarter of the population subject to a totally different system may have severe repercussions within Israel: "The question has to be asked whether such a dual system can remain stable indefinitely, whether in the long run the methods and mentalities bred by a colonizing military regime can be halted, hermetically sealed off, at an invisible line a few miles from Tel Aviv and Jerusalem. The future of Israel's constitutional system is now clearly hanging in the balance."[167] Some go a step further in expressing their concern over the effect of prolonged occupation. As early as 1986, former minister of justice Haim Zadok stated that the occupation had the effect of making Israel "not democratic, because it includes territories and population that fall outside the pale of democracy." More specifically,

> Within the state of Israel, inside the Green Line, everything looks nice and clean in terms of the rule of law. . . . When such a state of affairs continues for a long time, you have the danger that the situation in the territories will seep into the state of Israel. It was thus that the Jewish terrorist underground was born; it is thus that we now see attempts to undermine the authority of the government and its attorney general. I'm not saying this is a clear and present danger, but the situation has been going on for twenty years now, and the longer it continues, the greater the danger.[168]

The awareness of the asymmetries in the interactions resulting from the prolonged occupation of territories over people without equal civil and political rights (and the related socioeconomic discrimination) might be legitimate concerns for democratic Israelis of all persuasions. Yet it would be too simplistic to say that those who favor keeping the territories are unconcerned about democracy for Israel and those who support separating from the territories are motivated by democratic reasons only. Among the annexationists there are those who would agree to incorporate the Palestinians living there and to grant them full rights. At the other end of the spectrum, there are those who would call for abandoning the territories because the thought of incorporating a greater Arab population into the Jewish state is anathema.

Several observers have attempted to delineate the factors that contribute to the eventual determination of the standards of democracy in Israel. Karp suggests that we take into account several considerations when analyzing the preservation of Israeli democracy under such difficult circumstances: Israel has never experienced a peacetime democracy; the British Mandatory regime that preceded its independence (and from which Israel's legal framework was inherited) was antidemocratic and colonial in its nature; because of the unending security crisis, there has never been an opportunity to evaluate dispassionately the precarious balance between civil liberties and national security considerations in retrospect; a large segment of the population has come from countries without a democratic tradition; the religiously observant sectors of the Arab and Jewish populations may tend to ignore the secular standards appropriate for Western democracies; Israel is located in a region in which no other democracy has emerged so far; the residual trauma of the Holocaust has fostered the prevalent feeling that "never again" will the Jewish people tolerate any threat to its existence; the specific nature of the antiterrorist struggle involves the suffering of innocent Palestinians who may be perceived as supporting or cooperating in the commission of terrorist acts against Israel; and last, but not the least, the absence of a written constitution (or similar bill of rights) makes it more difficult to defend the individual against the excesses of the state.[169] Some of these considerations may fade away with time. However, others will persist unless lawmakers redress the existing or potential obstacles; few depend on external developments that are difficult to influence from within Israel. Hence, the overall balance sheet of the factors contributing to the preservation of Israeli democracy tends to indicate that, to date, the obstacles overshadow the prospects for amelioration.

Horowitz and Lissak have attempted to frame the main challenges to the democratic nature of Israeli society in the following three dilemmas. First is the dilemma between the minimal requirements of a democratic regime and the requirements of a more inclusive, open, and pluralistic democratic system. These requirements would include on the one hand political party pluralism, free elections, and a normal functioning of the parliamentary system, and on the other hand a democratic system that comprises clusters of channels of political participation and affirms democratic procedures for checks and balances, including criticism of public and official agencies that have a high degree of autonomy from the political party system. The second dilemma is found in the preference for respect of the rule of law and the freedom of the individual and civil rights over *raison d'état,* which is often based on national-ethnic factors that tend to belie the principle of the equality of all citizens. The third dilemma is the conflict between the necessity of a democracy to open up the rules of the game for all without the limitations of a national consensus and the inherent requirement of an infant democracy to act responsibly to proscribe the activities of groups perceived as attempting to undermine the state, the political regime, and the basic national consensus.[170]

There is general agreement that the intifada may accelerate the erosion of the standards of democracy in Israeli society, whether immediately or in the long-term. One dangerous development may be perceived in the lagging commitment to and respect for the rule of law. In some of the extraparliamentary extremist groups, the predominance of divine law over civil law and the devotion to the idea of supremacy over the whole of Eretz Israel has made having a Jewish state a higher priority than having a democratic state. Hence, the Council of Rabbis of Judea and Samaria *lex talionis* permits settlers to take justice into their own hands, even to the point of indiscriminately killing local Palestinians. Furthermore, in wide circles of Israeli society, such testing of the outer limits of the rule of law engenders an acceptance of the norm that an act, if not illegal, is legitimate.[171]

Another outgrowth of the intifada has been the rising confrontation and polarization within the political system and the active sectors of society. Additionally, the centrist forces that have so far helped the system cope with the situation have been weakened. Nonetheless, it would be premature to attribute all the signs of deterioration to the continuous occupation of the territories. Likewise, some of the positive trends that strengthen and maintain Israel's democracy (notably the derogation of censorship on theater plays, easy access to the Supreme Court for all citizens, and more democratization in the selection of candidates within the larger political parties) have evolved without any clear influence from or relation to the security situation. The pivotal question is whether occupation has been slowing down, perhaps even reversing in some spheres, beneficial processes such as these.

Our analysis has pointed to specific groups within society that appear to be the most susceptible to adopting and expressing values that may undermine the standards of democracy in Israel. Of these most exposed sectors in Israeli society, youth seem to be a sensitive cluster. It is difficult to determine whether extremist attitudes are part of the formative process of adolescence among Israeli youth or if they reflect a change in the society at large that will emerge over time and present itself as a element to be reckoned with in the political system. In addition, as shown in the mentioned studies, Orthodox Jews tend to be proportionally more affected by nonpluralistic attitudes that result in nondemocratic values. Other groups, such as Oriental Jews, even if they have been identified as more anti-Arab or more prone to have less acceptance of political dissent, may not give reason for concern in the long-term, given that the level of intermarriage among Jews from different ethnic origins is growing.[172] Although ethnic distinctions are blurring and may become less of a factor in shaping democratic values in the future, that does not necessarily mean intolerance will dissipate; it may simply go the other way and expand to wider circles. Indeed, some newly arrived Soviet immigrants, competing for manual jobs, have shown signs of asserting their priority rights over the natives.

However, we have to remember that the nature of democracy also requires the political participation and equal rights of the Arab minority in Israel. What was considered a temporary situation of occupation has become a semipermanent feature. This change in perception could percolate into an acceptance and understanding that "democracy for the Jews" may be a tolerable proposition.[173] But if Israel's democracy is reserved solely for Jews, if it is a "democracy for rulers" only, then Israel may no longer deserve to be called a democracy.[174] Furthermore, there are Jews of the left wing who are perceived by some Israelis as siding not only with the "Palestinian underdog" but with "the terrorists" as well. This image has fragmented Jewish society and will probably do so further.

Polarization in society also has had the effect of weakening the appreciation of professional groups and institutions in society that were previously held in much higher esteem and whose functions are essential to the proper functioning of a democracy. Suspicion toward journalists and intellectuals jeopardizes their ability to play their appropriate roles in democratic society as monitors and watchdogs against excesses of state power. The same is true with respect to such government agencies as law enforcement, and the military in particular, as well as the judiciary. There is an increasingly common belief on both sides of the political spectrum that these institutions have lost their moral standards and their impartiality. Without the trust and faith of the public, these institutions may find it increasingly difficult to carry out their crucial roles in democratic society in the future. As the southern European and Latin American experience shows, the breakdown of democratic regimes can be attributed to the development of serious cleavages and confrontations between the main political parties, as outgroups aim to paralyze the system rather than to function as a loyal opposition to the ruling coalition, thereby making governing nearly impossible.[175] The weakening of the center of the political spectrum may more seriously threaten the collapse of a regime than the activities of extraparliamentary groups at the fringe of the system.[176] Nevertheless, the emergence of extraparliamentary fringe groups who take the law into their own hands and often use violence can also paralyze regular parliamentary procedure by generating dynamics that are destructive to the democratic system. However, if the center of the political spectrum is strong, such extraparliamentary groups usually have only a negligible impact on the normal democratic life of a state and are denied the opportunity to use extremism as a trump card for imposing their will on society.

While the tendency of Israeli society has been to move toward intolerance, a portion of those who have been the targets of such intolerance may paradoxically have benefited indirectly from this trend. Those who have spoken out and criticized the curtailment of freedom in the postintifada period may have become marginally more active in reaction to the polarization of society. This increased activity will not alleviate the gravity of the situation, however. Watchdogs, monitors, and protestors against the excesses and abuses of power have had only a minimal impact on events. At the same time, however, their activities and criticisms have exacerbated the extremism of the other side. After a period in which Israeli society became noticeably more polarized in its reaction to the Palestinian uprising, the unprovoked attacks by Iraq in the Gulf War of 1991 renewed the consensus in Israel as to the threat of total annihilation posed by the Arabs. As a result, the ruling regime was temporarily able to consolidate its coalition and establish a more cohesive network of support for its policies against the Arab enemy. On the other hand, the decline of the intifada has produced a sensation among many Israelis, roughly equivalent to a cease-fire, that is evolving into the beginnings of a full-fledged peace process. To what extent the beginnings of this process can positively affect the rule of law or shift the focus from the injustices of human rights violations today to efforts for a better, more peaceful future is yet to be determined.

The concept of "benign occupation" may not come back into the Israeli lexicon. However, focusing only on the end of occupation without dealing with existing problems and concerns is not conducive to the maintenance and cementing of democracy in the Jewish state. So far, the Israeli democracy has managed to endure in spite of the hazards and intensity of the continuous dormant war situation, and it has done so in a region in which there are no other existing democracies. Indeed, no predictions can be made in terms of the speed or nature of any future deterioration in the standards of democracy in Israel. However, the years of struggle against a popular civilian uprising in the territories have exhibited the kind of polarization in the Israeli society that may foreshadow a future of alarming internal fragmentation and confrontation.

The problem can ultimately be summarized as an issue of commitment to democratic values. As Galnoor has recognized, "Our democracy in this country is not internalized. We have the external features of election, decisions made by a majority, and adherence to the independent judiciary.

However, the politicians have not adopted democracy as a way of life. There are no self-imposed restraints, as the politicians here do not have a democratic soul. Anything goes."[177] This reality stands in marked contrast to the high standards dictated by Israel's founding fathers, including the appeal to make the country "a light among nations." But such an entreaty was always pretense and hyperbole. I would suggest that perhaps there is an acceptable medium to be found between the two extremes of a prophetic dream and a reality dictated by wars and occupation.

Notes

1. I would like to express my gratitude to David Bobrowsky and Christine Quickenden for their extremely helpful assistance both in the researching and editing of this chapter. Additionally, Jorge Gordin's dedicated research efforts proved indispensable in the completion of this project.

2. Emmanuel Sivan, "The Intifada and Decolonization," *Middle East Review* (Winter 1989/1990), pp. 2–6.

3. Gad Barzilai, "Democratic Regimes During War and Post-War Periods: Israel from a Comparative Outlook," *International Affairs*, Vol. 54, No. 1–2, pp. 20–36.

4. Yoram Peri, "The Effect of the Intifada on Israeli Society," unpublished manuscript (1989), pp. 22–23.

5. Sivan, "The Intifada," p. 2.

6. Julian L. Simon, "Lebensraum—Paradoxically, Population Growth May Eventually End Wars," *Journal of Conflict Resolution*, Vol. 33, No. 1 (March 1989), p. 164.

7. *Ibid.*, p. 179.

8. Alan Dowty, "Jewish Political Traditions and Contemporary Israeli Politics," *Jewish Political Science Review*, Vol. 2, No. 3–4 (Fall 1990), pp. 55–84.

9. Even in the exceptional case of Great Britain, the non-English components (Scotch, Welsh, or Irish) did not have any ethnic or religious proximity to the colonial population (aside from the Scottish ancestry of the Falklanders).

10. See Rouhana and Ghanem, Chapter 7 in this book.

11. *Ha'aretz*, September 17, 1991, p. 4, in Hebrew.

12. Dan Horowitz and Moshe Lissak, "Democracy and National Security in a Protracted Conflict," *Jerusalem Quarterly*, No. 51 (Summer 1989), p. 3. For an analysis of the effects of Israel's "dormant war," see Yoram Peri, "The Arab-Israeli Conflict and Israeli Democracy," unpublished paper presented at the Hoover Institution (Stanford) conference on Israeli Democracy Under Stress, pp. 109–126.

13. Harold D. Lasswell, "The Garrison State," *American Journal of Sociology*, Vol. 46 (1941), pp. 455–467.

14. Barzilai, "Democratic Regimes," p. 24.

15. *Ibid.*

16. Barzilai eloquently states the point thusly: "As the Palestinian-Israeli intercommunal conflict has developed in intensity, it has produced further problems of non-governability, which in turn have led to Israel employing yet more considerable force against Palestinians and sometimes even against Israeli Arabs. If much more time elapses without the appearance of clear signs of the conflict abating, it could eventually spur the political establishment into using emergency laws, on a daily

basis, to prevent dissent among the Israeli population." *Ibid.*, p. 21.

17. The Proclamation of the Independence of Israel, May 14, 1948, declares that the state of Israel "will promote the development of the country for the benefit of all its inhabitants; will be based on the principles of liberty, justice, and peace as conceived by the Prophets of Israel; will uphold the full social and political equality of all its citizens, without distinction of religion, conscience, education, and culture; will safeguard the Holy Places of all religions; and will loyally uphold the principles of the United Nations Charter."

18. Michal Shamir, "Kach and the Limits of Political Tolerance in Israel," in Daniel J. Elazar and Shmuel Sandler, eds., *Israeli Odd Couple: The 1984 Knesset Elections and the National Unity Government* (Detroit: Wayne State Press, 1990), p. 161.

19. *Ibid.*

20. *Ibid.*, p. 164.

21. Kaufman defines the four main cleavages in Israeli society as 1) socioeconomic policies—support for a state-oriented vs. free-market economy; 2) religion and state—the religious-secular debate over the role of religion in the state and in society; 3) ethnic cleavages—cultural and socioeconomic differences between Jews of Ashkenazi (East European) and Oriental (Asian and African) origin; and 4) peace and security—the peace/war dimension related to the issue of territorial concession. See Edy Kaufman, "Intifada and Peace Process—Prospect for the Political Stabilization in the Middle East," Joint Research Programme Series No. 74 (Tokyo: Institute of Developing Countries, 1989), p. 13.

22. Michal Shamir and John L. Sullivan, "Political Tolerance and Intolerance in Israel," final report submitted to the U.S.-Israeli Binational Science Foundation (1982), p. 35.

23. Itzhak Galnoor, "Israeli Democracy in Transition," in Peter Medding, ed., *Israel, State and Society, 1948–1988* (Oxford: Oxford University Press, 1989), p. 126. Galnoor concludes, "As a result, none of the three internal social divisions reviewed herein developed 'normally' since 1948, because they became entangled in the web of Israel's external affairs. This fact has had a very important impact on the evolution of Israeli democracy, particularly after 1967."

24. A poll in the continuing survey of the Institute of Applied Social Research and the Smart Family Communications Institute, mentioned by Don Peretz and Sammy Smooha, in "Israel's Twelfth Knesset Election: An All-Loser Game," *Middle East Journal*, Vol. 43, No. 3 (1989), p. 389.

25. This study focuses on the weakening of these agencies' reputations in the eyes of the Jewish population. In another study, it was found that, in comparison, Israeli Arabs have lower confidence in the court, police, and other major Israeli institutions representative of Israeli democracy. See Elia T. Zureik and Aziz Haider, "The Impact of the Intifada on the Palestinians in Israel," *International Journal of Sociology of Law*, Vol. 19 (1991), p. 485.

26. Menachem Hofnung, "Israel—Security Needs vs. the Rule of Law," doctoral thesis submitted at the Hebrew University of Jerusalem (September 1989), English abstract, p. 8.

27. Asher Arian, "Israel's Democracy 1984," *Journal of International Affairs*, Vol. 38, No. 2 (Winter 1985), p. 263.

28. Asher Arian, *Politics in Israel* (New York: Chatham House, 1985), p. 262.

29. Dowty, "Jewish Political Traditions," p. 76.

30. Horowitz and Lissak argue that even if there were a high degree of acceptance of the basic norms of democratic institutions, "the degree of commitment to democratic ideology is evenly shared by all sectors of the Israeli political public,

and not always has there been agreement as to the contents revolving around the concept of democracy." See Dan Horowitz and Moshe Lissak, *Metsuka B'Utopia— Israel Chevra B'Omes Ieter* (Tel Aviv: Am Oved, 1990), p. 251, in Hebrew. Democracy in Israel, even prior to the establishment of the state, was based more on the political modus vivendi than on understandings of deeply rooted ideological values.

31. Ehud Sprinzak, "The Emergence of the Israeli Radical Right," *Comparative Politics* (January 1989), pp. 171–192.

32. *Ibid.*, p. 186.

33. Though considered to be less extremist than Moledet, Tehiya campaigned in 1988 on the platform of necessary deportation of 1,200 Palestinians so that the "intifada would die." Peretz and Smooha, "Twelfth Knesset Election," p. 391.

34. A term used by Sprinzak, "Radical Right," p. 179.

35. *Ibid.*, p. 189.

36. Horowitz and Lissak, *Metsuka B'Utopia*, p. 196.

37. Louis Guttman, "The Continuing Survey," Israel Institute of Applied Research, Jerusalem, August 1988.

38. Peri, "Effect of the Intifada," p. 20, quoting a heated debate on a comparison made by writer A. B. Yehoshua with the lack of German public response to the antidemocratic acts of the Nazis in their consolidation of power.

39. By comparison, 14 percent preferred "a strong man who will not be dependent on elections and on the Knesset." See the Van Leer Institute, "Political and Social Positions of Youth—1987," as reported in *New Outlook* (February 1988), p. 22.

40. *Ibid.*, p. 21.

41. Selected figures from "Survey of Youth Opinions," *Dahaf*, March 1986, in Hebrew.

42. Van Leer Foundation, "Political and Social Positions of Youth—1987."

43. Study conducted by the Israeli Institute for Military Studies in 1988 and published in *Israeli Democracy* (Fall 1990), pp. 21–31.

44. Survey reported by Peretz Kidron in *Middle East International*, September 28, 1990, p. 19. Findings also published in *Yediot Achronot*, September 18, 1990, in Hebrew.

45. See working paper of Orit Ichilov, "Hinuch Le'Ezrachut Be'Demokratia: Mediniut Ve'Tehanim" ("Education for Citizenship and Democracy: Policy and Contents"), Unit for the Sociology of Education and Community, School of Education, Tel Aviv University, January 1988, in Hebrew.

46. Aryeh Na'or, "The Bad Seed," *Yediot Achronot*, April 21, 1987. Na'or, a former Herut party member, served as cabinet secretary in the first Begin government. He added, "There is an organic link between xenophobia and antagonism toward any dissent, whether by the press or by other gadfly critics. There is a link between the inchoate fear of Arabs *qua* Arabs, and the fear of anyone who is different from the majority—whether this difference lies in ethnic origin, way of life, or personal opinions. Such mental associations are nothing new: We've already seen such things elsewhere in history. The only difference is that now we are the ones doing it: We, the offspring of the victims of anti-Semitism, now ironically display these same thought patterns among ourselves."

47. Shmuel N. Eisenstadt, *The Transformation of the Israeli Society* (Boulder: Westview Press, 1985), p. 533.

48. The components of Israeli nationalism are described as "territorial," "cultural," and "ethnic," the latter defined as "radical hostility to non-Jews." Although officially adopted by few political figures, such a definition has found many popu-

lar expressions of anti-Arab sentiment. See Charles S. Liebman, "Jewish Ultra-Nationalism in Israel: Converging Strands," in W. Frankel, ed., *Survey of Jewish Affairs—1985* (London: Associated University Press, 1985), pp. 28–50.

49. *Jerusalem Post*, weekly edition, January 17, 1992, p. 1B.

50. A study shows how particularly strong the increase in hatred toward Arabs was among Israeli high school students in general and among religious youth in particular. Scores for the 1988 survey resulted in the following breakdown, in answer to the question: "Do you hate Arabs?"

	Religious		Secular	
	Male	Female	Male	Female
Yes, all of them	26.2	33.2	13.2	10.6
Yes, most of them	24.4	30.1	19.2	17.6
Yes, some of them	32.5	26.6	32.9	35.0
Yes, only a few of them	11.5	7.25	23.0	24.4
No, I don't hate them at all	5.3	2.76	11.4	12.2

See Reuven Gal and Ofra Micelles, "Hatred on the Rise," *Israeli Democracy* (Fall 1990), p. 21.

51. Speaking at the Hebrew University, Rabbi Kahane started his speech with the introduction, "Greetings, Jews and dogs." The article reporting on it continues: "Only a democracy in a state of increasing arterial sclerosis could engage in a hair-splitting argument over whether or not Kahane's barking is racism." See Yotam, "Greetings, Jews and Dogs," *Davar*, March 19, 1985, in Hebrew.

52. Sprinzak, "Radical Right," p. 190.

53. Such an expression was formulated at the Van Leer Institute in Jerusalem by Abraham Ron, the head of the department in charge of religious vocational schools. See article by Aaron Geva, "Forty Percent for Kahane," *Davar*, June 16, 1985.

54. An illustration of such views is provided by Mordechai Nissan, who, based on the writings of Maimonides, believes that "Jews may tolerate the presence of non-Jews in the Land of Israel as long as non-Jews acknowledge their inferior status." Quoted by Liebman, "Jewish Ultra-Nationalism," p. 44.

55. Aryeh Dayan, "I Had the Privilege of Participating in Blowing Off Their Legs," *Koteret Rashit*, May 15, 1985, in Hebrew.

56. The terrorist Jewish underground included some leading members of Gush Emunim ("The Block of Faith") whose spiritual leaders were several rabbis, including Waldman and Levinger, as well as a number of Knesset members from several parties. An editorial entitled "With the Jewish Terror Trial" said that it is vital that leading rabbis and religious authorities, not to mention nationalist political leaders, come out at least with open condemnation of the kind of murderous acts that the Jewish terror defendants are said to have committed. See the *Jerusalem Post*, May 5, 1985.

57. See survey conducted by Ephraim Ya'ar, published under the title, "Who's Afraid of a Free Press?" *Israel Democracy* (Winter 1990), pp. 19–21.

58. See findings of Yochanan Peres, "Ethnic Relations in Israel," *American Journal of Sociology*, No. 6 (1971), pp. 1021–1047. The same article includes a paragraph from a publication subsidized by the Ministry of Education on the "seminary for Judaism in Ofra," which says that the natives (Arabs) "have no possible interest in democratic rights. They never had any democratic rights and they never had any political rights, only certain human rights."

59. Sprinzak, "Radical Right," p. 190.

60. Gal and Micelles, "Hatred," p. 23. The totals for the levels of strong hatred toward Arabs are: for Ashkenazi, 45.81 percent; for Orientals, 68.98 percent.

61. Yossi Yonah, *Oriental Jews in Israel and the Quest for Peace: The Myth of Cultural Hostility Towards Arabs* (Tel Aviv: International Center for Peace in the Middle East, no date), p. 2.

62. Johnny Goldberg and Yoram Peri, *Ha'im Hamizrahiim Nitziim Yoter?* ("Are the Orientals More Hawkish?"), (Tel Aviv: International Center for Peace in the Middle East, 1985), in Hebrew.

63. *Ibid.*, p. 28.

64. Yonah, *Oriental Jews*, p. 3.

65. Yoav Peled, "Socio-Economic Factors and Support for the Radical Right: The Case of the Kach Movement in Israel," Discussion Paper No. 9–89, The Pinhas Sapir Center for Development, Tel Aviv University, June 1989.

66. Arian, "Israel's Democracy," p. 269.

67. In relation to denial of Faisal Husseini's right, see "General Mordechai Closes the Streets of East Jerusalem to Prevent a Press Conference," *Ha'aretz,* October 10, 1980.

68. *Ma'ariv,* December 16, 1991, in Hebrew. The article entitled "Non-Moderate Physical Pressure" includes a detailed description of the brutality involved. Additionally, two of the members of the unit have been charged for attempts to intimidate the plaintiffs not to appear in court and substantiate their complaints.

69. What has gone unnoticed and unquestioned is that, to most Israeli Jews, being Israeli means being Jewish—and therefore, Israeli Arabs are seen as outsiders who have never integrated into the society and never could because they are always and only and essentially Arabs. See Lynne Belaief, "When an Israeli Arab Isn't an Arab," *Jerusalem Post,* December 27, 1990.

70. Peri, "Effect of the Intifada," p. 28.

71. The hostility of the most intransigent forces in the Arab world toward Israel and the opposition of Palestinian Arabs to occupation in the West Bank and Gaza are clearly sources of the Jewish population's lack of tolerance toward the Arab minority in Israel. See Sammy Smooha's notes from a lecture delivered at the International Conference on Education for the Prevention of Hatred, Haifa University, June 2–5, 1990, p. 2.

72. See, for example, Ian Lustick, *Arabs in the Jewish State: A Study in the Control of a National Minority* (Austin: University of Texas Press, 1980); David Shipler, *Arab and Jew: Wounded Spirits in a Promised Land* (London: Bloomsbury Publishers, 1987); Sammy Smooha, *Arabs and Jews in Israel* (Boulder: Westview Press, 1989); Elia T. Zureik, *The Palestinians in Israel: A Study in Internal Colonialism* (London: Routledge & Kegan Paul, 1979).

73. Alan Dowty, "Minority Rights, Jewish Political Traditions, and Zionism," in *Shofar,* Vol. 10 (Winter 1992), p. 30.

74. David Kretzmer, *The Legal Status of the Arabs in Israel* (Boulder: Westview Press, 1990).

75. "They [Israeli Arabs] are denied access to power and elite positions; their educational level, resources and opportunities are lower; they are worse off in income and all other measures of socio-economic status (such as housing); they are directly or indirectly discriminated against in the provision of universal welfare state services." See Stanley Cohen (with Mohammed Haj Yahia), *Crime, Justice and Social Control in the Israeli Arab Population* (Tel Aviv: International Center for Peace in the Middle East, 1989), p. 15.

76. Furthermore, a 1988 survey shows that 74 percent of the Jews said that the state should prefer Jews to Arabs, 43 percent favored the denial of the right to vote to Israeli Arab citizens, and 40 percent believed that Israel should use any opportunity to encourage Israeli Arabs to leave the country. Quoted in Smooha, lecture notes, p. 171.

77. Arab Knesset members have stressed that Israeli Arabs are represented in the Knesset, implying that the PLO is representative of those disenfranchised Palestinians in other lands.

78. The rejection by the Likud and other forces to the appointment of MK Abdel Wahab Daroushe of the Labor Party (then a coalition partner) as deputy education minister because of Zionist arguments was denounced as a travesty. The same forces did not object to the inclusion in the cabinet of ultra-Orthodox ministers of declared non- or anti-Zionist convictions. See editorial, *Al Hamishmar*, October 26, 1986, in Hebrew.

79. Reference to criminal file number 789/89, the State of Israel vs. Yousuff Abed-Elslam, as reported by *Kol Hayir*, January 11, 1991, pp. 46–47, in Hebrew.

80. See Noah Lewin-Epstein, "Arab Subordination and Education-Occupation-Mismatch," paper presented at the conference on Aspects of Integration of the Arab Community in Israel, Leonard S. Davis Institute, Hebrew University, Jerusalem, November 5–6, 1991.

81. In 1990 graffiti in perfect Hebrew was found on 250 gravestones in Haifa at the time of the desecration of the Jewish cemetery in Carpentras, France. Knesset member and retired general Rehavam Ze'evi immediately responded that "all French Jews should come to Israel. Does the desecration of Jewish graves in Israel itself prove that the Arabs should be removed from our midst?" He added that the perpetrators should "leave the country, if not voluntarily, then by force." Later, when it was discovered that an extreme messianic group was responsible for the desecration, a member of the group stated that he wanted "to unite the nation of Israel, which is involved in internal arguments while it faces the danger of Arab nations." See the article by Les Levidow, "Israel: a Paranoid Society," *Middle East International*, July 20, 1990, p. 17.

82. See Uzi Benziman, "A Painful Similarity: What the Lynching of Amnon Pomerantz (in Gaza) and the Assassination of Halhala Izat Mohamed (in West Jerusalem) Have in Common," *Ha'aretz*, September 25, 1990.

83. See articles in *Kol Hayir*, November 8 and 15, 1991. Three students were arrested, and most of the other interviewees justified not allowing Arabs to travel in "Jewish" buses on the grounds that Molotov cocktails were thrown at such vehicles.

84. Walid Sadik, "Response: An Unhealthy Situation," *New Outlook* (February 1988), p. 23.

85. See Zeev Schiff, "No More a Bridge for Peace," *Ha'aretz*, May 25, 1989.

86. Cohen, *Crime, Justice*, pp. 119–120.

87. See Mordechai Bar-On, *Shalom Achshav* ("Peace Now") (Jerusalem, 1988), in Hebrew.

88. Statements quoted by the "Voice of Israel," Jerusalem's radio news, on December 22, 1991, and the next day's *Ma'ariv*. This latter's newspaper included the reaction of MK Geula Cohen of the Tehiya Party, who supported the prime minister's criticism of the "collaborators with the [Arab] terrorist organizations," the "anti-national camp" that honors the "intifada's assassins." The reaction of MK Amnon Rubinstein, leader of the Movement for Change, was, "The statements of Shamir and Sharon in the Likud's Central Committee against the opposition are words of incitement that were so far unheard of in any democratic country and that were aimed at creating a campaign of violence and intimidation against anybody

who disagrees with the Likud position." (See *Ma'ariv*, December 23, 1991.) Shamir repeated an old expression of his regarding Peace Now, accusing the group of "assisting the most extreme of our enemies." See *Yediot Achronot*, March 6, 1989.

89. David Makovsky, "Poisonous Politics," *Jerusalem Post*, December 27, 1991, p. 1B. Reacting to MK Yossi Sarid's calling her "fascist," MK Geula Cohen said, "If I would be in charge of the police, you would have been under surveillance".

90. *Ibid.*

91. Yehuda Lahav, *Al Hamishmar*, April 16, 1986.

92. The interview took place in Jerusalem on December 14, 1991. Name withheld by request.

93. The threats against the daughter were received in phone calls asking the mother if the blonde girl was hers and stating that "we will slaughter her." The parents make a point to personally take her to and from school to ensure her safety. However, she still has difficulties sleeping at night.

94. The police recommended the installation of a comprehensive security system in the house, which makes it quite inaccessible. The family members also carry tear gas for self-defense, yet have refused so far to carry weapons.

95. MK Geula Cohen, quoted in *Yediot Achronot*, March 7, 1989.

96. MK Hanan Porat, as reported in *Yediot Achronot*, April 16, 1991.

97. *Ha'aretz*, May 23, 1990.

98. Sidra Ezrahi DeKoven, "Under the Barren Mulberry Tree: Violent Encounters in the City of Peace," *New Outlook* (August 1988), pp. 32–33. Reactions to signs stating "Deportation Destroys Democracy" and "American Immigrants Say: Don't Deport the Native Born" produced extremely violent oral reactions such as, "Don't deport him—hang him," "You too should be deported," and "First we will burn him—and then we will burn you." The author concludes, "The greater the hatred of the Other, the more we come to hate ourselves. . . . If one listens to the noises in the street, one begins to wonder if our society ever really internalized the commitment to pluralism, which would safeguard a plurality of opinions and options for action as not only legitimate but desirable."

99. Edy Kaufman, "Israeli Reactions to the Intifada's Violence," *Journal of Political Violence and Terrorism*, Vol. 88 (Winter 1991/1992).

100. Peri, "Effect of the Intifada," p. 2.

101. *Ibid.*

102. Middle East Watch, "The Israeli Army and the Intifada—Policies that Contribute to the Killings," a Middle East Watch Report, New York (August 1990). The IDF responded twice to the allegations, insisting that the report is biased, that it does not consider the danger that soldiers face when trying to disperse riots and catch terrorists, that it does not mention casualties from both sides, etc.

103. Yitzhak Rabin, "The Clubs, the Means and the Words," *Yediot Achronot*, November 2, 1990.

104. B'Tselem, "The Interrogation of Palestinians During the Intifada: Follow-up to March 1991 B'Tselem Report," Jerusalem, March 1992.

105. See Edy Kaufman and Nadir Tsur, "Walking on a Tightrope," *Present Tense* (September–October 1989), pp. 39–44.

106. Peri, "Effect of the Intifada," p. 27.

107. Gideon Fishman, a criminologist from Haifa University, showed that there was no increase in the murder rate, and the 6.1 per 100,000 was as low as the rate in Japan and Switzerland. See *Ha'aretz*, March 17, 1989.

108. *Jerusalem Post*, December 14, 1989.

109. See Mordechai Kaufman's statement in *Ha'aretz*, May 20, 1990.

110. MK Amnon Rubenstein, quoted in "Moral and Functional Deterioration in the IDF," *Yediot Achronot*, January 22, 1990.

111. *Ibid.*

112. The author is very familiar with one case that involved a Palestinian who worked in his house and was killed in 1988 by the border police while working in his field at the Dir al-Salah village.

113. Maintaining that lives were not in danger, the Labor-oriented newspaper *Davar* editorialized, "The historical meaning of the police's conduct in Jerusalem is that for the first time the police has opened fire at Israeli citizens, as part of its policy of maintaining law and order, even if the bullets were rubber rather than lead. . . . A policy of firing at an unarmed crowd which is endangering no one, is inconsistent with one of the holiest principles of a democratic regime." See Olek Netzer, "A Government Pulls the Trigger," *Davar*, January 14, 1990.

114. Research for Fuad Moughrabi and Elia T. Zureik, "Different Scales of Justice: Arab and Jew in Israel—Results of a National Survey," Occasional Paper No. 11, Series of Near East Cultural and Educational Foundation, Ontario, Canada, and International Center for Research and Public Policy, USA (ISBN 0-937807), no date, p. 11.

115. Avner Tavori, "Qualified Equality," *Davar*, January 6, 1987. "Our first lesson teaches that in a democratic country, every citizen is equal before the law. Right? Wrong. In the state of Israel, the police, charged with upholding the law, classify the citizenry in two separate categories." Strong criticism to the recording of a citizen's nationality as an undemocratic practice is expressed by MK Shulamit Aloni in "Who's Afraid of Israeli Citizenship?" *Yediot Achronot*, January 6, 1987.

116. See reports of investigation of the Shin Bet of the Yesh Gvul ("There is a Limit") organization, which advocates conscientious objection to military service in the Occupied Territories, in Danny Rubinstein, "West Bank Settlers Top of the List," *Davar*, January 17, 1989.

117. Avraham Burg, "The Police Listens to my Phone: There is Political Tapping in the State of Israel," *Ha'aretz*, June 16, 1991.

118. *Ha'aretz*, December 17, 1991.

119. "If we compare legal decisions concerning national security made during the State of Israel's early years to more recent ones, two developments are apparent: a change in the balance between legal and military criteria, and an enlargement of the scope of judicial review." See Amnon Goldenberg, "A Legal Perspective," *Israeli Democracy* (Fall 1990), p. 27.

120. Justice Aharon Barak, as quoted by Judith Karp in "Finding an Equilibrium," *Israeli Democracy* (Fall 1990), p. 27.

121. Moughrabi and Zureik, "Different Scales," p. 8.

122. Quoted by Darwish Nasser, "Stones in the Scales of Justice," *Ha'aretz*, March 3, 1988. See also Nasser, *Alarm Bells* (Jerusalem, 1989), in Arabic.

123. Moshe Landau, "The Limits of Pressure," *Israeli Democracy* (Fall 1990), p. 28.

124. Nasser, "Stones."

125. *Ibid.* Nasser provides five cases where the punishment for the killing of Palestinian Arabs resulted in sentences ranging between freedom and four months of actual time serving of the sentence in jail. In his view, "Arabs" are not murdered—they always get killed. It is the opposite for Arab suspects. According to Boaz Evron, "Since the trial of the Jewish underground, when several Jews were found guilty of the premeditated murder of Arabs, there have been many cases of Arabs killed by Jews and some of Jews killed by Arabs. . . . To the best of my

knowledge, not a single Jew has been found guilty of the murder of an Arab. . . . On the other hand, all Arabs who were suspected of having killed Jews were found guilty of murder." See Boaz Evron, "Occupation Corrupted Israeli Justice," *New Outlook* (May 1988), p. 8.

126. Arian, "Israel's Democracy," p. 263.

127. Shulamit Hareven, "Signs of Degeneration," *Yediot Achronot*, October 20, 1989.

128. David Kretzmer is mentioned within the speakers at a conference reviewed by Yoram Peri in "The Ailments of Israeli Society," *Davar*, December 24, 1989.

129. This is the title of an article by law professor and MK Amnon Rubenstein, "A Life-Saver for the Rule of Law," *Yediot Achronot*, December 25, 1989. While congratulating the court, Rubinstein calls the public's attention to an "unhealthy process" of widening the judiciary's intervention in an area that normally should have been confined to the military itself: the punishment of offenders. "Today, the Supreme Court is the only organ in the state's body that responds actively to injustice. Woe be us for having reached this state, but better this last way out than breaking the bones of the rule of law."

130. Horowitz and Lissak, *Metsuka B'Utopia*, p. 193.

131. Exceptional cases, such as the disclosure of the story of "Operation Moses" (the exodus of Ethiopian Jews via Sudan) disclosed in a West Bank Jewish settlers' magazine, *Nekuda*, were strongly criticized by most journalists from Israel and public opinion at large. See the interview with Brig. Gen. Yitzhak Shani, Chief Israeli military censor, in *Jane's Defense Weekly*, August 26, 1989.

132. According to the *IDF Journal*, "The Palestinian Arab press is problematic. They don't share the same security concerns of the Israeli press, and they don't share the neutral guest status of the foreign press corps. In fact, they are often a platform for incitement and fomenting violence. . . . This means that articles which do not endanger security and are allowed in Israel proper can be restricted in the administrative territories because they endanger public safety." See Michael Davis, "Censorship in a Democratic Society," *IDF Journal*, No. 16 (Winter 1989), p. 61. Such restrictions apply not only in the territories but also to the Arab papers of Jerusalem, the reunified capital of Israel, where the bulk of the Palestinian publications are located. The often arbitrary nature of the decisions has been described by Jack Khazmo, editor of the weekly *Al-Bayader al-Siyasi*, who maintains that decisions depend arbitrarily on the personality and mood of the censor, to such an extreme that "even statements by Israeli cabinet ministers have been cut out." Quoted by Ya'akov Ben-Natan in "Censorship—How Does It Work in Israel?" *Israeli Scene* (August 1988), p. 10.

133. Several dozen Palestinian journalists from East Jerusalem have been put under administrative detention without trial; weeklies and an information center have been permanently closed down. See Victor Cygielman, "When the Press is the Enemy," *New Outlook* (June 1988), p. 7.

134. Among the books censored are Shakespeare's *Hamlet*, the biography of Tolstoy by Henri Troyst, *Constitutional Law* by MK Amnon Rubinstein, and authors such as Solzhenitzyn, Sokholov, Jack London, as well as Israeli thinkers and statesmen. See Uzi Benziman, "Stupidity and Cruelty—Censorship," *Ha'aretz*, November 2, 1989. A comprehensive study was conducted by B'Tselem, "Censorship of Books" (Jerusalem, 1989). "At one time 1,500 books were on the black list, reduced by then–Minister of Defense Rabin in 1985 to approximately 350." See Ben-Natan, "Censorship," p. 13.

135. Ben-Natan, "Censorship," p. 11.

136. Laura Frucht, "Freedom of the Press and National Security: Are They Irreconcilable? *Israeli Scene* (February–March 1988), p. 7.

137. Rivca and Haim Gordon, "Racism in the Israeli Press," *Struggle* (March 1990), pp. 3–14.

138. Arian, "Israel's Democracy," p. 263. Seventy-five percent were in favor of freedom of speech, 14 percent were opposed, and 12 percent uncertain.

139. According to a survey published in the *Jerusalem Post International Edition*, August 27, 1988.

140. Ephraim Ya'ar, "Who's Afraid of a Free Press?" *Israeli Democracy* (Winter 1990), p. 19.

141. Journalist Danny Rubinstein was threatened and insulted with expressions such as "Arafat-lover."

142. See Hal Wyner, "Israeli Brutality, Press Timidity," *New York Times,* October 8, 1989.

143. "I have noticed that neither the facts I report nor the weight I attach to them are ever seriously challenged. The most common complaint, often put in far less polite terms by readers, has been that I am providing the anti-Semites with information." *Ibid.*

144. "More than ever, the TV journalists are aware of the existence of the 'client,' that amorphous creature who watches TV without really wanting to see anything. At the end of each evening's news broadcast, the TV station is flooded with calls from people who have been compelled to say: 'Why did you show the Peace Now demonstration, we're sick of those leftists. . . . Why do you interview Arabs on our own Jewish TV?'" See Lily Galili, "Israel TV: Siege and Self-Censorship," *Ha'aretz,* January 7, 1988.

145. "Much of the criticism was directed at foreign television networks. Israel's President Chaim Herzog said that "many of the recent incidents of unrest in Gaza and the West Bank began only when the television cameras were in place.'" See Frucht, "Freedom of the Press."

146. See interviews with Mordechai Kirshenbaum in *Hotem,* weekly supplement of *Al Hamishmar,* August 18, 1989.

147. Shilon contends, "It is the responsibility of the media, especially the television, to set the agenda for the public, and to cover extensively controversial issues, even if the public is initially not interested in them. . . . Supply of such information eventually creates demand by the public." See Leon T. Hadar, "Israeli TV Coverage of the Intifada: Throwing Stones at the Messenger," *Middle East Insight* (January–February 1990), pp. 27–28.

148. Stanley Cohen, "The Psychology and Politics of Denial: The Case of Israeli Liberals," *Psychologic Barrier to Peace* (occasional publication), pp. 10–23. "According to this secular theology, Israel is a democratic, liberal, peace-loving society committed to the rule of law. The liberal middle class (academics, professionals and, especially, lawyers) are the chief carriers of this self-serving myth." See also "The Human Rights Movement in Israel and South Africa: Some Paradoxical Comparisons" (Jerusalem: Harry S Truman Research Institute for the Advancement of Peace, 1991).

149. Yehoshafat Harkabi, *The Fateful Choices Before Israel* (Tel Aviv: International Center for Peace in the Middle East, 1986).

150. Rivca and Haim Gordon, "Academic Responses to the Intifada," *Struggle* (March 1991), pp. 3–12, in Hebrew. The researchers have charged a majority of university teachers with a "false platonic attitude, being a lack of will to speak up with decency, to address the existing situation, not to avoid the issues, to struggle for principles and to personally relate to what is happening." See p. 11.

151. See Daniel Williams, "Liberalism on Defensive in Once-Receptive Israel," *Los Angeles Times*, June 26, 1991.

152. *Ha'aretz*, May 28, 1990.

153. *Ha'aretz*, June 8, 1991.

154. *Los Angeles Times*, July 8, 1991, p. A10.

155. See Lily Galili, "The Hypocrisy of the Academy," *Ha'aretz*, December 20, 1989. p. 5.

156. In presenting the proposal to protest the violation of academic freedom of colleagues in the West Bank, "the professor compared the conduct of the Israeli government with that of the British government during the Mandate. Despite the fact that the Hebrew University and the Technion were centers of nationalist activity, and that many lecturers and students were members of rebel movements, the colonial regime did not close them down out of fear of public opinion back home. . . . But the shut-down of universities in the West Bank did not receive a hearing in the Tel Aviv University Senate. The Coordinating Committee, the academic body with executive powers, recommended that the issue be tabled. The reasoning was that it was political, and the Senate did not discuss political questions. University authorities checked to see if the issue had been raised at other universities, and members of the Tel Aviv University Senate were informed that other universities refrained from deliberating the matter as well." See Yonatan Shapira, "Where are the Guardians of Democracy?" *Ha'aretz*, January 17, 1989.

157. Sprinzak, "Radical Right," p. 182.

158. Interview with Y. Gorni in Aryeh Dayan, "We Racists," *Ha'aretz*, December 27, 1991. Speaking about Jabotinsky, the ideological founder of Prime Minister Shamir's political party, Gorni continues, "The classic Zionism did not conceive a situation in which the Arabs will be without rights. . . . There is no relation whatsoever between Jabotinsky and what's happening today in the Territories. Our aura of masters that accordingly everything is permissible to us, only because we are Jews, is dangerous."

159. Menachem Hofnung, "Security Needs," p. 8. See also his book, *Israel— Security Needs vs. the Rule of Law* (Tel Aviv: Nevo Publications, 1991), in Hebrew.

160. Michael Bar Zohar, *Facing a Cruel Mirror* (New York, Charles Scribners and Son, 1990), p. 5. According to the writer, the way to deal with the Palestinian awakening without affecting Israeli democracy was "unilateral autonomy in the West Bank."

161. Marver H. Bernstein, "Israel: Turbulent Democracy at Forty," *Middle East Journal*, Vol. 42, No. 2 (Spring 1989), p. 193.

162. Bar Zohar, *op. cit.*

163. Arian, "Israel's Democracy," p. 259.

164. *Ibid.*

165. Eisenstadt, *The Transformation of the Israeli Society.*

166. Sprinzak, "Case of Gush Emunim," p. 14.

167. Jonathan Frankel, "The State of Israel and the Liberal Crisis," *Jewish Quarterly*, Vol. 32, No. 4 (1985).

168. Interview with Hayim Zadok, *Politika*, April 1986, in Hebrew.

169. The last obstacle creates a vicious circle: "National security is one of the main factors impeding the legislation of a constitution, and the absence of a constitution results in a limited judicial review on matters involving security." See Karp, "Finding an Equilibrium," pp. 29–30.

170. Horowitz and Lissak, *Metsuka B'Utopia*, p. 197.

171. There is no better alternative to using the courts as little as possible in establishing the criminality of acts and leaving to individual morality and to leader-

ship in particular the greater share of behaving according to the spirit of the law. The continuous attempt to test the limits of interpretation of the written word, especially in a country without a constitution, is bound to stir serious commotions and cleavages in society, and increase criticism of the politicization of the judicial power. The subject is treated in both the universal and Israeli contexts by Steven Goldstein, "The Limits of the Judicial System," *Mishpatim,* Vol. No. 1 (July 1983). See especially section 4, pp. 21–24, in Hebrew.

172. Already there are many Israeli native-born respondents in surveys who refuse to be boxed into an Ashkenazi-Oriental (Sephardi) dichotomy. A study by Arian and Shamir in 1984 showed that 41 percent of native Israelis with native-born fathers, and about a third of both those whose parents were Ashkenazi or Oriental, refused to identify themselves either way. Quoted in Charles S. Liebman, "Jewish Ultra-Nationalism in Israel: Converging Strands," in William Frankel, ed., *Survey of Jewish Affairs—1985* (Cranbury, NJ: Associated University Press, 1985), p. 29.

173. Peri, "Effect of Occupation," p. 29.

174. *Ibid.*

175. Relating to the traumatic Chilean experience, a former rector of the capital's university cautions, "Democracy cannot be taken for granted. Not even a long-standing political tradition and democratic values can prevent the breakdown of democracy if confrontation and extreme polarization prevail over a lengthy period of time. Legitimacy erodes and institutions crumble." Edgardo Boeninger, "Lessons from the Past, Hopes for the Future," *Journal of Democracy,* Vol. 1, No. 2 (Spring 1990), p. 13.

176. Juan Linz, "Crisis, Breakdown, and Reequilibrium," in *The Breakdown of Democratic Regimes,* Juan Linz and Alfred Stepan, eds., Vol. 1 (Baltimore: Johns Hopkins University Press, 1978).

177. Makovsky, *op. cit.*

6

Attitudes Toward Democracy Among Israeli Religious Leaders

Charles S. Liebman

This chapter explores the attitudes of Jewish religious leaders in Israel (the religious establishment) toward democracy, the interrelationship between Judaism and democracy, and the implications of these for Arab-Israeli peace.

The question of the relationship between Judaism and democracy must trouble anyone who is committed to both. The *dati* (pl: *datiim*, the religious or Orthodox) population constitutes from 15 to 20 percent of the Jewish population of Israel. (Non-Orthodox Jews who consider themselves religious in one way or another—for example, Reform or Conservative Jews— are numerically insignificant, with negligible impact on the society.) Virtually every survey of Israeli Jews finds that among *datiim* there is less commitment to democratic values than among the roughly 40 percent of the population that defines itself as *masorati* (traditional).[1] The *masoratiim*, in turn, harbor fewer individuals with a strong commitment to democracy than do the roughly 45 percent of the population that defines itself as *hiloni* (secular). Differences remain when we hold constant for ethnic origin or education and therefore suggest that a religious factor of one kind or another does account, at least in part, for the differences among these population groups.[2] *Dati* Jews deem religious leaders the authoritative interpreters of Judaism. Therefore, any search for the relationship between religion and attitudes toward democracy must begin with the attitudes of religious leaders. However, we must first clarify what is meant by the relative lack of commitment of *dati* Jews to democracy.

Democratic attitudes or democratic commitment refers to a package of values. I think those who have expressed concern about the relative absence of positive attitudes toward democracy among *datiim* have not always focused on the important questions. For example, respondents are sometimes asked if they would give greater weight to a decision by the Knesset or a decision by rabbinical authority. This question does not adequately measure attitudes toward democracy among the religious population. One hopes that all citizens cherish certain principles to which they accord higher value than legislative law. In other words, under certain circumstances every Israeli ought to give greater weight to a moral authority or ethical code outside the elected system of government than to the decisions of any institution within the system. If this outlook leads to a violation of the law, then the democratic system requires that a citizen willingly pay the price for violating the law. Abie Natan's decision to meet with PLO leaders in violation of Knesset law is a good example of this principle. Natan violated a law he felt was foolish as well as unjust, but he also understood that the price of behaving in accordance with his own moral code in defiance of the law was a prison sentence. All human beings ought to be committed to a morality that might, theoretically, conflict with the decision of a democratically elected government.

Halakha (Jewish law) constitutes a system of morality as well as law for the observant Jew. A religious Jew, by virtue of being a religious Jew, is bound by *halakhic* decisions. This contract is the essence of a Jew's self-identity as *dati*. Hence, when asked a question about the relative weight he or she would give to a rabbinic or a legislative decision, the religious Jew will always answer that greater weight will be given to *halakha*. Whether the *dati* Jew would actually do so in practice is a different matter entirely.

Finally, it is difficult to imagine the circumstances under which the Knesset would pass a law contrary to that which all authoritative rabbinical voices interpreted as Jewish law. As Haim David Halevy, the chief rabbi of Tel Aviv, has suggested, this is a purely hypothetical case, and he finds difficulty in conceiving such a situation in reality.[3] I agree, although not for the same reasons the rabbi suggests. In order for such a situation to arise, two conditions would have to be met. The Knesset would have to pass such a law with all the consequences involved in deliberately defying the religious tradition, and the religious elite would have to interpret the law as contrary to *halakha* with all the consequences that such a defiance of the authority of the state would entail. In other words, not only would the present political constellation have to change, but the whole climate of attitudes toward Judaism, to be discussed below, would have to change as well. Let us assume that such changes did occur. All they would do is establish a situation no different, in theory, from that which arises when an individual is faced with a contradiction between positive law and his own moral convictions. The democratic system is in no danger as long as this sort of thing doesn't happen too often and too many people do not find the law incompatible with their moral conscience.

A second charge is leveled against the democratic propensities of the *datiim:* Their support for passage of "religious" legislation is interpreted as an effort at religious coercion, i.e., the violation of freedom of conscience. It seems to me that this charge is somewhat unfair. Much of the legislation that some religious parties, Agudat Israel in particular, has proposed may be neither fair nor wise. Such laws may have deleterious economic consequences for particular individuals (such as the prohibition against raising or selling pigs and pork products) or even the entire economy (such as the prohibition of El Al flights on the Sabbath or the restriction on factory operations on the Sabbath). In addition, some laws, such as those prohibiting bus transportation on the Sabbath, are a source of inconvenience, in some cases serious inconvenience, to many Israelis. The efforts to restrict abortion may have unfortunate effects on the health of women, although this is by no means assured. But I think it is a mistake to frame the debate over these prohibitions and restrictions in terms of democracy and religious conscience; I don't believe, in any event, that this is how the vast majority of Israelis see the issue. The real issue in the eyes of most Israelis is over the extent to which Israeli public life ought to reflect the Jewish nature of the state and to what extent the state may infringe upon the private rights of individuals.

All of the *dati* parties, including the most extreme, deny that they seek to impose religious law in the private domain, although some, as we shall see, do not object to such infringement in principle. In other words, while some religious parties would welcome a constitutional upheaval that would substitute religious law for Knesset legislation, no *dati* party seeks to generate such an upheaval. In this respect, it is worth noting, they differ from the fundamentalist parties in Islamic countries. In other words, even the most extreme *dati* parties accept, in broad outline, the rules of the democratic system, including individual liberties and freedoms. However, virtually all the political parties in the Knesset that represent a predominantly Jewish constituency favor publicly recognizing the Jewish nature of the state in some form or another. In fact, in 1985 the Knesset voted to prohibit a party from participating in Knesset elections "if its goals, explicitly or implicitly, or its actions include . . . negation of the existence of the State of Israel as the State of the Jewish people." In other words, no political party may challenge the Jewish nature of the state.

Israel pays lip service to the notion of the equality of all its citizens under law. In practice, however, there are measures of blatant discrimination that distinguish between Jew and non-Jew (although, like pre-1960 discrimination against blacks in the United States, this form of discrimination may be challenged). For example, the state does not accord national rights to non-Jews.[4] This policy has much more to do with Zionism than with Judaism. It is a commitment that about three-fourths of all Jews in Israel share.[5] But it is a mistake to think that commitment to a Jewish state is simply a euphemism for denying Israeli Arabs a right to national assertion. The vast majority of Israeli Jews also believe that Judaism, i.e., the religious tradition, ought to find expression in public life. The debate between the *dati* and non-*dati* parties over issues of religious legislation or religious coercion, therefore, is framed not in terms of a debate over the principle of democracy but over the interpretation of what the Jewish nature of public life means and what the private rights of individuals mean. Basic democratic principles are not at stake in this conflict in the sense that, when one principle is overturned (e.g., freedom of speech or minority rights), all other principles are endangered. Some political liberals may prefer to see the conflict in those terms, but this perspective distorts the nature of the debate as it takes place in the minds of most of the protagonists. Furthermore, doing so blinds us to the threats to basic democratic principles that do indeed arise from the *dati* quarter.

Even if we concede that *dati* support for religious legislation or their prior commitment to *halakha* over Knesset legislation is not a threat to democracy, the fact remains that *datiim* are more likely than non-*datiim* to favor censorship, restricting criticism of the government, and distinguishing between the rights and freedom of Jews and of non-Jews, even if the latter are citizens of Israel. The question, therefore, is whether these attitudes reflect positions that are shared by Jewish religious leaders—that is, by the Jewish establishment, the institutional guardians of Judaism—and, if so, whether those attitudes in turn reflect values that are inherent in the Jewish religious tradition.

Is There a Religious Establishment?

It might be argued that antidemocratic attitudes and tendencies within the religious population reflect those of one segment of *datiim*, not all. The Orthodox camp in Israel is quite divided. The basic division is between *haredim* (ultra-Orthodox, hostile to modernity, and anti-Zionist) and religious-Zionists (until recently characterized by a benevolent attitude toward modernity and less punctiliousness in religious observance).[6] Within each of these camps are subgroups whose animosity toward one another (at least among the *haredim*) sometimes leads to outbreaks of violence. Furthermore, the standard division of Orthodox Israelis into the *haredi* and religious-Zionist camps is complicated by the growing religiopolitical strength of *dati* Oriental Jewry—Jews who were born or whose parents were born in Arab-speaking countries. They don't fit neatly in either camp. But the question here is whether one can point to the development of religious attitudes common to all the Orthodox. I think it very clear that, dissenting voices to the contrary notwithstanding, one can increasingly do so with regard to some major issues, though not yet, as will be shown below, with regard to all of them.

A few decades ago, this was not true. Aryei Fishman has shown how the religious-Zionists integrated both Zionism and modernity into their religious formulations.[7] But the mood of moderation, openness to new ideas, and emphasis on the universalist dimension of Judaism no longer predominates within religious-Zionist circles in Israel. Instead, a new form of ultranationalist religious radicalism has gained ascendancy. Among *haredim,* ultranationalist ideals, phrased in religious rather than Zionist terminology, are expressed with increasing frequency. In many respects, therefore, the two religious strands are converging. This convergence is not evident in the assertions of the extremists and ideological purists in either camp but rather in its effect on the larger population of religious Jews who were heretofore identifiable as either *haredi* or religious-Zionist. Today, one can point to the emergence of new groups and/or changes in the ideology of established religious parties that integrate *both* strands.

Support for this approach is found in the growing usage of a label that was invented some ten years ago—*haredi-leumi* (a nationalist *haredi*). To the best of my knowledge, the term was first used by a moderate anti-*haredi* leader of the religious-Zionist youth movement, B'nei Akiva. He was very concerned with the growth of *haredi* tendencies within his movement, the denigration of secular education in particular, and unhappy, though perhaps less distressed, by the emergence of ultranationalist tendencies as well. The term *haredi-leumi* was certainly intended as a term of opprobrium. The term is now borne with pride by a growing number of religious schools, by a rapidly growing religious youth movement, Ezra, and by an increasing number of religious Jews who, according to a poll conducted by the religious weekly *Erev Shabbat,* decline to identify themselves as either *haredi* or religious-Zionist but prefer to be called *haredi-leumi.*

The growth of *haredi* parties and their ability to attract voters from non-*haredi* segments of the population has been accompanied, at the ideological no less than at the pragmatic level, by their de facto adoption of a nationalistic orientation and the muting of their ideological objections to Zionism,[8] although this tendency does not encompass all *haredim.* Moreover, even where the *haredi* parties adopt a dovish position on foreign policy issues at variance with that of the National Religious Party (NRP, the political arm of the religious-Zionists), that position reflects pragmatic considerations associated with the present condition of Jews. There is no affirmation among *haredim* about any basic or ultimate rights of the non-Jew, especially with regard to the Land of Israel. Indeed, surveys to which we shall return indicate that *haredim* are less tolerant of Arab rights than are religious-Zionists.

The real issue between *haredi* doves and the religious nationalists is whether or not Jews in Israel are still living under conditions of exile. The *haredim* claim that in a metaphysical sense the Jews still live in exile and therefore must act toward non-Jews with deference lest they irritate them and arouse their always latent feeling of anti-Semitism. Jews must acknowledge that their own power is inadequate to overcome Gentile animus,[9] for "since the beginning of time, there is an undertone of hatred between the Jew and the gentile. Either the gentile hates the Jew or the Jew hates the gentile. It is like a law of nature that is part of the laws of creation; just as there is light in the day and darkness at night."[10] Other voices can be heard within the *haredi* camp on attitudes toward non-Jews, but they are in the minority.

At the religious-Zionist end of the continuum, the National Religious Party and its constituents, heretofore characterized by religious moderation and by accommodation rather than rejection of modernity and secular culture, show increasing signs of asserting a rather reactionary interpretation of the religious tradition. This shift is evident in the increased allocation of school time to the study of sacred texts in religious-Zionist schools, in growing insistence on separation of the sexes in institutions identified with religious-Zionism, and in the rising emphasis on religious observance by many religious-Zionists. The National Religious Party's platform on the future of the territories has been radicalized and now virtually mirrors that of the extreme right, and other institutions of the religious-Zionist camp have adopted positions in other matters that increasingly resemble those of the *haredim*.[11] Thus, the counterpart to the nationalization of the *haredim* is the *haredization* of the religious-Zionists.

In summary, there is less point today than there was in the past in distinguishing among the segments of religious Jewry for purposes of assessing their relationship to democratic ideas and structures within Israeli society. This assertion does not mean that all religious Jews or religious parties are cut of one cloth; one can distinguish different orientations among parties, among groups within the parties, and among individual political and religious leaders. Nor have differences between *haredim* and religious-Zionists entirely disappeared (these are discussed in the following section). The major argument of this chapter, however, is that mainstream currents among religious-Zionists and *haredim* are becoming increasingly similar and are in conflict with assumptions, attitudes, and values that undergird a stable democracy. Given the democratic structure of the Israeli polity, the increasing involvement of *haredi* parties in the political arena may, over the long run, strengthen their democratic commitments. But, at least in the short run, this has not taken place. On the contrary, as we shall see, *haredi* participation in democratic processes may work at cross-purposes to both the assertion of minority rights in Israel and to the attainment of a peaceful settlement between Israelis and Palestinians.

Religious Leaders and Democracy

Statements by religious spokesmen about democracy generally refer to the formal properties of the system—majority rule and some guarantee of individual rights. Although some religious leaders have interpreted Judaism as being incompatible with democracy, others view the two systems as totally harmonious.[12] At the theoretical level, there are differences between *haredim* and many religious-Zionists on this point. Rare is the religious-Zionist spokesman who will admit an incompatibility between Judaism and democracy. One sometimes finds, especially among religious ultranationalists, statements about the foreign or non-Jewish nature of democracy, but these are unusual. Such is not the case in the *haredi* sector. Although the major *haredi* dailies, *Hamodia* and *Yated Ne'eman,* are generally circumspect, *haredi* leaders make no secret of the fact that the principle Ben-Gurion enunciated so often—that Israel is a state based upon the rule of law and not rule by *halakha*—is anathema to them. Indeed, rule of law is often mentioned as one of the major shortcomings of the Jewish state. Rabbi Eliezer Menachem Schach, the preeminent leader of one of the two major segments of the *haredi* public, protests that the secularists say, "Let us, the House of Israel, be like all the nations, a democratic state, a state of law and not a state of *halakha,* that is, a state with the laws of idol worshippers and not the laws of the Torah."[13]

On the other hand, even those who believe that democracy and Judaism are compatible with one another cannot reconcile the concept of majority rule at the theoretical level with a Jewish state governed in accordance with Jewish law. Authority in a democracy resides with the majority of the population, whereas in a religious state it resides with rabbinical sages.[14] The problem, however, is purely hypothetical, not only because such a state is so unlikely to ever be formed but also because Jewish law is subject to interpretation by the rabbis. Thus, the canon is far more flexible than one might otherwise imagine. It is really impossible to know how the rabbis would dictate where human authority resides if they were confronted with such a question at the practical level.

The real conflict between democracy and Jewish law is not in the realm of legislation by the Knesset or the theoretical mandates of *halakha* but in the role of the Jewish tradition in shaping attitudes and values that serve as preconditions to the functioning of a democratic system. As Nicholas Demerath observes, "Despite religion's prominence as a source of political legitimacy and campaign rhetoric, it is rarely a dominant factor in the affairs of state."[15] Still, the role of religion in forming the political culture of Israeli society, particularly of the religious sector, should not be minimized.[16]

The following is a list of attitudes or values that are important preconditions for the functioning of a democratic system and are probably influenced by religious commitment.

1. Basic respect for law and authority. Democracy places more limited means of coercive control in the hands of its political elite than does an authoritative system of government. Respect for law or the willingness of the citizenry to voluntarily acquiesce to laws they do not personally favor is

probably more important to the survival of a democracy than it is to other systems of government.

2. A large measure of tolerance for the opinions of others, regardless of how sharply one disagrees with these opinions and regardless of the type of person expressing the opinion.

3. Relatively greater concern about the process of the political system and relatively less concern about the outcome or output of the system.

4. As an extension of the previous point, high commitment to what Robert Bellah calls a liberal constitutional regime rather than to a republic.[17] In other words, low commitment to the notion that the state has a role to play in shaping the moral character of its citizens or in achieving some other preordained goal; a belief, instead, that government exists to serve the needs of its citizens as the citizens define their needs.

5. Given the presence in Israel of national and religious minorities who are self-conscious about their collective identities, a special tolerance toward non-Jews and some recognition of their group as well as their individual rights.

Other things being equal, high religious commitment is probably correlated with the first value—a respect for law and authority. That, at least, is my impression. Whether this correlation is empirically so, under what circumstances it is more or less so, and to what it is attributable awaits further study. If true, it may be accounted for by the generalized respect for law and authority that comes with religious socialization, but it may also stem from the relatively greater success of religious institutions in socializing their youth to the value of respect for law and authority (in other words, secular institutions seek the same goal but religious institutions socialize their youth more effectively). It also may stem from one or more other factors. Whatever the reasons, respect for authority and the rule of law, which is an important condition for the development of a stable democratic system, is in my opinion strengthened by religious commitment.[18]

However, the remaining values do not reinforce democratic ideals. Commitment to Judaism does not encourage a respect for the opinions of others or the rights of others to express themselves freely when such expression is contrary to basic beliefs of Judaism, especially when those who express this opinion are nonreligious Jews. This intolerance exists not only because expressions of such beliefs—for example, denial of the existence of God—is contrary to Jewish law, although this objection has led to demands for the censoring of plays;[19] it is deeper than that. The religious believer, other things being equal, is accustomed to the notion that there is an absolute truth, that right and wrong, morality and immorality, good and evil, are readily distinguishable. It is therefore folly to permit the expression of ideas and values one knows to be wrong, immoral, or harmful, especially when such notions are expressed by secularists, whose indifference, if not antagonism, to basic religious values suggests that they or their intent may be evil. According to a leader of the National Religious Party, art has a purpose; but instead of fulfilling that purpose, the theater, television, and press disseminate material offensive to religion and harmful to Israel's security. Everything published or presented to the public "must be in accordance with moral and educational standards," he argued on the floor of the Knesset.[20]

This sentiment is related to a central conviction in the thinking of religious Jews—the notion that a proper state is one that shapes the moral outlook of its citizens. It is therefore incumbent upon the state to adopt measures that will further this goal. A religious worldview socializes the Jew to the notion that the ideal state, the proper Jewish state, is not simply an instrument to serve a variety of interests or needs of the population but a framework that assists the Jew in his moral and spiritual elevation. This attitude is shared by all religious Jews, non-Zionists as well as Zionists.

The state, therefore, has a purpose. The religious Jew, to return to Bellah's distinction noted above, favors a republic, not a constitutional democracy. It is insufficient as far as religious Jews are concerned to be told that the government has adopted some law in accordance with "due process" (i.e., proper procedures) or that the majority of the population in addition to a majority in the Knesset favors a particular law. From a religious point of view, Israel has a special purpose, and no government and no majority has the authority to override that purpose. Thus, according to a resolution adopted by the Council of Jewish Settlements in Judea, Samaria and Gaza (a nonreligious body but one dominated by the ideology of the religious ultranationalists), if Israel should surrender sovereignty over Judea or Samaria it would "represent a prima facie annulment of the State of Israel as a Zionist Jewish state whose purpose is to bring Jews to the sovereign Land of Israel and not, perish the thought, to remove them from the Land of Israel and replace them with a foreign sovereignty."[21]

The idea of a republican rather than a constitutional democracy, the vision of a moral state rather than one that simply services its citizens' needs, is a Zionist no less than a Jewish ideal. Both Israel as a Zionist state and Israel as a Jewish state imply limitations on democracy. The notion that Israel has a moral purpose that Knesset law cannot overrule is not confined to the religious population.[22] Thus, for example, the Knesset's decision to prohibit parties that advocate abolishing the Jewish nature of the state passed with virtually no public protest.

However, it remains true that religious Jews interpret the consequences of Israel's condition as an ideological state more broadly than do nonreligious Jews. To put it another way: The policy consequences of Israel being a Jewish state are much broader from the point of view of the religious Jew than are the consequences of Israel's being a Zionist state to the secular Jew.

The most serious conflict between attitudes necessary for the maintenance of a stable democratic society in Israel and attitudes fostered by high religious commitment has to do with the rights of Arabs. Judaism in Israel has become increasingly particularistic and ethnocentric. It promotes little tolerance for the individual rights of non-Jewish citizens and even less for minority group rights. In the minds of most religiously committed Jews, the Arabs represent a danger and a security threat, and strong measures, including denial of their civil rights, are justified.[23] I would summarize the dominant tendency as one that grudgingly acknowledges the right of non-Jews to live in Israel in accordance with their religious or cultural norms but only insofar as their presence has no influence on other Jews or on the public life of the state. Even this tendency stretches the limits of *halakhic* tolerance. An article in *T'khumin,* the most distinguished annual dealing with matters of Jewish law and public issues from an Orthodox perspective, addressed the question of the status of Moslems in Israel according to Jewish law.[24] The author seems to phrase himself carefully, and there is no trace of polemic in the tone of the article, a fact that makes the conclusions all the more disturbing. According to the writer, under the ideal conditions envisioned by Jewish law, non-Jews in the Land of Israel ought to live in servitude to Jews. In fact, their very right to live in the Land of Israel is problematic. A Jew is permitted, though not required, to save non-Jews if their lives are in danger. However, the non-Jews ought not benefit from free public services. These, the author stresses, are basic principles according to which we want to build our society; the *halakhic* imperative to subjugate non-Jews living under Jewish rule may be relaxed because of political constraints, but we ought never lose sight of the ideal society to which Israel should aspire. (It is only fair to add that the editor of the volume challenged the author's understanding of *halakha* in a brief note at the conclusion of the article.[25])

Universalism, a central component in the American Jewish understanding of Judaism and one that extends to many Orthodox Jews as well, is deliberately rejected by mainstream Orthodoxy in Israel. The signs of Jewish particularism are quite noticeable. Everything is perceived from within a Jewish prism and judged from within a Jewish perspective. The rise of particularism has implications for the interpretation of morality as well. Emphasis on law and ritual means a deemphasis on the centrality of ethics. In addition, religious Jews in Israel have redefined the very term "morality" in particularistic rather than universalistic terms. According to the rabbi who pioneered the establishment of extremist education within the religious-Zionist school system, Jews are enjoined to maintain themselves in isolation from other peoples. Foreign culture is a particular anathema when its standards are used to criticize Jews.[26] There is no place in Judaism for "a humanistic attitude in determining responses to hostile behavior of the Arab population," says one of them.[27]

These attitudes and values derive from a religious perspective. Behind them lies a worldview formed in part by basic *halakhic* notions that divide the world into right and wrong, good and evil, pure and impure. True, these attitudes and values do not carry the force of *halakhic* norms in that they do not obligate anyone to observe them or follow them. Indeed, they are rarely articulated. They are conveyed by indirection and in a matter-of-fact manner as basic assumptions not only of Judaism but of human nature and the cosmos. For that very reason, they are more difficult to challenge and are more readily dispersed among population groups—especially poorly educated Jews from Islamic countries who are not punctilious in observing *halakhic* norms but who do internalize many presuppositions of the religious tradition as they are conveyed by the present religious elite. There is a parallel here to Hava Lazarus-Yafeh's observation that there is a basic Islamic orientation which, in denying that man is ever the measure of things "engendered a general mood, never a clearly defined political theory."[28] Similarly, deep suspicion of the non-Jew, the conviction that the non-Jew seeks to totally destroy all Jews, is deeply embedded in the religious culture. Not every religious Jew shares that belief. On the other hand, precisely because it is not articulated in specific *halakhic* norms, asserted as a tenet of Jewish faith, or formulated in an empirically testable statement, it possesses a mythical power to persuade without being easily refuted. The Holocaust, the enmity of the Arab states toward Israel, Arab terrorism against Jews, and Arab leaders' applause for or failure to condemn such attacks nourishes this suspicion and renders it plausible to nonreligious Israelis, especially but not exclusively those of more limited educational background. The difference between the religious and nonreligious sectors of the population, however, is that the suspicion and hostility not only is more widespread among the former but also receives specific theological sanction. Thus, for example, according to one *haredi* writer, "The Arab world that torments us is that which concludes the list of kingdoms that are destined to hinder Israel in its path in exile [an apparent reference to an interpretation of the book of Daniel]. It is the last [such world] and the righteous messiah, whose coming we await, that will overcome and conquer him."[29]

According to an American rabbi whose opinions are highly regarded in the *haredi* world, the October War is to be understood as "the wars of Satan—in the image of Egypt and Syria and other satanic figures—against the essence of Yom Kippur, and as a result, a war to totally uproot the essence of the Jew from all generations."[30]

An editorial in *Niv Hamoreh,* the journal of the association of *haredi* teachers, devoted a lengthy article explaining Arab hostility in general and the October War in particular. The article contained a number of themes that are not clearly sorted out. According to the author, Gentiles are the instrument of God and inflict His punishment upon the Jews. The particular sin of religious Jews was in being swept up by general currents in Israeli society that urged reliance on material forces rather than on God. The theme of Gentile enmity as ordained by God is found throughout biblical literature. The second theme, that Gentiles are willing instruments in the punishment of Israel, is also present, and the author seems to give it a particular emphasis. Whereas, according to the author, wars among Gentiles are fought for material reasons, their wars against Israel are always wars between profanity and holiness. "Hatred of the world for the nation of eternity" is the reality. The Gentile nations and the Jews "are two types of entities, which contradict each other like fire and water." Since the "refugees of European Jewry have gathered in the Land of Israel," the Land of Israel is now the focus of the Gentiles' hostility. The Arabs are seeking not land but rather the destruction of all Jews. The author then introduces a third theme: that victory is not far off. "The dark forces of Esau and Ishmael's seed sense how the ground is disappearing from under them" because the day of God is at hand.[31]

Having converted Arab hostility toward Jews and Israel into a matter of theological and even cosmic significance, distinctions between Arab states, or between Arabs living within Israel and other Arabs, are necessarily blurred. Indeed, the assertion of such distinctions would undermine the mythical construct. Hence, it is not surprising that religious Jews, who constitute the primary audience for these and similar articles, exhibit greater hostility for or suspicion of all Arabs, including those within the borders of Israel, or that they are relatively more amenable to proposals that would deny Arabs basic civil and political rights.

Not all religious leaders understand Judaism and its imperatives in the manner described so far. Talmudic masters, heads of one of the most prominent *yeshivot* (schools for advanced Talmudic study) in Israel, Rabbis Yehuda Amital and Aharon Lichtenstein argue for a very different interpretation of the tradition, one that places emphasis on the essential equality of all people because all are created in the image of God. Their theological perspective has not only led them to insist upon the equal treatment of Arabs and Jews within Israel but has led them to adopt positions on Arab-Israel relations that are far more accommodating than those of the National Religious Party, from which they seceded. In addition, a large minority who define themselves as *dati* and are committed to observance of the Torah would grant Israeli Arabs equality. A recent survey of attitudes toward Arab rights in Israel among all Israeli Jews offered respondents three alternative choices on their attitudes toward Arab rights in Israel. The first choice was that only Jews have rights, the second choice was that only Jews have national rights but Arabs have individual rights, and the third choice was that both Jews and Arabs have individual as well as national rights. Among the general population, 62 percent chose the second or third option; 26 percent chose the third option—i.e., they were prepared to grant Arabs national as well as individual rights. Among those who defined themselves as *dati*, 44 percent chose the second or third option, 13 percent choosing the national rights alternative. Among those who defined themselves as *haredim*, 24 percent were prepared to grant individual rights to Arabs, and 8 percent were even prepared to grant them national rights.[32]

Attitudes Toward Peace Among Religious Leaders

The value of peace is deeply rooted in the Jewish tradition. Whereas this is true of other religious traditions as well, the Jewish tradition probably goes further in anathematizing war and everything connected to it. War is viewed as a necessity under certain conditions, but neither war, nor the instruments of war, nor those who carry out the war are idealized. In this regard, Rabbi Zvi Yehuda Kook, sometimes referred to as the spiritual grandfather of Gush Emunim, and his spiritual heirs represent a minority.[33] Their position may yet become the normative one among religious-Zionists, as it already has among the ultranationalists, but their sanctification of weapons of war in the hands of Israel is still quite foreign to *haredim*. (The transformation of the tradition in the hands of the ultranationalists is a point to which I return.) However, among virtually all religious leaders, even among the ultranationalists, and especially among *haredim*, the issue is not the value of peace but rather the price or the sacrifices one is prepared to make for peace. A second issue, one too often overlooked, is the question of the priority accorded to securing peace on one's political agenda.

Peace, from a religious point of view, is not an entirely unmixed blessing. Rabbi Schach's central role within *haredi* Jewry has already been alluded to. According to him:

> Even though all of us desire and yearn for peace with our neighbors . . . I am very very suspicious of this peace. In our present situation [the absence of peace], we are assured that young men and women from among our people and from Egypt and other Arab countries do not come to Jerusalem to study in the university, and a great deal of assimilation is thereby prevented. But when there will be peace with our neighbors, young men and women from Israel will certainly travel to Beirut and Cairo to study there, and they [gentiles] will come from there to study in the university in Jerusalem. What will prevent assimilation? Will nationalism prevent it? Don't we see what nationalism means to them? [suggesting that nationalism is no barrier to the assimilation of secular Israelis][34]

But this comment is really an aside on the nature of Israeli society. When

Schach addresses himself directly to the issue of peace, he is forthright in his emphasis on its importance:

> We are obligated to agree to any step on behalf of peace and in any manner. We are obliged to accept any compromise that will hasten the peace, for much shedding of blood can be avoided by peace.[35]

This statement might appear related to Schach's support for the Camp David agreement, his opposition to the annexation of the Golan Heights and to the 1980 law declaring the unified city of Jerusalem the capital of Israel, and his critical remarks about the settlement in the Occupied Territories.[36] However, such an interpretation would misrepresent the priority that the desire for peace has on the religious agenda in general and the *haredi* agenda in particular. Here we must distinguish between two basically different political orientations, one that is characteristic of religious-Zionists and the other of *haredim*. As Eliezer Don-Yehiya has pointed out, religious-Zionism, from the outset, was sympathetic to political activism. *Haredim,* at least until most recently, are oriented toward political quietism, especially in matters that do not affect their ability to fulfill religious commandments.[37] The ultranationalists who increasingly dominate religious-Zionists circles are convinced that a greater Land of Israel under Jewish control is not only desirable and necessary for purposes of security but also a positive religious commandment they are obliged to fulfill. This interpretation of sacred text is nourished by the nationalists' activist orientation, which in turn strengthens their sense that the religious command to settle the Land of Israel is one that demands immediate fulfillment. The *haredim,* who have internalized a more passive political orientation—one they not surprisingly, though somewhat inaccurately, attribute to the Jewish tradition itself—interpret sacred text in congruence with that orientation. Thus, they do not interpret scripture in a manner that imposes immediate political obligations upon them. Their quietism is nowhere better expressed than in Schach's rationale for opposing measures such as the annexation of the Golan Heights or the declaration of Jerusalem as the unified capital of Israel. These steps, he argues, only serve to irritate the Gentiles. The Jews, in an analogy *haredi* leaders often invoke, are comparable to a lamb among seventy wolves. The lamb is defenseless. It cannot possibly resist its enemies. It must exercise the severest caution in order not to antagonize them. The Jews' ultimate hope rests only in salvation from God. Rav Schach is no less ethnocentric and xenophobic than the ultranationalists of Gush Emunim. Nor, as he himself says, does he have any doubt that the Land of Israel in its entirety will belong one day to the Jews. But the timing and manner in which the Jews will acquire the land is to be determined by God. Jews have no obligation in this regard. Their responsibility is to study and observe the commandments of the Torah and trust in God, not in secular or military power or solutions.

It would be misleading to argue that the issue of Arab-Israeli or Palestinian-Jewish relations and the issue of peace are of secondary importance to most *haredi* leaders. They are, however, not issues that rank high on their agenda of activity, because most *haredi* leaders do not believe there is much that Jews can do about them. In a proximate sense, the issues of peace or war, retaining or returning territory, will be resolved by the Gentiles. In the ultimate sense they are determined by God, who, especially in matters concerning the Jews, guides the decisions of the Gentiles. Hence, the best hope for Jewish security and for peace is to obey God's laws and trust in Him. But this outlook also means, as already indicated, that they will do little in pursuit of peace. When forced to choose between joining a Labor-led government or a Likud-led government, Rabbi Schach chose the Likud. In an address to a mass rally of his followers on March 26, 1990, nationally televised, he stressed the paramountcy of observing Jewish law and disdain for those who violate it. In this matter, the Labor Party, by virtue of its behavior in the 1940s and 1950s, was deemed less trustworthy than the Likud. A view attributed to Schach was that the nations of the world would force Israel to surrender the West Bank and Gaza regardless of who was in office. Therefore, peace and order within Israel could better be maintained if Likud rather than Labor presided over the surrender of the territories. This example demonstrates that *haredi* parties march to tunes that are different from those of the non-*haredim* and provides additional evidence of the futility of assessing *haredi* attitudes on issues that seem so important to the non-*haredi* public.

Not all *haredi* leaders, however, share Schach's political orientations or his political independence. We may distinguish his position from that of others in three respects. First, many *haredi* leaders are less dovish than he. For instance, Rabbi Menachem Mendel Schneersohn, the Lubavitcher rabbi, is an adamant hawk who even opposed the 1985 Israeli withdrawal from Lebanon and has threatened to vilify former Prime Minister Shamir if he proposes any form of Palestinian autonomy. None are as hawkish as Schneersohn, but within *haredi* circles voices can be heard that oppose Israeli withdrawal from the territories, generally for reasons of security and distrust of Arab promises. Political scientist Ephraim Inbar, under the auspices of the Leonard Davis Institute of Hebrew University, interviewed all *haredi* members of the Knesset regarding views on the Arab-Israeli dispute. The most striking result of this as-yet unpublished study is that the range of views among *haredi* Knesset members parallels the range of views extending from the left wing of the Labor Party to the right wing of the Likud. But these are personal views of the Knesset members and play a relatively minor role in their Knesset voting; they are subordinated to issues deemed critical by the *haredim* themselves.

Schach's position can be distinguished from that of other *haredi* leaders in a second respect: His authority over his followers is absolute. The same is true of some other *haredi* leaders, such as the Lubavitcher rebbe, but it is not true of all of them. The most important *haredi* leader who cannot impose absolute authority in political matters, who indeed finds that he must often be attentive to his followers' sympathies lest he lose his position of eminence, is Rabbi Ovadia Yossef, former Sephardi chief rabbi and spiritual leader of the largest *haredi*-style party, Shas. Yossef is a political dove. Shas's constituents are Oriental Jews, probably all of whom are religiously traditional, but the majority are not *haredi*; i.e., they are not strictly punctilious in their religious observance nor do they identify themselves as part of the *haredi* community or share all the worldviews prevalent there. They have strong, decidedly hawkish political opinions, and they conveyed a message to Yossef on one occasion (by demonstrating in front of his home) that they will resist Shas support for the Labor Party and will not tolerate endorsement of more than minor political concessions to the Palestinians. Ethnocentrism and thorough distrust of the Palestinians more than commitment to a greater Land of Israel lies behind these attitudes.

The third respect in which Schach's position is distinctive, or at least increasingly distinctive within the *haredi* sector, is his passive political orientation. I have indicated that the *haredi* worldview is characterized by political passivity. But it is my impression that this attitude is changing. I believe the orientation remains normative within *haredi* circles because a core group of leaders still adheres to it. But this aspect of their worldview is, to borrow a phrase from Peter Berger, increasingly implausible with the reality experience of *haredim*. Their continued adherence to the notion that worldly activism in the political realm is futile does not accord with their own experiences in Israel or with Israel's success against its enemies, a success they applaud and which they appreciate as being explained by more than God's will. Once Schach and a few others of his generation are gone—and given their age this is likely to come sooner rather than later—the *haredi* mood will turn increasingly activist. This part of the process of modernization even the *haredim* are unable to totally resist. It is explained, first and foremost, by the involvement of *haredim* in Israeli politics, an involvement that, as Menachem Friedman points out, was required to secure public funding to support their growing numbers.[38] The parties and other political instruments that the *haredim* established to further their immediate self-interest now generate an independent pressure on behalf of political activism. The more political activity there is, the more the status of the politicians and their periphery is enhanced. Second, the political experience accustoms *haredim* to the notion that politics are an important instrument for securing objectives. Third, *haredim* do not live in total isolation from the non-*haredi* society, least of all in matters affecting security. They are swept up in the current of Israeli thinking that insists on active measures in defense of Israel's interests. If, as I expect, the Jewish ethnocentrism and xenophobia of *haredim* is combined with more activist political tendencies, the outcome, at least in the short run, will be *haredi* support for policies that are inimicable to peace. It is my impression that similar developments are occurring in the Arab world.

Religious Changes in Israeli Life

This chapter has argued that among religious Jews in general and their leaders in particular, tendencies inimicable to both democracy and a peaceful settlement of the Israeli-Palestinian issue seem to be ascendent. These tendencies, I have suggested, stem less from the imperatives of *halakha* than from assumptions, moods, and a general orientation present within the religious public. But moods, attitudes and even general orientations are amenable to development and change without having to overcome legalistic hurdles. Indeed, attitudes and values concerning the Jewish tradition have undergone dramatic change, as I have tried to show elsewhere.[39] Regardless of how one evaluates the weight of Jewish tradition, it is not one-sided. The option of interpreting it in a more liberal, humanitarian, universalist vein compatible with the maintenance of stable democratic structures exists. The question, therefore, is: Why is this interpretation virtually absent in *dati* circles in Israel? Why has Judaism in Israel undergone a transformation in the direction of particularism and ethnocentrism rather than moralism, universalism, and political liberalism—in other words, why has Israeli Judaism become less rather than more compatible with the preconditions for a stable democratic society?

There are a number of answers to this question—historical, sociological, and political. The most obvious factor is that when religious Jews, leaders as well as masses, express values we define as antidemocratic, they do not see democracy as the critical issue. They are not acting out antidemocratic scenarios in any deliberate fashion. Unlike fascists, for example, even the most particularist and authoritarian *dati* spokesmen do not view their behavior or ideology as contrary to democracy. Democratic values and norms are simply not a referent. These leaders believe they are behaving in accordance with the precepts of Judaism, but more specifically they are acting to strengthen the security and well-being of the Jewish people. *Haredi* Jews not only believe they are better Jews because they are more pious, devout, and religiously observant; they are also convinced that they care more than anyone else for other Jews. The *haredi* press delights in drawing invidious comparisons between *haredim* who care for Jews and the Israeli left wing, which they charge is concerned only for the rights of

Arabs. Religious-Zionists of all stripes—not only the ultranationalist settlers of the Occupied Territories, who are not necessarily the most antidemocratic in attitude—firmly believe that they are the better Zionists and that the values and ideals they espouse are, with the exception of the desire to impose religious law, totally consistent with the values and ideals of the Zionist pioneers, whom they hold in the greatest esteem. In other words, attitudes and values that the observer labels antidemocratic and threatening to social order, freedom of choice, and basic human decency are viewed by many if not a majority of *datiim* as part of the struggle for Jewish security and well-being. Meir Kahane was no hero in most *dati* circles, but many of them believed that his basic error was that he was too zealous on behalf of ideals all Jews share, or at least ought to share. Many *datiim* and, according to some surveys, a majority of *dati* youth identified with his values. That is the difference between attitudes toward Kahane and attitudes toward a figure such as MK Yossi Sarid (who is a special focus of hatred) or the Citizens' Rights Movement. Kahane, they will tell you, may have gone too far, but he went too far in a proper cause. The Zionist left has gone too far in the wrong cause.

Another explanation for changes in religious attitudes toward democracy in general and the rights of the Arab minority in Israel in particular must be understood in light of changes that have taken place within Israeli society as a whole. Religious spokesmen need no longer concern themselves with secular alternatives to the religious tradition. They need no longer respond to alternative concepts of Judaism that stress universalist or ethical components within that tradition, because secular Judaism no longer poses an ideology that competes with religious Judaism.[40] Therefore, religious figures most capable of leading the battle against secularists—politicians and especially religious intellectuals—find that their influence has declined and that the balance of authority within the religious world has shifted in favor of the rabbinical elite, who by virtue of their narrow training and significant referents tend to be more particularistic and xenophobic.

The Jewish tradition, which the rabbis insist is theirs alone to interpret, is not, as I noted, the same tradition over which they held sway in the past. The transformation of the tradition has taken place independently of the influence of the rabbinical elite. The tradition has been nationalized among nonreligious as well as religious Zionists through a selective interpretation of sacred texts and Jewish history. Emphasis is given to the sanctity and centrality of Eretz Israel, the Land of Israel. In the past, Zionists celebrated their radical departure from the Jewish tradition in their efforts to reclaim and settle the Land. Today, Israelis celebrate their continuity with the tradition in this regard. What is all the more remarkable is that Eretz Israel has come to symbolize both loyalty to the state of Israel and loyalty to Judaism. Baruch Kimmerling points out that the term "Eretz Israel" has increasingly replaced the term "state of Israel" in the pronouncements of national leaders, especially those on the political right.[41] To be a good Jew means to live in the Land of Israel under conditions of Jewish autonomy.

The nationalization of the Jewish tradition means its particularization as well. I don't wish to argue that this process constitutes a distortion of the Jewish past. I suspect that the effort to interpret Judaism as moralistic and universalistic, an effort that is basic to American Judaism, is less faithful than is the Israeli version to what Jews throughout the ages have understood as their tradition.[42] But the present interpretation also contrasts with the Zionist effort to "normalize" Jewish existence. Classical Zionists suggested that anti-Semitism was a consequence of the peculiar condition of the Jews as perennial guests or strangers in countries not their own. It was not, they claimed, the result of any special animus toward Jews as such. Zionists believed that once the Jews had a country of their own, their condition would be normalized and anti-Semitism would disappear. The Zionists were aware of the fact that this cornerstone of their credo contradicted traditional Jewish conceptions of anti-Semitism.

Israeli Jews no longer, for the most part, believe this to be true. Anti-Semitism, they are likely to believe, is endemic. "The world is all against us," as the refrain of a popular song went, suggesting that there is nothing Jews in general or Israelis in particular can do to resolve the problem. The Jew is special because he is hated, and he is hated because he is special. This is the lesson of Jewish history, and it serves to anchor the state of Israel within the currents of Jewish life. But it is also the cornerstone of *haredi* political conceptions and it reinforces their worldview and strengthens their self-confidence. In summary, Zionism, the ideology of Jewish nationalism, has been transformed and integrated into the Jewish tradition. The tradition, in turn, has been nationalized. Erik Cohen describes this trend as "a reorientation of the basic principles of legitimation of Israel: a trend away from secular Zionism, especially its pioneering-socialist variety, towards a neo-traditionalist Jewish nationalism which, while it reinforces the primordial links among Jews both within Israel and the diaspora, de-emphasizes the modern, civil character of the state."[43]

The Impact of a Democratic Environment on the Religious Establishment

Balancing this dismal picture is the fact that the religious parties have been affected by the democratic structure of Israeli political life. The majority of Israeli Jews harbor a feeling of sympathy for the religious tradition. Indeed, when asked about their religious identification, between 35 to 40 percent, as I noted, prefer to define themselves as "traditional" rather than "secular." Many are distressed, though not to the point of doing much about it, by the ignorance of religious rites and customs that they find among their own children. But even this general mood is often accompanied by anticlerical feeling. Under the circumstances, religious leaders are reluctant to demand the total imposition of Jewish law, even if they might harbor the hope for such an eventuality. What they have called for, in more outspoken terms, is the maintenance of what is called a "Jewish street," i.e., the conducting of *public* life in accordance with Jewish law. In fact, they have been more anxious to maintain victories already secured than to expand the scope of religious law.

The key demands of the religious parties in the 1988 Knesset elections, were, in fact, defensive demands. In many instances, the religious parties simply sought to retain the fruits of legislative and administrative victories they had secured in the past. The most important of these included upholding municipal ordinances mandating that places of amusement be closed on the Sabbath. A 1988 court decision held such ordinances invalid because the Knesset had never explicitly empowered local councils to pass such laws. Closely related was the demand for the expansion of the authority of rabbinical courts in matters of personal status (especially marriage and divorce), an authority that has undergone some erosion by virtue of decisions by secular courts. However, for the *haredim,* the most important defensive demand was the continuing assurance that *yeshiva* students (which includes virtually all *haredi* youth) would continue to benefit from draft exemptions as long as they are enrolled in *yeshivot.*

A second type of demand included increased benefits, or what the religious parties called "equalizing" public funding for their educational and philanthropic institutions. The *haredi* parties also called for greater housing benefits for young couples, and one *haredi* party was especially interested in having its schools recognized on the one hand as an independent system eligible for public funding while continuing to enjoy administrative autonomy on the other hand. These demands, while marginally burdensome to the Israeli taxpayer, hardly presaged an onslaught on the democratic structure of the Israeli polity or, for that matter, on individual religious freedoms.

An effort to expand religious influence in Israeli society was reflected in two types of demands. One was of a generally symbolic nature. For example, amending the Law of Return to preclude recognition by the state of Israel of non-Orthodox conversions performed abroad (popularly known as the "Who is a Jew?" law) would have affected no more than a handful of Israelis but was of great symbolic importance because it would have established the authority of Orthodox rabbis in determining whom the state of Israel recognizes as a Jew. The second type of demand was in the area of culture and education. Proposals in this regard were rather vague. They included the demand that the government ought to introduce more Jewish (that is, religious) education. The National Religious Party also talked about the need for more national (that is, ultranationalist) education. There were also hints at the need to preserve Israeli culture against negative influences (an allusion to pornography and probably to antireligious and/or antinationalist expressions as well). Opposition to the construction of the Mormon University (in fact, a branch of Brigham Young University) on Mount Scopus in Jerusalem also falls into this category. These demands, it should be noted, were phrased very carefully, generally in a positive rather than a negative vein, under category headings that talked about the need for the unity of the Jewish people. All the demands were surrendered in the negotiations over the establishment of a coalition government following the election and have not been raised since then. Following the dissolution of the unity government between Likud and Labor in 1989, the religious parties held the balance of power. Most of them refused an alliance with the left despite evidence that the Labor Party would concede to virtually any demand they made. Their demands from the Likud were fairly modest in the realm of legislation: no amendment to the "Who is a Jew?" law, no banning of the Mormon University, no censorship of pornography, no changes in the secular school system. A law banning the sale of pork products passed its first readings, but as of the beginning of 1992 it had still not been enacted into final law and appeared unlikely to be enforced if passed. Other laws that were enacted included legislation restricting the procedures whereby women could request legal abortions. It is not clear whether that law has affected the number of legal abortions performed in Israel. A law permitting local municipal councils to determine whether places of entertainment may or may not open on the Sabbath could actually serve to extend rather than restrict the number of such places now open. By the beginning of 1992, over a year after the law was enacted, only one municipality adopted an ordinance in accordance with its provisions. The city of Netanya decided to allow movie theaters in one section of the city to remain open on the Sabbath and prohibited showings in another section. Most extraordinary is the fact that the compromise to close movie theaters in one section and allow them to remain open in another section received the blessing of outstanding *haredi* leaders.[44] Even this ordinance is being challenged in the courts. Finally, a law banning lascivious advertisements was enacted; its consequences are hardly felt.

How are we to account for the generally moderate nature of religious party demands? *Haredi* parties increasingly attract nonreligious voters. Shas's attraction to ethnic nonreligious voters is well known, but the fact that Agudat Israel has become an increasingly attractive option to voters of low socioeconomic status has received less attention.[45] The success both these parties had in attracting such voters and the fact that they became outlets for social protest among some nonreligious Jews may have led the parties themselves to temper the narrowly religious focus of their demands.

Moreover, more active participation in the democratic process may have sensitized party leaders to the fact that making excessive demands in the area of religious legislation threatens them with public backlash.

According to the leading *haredi* representative on the Netanya city council, *haredi* rabbis agreed to the compromise because the outcome of a battle to close all the theaters was unclear and the result might have been "opening all of the city on Sabbaths and holidays."[46] The religious parties are aware of their minority position in Israeli society and are anxious to avoid confrontations with the nonreligious majority at both the political and the social levels—confrontations they can only lose.

Finally, benefits from public funds that the leaders of the secular parties have showered on the *haredi* parties may be the most important factor in moderating demands for religious legislation. Large segments of *haredi* society benefit from these funds and are unwilling to jeopardize them by raising demands the majority will refuse to meet. It is especially dangerous for a religious party to raise demands of a religious nature that go unmet. They then stand charged with compromising religious principle for the material benefits derived from participation in a governing coalition. They may prefer, therefore, to moderate their demands to begin with.

Can Democracy Survive in a Jewish State?

The answer to the question "Can democracy survive in a Jewish state?" is that of course it can, assuming we are flexible about what we mean by democracy and what we mean by a Jewish state. If democracy means a state without moral purpose, one that functions simply to attend to the interests of its citizens as they define them, to provide the services its citizens demand without an effort to further some ultimate vision of the good society and the good citizen, then democracy is incompatible with a Jewish state, a Zionist state, or any other kind of ideological state. If by a Jewish state we mean a theocratic state, one ruled by a religious elite or even one in which the laws are subject to the approval of a religious elite, or a state in which the Torah is the ultimate constitutional authority, then democracy and a Jewish state are also incompatible.

But if by democracy we mean majority rule, individual liberties, and minority rights guaranteed by law within a set of parameters derived from a reasonable understanding of Judaism and the Jewish tradition, then democracy and a Jewish state are not incompatible, although reconciling the two may require painful compromises for those committed in good faith to only one or the other. Separation of religion and state is no solution, because a Jewish state is by definition one in which religion plays a public role and is accorded public status.

The resolution lies in a less than perfect accommodation. The route to that accommodation rests in part on efforts of all the parties to find such an accommodation and no less importantly on the definitions accorded to democracy and especially to Judaism. It should be clear that everyone has a stake in how everyone else defines these concepts.

Notes

This is a substantially revised version of an essay "Religion and Democracy in Israel," appearing in Ehud Sprinzak and Larry Diamond, eds., *Israeli Democracy Under Stress: Cultural and Institutional Perspectives* (Boulder: Lynne Rienner, 1993). Sections from that essay were originally published in "Jewish Fundamentalism and the Israeli Polity," in Martin E. Marty and R. Scott Appleby, eds., *Fundamentalisms and the State* (Chicago: University of Chicago Press, 1993).

1. There are a number of such studies, but the most detailed appear regularly in articles authored by Yochanan Peres and Ephraim Yaar in the periodical *Israeli Democracy*, published by the Israel Democracy Institute.

2. The most recent survey is Yochanan Peres, "Religiosity and Political Attitudes," *Demokratia* (Winter 1992), pp. 26–31, in Hebrew; published as a supplement to *Ma'ariv* by the Israel Democracy Institute.

3. Haim David Halevy, *Dat V'Medina* (Tel Aviv: Arzi Printers, 1969), pp. 49–60, in Hebrew.

4. See David Kretzmer, *The Legal Status of the Arabs in Israel* (Boulder: Westview Press, 1990).

5. This particular finding is described below.

6. The most comprehensive work on contemporary *haredi* society in Israel is Menachem Friedman, *The Haredi (Ultra-Orthodox) Society—Sources, Trends and Processes* (Jerusalem: The Jerusalem Institute for Israel Studies, 1991), in Hebrew.

7. Aryei Fishman, "'Torah and Labor': The Radicalization of Religion within a National Framework," *Studies in Zionism*, No. 6 (August 1982), pp. 255–271; "Tradition and Renewal in the Religious-Zionist Experience," in Abraham Rubinstein, ed., *In the Paths of Renewal: Studies in Religious Zionism* (Ramat-Gan: Bar-Ilan University Press, 1983), pp. 127–147, in Hebrew; and Fishman's introduction and the collection of documents in *Hapoel Hamizrachi: 1921–1935* (Tel Aviv: Tel Aviv University, 1979), in Hebrew.

8. Yosef Fund, *Agudat Israel Confronting Zionism and the State of Israel—Ideology and Policy*, doctoral thesis, Bar-Ilan University, 1989, in Hebrew.

9. See, for example, "Yated Hashavua," *Yated Ne'eman*, November 1, 1991, p. 9. The author amasses a variety of sources, including recent statements by *haredi* leaders, to prove his point.

10. Aharon Sorsky, "You Have Chosen Us From Amongst All the Nations," *Diglenu* (Sivan 1974), p. 6, in Hebrew.

11. It is worth noting that despite the adoption of increasingly hawkish positions by the National Religious Party, it is still failing to satisfy many of its ostensible constituents. A poll among twelfth-grade students in a prominent religious high school in Tel Aviv, one that attracts predominantly middle class non-Oriental students, showed that only 15 percent would support the NRP. Thirty-five percent said they supported parties to the right of the Likud and 25 percent said they supported the Likud. *Ha'aretz*, March 8, 1992, p. 4.

12. The late Rabbi Meir Kahane, though not a renowned rabbinical scholar, nevertheless anchored himself in rabbinic text and certainly represented one stream within the Jewish tradition. According to Kahane, "The liberal west speaks about

the rule of democracy, of the authority of the majority, while Judaism speaks of the Divine truth that is immutable and not subject to the ballot box or to majority error. The liberal west speaks about the absolute equality of all people while Judaism speaks of spiritual *status*, of the choseness of the Jew from above all other people, of the special and exclusive relationship between G-d and Israel." Meir Kahane, *Uncomfortable Questions For Comfortable Jews* (Secaucus, N.J.: Lyle Stuart, 1987), p. 159.

Other rabbis, less politically extreme than Kahane, express opinions that range along a wide spectrum. Zvi Weinman writes that even if all the Knesset members were religiously observant Jews, the democratic system would be tainted because it can in theory decide matters contrary to the Torah. See Weinman, "Religious Legislation—A Negative View, *T'khumin*, Vol. 7 (1986), p. 521, in Hebrew.

A more subtle objection to democracy is contained in the notion that belief in the equality of all men, along with the absence of monarchy and the deference paid to a king, undermines the notion of God as king. In the following quotation there is no direct objection to democracy, but the observation concerning the consequences of democracy implies a negative evaluation: "In contemporary democratic society there are no kings and there are no counts. The relationship toward the elected officials is only as 'the first among equals' and the sense of elevation and self abnegation is absent. . . . And since human beings are proud and filled with the sense of equality and their own self importance, it is difficult for them to accustom themselves to the idea that there is after all a King above them, for whom their importance is as nothing and whom they are obliged to serve as slaves. And in the absence of a wish to feel enslaved, humans are swept, in their desire for self justification, to a denial of the existence of the King." Rabbi Moshe Rubinstein, "Causes for the Undermining of Faith in the Modern World," *Diglenu* (Nisan 1981, p. 16, in Hebrew).

On the other hand, according to another distinguished rabbi, "the democratic approach, whose substance is consideration for the will of the people, their demands and their needs, is among the foundation stones of Israeli *halakha*." Nathan Zvi Friedman, "Notes on Democracy and *Halakha*," *T'khumin*, Vol. 4 (1984), p. 255, in Hebrew. Eliezer Schweid concludes his discussion of Rabbi Chaim Hirshenson's ideas about a democratic state according to *halakha* with the observation that "the political system that the Torah intended is democratic in its basis." Eliezer Schweid, *Democracy and Halakha: Reflections on the Teachings of Rabbi Chaim Hirshenson* (Jerusalem: Magnes Press, 1978), p. 75, in Hebrew. Finally, to Rabbi Sol Roth, "it is clear that the fundamental principles of democracy, namely, representative government and rule by majority, inhere in a Jewish tradition." *Halakha and Politics: The Jewish Idea of a State* (New York: Ktav, 1988), p. 141.

13. Eliezar Menachem Man Schach, *Sefer Mikhtavim V'Ma'amarim* (Bnei Brak, 1988), pp. 6–7. The citation is from a letter written in the summer of 1977 in the wake of the electoral victory of the Likud. The purpose of the letter is to assure Rav Schach's correspondent that nothing has changed.

14. This is the thrust of a very straightforward article by Rabbi Haim David Halevy, "Majority and Minority in a Democratic Jewish State," in *Yahadut V'Demokratia* (Jerusalem: Department of Torah Culture, Ministry of Education and Culture, 1989), pp. 29–40, in Hebrew.

15. N. J. Demerath III, "Religious Capital and Capital Religions: Cross-Cultural and Non-Legal Factors in the Separation of Church and State," *Daedalus*, No. 120 (Summer 1991), p. 38.

16. The argument that religion may exercise great political efficacy by influencing the religious culture without necessarily possessing great structural or insti-

tutional influence is developed at the theoretical level in N. J. Demerath III and Rhys H. Williams, "Religion and Power in the American Experience," in Thomas Robbins and Dick Anthony, eds., *In Gods We Trust: New Patterns of Religious Pluralism in America,* 2nd edition (New Brunswick, N.J.: Transaction Books, 1991), pp. 427–448.

17. Bellah distinguishes between liberal constitutionalism, built on the notion that "a good society can result from the actions of citizens motivated by self interest alone when those actions are organized through proper mechanisms," and a republic, which "has an ethical, educational, even spiritual role." Robert Bellah, "Religion and the Legitimation of the American Republic," in Robert Bellah and Philip Hammond, *Varieties of Civil Religion* (New York: Harper and Row, 1980), p. 9. The point and its application to Israeli society are discussed more fully in Charles S. Liebman and Eliezer Don-Yehiya, "The Dilemma of Reconciling Traditional Culture and Political Needs: Civil Religion In Israel," *Comparative Politics* (October 1983), pp. 53–66.

18. On the topic of the lack of respect for the authority of law in Israel, see Ehud Sprinzak, *Every Man Whatsoever Is Right in His Own Eyes: Illegalism in Israeli Society* (Tel Aviv: Sifriat Poalim, 1986), in Hebrew.

19. The effort, for example, to remove or at least censor the play *The Messiah* because of exclamations of heresy is described in Uri Huppert, *Back to the Ghetto: Zionism in Retreat* (Buffalo: Prometheus Books, 1988). Although the book is a polemic, extremely one-sided, and misleading in many respects, the treatment of this incident is, to the best of my knowledge, an accurate one. On the other hand, the minister of interior, Aryei Deri, a leader of Shas, the most ostensibly "primitive" of all religious parties, abolished the censorship of plays in an order issued in August 1989.

20. The speech by Rabbi Haim Druckman was reprinted in *Nekudah,* March 2, 1983, and is described in Charles S. Liebman, "Jewish Ultra-Nationalism in Israel: Converging Strands," in William Frankel, ed., *Survey of Jewish Affairs, 1985* (London: Associated University Press, 1985), pp. 28–50.

21. The statement was issued November 4, 1985, reprinted in *Davar,* November 22, 1985, and translated into English in International Center for Peace in the Middle East, *Israel Press Briefs* 40 (December 1985), p. 17. There are many similar statements.

22. In addition to Sprinzak, *Every Man Whatsoever,* see Boaz Evron, *A National Reckoning* (Tel Aviv: Dvir, 1988), pp. 392–395, in Hebrew.

23. Religion acts independently of education and ethnicity in the formation of Jewish attitudes toward Arabs. The religious Jew is more likely to harbor prejudice and less likely to respect the political rights of Arabs. Ephraim Yuchtman-Yaar's chapter, "The Israeli Public and the Intifada: Attitude Change or Entrenchment?" in Ehud Sprinzak and Larry Diamond, eds., *Israeli Democracy Under Stress: Cultural and Institutional Perspectives* (Boulder: Lynne Rienner Publishers, 1993), provides additional documentation to a phenomenon which is supported by every survey of Israeli public opinion with which I am familiar.

24. Elisha Aviner, "The Status of Ishmaelites in the State of Israel According to *Halakha,*" *T'khumin* 8 (1987), pp. 337–359, in Hebrew.

25. Overtones of this attitude in the political realm are to be found in an incident that occurred during the tense days preceding the January 15, 1991, deadline for an Iraqi withdrawal from Kuwait. The general secretary of the National Religious Party demanded that, in the event that Israel calls up reserves as a consequence of a U.S.-Iraqi conflict, activists from the Peace Now movement not be drafted. He indicated that the Palestinian population in the West Bank and Gaza

might respond to the war by heightening the intifada. In such a case the Israeli army would have to resort to harsh measures, and Peace Now activists, according to the general secretary, would be unwilling to participate in such measures and might create a false impression in the world media (*Ha'aretz,* January 11, 1991, p. 3.). Underlying this demand, in my opinion, was the belief (hope, fear) among some Israelis and Palestinians that a U.S.-Iraqi war would serve as the pretext for the Israeli army to undertake a massive expulsion of Palestinians.

26. Cited in Liebman, "Jewish Ultra-Nationalism in Israel," p. 46.

27. *Ibid.*

28. Hava Lazarus-Yafeh, "Political Traditions and Responses in Islam," in Israel Academy of Sciences and Humanities, *Totalitarian Democracy and After* (Jerusalem: Magnes Press, 1984), p. 131.

29. Aryei Rosen, "In the Fury of Days of Fire and Blood," *Diglenu* (Heshvan 1973), p. 4.

30. Simha Elberg, "The Yom Kippur War," *Diglenu* (Adar 1974), p. 3.

31. *Niv Hamoreh,* No. 46 (Kislev 1973), pp. 3, 17.

32. Peres, "Religiosity," p. 30.

33. Zvi Yehuda Kook, "The Sanctity of the Holy People in the Holy Land," in Yosef Tirosh, ed., *Religious Zionism and the State* (Jerusalem: World Zionist Organization, 1978), pp. 140–146, in Hebrew.

34. Schach, *Sefer Mikhtavim,* p. 7.

35. *Ibid.,* p. 18.

36. *Ibid.,* pp. 15–45.

37. Eliezer Don-Yehiya, "The Book and the Sword," in Martin Marty and Scott Appleby, eds., forthcoming.

38. Friedman, *The Haredi.*

39. Charles S. Liebman, "Attitudes Toward Jewish-Gentile Relations in the Jewish Tradition and Contemporary Israel," Occasional Papers, Kaplan Centre, University of Cape Town, 1984; and Charles S. Liebman and Steven M. Cohen, *Two Worlds of Judaism: The Jewish Experience in Israel and the United States* (New Haven: Yale University Press, 1990).

40. Yisrael Segal, a senior editor for Israeli television, was raised in a haredi home and left the world in which he was brought up for the secular world. He reports about the experience of a young haredi who came to him for help in escaping the haredi world in "An Adopted Son of God," *Politika,* No. 41 (November 1991), pp. 43–45, in Hebrew. The effort to escape failed, and Segal notes the basic problem: "Whereas in the first generation of those who abandoned religion . . . the Zionist vision awaited at the threshold, and whereas at the time of the [Zionist] pioneers who left the path of religion, a faith in marxism and a dream of paradise on earth [could provide a substitute] . . . in Israel of the 90's what awaits one who leaves [religion] is a world devoid of absolute values: a difficult daily struggle with a grey, complex, often tortured reality."

41. Baruch Kimmerling, "Between the Primordial and the Civil Definition of the Collective Identity: *Eretz Israel* or the State of Israel?" in Erik Cohen, Moshe Lissak, and Uri Almagor, eds., *Comparative Social Dynamics: Essays in Honor of S.N. Eisenstadt* (Boulder: Westview Press, 1985), pp. 262–283.

42. I explore this notion in greater detail in "Ritual and Ceremonial in the Reconstruction of American Judaism," in Ezra Mendelson, ed., *Studies in Contemporary Jewry VI* (New York: Oxford University Press, 1990), pp. 272–283.

43. Erik Cohen, "Citizenship, Nationality and Religion in Israel and Thailand," in Baruch Kimmerling, *The Israel State and Society* (Albay: SUNY, 1989), p. 70.

44. *Ha'aretz,* November 7, 1991, p. 5.

45. Eliezer Don-Yehiya, "Religion and Ethnicity in Israeli Politics: The Religious Parties and the Elections to the 12th Knesset," *Medina Mimshal Vihasim Benleumiyim,* No. 32 (Spring 1990), pp. 11–54, in Hebrew. Don-Yehiya develops this point in some detail. See also U. O. Schmelz, Sergio DellaPergola, and Uri Avner, "Ethnic Differences Among Israeli Jews: A New Look," in David Singer, ed., *American Jewish Year Book 90* (Philadelphia: Jewish Publication Society, 1990), pp. 3–206. The point is made in a passing reference on p. 101.

46. *Ibid.*

7

The Democratization of a Traditional Minority in an Ethnic Democracy: The Palestinians in Israel

Nadim Rouhana
As'ad Ghanem

This chapter uses the concepts and tools of political socialization to examine the ongoing process of democratization of a traditional community living in an ethnic democracy: the Palestinian community in Israel. Unlike other Third World people living in Western societies, the Palestinian citizens in Israel did not immigrate to the new system; rather, the system was imposed upon them. This distinction is important for three main reasons: *First,* immigrants who willingly choose to leave their homeland and move to a new country might do so because they believe in and wish to be governed by the values of the new system, including democratic values. The Palestinians in Israel made no such choice; in 1948, a new state was forced upon them in their homeland, involuntarily making them citizens of the newly established state of Israel. *Second,* unlike immigrants who leave their communities behind and assimilate into their new society, this community remained together in toto. Though truncated from the larger Palestinian society, the community maintained characteristics of a coherent group, living in more than a hundred Arab towns and villages (and in Arab quarters in cities with Jewish majorities). All the traditional links and structures—the extended family and the patriarchal relations therein, forms of subsistence, community networks, religious traditions—remained virtually intact in the new, Western-oriented, modern Israeli system. *Third,* the new system was established to serve the goals of a national group—the Jewish people—to the exclusion of this community, thereby introducing the potential for ongoing conflict.

Understanding the democratization process, the tensions emanating from the social differences between the new majority and the indigenous minority, and the contradictions of the political framework in which democratization is occurring will shed light on the paradoxes that characterize democratization in the Third World—the Arab world in particular—and in conflict situations. Such an understanding will also help us develop hypotheses on the implications of the democratization of this community for future Israeli-Palestinian interactions. The Arabs in Israel, who constitute a significant segment of the Palestinian people, are loyal to larger Palestinian goals and aspirations and at the same time are Israeli citizens with many democratic tools available to them. While they are keeping a low profile in the ongoing process of negotiations between Israelis and Palestinians, they might also have the potential to change the shape of future political arrangements between the two groups if they choose to articulate and express their political objectives democratically.

This chapter is divided into three main parts. In the first part we examine the factors that influence the democratization process of the Palestinians in Israel—both local and systemic factors, and the interaction between the two. In the second part, we examine paradoxes of the democratization process, some of which emanate from the contact between a Third World community and a modern setting, some from the conflict situation, and some from unique characteristics of the case under study. The third part examines the implications of a peaceful settlement for the democratization of other groups in the area and for future Israeli-Palestinian interaction.

Factors Influencing the Democratization Process

As indicated by Rothstein, democracy is a contested concept; there are "no perfect democracies in the developed or the developing world."[1] While certain ideal democratic characteristics have been posited in the context of the developed world,[2] the definition of such characteristics in a Third World context is more complex. In both cases, however, the discussion of democracy focuses on the systemic level of the type of government and political regime and its relevance to democratic transformation.

In this chapter, the emphasis is placed on individuals and their interaction with the governing system—how individuals are affected by the system and how the system is modified in response to individual change. Democratization, therefore, is defined here as the individual's embracement of democratic values based on rational/legal sources of the legitimization of authority, as defined by Weber,[3] and the endorsement of democratic procedures in the interaction between authorities and citizens based on that legitimacy. Democratization is thus part and parcel of the collective political socialization determined by the interaction between the polity and the system. Accordingly, democratization of the Arabs in Israel is determined by the interaction between Israeli policy toward the Arabs and internal developments within this community. The first part of this chapter will discuss in brief the Israeli policy toward the Arabs, internal developments within this group, and the interaction between the two.[4]

The Framework of Israel's Policy Toward its Arab Citizens

Israel's policy toward its Arab population was formatively shaped by three overriding ideas:[5] that Israel was established as the state of the Jewish people; that it is a Western democracy; and that Israel has special security concerns about its Arab population that will prevail as long as the conflict with all Arabs is not resolved.

According to the first idea, Israel was established to construct a Jewish society. Its responsibility expands beyond its borders to include the Jews all over the world; therefore, "in-gathering the exiles" is given the highest priority. The meaning of a Jewish state is reflected not only in the national, official, cultural, and political symbols and means of expression of the state but also in the perception that Israel as a homeland belongs exclusively to the Jewish people rather than to its Jewish and Arab population. Most national priorities, projects, and institutions are exclusively Jewish, arguably harnessing Arab resources to serve Jewish goals.

According to the second idea, Israel was established as a democratic state applying the principles of liberal democracy. Indeed, as far as its Jewish population is concerned, Israel enjoys democratic standards similar to those of well-established Western democracies. As far as the Arab population is concerned, the vast majority of Arabs were granted citizenship after the establishment of the state. The Arabs enjoy complete freedom of worship and formal equality before the law, with the significant exception of the law of return and nationality. To what extent Arabs in Israel actually enjoy the fruits of Israeli democracy is debatable. But most researchers agree that Arabs, while benefitting from democracy, don't enjoy full equality.[6]

Finally, Israel's national security needs markedly influenced its policy toward its Arab citizens. After all, Israel was imposed on its Arab citizens against their will and immediately became embroiled in a zero-sum conflict with the Palestinians and other Arab states. It was frequently argued that an Arab population feeling nationally and culturally connected to Palestinians or to the Arab nation could be a security burden. Israel, therefore, took steps to abort and prevent any security offenses that Arabs might want to commit individually or collectively.

This triangular foundation underlying Israel's policy toward its Arab population is fraught with contradictions. The second and third principles are in conflict: While tension between security requirements of democratic states and the practice of the rule of the law increases during wartime, Israel took this tension to an extreme.[7] The way Israel defined its security needs necessitated curtailing the Arabs' democratic rights. Pinkas,[8] for example, argues that security in Israel has institutional expressions far beyond any comparable democratic state: "The Israeli public and body politic comfortably assume that if certain democratic rights are suspended or civil rights infringed it is permissible if it is in the name of security."[9]

Similarly, the first and second principles are fundamentally at odds: A state that is defined as belonging only to one people when its population is composed of two cannot offer equal opportunity and an equal voice to all its citizens. But it was, in part, this tension between the three principles that enabled Israel to enact discriminatory policies toward the Arab population. These contradictions are becoming increasingly apparent to the Arab population.

The main contradiction in this triangle, between being a democracy and being a Jewish state, has profound implications not only for the democratization of the Arab population but also for the future of democracy in Israel.[10] It is not at all clear, for example, that most Israelis consider being a democracy of greater importance than being a Jewish state and that, if forced to choose, they would opt for democracy. Although Israeli society has thus far been spared the torment of such a choice simply because the conflict was successfully buried under the excuse of "security considerations," developments in the relationship between the two societies are bringing this conflict to the surface.

The triangular foundation described above does not imply that the three ideas contributed equally to Israel's policy toward its Arab citizens or to the democratization process. The principle that Israel is the state of the Jewish people is the driving force behind most of Israel's policies toward its Arab population. Although this principle's importance overrides the importance of democracy, the idea of a democratic state nonetheless has deeply affected the democratization process.

Internal Developments

Internal changes within the Arab community have provided the social and political grounds for democratization. Among the most important of these factors are demographic growth, the social transformation of the traditional Arab family, and political involvement in the Israeli system.

Demographic growth. The demographic growth of the Arab population and the physical expansion of Arab towns and villages is the most conspicuous change in the Arab community since the creation of Israel. By the end of 1990, the nation had 713,400 Arab citizens (not including the 146,300 Arab residents of Jerusalem who are not Israeli citizens and 15,300 Arabs in the Golan Heights).[11] This total represents 15.3 percent of Israel's citizenry. According to figures worked out from the most conservative estimates of the Israeli Bureau of Statistics, the Arab population will number 922,990 citizens in the year 2000 (East Jerusalem's Arab community will grow to 191,700). The percentage of Arabs would depend on the future of Jewish immigration.

The increase in the Arab population created large towns. Of the 112 towns in Israel with more than 5,000 residents, 41 are Arab; 15 of those have more than 10,000 residents. Although territorial expansion has failed to match population growth, it is unmistakably visible. Physical continuation between towns is developing, laying the groundwork for Arab metropolitan areas in parts of the Galilee and in the Triangle region. In addition, Arabs live in six mixed cities: Haifa, Ramle, Lydda, Jaffa, Acre, and Upper Nazareth, which was established as a Jewish city. Recently, Arabs have been moving into Carmiel, Rehovot, Hadera, Nahariya, Eilat, and Beersheba.[12]

The increase in their number and the expansion of their physical habitat have created self-confidence and a heightened sense of community among the Arabs. Demographic growth has also opened up the possibility of developing distinct and vibrant forms of cultural life, massive political organizations, and diverse economic enterprises. It made possible dynamic political activity through the establishment of independent political parties or participation within the Jewish parties, and the gradual development of groups with distinctly different political orientations. The interaction between these groups produced political pluralism within the community.

Social and Economic Changes

Social and economic changes in Arab society have expedited the process of political change and contributed to the democratization of this community. While Israeli authorities encouraged the existing traditional and segmented structure of the Arab population because it facilitated the state's strategy of control,[13] they often unwittingly accelerated democratization with some of their policies.

Massive expropriation of Arab land inadvertently created a background against which deep changes in the socioeconomic structure and social values could occur.[14] While Arab rural society was transformed in the early years of the state into an unskilled proletariat,[15] the last fifteen years have witnessed the emergence of a skilled, industrialized proletariat. Similarly, a burgeoning middle class made up of professionals, small contractors, and businessmen is also emerging, but there are no signs of a middle class based on the productive industrial sector because industrialization is virtually nonexistent in the Arab community.

To cope with the new reality, Arabs had to change their social values and attitudes toward modernity. One direct outcome of land expropriation was the drastic decrease in farming, which had been the main source of income for the vast majority of Palestinians. Land was farmed by whole families with the father, the sole landowner, as the central figure of authority. The loss of land meant young workers went to work outside the family property—in workshops, farms, and businesses outside their own villages, usually in Jewish urban areas. This type of employment gave them an unprecedented degree of economic independence.

Working in the cities has had other ramifications as well. While most workers commute on a daily basis, many stay in the Jewish settlements for a week or longer at a time. It is in the work setting that most social interaction between Arabs and Jews takes place. When they have pursued these relations beyond the workplace, Arabs have been exposed to an alternative set of social relations within the family (including child rearing), between families, and between the sexes. Working in modern surroundings also has necessitated changes in work-related values, such as respect for manual work, efficacy, and so forth. The relatively democratic interactions in the workplace and the way unions operate also changed Arab workers' values.[16]

The loss of land and the associated changes revolutionized relations within the family. The economic basis for patriarchal control over the children eroded, and the father's authority declined. Perhaps the greatest blow to parental authority in general came from a reversal of dependency: Parents became reliant on their children because the younger generations were more educated and consequently more versed in the political and social language of the new system. Within the context of this more egalitarian relationship, children began to oppose authority and take part in decisionmaking. That change became most apparent in their gaining the power to choose their own professions, marriage partners, living arrangements after marriage, child-rearing methods, and future plans.[17] The new patterns of interaction among family members were reflected in patterns of social relations in the society. Traditional respect for the elderly, a direct derivative of paternal authority, came under question, and extended-family affiliation lost its functional justification (though new functions might have arisen, as we will argue later). The weakening of extended-family ties eroded the status of the extended-family leadership, which epitomized traditional legitimacy.

A third factor that accelerated the democratization process was education. Israeli authorities took complete control over the Arab educational system. The curriculum was emptied of any content that referred to national consciousness, patriotism, national pride, historic roots, and the like.[18] Learning was completely overhauled to emphasize Zionist points of view, Hebrew literature, and some biblical studies. Perhaps most detrimental to the Arab educational system was the authorities' tight control of teacher appointments. Until the 1960s many teachers were appointed not on merit but out of "security considerations," with security broadly defined to include political activity, party affiliation, and national consciousness. This practice was meticulously followed in elementary schools, which were and still are under the complete command of the Ministry of Education and Culture. Since jobs for educated Arabs were scarce, teacher appointments became a key means of control and a form of reward for cooperating with family chiefs, traditional leaders, and sometimes directly with the authorities. Until now, teachers colleges have to clear Arab applicants with security agencies before accepting them.

In addition to damaging education itself, this process led to a free-fall in the traditional prestige that teachers enjoyed, disrespect for the curriculum, and a deep mistrust in a system that required teaching the Bible but not the Muslim Quran, Zionist nationalism but not Palestinian nationalism, and nationalistic Hebrew literature but not Palestinian literature. The whole educational message was received with suspicion and sarcasm, which ultimately resulted in its psychological rejection. The end result was the delegitimization of the educational system as a source of political socialization. Indeed, Arab youth looked for their political education in outside agencies such as political parties, media, peer groups, unofficial activities, and so on.[19] The students often became the political educators of their teachers.

It was not until the mid-1970s that the grip of the Ministry of Education was loosened because of the increase in the number of Arab towns whose local governments controlled hiring and firing in high schools. Around the same time, sweeping change in local governments began. Governments associated with the governing Labor Party were replaced by governments under the control of the Democratic Front for Peace and Equality (centered around the Israeli Communist Party) or independent mayors. High schools became staffed with university graduates who brought to the system the new methods, values, and democratic practices they had learned in the Israeli university system. The traditional student-teacher relationship based on awe, obedience, and unquestioning acceptance was gradually giving way to more democratic relations, intellectual openness, and the right to question authority.

Educational developments facilitated the process of social and political democratization. Indeed, educational changes in the Arab community over the last four decades are most visible. For example, in the 1990–1991 academic year,[20] there were 235,557 Arab pupils in the Israeli educational system.[21] Of those, 40,271 were in secondary schools (compared to a few dozen in 1948); this figure had quintupled in twenty years.[22] Between 1948 and 1971, the total number of Arab university graduates (i.e., those who hold a B.A. degree or higher) was estimated to be 600. A survey found that a total of 328 Arabs had graduated from Israeli universities during the whole period between 1961 and 1971. In 1961 there were six graduates; in 1971 there were 82 graduates.[23] Now the number is estimated to be more than 1,000 per year. According to the latest figures,[24] non-Jewish students (mainly Arabs) constituted 6.7 percent of the Israeli undergraduate body (or

3,146 students) in the 1989–1990 academic year, 3.5 percent of M.A. students (563 students), and 3.5 percent of Ph.D. candidates (137 candidates). The number of Arabs with academic degrees is estimated to be 15,100, which represents 3 percent of Arabs aged fifteen and over. Those with thirteen to fifteen years of education number 30,700, constituting 6.1 percent of the same population group.[25]

A fourth factor that expedited democratization was the entry of women into the labor force. An economic crisis in the late 1970s and early 1980s and the increase in the standard of living made Arab society more accepting of women's entry into the labor market. The changing patterns of interaction within the nuclear family, described above, facilitated this acceptance. Though incremental, change occurred rapidly. By now the majority accepts women's work as natural. Many Arab women work in local branches of Israeli textile companies, which opened factories in Arab villages to hire women who preferred not to leave the village. Although accused of exploiting women as cheap laborers, they nonetheless have given many women the economic bases for increased independence and control over their own lives and reduced their subjection to the authority and control of the family, particularly their father and brothers.

The rise in educational levels has included Arab women, too. Girls comprise 48.3 percent of Arab high school students and 47.3 percent of intermediate school students.[26] There has been a dramatic increase in the number of women with university and professional degrees: lawyers, physicians, engineers, and others. Some are also in journalism, sports, and theater. Some university graduates tried to popularize and adapt principles of women's liberation to Arab culture. Lately, Arab women have established a number of independent organizations to defend the status of women and their rights.[27] The Arab-dominated political parties also have active women's organizations.

Independence from the family, once unthinkable for women, is now gaining acceptance. Some women leave home to live in the mixed cities for work or study. There they can liberate themselves from family limits and the influence of brothers, fathers, and other men in the family. Once they marry, the pattern of relations within their own families—husband and wife, children and parents, etc.—approximates a Western one more than it does a traditional Arab one.

These new lifestyles do not mean that all Arab women are changing their values. Because of the rapid change that occurred in a limited period, Arab society has a full spectrum of women, from the most traditional to the most liberated. Yet the overall change in women's status is unmistakable. It has added yet another dimension to the deepening evolution in social values and to the acceptance of democratic principles of interaction within the family.

In sum, Israeli policies and the ensuing changes in Arab society destabilized agencies that are essential for inculcating authoritarian and traditional attitudes: the family and the schools. The family authority structure was severely disrupted as fathers lost their means of control over their children—land ownership and cultivation. And, paradoxically, the authorities' tight control over the educational system weakened the status of the authority figures within it and increased students' relative power.

Political Experience and Involvement in the Israeli System

The factor that had the greatest influence on the process of democratization is Arab involvement in the Israeli political system. Unlike Palestinians in the West Bank and Gaza, who have watched Israeli democracy from afar while suffering the brunt of Israeli military occupation, the Palestinians in Israel have learned about Israeli democracy through observation and participation. As mentioned earlier, Israeli democracy is constrained for Arab citizens by other state considerations, yet there is no doubt that participation in a democratic system has gone a long way toward instilling democratic values and introducing democratic practices. The Israeli system has influenced the Arabs' democratization in the following ways.

Close observation. Dependency upon the system has made most of the new generation bilingual and bicultural. Hebrew is mandatory in Arab schools from the second grade. Having lost trust in the state-run Arabic media, Arabs turned to the Hebrew media as a source of news.[28] Many educated Arabs became comfortable with both Arab and Jewish cultural works.

Politicization, the ongoing Palestinian-Israeli conflict, and near-total dependency has made many Arabs highly aware of the Israeli political system, the way it works, its values, the ideologies of the various parties, and the function of various institutions such as the Supreme Court and the state comptroller. Generally speaking, Arabs are versed in Israeli politics; educated Arabs might be more aware than their Jewish counterparts of the ideological positions of various parties and of Israeli policy vis-à-vis the Arab minority or the Palestinians.

Participation in parliamentary elections. Arabs have voted in every Israeli parliamentary election. In a state that relies on the parliamentary system and in which the parliament places checks and balances on the executive branch, controlled groups or protest groups often choose to affect policy in the Knesset. Participating in elections and winning a number of representatives might give the group influence over allocation of resources and distribution of power. In Israel, the government is not only subordinated to the checks and balances of the Knesset but also receives its confirmation by a simple majority of 61 Knesset members. In a multiparty system in which no one party controls the majority, a coalition between the two major parties or between one of the two major parties and smaller parties is required to achieve parliamentary majority. In exchange for coalitional support, a party might grant government participation, but it might also pay back the support by other means, such as increasing budgets, improving services, and/or granting consultation in decisionmaking. While the extent to which Arabs can influence the system is debatable, surveys show that most Arabs believe it is possible to improve their situation through parliamentary politics; only a small minority does not share this view.[29]

Indeed, from the first to the sixth Knesset, despite a slight decrease in the percentage of Arab voters, their percentage exceeded the percentage of Jewish voters. For the second Knesset (1951) the percentage of Arab valid votes (to total of potential Arab votes) reached 86 percent, and for the third (in 1955) it peaked at 90 percent.[30] These numbers do not necessarily demonstrate belief in the utility of parliamentary elections or commitment to the democratic process; at that time, it was more a reflection of the mechanism of external state control, or of internal *hamula* (extended-family) control. Since the third Knesset elections in 1955, the percentage of valid votes has dropped, reaching 68 percent, 72 percent, and 70 percent in the last three Knesset elections. During this period, the pattern of voting changed and support began shifting from Zionist parties and their Arab surrogates to Arab-dominated parties.[31] By 1988 Arab-dominated parties received about 60 percent of the Arab vote. The experience of organizing parties, campaigning for them, voting for them, and running them has added tremendously to Arab democratization.

Of the many groups, parties, and organizations that are active in the Arab sector, all but Abna' al-Balad and a branch of the Islamic movement want to be part of parliamentary elections. Abna' al-Balad (active in some villages in Galilee and the Triangle and among university students) rejects participation in elections and parliamentary politics on principle. The movement disavows the present regional arrangement and calls for the establishment of a secular state in all of historic Palestine. It does not participate in Israeli parliamentary politics because, in its view, participation represents recognition and acceptance of the present arrangement, which it does not wish to grant. A branch of the Islamic movement, particularly that under the influence of Sheikh Kamel Khatib of Kofr Kanna, also adheres to nonparticipation.[32]

Organizing and leading opposition parties. In opposition parties, Arabs have learned about the democratic system's advantages and limitations through practice. The contribution of this experience to democratization might be even greater than that of involvement within the governing parties. In this regard, the influence of the Israeli Communist Party should be examined, because until the early 1980s it was the dominant force in Arab political life. Both its ideology and its methods affected the democratization process, albeit in contradictory directions.

On the one hand, the party encouraged and enhanced democratic practice vis-à-vis the authorities. The party perceived itself as a genuine part of the Israeli system. Its criticisms of Israeli policies were and are rooted in genuine, even patriotic, concerns for Israel and its future in the region and deep concern for the Arab population and the Palestinian people. The Communist Party used the democratic means provided by the system without hesitation. The protests the party organized and led, the new modes of political expression it introduced (such as the harsh criticism of authority), and its challenge to the system through parliamentary and extraparliamentary activities, all carried out meticulously within the framework of Israeli law, left deep impressions on the Arab population. On the social level, the party relentlessly attacked traditional sources of loyalty, such as family and religious affiliation, and encouraged new sources, such as national affiliation, political and class consciousness, and ideological commitment. It also advocated equal rights for women, educated against anti-Semitism, and promoted genuine forms of Arab-Jewish relations in the country within its own ranks. In the absence of a trustworthy and capable agent of political socialization, the party provided the main source of ideological, political, and social education for many Arabs, particularly the younger generations. All of this activity contributed to the political and social democratization of the Arab population vis-à-vis the system and the authorities.

On the other hand, the party might have hindered the internal democratization of the Arab community insofar as freedom of expression and opinion went. For a long time, until 1989, the party employed the equivalent of "intellectual terror" in its debates when it encountered any political views that did not fit the party line. It considered its views the absolute balance, the outcome of a *chef d'oeuvre,* and behaved as if any deviation in either direction would harm the collective interests of the community and the larger national interests.

The Communist Party came very close to claiming sole representation of the Arabs in Israel, particularly after the establishment of the Democratic Front for Peace and Equality in 1977. It tried to prevent the rise of other forces that emerged to claim representation, using severe criticism, ridicule, and even public skepticism of these forces' national loyalties and political motives. But with the emergence of new political forces, the internal weakening of the party, and the collapse of the Soviet bloc, the party changed course and gave up its "soleness" of representation. It accepted the new Arab parties as legitimate and began calling for mutual respect, cooperation, and coordination.

The party's "intellectual terror" has been abruptly replaced by an approach toward the other parties that is laying the foundation for a national democratic politics in which the multiparty system can genuinely represent the different orientations of the Arab public. In the 1989 Histadrut elections, the party coalesced with the other two Arab-dominated parties (the Progressive List for Peace and the Arab Democratic Party) to run in one unified list. This strategy was drastically different from the 1988 national elections, in which the party harshly attacked the two parties' legitimacy and refused even to negotiate an agreement with either of them on excess votes,[33] wasting thousands of votes given to all three parties.[34]

Organizing legal extraparliamentary protest. Given the rise in Arab demands and the failure of parliamentary methods to bring about significant achievements, extraparliamentary protest has been steadily increasing. It is now a popular form of protest that Arabs use regularly. Activities include general and local strikes, demonstrations, distribution of leaflets, and writing in Hebrew newspapers and magazines to influence the Jewish majority and the decisionmakers. Surveys show that Arabs in Israel are highly committed to this method in order to enhance their status and achieve their goals.[35] Unlike parliamentary struggle, extraparliamentary tactics are accepted by all political parties and factions and supported by political and social organizations.

Arab citizens also use this method to protest Israeli policies toward Palestinians in the Occupied Territories. During the uprising, the number of organized protests against Israeli policies in the territories increased sharply.[36] This rise demonstrates the Arabs' deeper understanding of the democratic system and increased ability to maneuver within it.

The process of decisionmaking about using extraparliamentary protest provides the strongest indicator of the depth of the democratization process among the Arab political elite. Decisions about national strikes and regional demonstrations are discussed in the Monitoring Committee on the Affairs of Arab Citizens (FCAAC, or *Lajnat Mutaba'at Shu'un Al Muwatineen Al Arab*) which is composed of Arab mayors, Arab Knesset members (including those with Zionist parties), representatives of political movements and social organizations, and representatives of student unions. Decisions are passed by simple majority. Without exception, the minority has abided by majority rule despite frequent deep disagreements with these decisions.

Paradoxes of Democratization

Underlying the democratization of the Arab society in Israel, as noted, is the gradual transformation of patterns of interaction with authority from traditional bases to legal/rational bases, as broadly defined by Weber.[37] When examining this transformation, we uncover a number of paradoxes that reflect the contradictions of Israeli policies and the complexities of the rapid internal changes in this community. Five main paradoxes are described below:

1. *Increasingly active political participation in the national system versus constantly limited civic competence.* Civic competence is used to define the extent of an individual's or group's political influence over governmental decisions, or the degree to which government officials act to benefit a group or an individual because the officials believe they will risk some deprivation if they do not act.[38] The limited civic competence of the Arab minority as a whole has not increased with their participation in national elections.

While the percentage of Arabs who participate in national elections has not changed drastically since the first Knesset elections, the nature of the process has been transformed. In the first few elections, Arab slates that claimed to be independent but were actually initiated, organized, and completely controlled by Zionist parties competed for the Arab vote.[39] These slates, represented by co-opted leaders and based on extended family and religious affiliation, addressed in the Arab voter parochial loyalties of religion and extended family and were assisted by the Israeli system of control. But these slates gradually lost their base of support and were replaced by three Arab-dominated parties that responded to the increase in political and national consciousness and the rise in demands for equal distribution of resources. Yet this change did not by itself bring about any improvement in the Arabs' condition. The parties have very limited influence on governmental decisions regarding the Arab minority and on the decisionmaking process in general. Despite their number (six Arab and Jewish Knesset members in the three Arab-dominated parties), their coalitional weight, and therefore potential influence, is limited—because Arab parties are viewed by Zionist parties as illegitimate partners in any governmental coalition.

Whatever gains the Arabs achieved in promoting their interests as a national community were mainly secured through extraparliamentary protest. In 1976, after a national strike and many demonstrations, they were able to achieve a government freeze on most land expropriations. Likewise, they extracted promises from government officials to increase the budgets of their local governments only after mayors held a number of sit-in strikes in front of the prime minister's office. (Unlike national interests, local interests of individual towns were also served by the particular relationship of the local town government with the authorities).

2. *Increasing support for achieving equality integratively within the state as an essential element of consensus versus increase in differential national organizations.* Calling for full equality within the state had become an element of the national Arab consensus by the mid-1980s. This demand has become a cornerstone in their collective bargaining with the

state to improve their status. It is gaining more importance and vigor in light of regional developments. Of major importance were the Palestinian uprising in the Occupied Territories and the ensuing two-state solution espoused by the Palestine National Council (PNC) in 1988. After these developments, it became clear to the Arab citizens of Israel that if a negotiated settlement were achieved, their final collective political future would be within the state of Israel.

But hand in hand with the growing insistence on full equality within the system, Arabs were establishing national organizations all over the country. The effort was pioneered by student associations in the early 1970s and followed by many others: high school students, heads of local governments, academics, the Committee for the Defense of Land, physicians, social workers, writers, artists, etc. This effort culminated in the aborted effort to hold "the congress of Arab masses" in 1980, which was to have representatives of the groups mentioned above and include the whole political spectrum. The congress was outlawed by an order from the defense minister, Menachem Begin.[40] In 1982 the FCAAC was established. Some observers consider this effort to represent the preparation of national infrastructure prior to demanding autonomy.

While we doubt that the effort was directly motivated by such considerations, it is not unlikely that if they are frustrated by the impossibility of achieving equality within the Israeli system, Arabs will consider alternative arrangements with Israel, including autonomy. Indeed, when two professors in a West Bank university advocated institutional autonomy in a local paper,[41] their article stirred a lot of debate and gained substantial attention in the community.

3. *Despite the recent increase in "security violations," a consensus was solidified that political struggle should be conducted solely within the framework of Israeli law.* Since the Arabs organized a national strike on December 21, 1987, to protest Israeli policies toward the uprising, the Israeli media and security establishment have given increasing attention to a rise in the number of "security violations" by Arab citizens.[42] Although there was an increase in acts of solidarity with the uprising, the extent of increase in security violations depends on how one defines "security violation [e.g., slogans in support of the uprising, raising a Palestinian flag, etc.]." The reaction of the Israeli public, media, and establishment was to express profound concern about any attempt by Arabs to act outside the laws of the country. In reaction, the whole Arab political spectrum asserted a collective desire to keep acts of protest within the framework of Israeli law.[43] So despite the increase of extraparliamentry protest since the beginning of the uprising, there was a meticulous effort exerted by Arab leadership to keep all acts legal and all expressions within the law. This attitude was shown to have support by consensus in in-depth interviews we conducted with representatives of all political groups in the Arab community.[44]

This respect for legal boundaries is also supported by the Arab public, as demonstrated in attitude surveys.[45]

4. *Despite the impossibility of electing a national leadership, the FCAAC is a de facto leadership for the Arabs in Israel.* It is inconceivable at the present time that the Arabs in Israel would be allowed to elect national leaders. They have not called for such elections because of the profound political implications of such a move. Instead, they have established their own parties to run in Israeli national elections and have elected their own local governments. Yet it seems that de facto national leadership has emerged without national elections in the form of the FCAAC.

The center of the FCAAC is a smaller committee of the Arab mayors. However, members of the FCAAC are locally elected (except for the Knesset members, who are nationally elected). As local elections are influenced by parochial loyalties, this national leadership does not necessarily represent the real aspirations and interests of the Arabs in Israel as a whole. Furthermore, even the Arab Knesset members are elected as representatives to the Israeli legislature, not as national leaders. Yet the FCAAC—which represents all the political groups in the community including Abna' al-Balad, the Islamic movement, and Arab members of Zionist parties—is considered by many in the Arab public and the establishment to be the de facto Arab national leadership.

5. *The increasing appeal to broader loyalties for national elections (national, political, ideological, identity) versus almost stable recourse to traditional loyalties in local elections.* The changes in the social and economic structure and values of the community made it impossible for the parochial loyalties of extended-family affiliation, religious belief, and region of residence to attract large numbers of Arab voters. By 1984 the Arab slates associated with Zionist parties disappeared from the political map, making way for parties that call upon broader loyalties such as political goals, national identity, and collective concerns. Even the Arab Knesset members in Zionist parties adhere to the political consensus that has been shaped by these new parties and address their constituencies using the elements of the consensus.

This transformation in the nature of participation in national elections does not mean, however, that parochial loyalties have disappeared. All of them are at work to some extent, at least in mobilizing some constituencies and motivating some voters. Even some of those who voted for the Communist Party did so at times out of parochial loyalty. Yet it is reasonably safe to state that whatever parochial loyalties persist among Arab voters, it would be impossible to successfully mobilize a national party based on any or all of them.[46] However, loyalty to the extended family might still be the main mobilizer in local elections, and religious affiliation might still play a significant role in religiously mixed towns.

To explore the extent of importance of the *hamula*-based vote in local elections, we examined the three most recent local elections (in 1978, 1983, and 1989) in all fifty-three Arab cities and towns that have local governments. We focused on the effect of *hamula* and religious affiliation on the election of municipal council members and mayors, who since 1978 have been directly elected by voters. The data were collected from the publications of the National Supervisor on Elections in the Department of the Interior. When data were missing, we conducted personal interviews with mayors and secretaries of local councils.

Our findings show that in all three elections in all fifty-three localities, there were only two cases in which a national political party won the office of the mayor independently of *hamula* or religious group support: Nazareth, where the Democratic Front for Peace and Equality (centered around the Israeli Communist Party) has won all elections since 1975, and Kofr Yassif, where the same party has won all elections since 1978. In either case, no *hamula* or religious politics were involved in the election process. In the remaining fifty-one localities, however, not one mayor was elected solely on an ideological or partisan basis. Winning was determined by *hamula* or religious group support, though in many cases the mayor was supported both by the *hamula* and by a party. All mayors in these cases were members of the largest *hamula* or religious group (or both) or affiliated with a coalition of *hamulas* in the town. The extent of *hamula* support varied from place to place. In some cases, for example, *hamula* lists existed on their own, while in other places they were supported by national political parties. Except for Abna' al-Balad and the Islamic movement in some cases, all political factions supported *hamula*-based elections.

Not only did mayors rely on *hamula* support, they also occasionally used various means that Zionist parties had used in the past, such as personal benefits, co-optation, and sometimes even bribes, to gain the support of family chiefs.

Hamula-based voting might be becoming even stronger instead of weaker. One indication is the difference in voting percentages for the Knesset and for local governments. For the last three Knesset elections (1981, 1984, and 1988), the percentages of Arab valid votes were 68 percent, 72 percent, and 70 percent, respectively. But for the local elections they were 87.9 percent, 88.9 percent, and 90.4 percent, respectively, consistently higher than for the Knesset elections and showing a slight increase. So it seems that *hamula*-based voting is resisting change in local elections but not in the Knesset elections. This differential change requires some explanation.

While it might be the case that many voters believe in family loyalty and that their support for a *hamula*-based list emanates from that loyalty, many others use family as a political tool. For example, an increasing number of young educated mayors who are familiar with democratic values and practices from their involvement in national politics are nonetheless elected to head local governments by *hamula*-based lists. They seem to be using the *hamula* support as a political tool to attain broader goals. *Hamula* support in local elections was also legitimized by the Democratic Front for Peace and Equality, which realized that to win some of the local elections it had to cooperate with *hamula* leaders. For a long time it advocated anti-*hamula* democratic education, as well as the slow but thorough process of change that such education would have entailed. But when this change came too slowly, the desire to control the local authorities overcame the trend against *hamula* policies.

Local elections themselves might have reinforced the *hamula*-based voting trend. After all, the local town councils control many resources and benefits that matter to town residents, including municipal hirings, zoning of development areas, budgets, and the education department. *Hamula* support for a candidate will affect distribution of jobs and local development to *hamula* members. A *hamula*, for example, can pressure the mayor to appoint a teacher, principal, town supervisor, etc., in exchange for votes. The teacher himself becomes tied to the family in return for its commitment and help. This way, the local government and the resources it controls became a tool in the hands of family chiefs to control family members, especially some of the young and educated who needed employment. *Hamula* voting is thus re-entrenched.

Although it would seem important for the extended family to vote only for family-based or family-supported lists in the local elections, such is not necessarily the case in Knesset elections. It is often in the family's interest to diversify its votes in national elections to increase its negotiating power vis-à-vis its main party of support. Although this diversification might begin as *hamula* interest-based behavior, over time it can change the basis for voting decisions by introducing diversity of views, legitimizing voting for different parties, and enriching political discussion.

For whatever reasons, it seems that among Arabs the political culture of local elections is distinctly different from the political culture of national elections. On the surface local Arab politics may appear to be conducted democratically, but the underlying values and means of gaining support are actually impeding democratization.

We conclude that while Arab society in Israel is not completely democratized, it is undergoing a rapid and advanced process of democratization. As in any process of collective social change, it is not unusual for conflicting values and practices to coexist. After all, sociopolitical change does not imply the instant replacement of one value system by another, but rather the gradual, sometimes haphazard introduction of new elements, their practice and internalization.

Facilitating this process of change is the fact that democratization at the national systemic level serves Arab national interests. Compared to the

Jewish majority, Arabs as a group suffer from structural discrimination and enjoy few of the country's resources and little state power. It is thus in their interest to have a completely democratic and egalitarian system. Democratic arguments therefore serve the instrumental needs of the Arab minority. Once values are advocated—even if only superficially or out of pragmatic considerations—the way to their internalization opens, and people gradually make democratic values an integral part of their value system. The instrumental worth of the democratic value becomes secondary to its worth as a prized expression of belief and ideology.

While our study of local elections raises profound questions about the extent of democratization among Arabs in Israel, their political behavior on the national level shows an advanced stage of democratization. They practice democratic partisanship[47] as expressed by the acceptance of the rules, laws, and customs of political competition, and they express their political feelings openly vis-à-vis other groups and parties in their community. Political pluralism is reflected in the legitimacy granted to the representation of various parties—Rakah, the Progressive List for Peace (PLP), the Democratic Arab Party (DAP), and sometimes even to some Zionist parties. As mentioned earlier, this pluralism was recently apparent in the political cooperation between the PLP, Rakah, and the DAP, which joined forces in one unified list in a 1989 Histadrut election, as mentioned above.

Democratization and Peaceful Settlement of the Palestinian-Israeli Conflict

Democratization and shared democratic values are not panaceas for resolving conflicts. When conflicting groups share the values of democracy, they are perhaps more likely to peacefully resolve disputes and avoid the eruption of violence. But there are no indications that this shared value can override the national, religious, and ethnic identities that might still be in conflict between two democratic collectives. In some cases, democratic expressions can increase conflict rather than decrease it, at least in the short run. Notice, for example, how democratization in Jordan gave voice to public opposition to the US intervention in the Gulf and made conflict between Israel and Jordan more likely, while the nondemocratic regime in Syria suppressed public feelings and reduced the likelihood of open conflict with Israel.

In our case, some observations are in order about the implications of democratization for a peaceful settlement of the Israeli-Palestinian conflict and the likely effect of a peaceful settlement on the process itself:

1. *It is highly likely that Arabs in Israel will continue to use only democratic and legal means to resolve their conflict with the state and to change*

their status within it. It is extremely unlikely that Arabs will resort to violence either to promote their own equality or to support Palestinians in the Occupied Territories. This preference is becoming even clearer after five years of the uprising in the Occupied Territories. A distinction should be made between *support for* the uprising, which was and is taking place, and *participation in* the uprising, which is unlikely.[48]

This distinction by itself is very important because the issues of dispute between Arab citizens and the state are vital and sometimes emotional for both groups. The extent of democratization that Arabs achieved has defused the potential for violence. Arabs' consensus on struggle within the law lessens the likelihood of violence on the Arab side, and the cooperation of some police departments with Arab leaders before Land Day demonstrations and strikes in light of the experience of 1976[49] decreases the likelihood of violence on the authorities' side.

2. *The combustive issue of the Arabs' status in a future settlement of the conflict will remain suppressed for the time being.* Although some Arab political factions think now is the time to raise it, the majority still do not. The democratic political pluralism that Arabs have achieved excludes the possibility of its one faction's imposing view on the whole public. In effect, it guarantees that unless and until a majority of Arabs agree that the issue should be openly raised, it will remain in the background. Raising the issue at this time would ostensibly complicate the peace process; by not raising it, the Arabs are in fact contributing to the likelihood of that process's success.

3. *Arabs will decide democratically about the form of their relationship with Israel and a Palestinian state.* Democratic pluralism allows for and requires public debate on any changes in the status quo. If the question of autonomy, for example, is to be raised as a possible political arrangement, it will go through intensive democratic examination by the various parties and factions. Once a political idea has gained support, it is unlikely to lose it, given the process by which support is gained in this political atmosphere. Hence, the three elements of consensus—equality for the Arabs in Israel, statehood for Palestinians in the Occupied Territories, and struggle within the framework of Israeli law—are of cardinal importance to the Arab minority as a whole.

4. *A peaceful settlement of the Israeli-Palestinian conflict might also influence the democratization process.* Paradoxically, we believe, a settlement might strain Israel's democratic nature, at least in the short run. A settlement will inevitably prompt the state and large segments of the Jewish public to emphasize the Jewish nature of Israel and the fact that it is the exclusive possession of the Jewish people. At this level of political consciousness, Arabs will point out that such an attitude contradicts democratic values and equality. While democracy is highly valued by many Jewish Israeli citizens, the Jewishness of the state, particularly after painful with-

drawals from the Occupied Territories, might be more precious, and securing it could lead to suppression of Arab demands for openness, equality, democratization, and inclusion. This might be one of the serious setbacks of Israeli democracy within the 1967 borders.

5. *Democratic interactions between Israel and its Arab citizens will probably have a positive impact on Israeli-Palestinian interaction.* But it is only after Israel resolves the conflict between being a state of the Jewish people and being a democracy that the Arabs will be able to become genuine partners with the state. Indeed, the old adage that Arabs could be a bridge for genuine peace and reconciliation between Israel and the Palestinians requires that both sides follow democratic rules.

6. *The possible setback of democracy after a settlement with the Palestinian people will bring about strategic alliances between some Israeli political forces and some Arab political groups or parties.* Although some cooperation was once imposed by the Israeli Communist Party under strict conditions, the road will become more open for broader cooperation across national lines in conditions of peace. The submergence of security concerns should enable Israel to serve as a democracy for all its citizens. Cooperation and future strategic alliances between Arab and Jewish citizens based on voluntary democratic bases can open the road for the development of new shared identities and values that supersede separate national identities if these two groups are to coexist equally in the same land.

Notes

1. See Robert Rothstein, Chapter 2 in this volume.
2. See Rothstein's review, Chapter 2 in this volume.
3. M. Weber, "The Three Types of Legitimate Rule," in A. Etzioni, ed., *A Sociological Reader on Complex Organizations,* 2nd edition (New York: Holt, 1969), pp. 6–15. According to Weber, legitimacy of authority rests on enactment. He argues that "the basic idea is that laws can be enacted and changed at pleasure by formally correct procedures."
4. For a more detailed discussion, see N. Rouhana, "The Political Transformation of the Palestinians in Israel: From Acquiescence to Challenge," *Journal of Palestine Studies,* Vol. 18, No. 3 (1989), pp. 38–59.
5. For more details on the conceptual framework for analyzing Israel's policy toward its Arab population, see Rouhana, "Political Transformation," pp. 39–40.
6. For example, see I. Lustick, *Arabs in the Jewish State* (Austin: University of Texas Press, 1980), Chapter 5; D. Kietzmer, *The Legal Status of the Arab in Israel* (Boulder: Westview Press, 1990), Chapter 6; and Elia Zureik, *The Palestinians in Israel* (London: Routledge & Kegan Paul, 1979).
7. See Alon Pinkas, "Garrison Democracy," Chapter 4 in this volume.
8. *Ibid.*
9. *Ibid.*
10. We disagree with Pinkas, who argues that the tension between the two is increasing in the Occupied Territories and decreasing in Israel proper. We think the

tension is also increasing in Israel as the Arab population becomes more aware of the inherent contradictions described above. See Rouhana, "Political Transformation," for elaboration on the growing awareness of this contradiction.

11. Figures in this section are quoted or worked out from *The Statistical Abstract of Israel* (Jerusalem: Central Bureau of Statistics, 1991). In this source, the total figure of Arabs in Israel includes the Arab residents of East Jerusalem; the number of Arabs in Jerusalem should be subtracted from the CBS figure in order to arrive at the number of Arab citizens of Israel within the 1967 borders. (Some Arabs in Jerusalem are Israeli citizens, but their number is negligible for this calculation).

12. See Arnon Sofer, "The Arabs of Israel—From Village to Metropolis, What Next?" *Hamizrah Hehadash*, Vol. 32, pp. 97–105, in Hebrew; and A. Sofer, "Geography and Demography in Eretz Yisrael in the Year 2000," in Alouph Hareven, ed., *Another War or Towards Peace?* (Jerusalem: The Van Leer Institute, 1980), in Hebrew.

13. For a detailed discussion of how Israel's policies were designed to preserve and strengthen segmentation of the Arab community see Lustick, *Arabs*, Chapter 4.

14. E. T. Zureik, "Transformation of Class Structure Among Arabs in Israel: From Peasantry to Proletariat," *Journal of Palestine Studies* 6 (1976), pp. 39–66.

15. N. Makhoul, "Changes in the Employment Structure of Arabs in Israel," *Journal of Palestine Studies* 10 (1981), pp. 77–102.

16. Some of the value change is described in S. Smooha, *The Orientation and Politicization of the Arab Minority in Israel* (Haifa: Haifa University Press, 1980).

17. For a discussion of land loss and its impact on relations within the family see H. Rosenfeld, "The Class Situation of the Arab National Minority in Israel," *Comparative Studies in Society and History* 20 (1978), pp. 374–407; and H. Rosenfeld, "The Class Situation of the Arab National Minority in Israel," *Mahbarot Limihkar Olibikoret* 3 (1979), pp. 5–40, in Hebrew.

18. For early discussions of education, curricula, and national identity, see Y. Peres, A. Ehrlich, and N. Yuval-Davis, "National Education for Arab Youth in Israel," *The Jewish Journal of Sociology* 12 (1970), pp. 147–164; and S. Mar'i, *Arab Education in Israel* (Syracuse: Syracuse University Press, 1978).

19. For an extended discussion, see R. Lazarowitz, N. Rouhana, J. E. Hofman, and B. Beit-Hallahmi, "Impact of Curricula on Shaping the Identity of Jewish and Arab Students in Israel," *Studies in Education*, No. 19 (1978), pp. 153–168, in Hebrew.

20. Figures in this section are obtained from *The Statistical Abstract of Israel,* 1991.

21. Figures on the educational system, as provided in *The Statistical Abstract of Israel,* 1991, include students in East Jerusalem and the Golan Heights.

22. For elaboration on reasons for the increase in the number of Arab students in all levels of education, see M. Al-Haj, *Education and Social Change among Arabs in Israel* (Tel Aviv: International Center for Peace in the Middle East, 1991), pp. 71–83.

23. The figures provided in the text are based on Eli Rekhess, *A Survey of Israeli Arab Graduates From Institutions of Higher Learning in Israel—1961–1967*, mimeograph, The Shiloah Center, Tel Aviv University, 1974.

24. *The Statistical Abstract of Israel,* 1991.

25. These figures fail to come close to comparable percentages of the Jewish population, which stand at 12.2 percent for the first and 16 percent for the second. Yet they represent a multifold increase in comparison to figures in the Arab popula-

tion from previous years. For more details, see Table 22.1 in *The Statistical Abstract of Israel,* 1991.

26. For more details, see Table 22.16 in *The Statistical Abstract of Israel,* 1991.

27. Three main organizations were established in the Galilee, the Triangle, and Haifa. Some became visible when they demonstrated against incidents in which women were killed for "violating the honor of the family," a term that means having a sexual relationship before or outside marriage.

28. See the results of a survey conducted in 1976 and published in S. Smooha, *Arabs and Jews in Israel* (Boulder: Westview Press, 1989), p. 46.

29. Smooha (*Arabs and Jews,* p. 126) reports that his surveys show this minority to be 17.6 percent.

30. For a discussion of Arab voting patterns until 1984, see N. Rouhana, "Collective Identity and Arab Voting Patterns," in A. Arian and M. Shamir, eds., *Elections in Israel—1984* (New Brunswick, N.J.: Transaction Books, 1986).

31. For an elaborate discussion of the change in Arab voting patterns, see *ibid.*

32. Khatib confirmed this in an interview on October 5, 1990. He used explanations similar to those of Abna' al-Balad.

33. According to surplus vote agreements, one of the two parties becomes eligible for the surplus votes of the other, depending among other things on the size of the surplus votes of each and the number of candidates each party wins.

34. None of the Zionist parties agreed to have an excess vote agreement with any of the three Arab-dominated parties.

35. Smooha, *Arabs and Jews.*

36. See a discussion of change in mass political activity after the uprising in N. Rouhana, "Palestinians in Israel: Responses to the Uprising," in R. Brynen, ed., *Echoes of the Intifada: Regional Repercussions of the Palestinian-Israeli Conflict* (Boulder: Westview Press, 1991), pp. 97–115.

37. Weber, "Three Types."

38. This definition is based on Almond and Verba's discussion of citizen competence and subject competence. See G. Almond and S. Verba, *The Civic Culture: Political Attitudes and Democracy in Five Nations* (Boston: Little, Brown & Company, 1965), Chapters 6 and 7.

39. Lustick, *Arabs;* Rouhana, "Collective Identity."

40. For details, see *The Prohibited Conference* (Haifa: Al-Ittihad Press, 1981), published by the committee for rescinding the decision to prohibit the conference of Arab masses.

41. The article was published by A. Bishara and S. Zeidani in *Al-Arabi,* December 29, 1989, in Arabic.

42. See Rouhana, "Palestinians in Israel."

43. *Ibid.*

44. This was discussed extensively in a paper delivered by N. Rouhana in 1991. The paper, entitled "Palestinianization Among the Arabs in Israel: The Accentuated Identity," was presented at the Moshe Dayan Center for Middle Eastern Studies at Tel Aviv University in a conference on The Arab Minority in Israel: Dilemmas of Political Orientation and Social Change.

45. Smooha, *Arabs and Jews.*

46. It seems the Islamic movements in Israel can mobilize broad support, but so far they haven't shown any intention of establishing a national party and run for elections to the Knesset. In the 1989 local elections, they made remarkable gains, winning five local governments. However, a party led by the Islamic movement, if established, should not be seen as relying on parochial religous affiliation but rather on a developed social and political ideology arguably anchored in Islam.

47. This definition is based on Almond and Verba, *Civic Culture,* Chapter 5.

48. Rouhana, "Palestinians in Israel."

49. On March 30, 1976, the Arab community declared a strike to protest the expropriation of Arab land by the authorities. In response, police and army units entered Arab towns, and clashes resulted in the killing of six Arab citizens. Since then, Arabs have commemorated that day as Land Day.

THE PALESTINIANS:
CRAFTING DEMOCRACY

8

Democracy and the Arab World

Shukri B. Abed

A quick look at the political map of the Arab world reveals that of the twenty-one Arab states, only one—Lebanon—boasts anything even approximating a Western-style democratic regime. And even this lone Arab country, with its Western-style parliamentary system, has been on the verge of collapse for years—precisely because of the inherently *nondemocratic* principle embodied in the Lebanese constitution: Maronite Christians were granted certain privileges over other major religious groups (the Druze, the Muslims, and even other Christian sects).

The Sudan is another example of the fragility of the liberalization movements afoot in certain Arab countries. Only five short years ago, in the mid-1980s, the Sudan was perceived as the Arab country with potentially the most liberal and open political system. Suwar El-Dhahab, leader of the group of officers that overthrew Numeiri, set up a transitional government that included civilians. Soon thereafter he allowed parties to organize, and in April 1986 elections were held for a new parliament. A coalition government was formed, headed by Sadiq al-Mahdi, and the democratization process seemed well on its way. In June 1989, however, this process was reversed, when Brig. Gen. Omar al-Bashir forced the elected government of Sadiq al-Mahdi out of power. Since then the country has been under military rule, and supporters of the military government have not shrunk from the use of any means to suppress their opponents. To quote Benaiah Yongo-Bure:

> Repression has prevailed in Sudan in every period, but whereas earlier it had targeted particular groups, the present regime spares no sector of society. Previous governments have operated on the basis of the same dogma of Islamizing and Arabizing the country, but they have felt constrained, for a variety of reasons, from vigorously enforcing their cultural and political hegemony. The regime of Omar al-Bashir has shed all constraints and hesitancy.[1]

As bleak as the outlook for democracy appears to be in Lebanon and the Sudan, a number of Arab countries have taken steps toward democratization of their regimes: Egypt, Jordan, Tunisia, and Algeria have all tried their democratic wings in recent years.[2] Although it is not my intention in this chapter to catalogue in detail specific steps taken by the various Arab countries to meet the minimum requirements that might entitle them to the designation "democracy"—if in name only—I would like to document in a cursory manner some of the more recent democratic stirrings in the Arab world and then move to an examination of the applicability of democracy as developed in the West to the Arab world.[3]

For several years, Egypt has allowed a multiparty system as well as a relatively free press, both of which provide a forum for opposition parties to express their views on political and social matters. Almost two years ago, the pragmatic king of Jordan allowed Muslim and leftist forces to run for election in the Jordanian Parliament. The Muslim forces and their supporters won about thirty-five out of eighty seats in these elections. Several women also ran for election, although none successfully. Incidentally, this was the first time in twenty-six years that elections were held in Jordan.

In June 1990 municipal elections were also held in both Algeria and Tunisia. In Algeria these were the first free elections since independence from French occupation in 1962 and involved ten recently established parties. These same two North African countries have initiated other types of reform as a consequence of internal upheaval. In Tunisia the catalyst for change was President Zain al-'Abdin's replacement of longtime head of state Habib Bourghiba; in Algeria the catalyst proved to be the massive demonstrations of 1988, the most violent events to have rocked this country in its recent history. Yet both countries sacrificed their embryonic democracies when faced with the spectre of fundamentalist takeovers. In Tunisia the democratization process stalled when the government countered Muslim-led demonstrations by arresting most of the movement's leaders. In Algeria the process was allowed to continue somewhat longer, leading to the aforementioned recent elections and the Islamic Salvation Front's landslide victory. However, as the election results were not to the incumbent government's liking, the Algerian president promptly resigned, clearing the way, or so it seemed, for a military takeover.

As the Gulf crisis evolved, many observers expected Kuwait's addition to this list of Arab countries dabbling in democracy. Even before the Gulf emirate's occupation by Iraqi forces on August 2, 1990, democratic movements were gathering force within its borders. With Iraqi troops still occupying the country, the hopes of prodemocracy forces were raised when the exiled emir of Kuwait met with the opposition leadership on October 15, 1990, in Jedda, Saudi Arabia. With the ruling family at its most vulnerable, pressure was applied to abolish censorship of the media and to reinstate the Kuwaiti House of Representatives, banned by the emir in 1986 at the peak of the Iran-Iraq War on the grounds that there was a need to unite the nation in the face of crisis. (The implication, of course, is that democracy is an inherently chaotic and divisive form of government.) The emir promised certain reform measures in the country's political system. He apparently even committed himself to allowing a kind of power sharing with the opposition once his regime was restored. With Kuwait's liberation, however, the emir and his family seemed to lose their enthusiasm for instituting definite steps toward democratization in their country.[4]

Even the rigid rulers of the Saudi royal family are facing some pressure for change. On November 6, 1990, Saudi women literally "sat in the driver's seat" for once and drove in a convoy of forty cars through the streets of Riyadh, defying the strictures of the rigid, conservative, male-dominated Saudi society. Some say these Saudi women were inspired by the presence of the US troops in their country, particularly by the presence of many female soldiers among these troops. More recently, on March 1, 1992, King Fahd issued a decree aiming at liberalizing the political system of Saudi Arabia.[5] Regardless of the scope of the recommended changes, this decree might provide a window of opportunity for some liberalization not only in Saudi Arabia but also in the rest of the Gulf states.

Let us return to the case of Algeria for a closer look. Were democratic reforms simply pushed too far too fast, thereby evoking a repressive backlash from a government suffering from political cold feet? Or was there more to the story than first meets the eye? For not only does the recent parliamentary balloting represent the first free election ever held in Algeria, it also represents, as we shall see, the Arab paradox par excellence.

Forty-nine parties competed in the elections held on December 27, 1991, but it was the Islamic Front that came out on top, winning 188 seats, just 28 short of a majority in the 430-member Parliament.[6] The Islamic Salvation Front was widely expected to win these twenty-eight additional seats during the second round of elections, scheduled for January 16, 1992, which led to speculation that, once in power, the Front's members would impose Islamic law (*shari'ah*) as Algeria's constitution. Anticipating that Algeria's democratic process was paradoxically hurtling the nation toward a theocracy, secular forces in Algeria, including women's organizations, launched massive demonstrations demanding cancellation of the second round of the elections.[7] The independent press in Algeria also demanded that something be done to thwart a fundamentalist takeover. Reports spread that Algerian army and security forces were being deployed across the country, which, according to a Western diplomat, is just what took place before the army imposed martial law last June.[8]

Algeria's dilemma became immediately apparent. The Algerian government did indeed eventually enlist the help of the military to cancel the second round of elections, but in so doing it resorted to nondemocratic means and interfered forcibly with the democratic process. Yet had the government stayed its hand and allowed the second round of elections to take place, it would have risked a victory by the Islamic Salvation Front, the imposition of the Islamic *shari'ah*, and the establishment of (inherently nondemocratic) theocratic rule. This no-win situation illustrates some of the problems involved when democratic *proceedings* are encouraged where democratic *prerequisites* are lacking.

From the preceding discussion of the situation on the ground, we cannot help but note that the Arab world's progress toward democratization has thus far been fraught with tremendous difficulties. The results to date would certainly seem to call into question the agenda of those who prescribe democracy as a cure for all ills in the Middle East region. Or is it perhaps that the Arabs simply *don't understand* democracy, or that they just *aren't good at it?*

Let us first dispel the notion that democracy as a concept is something new and unfamiliar to the Arabs. The term "democracy" in its Greek context was known at least to some Arab intellectuals in the early days of Islamic history, probably through translations of Greek political works into Arabic. The Arab philosopher Alfarabi, for example, discusses the concept of democracy as early as the tenth century in his *Al-siyasah al-madaniyyah* (The Political Regime). Alfarabi describes what he calls "the democratic city" (*al-madinah al-jama'iyyah,* literally "the collective or pluralistic city"),

> in which each one of the citizens is given free rein and left alone to do whatever he likes. Its citizens are equal and their laws say that no man is in any way at all better than any other man. Its citizens are free to do whatever they like; and no one, be he one of them or an outsider, has any claim to authority unless he works to enhance their freedom.[9]

Alfarabi then adds that those who rule the citizens of the democratic state "do so by the will of the ruled, and the rulers follow the wishes of the ruled. Close investigation of their situation would reveal that, in truth, there is no distinction between ruler and ruled among them." For Alfarabi, the democratic state was not the ideal or virtuous state he himself was prescribing. Yet "the construction of 'virtuous' cities and the establishment of the rule of virtuous men are more effective and much easier out of the indispensable and democratic cities than out of any other ignorant city."[10] As Alfarabi understood it, then, the democratic city is the closest possible approximation of his ideal state; it is the type of state out of which the ideal state will eventually emerge.

Alfarabi's tenth-century concept of the democratic state was quite different from those that have developed in Europe and the United States during the last two centuries. Yet the above quotation demonstrates that the Greek-based idea of democracy was known to the Arabs many centuries before the Western states adopted and developed it.

"Democracy" (*dimuqratiyyah*)[10] in its modern European sense was introduced to the Arab world about two hundred years ago and has subsequently been the subject of heated debate within important circles in the Arab world. For the past two centuries, since the Arabs' second major cultural confrontation with the West—the first being the transmission of Greek science and thought in the eighth, ninth, and tenth centuries—Arab thinkers have been debating the value of importing and implementing Western concepts, including political ones and above all those related to the Western concept of democracy. The Egyptians Rifa'a Badawi Rafi' al-Tahtawi (1801–1873) and Muhammad 'Abdu (1849–1905); the Tunisian Khayr al-Din al-Tunisi (1820?–1889);[12] Jamal al-Din al-Afghani (1839–1897);[13] and the Syrian Rashid Rida (1865–1935), to mention only a few, expended a great deal of their considerable intellectual energy exploring the question, "How can Muslims take their deserved place in the modern world while remaining Muslims?"[14] In a comprehensive article on this topic written in 1963, Malcolm Kerr stresses that postmedieval debates concerning the question of democracy in the Arab world "can be traced well back into the nineteenth century," and that "there has been no lack of Arab thinkers and statesmen who have told their people that to have constitutional democracy it was necessary to develop certain qualities of citizenship, a certain attitude toward science, a spirit of tolerance, a concept of secularism, and so forth."[15] Kerr's article summarizes in an illuminating fashion some of these debates through the early 1960s, the peak of Gamal Abdul Nasser's pan-Arabism.

These debates, however, have continued and indeed intensified, throughout the past three decades. They are a subset of more comprehensive debates on Islam and modernity, exploring the question of whether the Muslim countries need to adopt, adapt, or reject the technological, scientific, and political achievements of the West. The crushing defeat of the Arab armies in 1967 and the continuing technological stagnation of the Arab world has once again brought to the fore thorny questions concerning the ability of Arab society and culture to catch up with, let alone challenge, the more technologically advanced Western civilization. Democracy's applicability or inapplicability to the Arab world is by no means the only question raised, yet it is certainly a major issue around which contemporary debates are focused among intellectuals (both male and female)[16] and on the mass level.

An echo of these debates may be found in an almost 900–page volume summarizing views of prominent Arab intellectuals on democracy expressed during a five-day convention held in Cyprus in 1983.[17] This volume was preceded by a series of articles published during 1979 and thereafter in *Al-mustaqbal al-'arabi* (The Arab Future), as well as by a series of articles written in English and published in *The Cairo Papers in Social Science*,[18] also dealing with the question of democracy and the Arab world.

Although these papers express a universal dissatisfaction with the state of affairs prevailing in Arab countries vis-à-vis human rights, freedom of speech, power sharing, and the public accountability of the Arab rulers, their authors highlight the difficulties involved in attempts to rectify these sociopolitical flaws. There is far more agreement in describing the situation than in prescribing solutions; that is, almost all agree on what is, but there is little consensus on what ought to be.

To begin with, not everyone in the Arab world is convinced that lack of democracy is the cause of Arab countries' social and political malaise. Rather, some believe, this lack is only a result, a reflection of these miseries. In the eyes of such thinkers, democracy is a natural development of changing socioeconomic conditions and therefore not something that can be arbitrarily imposed on any given society. Such conditions as prosperity, literacy, a well-developed middle class, and an enlightened leadership are viewed as necessary and perhaps sufficient conditions for the emergence of democratic forms of government.[19]

Second, and perhaps more important, not everyone in the Arab world agrees that Western-style democracy is even applicable to Arab countries. Here one can point to three major streams: unqualified acceptance, absolute rejection, and selective borrowing.[20] That is, there are those who want sweeping and radical changes to transform Arab society into a "modern" society, including adoption of the Western political system in all its details. Others patently reject all Western political concepts on the grounds that Islam has and *is* its own political system. Finally, some—such as the reformists of the Arab renaissance (*nahdah*) movement—simply wish to revise the system without making drastic changes. In the eyes of this latter group, the Arabs ought only to amend their civilization by introducing selected foreign elements to their politics and culture.

According to the rejectionist stream, the Islamic system worked in the past and is capable of working at any time and in any place because it is a divinely inspired system. Although the holders of this view belong to various distinct Islamic groups, we will, for convenience, refer to them together as revivalists or fundamentalists. These groups are a very powerful element in the Arab world and are likely to have a major impact on future political developments. The tip of the iceberg of their potential as an organized political group may be seen from the following facts: 1) The Islamic forces won a massive victory in the recent elections in Algeria;[21] 2) In Jordan, where only a limited type and extent of elections have been allowed, the Islamic movement[22] has made substantial showings; and 3) In the Sudan, Islamic *shari'ah* is now enforced, and the Islamic movement seems to be backing the ruthless absolute rule of al-Bashir.

In at least one of the above-cited cases (the Sudan), Muslim fundamentalists joined forces with a reactionary, absolutist ruler to establish a theocratic Islamic regime. Fear that this trend would be repeated has paradoxically prompted the abrogation of free elections in Algeria. But is this pairing of Islamic and reactionary forces inevitable?

Indeed, all too frequently, the pro-Islam view translates into an implacable stance that dismisses democracy along with all things Western. The modern *salafiyyah* school, for example, expresses itself in several works published this decade. One of these works considers democracy an imported idea that has no room in Islam and asserts that its supporters, "those who were schooled in Western Civilization, should be fought against."[23] Another book, of which several editions have been published during this decade, claims that the spread of the democratic idea in the Arab homeland has been "one of the methods of cultural invasion of the Islamic World."[24]

Yet according to many defenders of the "Islamic solution," Islam is in and of itself liberal and democratic and therefore compatible with the ideas of the modern world. Islamic terms—such as *ahl al-shurah* (counselors of the ruler), *bay'ah* (acclamation or swearing of allegiance by the people to the caliph), *ahl al-hall wa-'l''qd* (electors of the caliph, or literally, "those who loose and bind"), *ahl al-'adl wa'-l-insaf* (people of justice and equality), *ahl al-ijma'* (jurists whose consensus on legal questions is authoritative), *ulu 'l-amr* (literally, those in authority, who according to the Quran [IV:58] must be obeyed along with God and the Prophet), and *ummah* (the community of believers)[25]—symbolize in the eyes of many Muslims the democratic spirit of the first generations of Muslim history, the period of *al-khulafa' al-rashidun* (i.e., the rightly guided caliphs), or more particularly that of the first two caliphs who succeeded the Prophet Muhammad—Abu Bakr and 'Umar. According to Montgomery Watt, this period is often idealized by Muslim thinkers and cited as evidence of democratic practices in Islamic history.[26] This idealization of the early period of Islam may not only be found in the writings of such thinkers as Rashid Rida and Abdel Razzaq Sanhoury of the early twentieth century,[27] but also in present-day discussions.

It is hardly fair, then, to portray Islam as inherently antidemocratic and the single greatest obstacle to political progress in the Arab world, especially when a wariness and suspicion of democracy and other Western exports is shared by many staunchly opposed to the Islamic movement. Like their Muslim fundamentalist counterparts, Arab Marxists and leftists often argue (though perhaps for different reasons) that Western-style democracy is not necessarily the best form of government for the Arab countries. True, Nasser, the most celebrated leader of Arab nationalism, often spoke of democracy, and he included the statement that "freedom of speech is the first introduction to democracy" in many of his lectures. Yet for him Western concepts did not automatically apply to the Arab situation. Rejecting Adam Smith's theory of supply and demand as irrelevant to Egyptian realities, for example, Nasser went on to say:

When I find a suitable book on the nature of our economy, on our experience, then I will feel that this book constitutes a large part of the theory,
and that we have actually begun to lay the foundations. But when I realize
that these economics books are merely a repetition of what we were
taught at the Law Faculty in 1936, then I am filled with endless disappointment.[28]

The prominent Egyptian writer Nawal Sa'dawi argues that the real distinction is between capitalist democracy and socialist democracy, rather
than between Western and Eastern democracies. According to Sa'dawi,

[You] cannot have real freedom in capitalist society; it is impossible. And
you cannot have real freedom for women in a capitalist society. The problem in capitalism is that you are supposed to have freedom in the economic sphere, but what you actually have is domination by the people who
have money. . . . How can I be free if I am taking my food from my enemies, for instance? If I criticize the United States and criticize Zionism
and criticize capitalism, and at the same time depend economically, take
my wheat and bread from the United States, how can I say I am independent? It is a paradox.[29]

According to Sa'dawi, therefore, Western-style democracy, or what she
calls "capitalist democracy," is inapplicable to the Arab world under current economic conditions.

A similar theme is echoed in the writings of the Marxist Samir Amin,
who argues that "Western bourgeois democracy" is based on three basic
principles—economic freedom, legal equality for every citizen, and government noninterference in the private lives and personal opinions of people—that are not applicable in the Arab world, except perhaps in a rudi-
mentary form. Then he concludes that neither this concept of democracy
nor the socialist concept of democracy "fit our conditions and the needs of
our contemporary Arab society."[30]

Having stated in general terms some of the opinions vis-à-vis the
applicability and implementation of Western-style democracy in the Arab
world, let us discuss the roots of the sociopolitical situation in the Arab
world and how these affect future prospects for democracy in the region.
"For more than a thousand years," says Bernard Lewis,

Islam provided the only universally acceptable set of rules and principles
for the regulation of public and social life. Even during the period of maximum European influence, in the countries ruled or dominated by
European imperial powers as well as in those that remained independent,
Islamic political notions and attitudes remained a profound and pervasive
influence.[31]

In another passage he adds:

The very notion of something separate or separable from religious authority, expressed by Christian languages by such terms as lay, temporal, or
secular, is totally alien to Islamic thought and practice. It is not until relatively modern times that equivalents for these terms were used in
Arabic.[32]

These two passages summarize the situation of the Arab world after
the demise of the Ottoman Empire, which had been a thoroughly Islamic
regime. The secular alternative introduced by the new occupiers, the
Europeans, was still alien to the East and could not adequately substitute
for the loss of the Islamic basis for managing the political and social affairs
of the region. True, the new regimes in many of the Arab countries did
model themselves on European modes of governance, but only externally.
By this I mean that they adopted often meaningless components of the
European political model without many of democracy's basic elements—
namely, actual participation by the people and suitable socioeconomic conditions. The Arab rulers either were appointed by an external power or, as
was the case during the second half of this century, appointed themselves
by coup d'état. In either case, they were not elected by the people, as would
be required by the most basic democratic system. In other words, there was,
and still is, a legitimacy (*shar'iyyah*) problem for these leaders, which has
been a major theme in the writings of both Western and Arab scholars who
deal with the Arab world.[33]

The rulers of Saudi Arabia and the other Gulf states had a relatively
easy task overcoming any dearth of legitimacy they might have suffered.
Because of the traditional structure of these societies, in which tribalism
and religion are extremely strong, the rulers did not need to justify their
authority in the eyes of their people; the structure itself was their legitimacy. In the words of Michael Hudson:

The locus of legitimacy [in Saudi Arabia] is not to be found in the people;
instead, the Good Society (which the Saudis as good Muslims wish to create) emerges through a leadership imbued with Islamic values and a society governed by Islamic law and teachings. In short, the totality and
coherence of Islam is so ingrained in Saudi culture that it still serves as a
potent integrating mechanism. The present leadership enjoys Islamic
legitimacy; this is its most formidable political resource. Similarly, the
idea of family rule is apparently still widely accepted, especially at the
mass level.[34]

In fact, the Saudis do not see the need for their people's approval
because, in the words of one Saudi official,

Islam is the most progressive, even revolutionary, system in the world. It
is certainly more satisfactory than the electoral system of the West in
which . . . presumably educated voters are shown to vote on irrational

grounds, parties express only narrow, selfish interests, and moneyed corruption is widespread. If such abuses and distortions affect Western
democracies, the system would hardly be suitable for a less-developed
society like Saudi Arabia.[35]

According to this same official, the Islamic system of Saudi Arabia is a
close, real, and practical expression of the general will.[36] Saudi satisfaction
with the *shari'ah* as the basis of their constitution is echoed in a 1963
speech by Prince Faisal, given one year prior to his ascension to the throne:
"What does a man aspire to? He wants 'good.' It is there in the Islamic
shari'ah. He wants security. It is there also. Man wants freedom. It is there.
He wants remedy. It is there. He wants propagation of science. It is there.
Everything is there, inscribed in the Islamic *shari'ah*."[37]

Of course, this is not to say that the other Gulf states subscribe to the
Saudis' extreme Wahabi position. Kuwait, for example, has a much more
liberal social, political, and religious attitude, which is reflected in an
active opposition movement percolating beneath the surface of this
sheikhdom. Yet the traditional structure of the Gulf states is in general very
strong and likely to continue to resist, in varying degrees, any radical political or social change for many decades to come. This structure, one should
add, would have been much less immune to external influences and change
were it not for the virtually unlimited financial resources of these countries,
which have made them welfare states able to satisfy the needs of each and
every citizen. Just as general prosperity is considered a factor conducive to
the development of democracy, it can also contribute to the support of an
autocratic regime, if widely shared as in the Gulf states.

Societies do not change unless there are compelling economic or ideological causes that force these changes. The wealthy traditional societies
are satisfied with the Islamic ideology and certainly do not have economic
problems. Their wealth—great enough to be shared with the general populace without making a significant dent in the conspicuous consumption of
the ruling class—has killed any desire that might have existed for a change
in ideology; it has even clouded the perception that the modern era might
require a new or modified outlook. With money readily available in the
Gulf states, the most advanced technological products can be bought, and
there is no incentive to encourage domestic productivity. Even the minds
and pens of those who might have raised public awareness of the need for
change can be bought.

The story in Arab countries outside the Gulf region is quite different.
Although none of these countries has officially separated state from religion, their ideologies have been based on secular notions, primarily nationalism, which is itself a Western transplant. Even before the era of independence in the modern Arab world, the general orientation of Egypt, Syria,
Iraq, Lebanon, Libya, Tunisia, and Algeria was not religious. It became

even less so with the wave of revolutions against Western colonial powers and/or their puppets. Egypt led off with its revolution against the British puppet King Faruq in 1952, followed by Tunisia's rebellion against the French in 1956, Iraq's against the British-supported monarchy in 1958, Algeria against France in 1962, North Yemen's against the monarch in 1962, South Yemen's against the British in 1967, Libya's against King Edris al-Sunusi in 1969, and the Sudan's in 1969.

The new rulers clearly adopted Arab nationalism as their ideology. Nasserism in Egypt and Ba'thism in Syria and Iraq[38] became its two major strains. The new rulers of most Arab countries derived their legitimacy and authority from this ideology. Nationalism became the weapon with which they fought not only against Western imperialism but also, and primarily, against the dissenting voices within their own borders. Arab nationalism attempted to replace Islam and tradition in these countries after the demise of the Ottoman Empire. Just as a combination of Islam, traditional family structure, and oil money is used by the ruling family in Saudi Arabia to maintain and secure its rule, Arab nationalism has been used by Nasser, Assad, Saddam Hussein, Muammar Qaddafi, King Hussein of Jordan, the rulers of the former North Yemen, and Numeiri in the Sudan (at least, until he allied himself with the Muslim forces and unilaterally imposed Islamic law in September 1983)[39] to secure their unchallenged and absolute rule.

To recapitulate, then: Because of the historical circumstances of the past two hundred years, and particularly since the demise of the Ottoman Empire in 1917, most Arab countries have actually lost Islam as their primary identity. Many Arab leaders have attempted to design a new ideology for their respective countries that is compatible with Arab nationalism and in some cases (e.g., Qaddafi in Libya and perhaps Sadat in Egypt) with Islam, at least as they choose to interpret it. However, the defeat in 1967 of Nasser, the symbol of Arab nationalism, and that of Saddam Hussein, the self-styled reincarnation of Nasser, in 1991, along with nationalism's failure to solve social, economic, and political problems in the Arab world, has weakened this ideology substantially—or rather revealed a weakness that was there all along.

When nationalism peaked in the early sixties, it already faced both external and internal problems. Because it was meant to fight external powers that were perceived as obstacles to Arab independence and unity, it had to withstand pressure from countries that were stronger and more technologically advanced. In some cases its adherent even had to engage in war with such countries (Egypt against Israel, France, and Britain in 1956; Egypt and Syria against Israel, with help from the United States, in 1967; Lebanon against Israel in 1982; and Iraq against the coalition forces in 1991). And as nationalism meant to introduce social justice and a better distribution of wealth among its citizenry, it also faced bitter resistance from the feudal upper classes, who stood to lose their privileged status under the new order.

Nationalism, as the rallying point—indeed, the new identity—of certain Arab countries in the sixties and seventies, had to deal with other older and more deeply rooted religious and ethnic identities. Nasser, for example, waged a constant battle with the Islamic movement in his country, and in 1966 the leader of this movement, Sayyid Qutb, was executed. Saddam Hussein in Iraq, and those who preceded him, have engaged in an ongoing struggle with the Kurds in northern Iraq and, to a lesser extent, with the Shi'ah Muslims to the south. The Sudan is embroiled in a chronic state of war with its non-Arab minority in southern Sudan. Jordan, plagued by lack of natural resources, also faces an acute crisis and a real legitimacy problem, in that half its population is comprised of Palestinians, most of whose loyalty lies elsewhere. Morocco, too, is torn by long-standing conflicts between the mountain people of Berber background and the Arab culture of the coast,[40] as well as by the Sahara conflict.

Arab nationalism has so far failed to address these challenges successfully. The rulers who have tried to derive their legitimacy and authority from nationalism find themselves in need of increasingly oppressive methods to maintain their rule. This ideology has thus far reneged on its promises of Arab unity, independence from foreign domination, social justice, and the liberation of Palestine. Its failure puts mounting pressure on Arab rulers, and they have tended to react by clinging more and more desperately to their "thrones," becoming ever more oppressive and intolerant of opposing ideas and views.

Is this a uniquely Arab phenomenon? To be sure, there are authoritarian elements in Arab civilization and society[41] that might encourage us to adopt the simplistic explanation that the lack of democracy in the Arab world is attributable to pervasive cultural (particularly Islamic) influences. Islam as a religion does present itself as a comprehensive system of thought, embracing both heavenly and worldly matters: God rules all aspects of our lives—politics, society, ethics, man-God relations, even science—and we owe Him absolute obedience. In a sense, the ruler is a concrete realization of God on earth, and absolute obedience to God is transferred to absolute obedience to his representative on earth. This phenomenon was certainly true of the Prophet Muhammad and of the first caliphs. Their authority was believed to be sacred, as it was God-given and therefore it had to be obeyed without qualification.[42]

In a democratic regime, power is at least theoretically in the hands of the people, and they alone can empower their rulers to manage their affairs. Citizens of a democratic state are expected to realize the power they possess and use it; they are not encouraged to appeal to external or metaphysical forces to manage things for them. Islam, however, is a theocratic system, within which men are viewed as relatively powerless; an omnipotent deity is in charge not only of their ultimate destiny but of every aspect of their daily lives. The theocratic view fosters a total dependency on external forces, rendering the individuals themselves powerless and even useless. According to this view, there is always an external power that decides for the individual: God or his representatives on earth.

It is true, as we have seen, that many Muslim fundamentalists view the turning away from Islamic values and leadership since the fall of the Ottoman Empire as a major cause for the decline of the Arab world. They hope that by returning to Islam, the Arab world will regain its former power and stature. It is also true that democracy as a concept is often associated with Western cultural imperialism and therefore repudiated by important segments of Muslim society. Yet to explain the lack of democracy in the Arab world solely on the basis of religious factors is to assume that the lack will persist as long as Islam is a significant social factor—or, conversely, that the Arab world must relinquish Islam if it is to progress toward democratization. Can the apparent preference for a hierarchical, autocratic structure in the Arab governments of today indeed be attributed to a religious worldview deeply imbedded in the Muslim consciousness? That is, are Islam and democracy mutually incompatible? Or are there perhaps additional forces at play here?

Contemporary Arab intellectuals dealing with such questions as prospects for democracy in the Arab world tend to reject facile religious explanations.[43] The newest generation of Arab thinkers, like their precursors in the nineteenth century, have realized that achieving democracy involves more than imperfectly masking tribal and hierarchical structures with a parliamentary facade; it embodies the development of a distinct system of social values, and the march toward democracy in the Arab world must progress via socioeconomic reforms. As Dessouki observes,

> In attempting to answer these questions [of democracy in the developing countries], we must examine the conditions or requirements for a viable democratic system. Democracy is not merely a multiparty system—rather it is a state of mind and an orientation. Democratic institutions such as political parties may be a necessary condition but in themselves they are not sufficient. Democracy involves certain norms and values, as well as a number of socio-economic requirements; to the extent that these requirements exist in a society, or that the democratization process enhances their emergence, we can talk of a viable democratic system.[44]

The fact, then, that the Arab states have not yet wholeheartedly adopted Western-style democracy as the basis for their political systems is not indicative of a lack of understanding of the ideals this notion carries with it, nor of a disregard for or a belittling of the values of democracy. Rather, it signifies a questioning of the acceptability and applicability of Western democracy to the socioeconomic and political conditions in the Arab countries *as they are today*. This questioning, in and of itself, is a very healthy sign, a sign that Arabs are well aware of what is unique about their culture and of the important ways it distinguishes itself from the cultures of the West. It is a sign that although they recognize the benefits accompanying the progress their Western counterparts have made in the areas of democratization, social equality, and human rights, they are also painfully aware of the accompanying costs and not at all sure they wish to pay them.

A quick look at the Western European and North American countries where democracy has best succeeded to date reveals a number of factors common to all, suggesting at least a correlation, if not a causal link, between these factors and the development of democracy. They include a fairly high rate of literacy, a relatively affluent economy (generally urbanized and industrialized with a broad economic base), a fairly homogenous population (ethnically, linguistically, and socially) with a strong middle class, grassroots microdemocratic structures (town and county governments, worker's associations, etc.) providing a backbone for a democratic macrostructure, and skilled and efficient leadership.[45] How does the Arab world measure up in these areas? The Arab countries are not monolithic. Each country has its own unique historical, social, and economic conditions. The distinction made earlier between the Gulf states and the rest of the Arab countries is an example of the important differences that exist. Any serious study of the prospects for democracy in the Arab world must take into account the specific conditions in each country.[46] What follows is a general overview for the region.

Rate of literacy. Whereas the average illiteracy rate for European and North American countries is 1 to 2 percent (and nowhere more than 17 percent),[47] the illiteracy rate in the Arab world ranges from 25 to 35 percent (in Lebanon, Jordan, Iraq, and among the Palestinians) to 77 percent (in Yemen and the Sudan).[48] Whereas a high percentage of literacy by no means guarantees democracy,[49] it is worth noting the correlation between *il*literacy and *lack* of democracy. In other words, a high rate of literacy is a necessary but not a sufficient condition for the development and maintenance of democracy. Furthermore, whereas a liberal education would tend to inculcate liberal values (among them a belief in democracy), this is not the type of education most prevalent in the Arab world, and an education that inculcates illiberal values may promote autocracy.[50] So it is not just a question of technical literacy, but also of the type of education a population is receiving.

Affluence and a broadly based economy. There is no need to document the poverty existing in the Arab world as a whole. In the majority of Arab countries, there are huge disparities between the rich and the poor, and the poor far outnumber the rich. Yet as we have seen, even in those Arab countries possessing immense oil wealth, the triple yoke of family and tribal structure, Islam, and unlimited amounts of money *widely shared* seems to represent a very effective means of maintaining the status quo.

Homogeneity. While a homogenous society is certainly not a prerequisite for democracy (witness Switzerland and the United States), lack of homogeneity renders the development of democracy particularly difficult and puts tremendous stress upon democratic structures once in place, especially when racial and ethnic rivalries are bitter and longstanding.[51] Whereas the Gulf states have been blessed with not only relatively homogenous populations but also unlimited sources of wealth to support stability within their borders, other Arab countries possess neither advantage. No single element is strong enough to ensure stability, hence the constant search of these countries for solutions to reach and maintain social, economic, and political stability.

Ethnic diversity, heterogeneity, and social pluralism exist in many Arab countries, including Iraq, Syria, Algeria, Morocco, and Yemen. These countries have not suffered as much from ethnic violence as have Lebanon and the Sudan, somehow managing, primarily because of historical circumstances, to maintain unified national identity and "to accommodate divergent communities and groups within a relatively unified social and national order."[52] Yet this accommodation of private and distinctive identities within the national identity was not achieved through a democratic process (as in Switzerland or Belgium, for example). In none of these countries, in other words, has the *social* diversity been translated into *political* pluralism. Rather, the reconciliation of private and public identities has been achieved either through unifying, if cruel, historical circumstances, as was the case for Algeria in its bloody and bitter war of liberation against French imperialism, or through oppressive means, as in Iraq (the Kurds in the northern part of the country).[53]

As we saw earlier, the two highly heterogenous societies, Lebanon and the Sudan, "have fluctuated between conflict, including sustained violent encounters between self-assertive communities, and accommodation."[54] However, "accommodation" in these two cases has meant adoption by the elites of the different communities of a policy of coexistence without compromising their separate identities. And the attempts to contain these conflicts by "the use of some conflict-regulating practices, the management of differences, and consociational democracy have not been successful. The elites failed to accommodate the divergent interests of their communities."[55]

Given the ethnic problems in many of the Arab countries, there is a genuine fear of further disintegration in the Arab lands. The events in Lebanon over the last fifteen years, the potential threat of dividing Iraq into three parts along religious and ethnic lines in the aftermath of its defeat in early 1991, the problems facing the Sudan, and the negative examples of the current civil war in Yugoslavia and the disintegration of the Soviet Union most likely represent proof to those who believe that a strong central authority, not a democracy, will be required to maintain the geographic and political unity of Arab countries such as Iraq, the Sudan, Egypt,[56] and Lebanon, where ethnic and religious problems are highly threatening to stability.

Existence of intermediate microdemocratic structures. The definition of the relationship between the state and the individuals belonging to that state is always a complex matter. The distinction between the state's or the community's interests and the individual's interests is a matter of degree that varies with the conditions of a given society.[57] In modern Arab states, the line is drawn in such a way that the individual's interests are swallowed almost entirely within those of the community. The deeply rooted sense of *ummah,* of the priority of the collective over the individual, has expressed itself in the very structure of the modern Arab states. These states have a monopoly on all aspects of life, and there is very little room for individual input or private grassroots initiatives. As Polk describes it:

> Since the Arab country had no tradition of private enterprise, everything depended upon the state. As in ancient Egypt and Mesopotamia, the state alone was believed to have the capacity to organize resources. Even in conservative Saudi Arabia, it is the state that sets the goals, provides the capital, mobilizes the manpower, and often buys the product of nascent industry. The state has a monopoly on education, health care, social welfare, law and internal security—most of which were traditionally not thought of as parts of its role. With this scheme of state intervention in the lives of citizens, the Arabs are finding two kinds of failure. First, like the Russians, many see waste, corruption, inefficiency, lack of incentive. . . . The second kind of disillusionment is of a different sort. It is the growing belief that the road to the "good life," whatever that may be, does not run through materialism.[58]

Muslih and Norton provide further details:

> Today the principal growth industry in the Middle East is pervasive, centralized government, heavily bureaucratized and militarized. In Egypt, Iraq, and Syria the number of government employees increased about nine-fold over the span of approximately 20 years. If members of the armed and security services are added, the government employs more than one-fourth of the working population. Needless to say, increased dependence on the state as a source of livelihood undermines the democratic impulse because, economically speaking, the employee is in no position to bargain with the employer over political and civil liberties.[59]

Authoritarian regimes certainly are not something inherently or inevitably Arab. From the above description, it should be clear that the Arab countries are part and parcel of the socioeconopolitical phenomenon called the Third World. And as far as Third World countries are concerned, it is still unclear what type of regime is most suitable for them. It is unclear whether Western democracy can be applied to countries whose conditions are diametrically opposed to those in which this concept has evolved naturally. Most Third World leaders, those of the Arab world included, believe that socioeconomic and national liberty must be given precedence over political and personal liberty. The latter, in their view, is an outgrowth of the former and will follow once the first is attained. Robert L. Rothstein summarizes this point as follows:

> In both the Third World and the First World it became fashionable to denounce democracy as an inappropriate shortrun goal for poor countries, a form of government and a system of values imposed on the former Colonial areas by the West. That attitude still persists in many Third World countries where democracy is resisted not only because of fears that it will impede development but also because of fears that it will exacerbate internal divisions—and, of course, threaten elite prerogatives.[60]

In a recently published article dealing with democracies in Africa, another contemporary scholar, Jon Kraus, argues that the brief periods of democratic rule in some African countries have brought about "disillusions and disappointment with democratic governments" and that in Sierra Leone, Somalia, Benin, and Sudan they have "deepened the chasm between the Arab-Muslim north and the Christian-animist southern regions."[61]

It is hardly true to state that *all* Arab leaders in the last few decades have been incompetents, traitors, or the like. After the Arab countries' respective bids for independence, the leaders of the less fortunate Arab countries truly and genuinely believed that the best way to deal with the enormous internal and external problems facing the Arab nation as a whole and their individual nation-states in particular was strong leadership. No one, for example, doubts Nasser's devotion to the goals of Arab nationalism, but Nasser, despite his charismatic leadership, was an authoritarian leader who had to overlook the questions of human rights, freedom of speech, and public accountability in order to maintain his regime. He genuinely believed that finding solutions for Egypt and the Arab world took priority over any other considerations. Even prominent Arab intellectuals have been willing to defend this principle, as can be seen from the lengthy quotations in Kerr's article by professors such as the Syrian 'Abdallah al-Da'im,[62] the Palestinian Fayez Sayegh,[63] and Ba'th Party founder Michel 'Aflaq.[64]

Given the economic weakness of many Arab countries (Egypt, Syria, Sudan, Yemen, and Jordan, to mention only a few) and the new world order (disappearance of the Soviet Union and the enhanced position of the United States), Western countries and the United States in particular could use their economic leverage over the Arab countries to push for democratic reforms. In addition to the direct aid they give to countries such as Egypt, Western countries have enormous influence through institutions such as the World Bank and the International Monetary Fund.[65] Instead, the U.S.-supported Arab regimes have enhanced their positions, in part because of this support.

From the United States's point of view, it is convenient to maintain control of these countries through an individual or a family that can be easily manipulated. For example, it is much easier to convince the royal family of Saudi Arabia to allow the deployment of U.S. forces in that country than it is to wait for an elected parliament to agree to such a deployment.[66] Any democratically elected representative would have expressed reservations concerning the massive deployment of foreign troops in an Arab country for the purpose of fighting another Arab country. It would have taken more than one visit from the U.S. defense secretary to convince the rulers of Saudi Arabia to agree to such a massive deployment had these rulers been democratically elected. They would have been concerned about the response of their constituency.[67] The issue for the United States is not so much pushing for democratic reforms as supporting the regimes that best serve its interests. The slogan of democracy is enthusiastically applied when nondemocratic regimes do not serve U.S. and Western interests, as in the case of Nicaragua, when U.S. interests were threatened by a Marxist regime, the Sandanistas. However, democracy was not an issue the liberators of Kuwait from Iraqi occupation concerned themselves with. The Kuwaiti case is best summarized by Adeed Dawisha:

> The president [of the United States] was far less assertive on the questions of democratization and human rights in the Gulf States. Between March and October 1991, the press and international organizations reported widespread abuses of human rights in Kuwait. . . . Yet on the few occasions when the President felt compelled to respond to the mounting criticism of Kuwait's human rights record, he seemed to excuse the behavior of the country and its emir.
>
> Nor was the President especially concerned that Kuwait's ruling Sabah family dragged its feet on promises to democratize the political system—promises it made while in exile. Bush reminded his critics that the United States had fought the war not to institute democracy in Kuwait, but to liberate the country from Iraqi occupation.[68]

Democracy is not just a political system; above all it is a social phenomenon that eventually translates into a political system. Any attempt to liberalize or democratize a political system without paying close attention to the economic and social (including religious) factors of the Arab societies is putting the cart before the horse. Democracy is an evolving concept that does not exist in a vacuum; rather it expresses certain social values and economic conditions. Democratizing the political system without changing the reality it reflects will sooner or later backfire. We ought, therefore, to ask: Can a democracy, be it the most primitive or the most advanced type, succeed when conditions of enormous economic disparity prevail, as is the case within and among the various Arab countries? Can the Arabs really have Western-style democracy as their model when threatened with territorial divisions and when facing growing Islamic resurgence, partly in reaction to this very same Western orientation?

When we talk about "Western leverage," we should not understand it as being exercised to impose a new political system on client states. The maximum we can hope for at this stage is a change in attitude on questions such as human rights and freedom of speech as the first step toward tipping the balance in favor of the individual, who is currently swallowed up in the state apparatus. Like democracy, human rights and freedom of speech are broad and relative concepts. Yet perhaps they are easier to begin with as they are less abstract and more narrowly defined than democracy; indeed, they are components of it and therefore can serve as a point of departure. In the words of Giovanni Sartori:

> New states and developing nations cannot pretend to start from the level of achievement at which the Western democracies have arrived. In fact, no democracy would ever have materialized if it had set for itself the advanced goals that a number of modernizing states currently claim to be pursuing. In a world-wide perspective, the problem is to minimize arbitrary and tyrannical rule and to maximize a pattern of civility rooted in respect and justice for each man—in short, to achieve a humane polity. Undue haste and overly ambitious goals are likely to lead to opposite results.[69]

In light of such wise words, it would seem the Arabs are far more cognizant than their Western patrons of the pitfalls that strew the path to democracy for developing nations. The debates raging in the Arab world today over democracy and other Western notions signify a wealth of independent intellectual energy and a pluralism of opinion that must be the envy of any democratic society. Such debate ensures that if and when the Arab countries, singly or in groups, commit themselves to supporting democratization within their borders, the type of democracy implemented will be peculiarly Arab and therefore appropriate to the Arab societies. The West can only do the citizens of the Arab world irreparable harm by hurrying the process along and cutting short the debates of the Arabs before they have fully explored all the nuances of this immensely complex issue and settled on a type of government that is right for them.

Notes

1. *Middle East Report* (September–October 1991), p. 9.
2. The Palestinians as a nation may also be included among the Arab nations in this category. There are many indications that the Palestinians have made sub-

stantial progress in terms of democratization. In fact, the unique circumstances of the Palestinians render them a candidate to lead the first full-fledged Arab democratic state. See Shukri Abed, "Will a Palestinian State Be Democratic?," *Jerusalem Post*, March 30, 1989, p. 4.

3. For various points of view on the question of "Democracy in the Arab World," consult *Middle East Report*, No. 174 (January–February 1992). See also Michael Hudson, "After the Gulf War: Prospects for Democratization in the Arab World," *Middle East Journal* (Summer 1991), pp. 407ff.

4. On January 13, 1992, the Kuwaiti authorities were finally reported to have lifted the ban on a free press, perhaps a first step toward fulfilling their promise of more than a year ago.

5. See *Al-majallah*, No. 630, March 4–10, 1992, and the *New York Times*, March 2, 1992.

6. *New York Times*, January 3, 1992, p. A3.

7. *Ibid.*

8. *New York Times*, January 9, 1992, p. A3.

9 Abu Nasr Alfarabi, "The Political Regime," trans. Fawzi Najjar, in Ralph Lerner and Muhsin Mahdi, eds., *Medieval Political Philosophy* (New York: The Free Press of Glencoe, 1963), pp. 50ff.

10. *Ibid.*

11. For the entry of the term *dimuqratiyyah,* along with other political terms, into modern Arabic, see Ami Ayalon, "Dimuqratiyyah, Hurriyya, Jumhuriyya: The Modernization of the Arabic Political Vocabulary," in *Asian and African Studies* (Journal of the Israel Oriental Society), Vol. 23, No. 1 (March 1989), pp. 23–42.

12. On Tahtawi's and Tunisi's attempts to reconcile the modern concept of democracy with Islamic political concepts, see Ahmad Sidqi al-Dajjani, "Tatawwur mafahim al-dimuqratiyyah fi'l-fikr al-'arabi al-hadith [The Evolution of the Concept of Democracy in the Modern Arab World]," in *Azmat al-dimuqratiyyah fi'l-'alam al-'arabi* [The Crisis of Democracy in the Arab World], 2nd edition (Beirut: Markiz dirasat al-wihdah al-'arabiyyah, 1987), pp. 117ff. [Henceforth, *Azmat*].

13. About the obscurity of this scholar's origins (Was he Afghani, as his name suggests, or Persian, as some of his detractors claim?), see Albert Hourani, *Arabic Thought in the Liberal Age: 1798–1939* (Cambridge: Cambridge University Press, 1962), p. 108.

14. See Hourani, *Arabic Thought*, p. 95.

15. Malcolm Kerr, "Arab Radical Notions of Democracy," in Albert Hourani, ed., *Middle Eastern Affairs*, No. 3 (1963), St. Anthony's Papers, No. 16, p. 10.

16. See Kevin Dwyer, *Arab Voices: The Human Rights Debate in the Middle East* (Berkeley: University of California Press, 1991), Chapter 11.

17. See *Azmat*. It is important to draw a distinction between the Arab leaders and the Arab intellectuals with respect to democratic leanings. Most revealing, for example, is the fact that the conference on whose papers the *Azmat* volume is based, a conference that ostensibly dealt with problems of the Arab world, was not held in an Arab country. What is worse, no Arab country was even willing to host the conference, according to the volume's introduction, written by Sa'd al-Din Ibrahim (p. 14). Thus, while contemporary Arab thinkers clearly feel democracy is a topic worth discussing, contemporary Arab rulers apparently do not.

18. *The Cairo Papers in Social Science* (Cairo: The American University in Cairo, 1978).

19. For such views as these, see the article by Bassam Tibi, "Al-bina' al-iqtisadi al-ijtima'i li-l-dimuqratiyyah" [The Economic and Social Foundations of Democracy], in *Azmat*, pp. 73ff. See also Charles Philip Issawi, "Economic and Social Foundations of Democracy in the Middle East," in *International Affairs*, Vol.

32, No.1 (January 1956), which is quoted in Tibi's article and (according to the introduction of *Azmat*, p. 16) was the basis for Tibi's original presentation at the Cyprus conference. Tibi quotes another important source for this view, namely that of 'Abd al-'Aziz al-Duri's "Al-dimuqratiyyah fi falsafat al-hukm al'arabi [Democracy According to the Arab Philosophy of Government]," in which the author suggests, "Democracy is not a sheer abstract theory, but rather it is tied to certain political [and] economic conditions" (*Azmat*, p. 74).

20. Al-Dajjani, "Tatawwur mafahim al-dimuqratiyyah fi'l-fikr al-'arabi 'l-hadith," in *Azmat*, p. 117. See also Issa J. Boullata, *Trends and Issues in Contemporary Arabic Thought* (Albany: State University of New York Press, 1990), pp. 3ff.

21. Among the relatively small Arab community inside Israel, the Muslim movement has also become a major factor in the municipal elections and is eminently capable of gaining four to five seats in the Knesset should its leaders decide to run in the forthcoming Israeli general elections, scheduled for June 23, 1992.

22. The "Islamic movement" is a term broadly used to indicate all Islamic parties in Jordan, the major one of which is the Muslim Brotherhood. See Beverly Milton-Edwards, "A Temporary Alliance with the Crown: The Islamic Response in Jordan," in James Piscatori, ed., *Islamic Fundamentalism and the Gulf Crisis* (Cambridge, Mass.: American Academy of Arts and Science, 1991), p. 88.

23. Yusuf al-Qaradawi, *Al-hulul al-mustawradah wa-kayfa janat 'ala ummatina* [The Imported Solutions and How They Harmed our Nation] (Beirut, 1980), pp. 49ff, quoted in Tibi's lecture in *Azmat*, p. 87.

24. 'Ali M. Jraisheh and Muhammad Sharif al-Zaibaq, *Asalib al-ghazw al-fikri li-l-'alam al-islami* [The Methods of Cultural Invasion of the Islamic World] (Cairo, 1978), quoted in Tibi's lecture in *Azmat*, p. 87. Tibi comments on this position as follows: "Thus the fight against cultural invasion becomes the fight against democracy and its supporters, and the struggle for Islam turns into a struggle against democracy."

25. Kerr, "Radical Notions," p. 15.

26. Watt, *Islamic Political Thought*, pp. 36–37.

27. See Kerr, "Radical Notions."

28. Quoted in Kerr, p. 33.

29. Dwyer, *Arab Voices*, p. 187.

30. Samir Amin, "Mulahzat hawla manhaj tahlil azmat al-dimuqratiyyah fi'l-watan al-'arabi [Notes on the Methodology of Analyzing the Crisis of Democracy in the Arab Homeland]," in *Azmat*, pp. 307, 317.

31. Bernard Lewis, "State and Society Under Islam," *The Wilson Quarterly*, Vol. xiii, No. 42 (Autumn 1989).

32. *Ibid.*, p. 41.

33. See particularly M. Hudson, *Arab Politics: The Search for Legitimacy* (New Haven: Yale University Press, 1977) Sa'd al-din Ibrahim, "Masadir al-shar'iyyah fi anzimat al-hukm al-carabiyyah [The Origins of Legitimacy for the Arab Regimes]," in *Azmat*, pp. 403ff.

34. Hudson, *Arab Politics*, pp. 176–177.

35. *Ibid.*

36. *Ibid.*

37. Quoted in John L. Esposito, *Islam and Politics* (Syracuse: Syracuse University Press, 1984), p. 103.

38. According to Muhammad Muslih and Augustus Norton, Ba'thism "also has a significant following in Lebanon, as well as in Mauritania and Yemen." See Muslih and Norton, "The Need for Arab Democracy," *Foreign Policy*, No. 83 (Summer 1991), p. 7.

39. See *Middle East Report* (September–October 1991), pp. 3ff.

40. Hudson, *Arab Politics*, p. 209.

41. According to contemporary sociologist Halim Barakat, the Arab family, which is "the center of social and economic activities" in both traditional and contemporary Arab societies, is "patriarchal; pyramidally hierarchical, particularly with respect to sex and age; and extended." Barakat goes on to tie the hierarchical family structure into the political structure as follows: "The same patriarchal relations and values which prevail in the Arab family seem also to prevail at work, at school, and in religious, political, and social associations. In all of those, a father figure rules over others, monopolizing authority, expecting strict obedience and showing little tolerance of dissent. Projecting a fatherly image, those in position of responsibility (as rulers, leaders, teachers, employers, or supervisors) securely occupy the top of the pyramid of authority. Once in this position, the patriarch cannot be dethroned except by someone who is equally patriarchal." See Barakat, *Contemporary Arab Society*, forthcoming.

42. The position of the ruler in Islam is dictated by the Quran itself. Sura 4 [*al-Nisa'*, or "Women"]: 59, for instance, demands that one obey the rulers the same way one obeys God and his messenger. "O ye who believe! Obey Allah, and obey the Messenger, and those charged with authority among you." Such statements—mentioning obedience to God, the Prophet, and the ruler in a single syntactical breath—can easily be interpreted to mean that obedience to the ruler is absolute and should not be challenged, as his word is similar to the word of God.

43. See, for example, Sa'd al-Din Ibrahim, *op. cit.*, p. 403. See also Khalid al-Nasir, "Azmat al-dimuqratiyyah fi 'l-watan al-'arabi [The Crisis of Democracy in the Arab Homeland]," *Al-mustaqbal al-'arabi*, No. 55 (September 1983), pp. 79ff.

44. Ali E. Hillal Dessouki, "The Transformation of the Party System," in *The Cairo Papers in Social Science* (New York: American University in Cairo, 1977–1978), pp. 21–22.

45. The majority of these points are discussed by Giovanni Sartori in "Democracy," in David L. Sills, ed., *The International Encyclopedia of the Social Sciences*, Vol. 4 (The Macmillan Company and The Free Press, 1968), pp. 112–121. Sartori warns repeatedly that the search for "causal links" is a complex one; that one must differentiate, for example, between factors conducive to *emerging* democracy as opposed to those conducive to the successful *continuation* of democracy, and that many of the cited factors may be the *result* rather than the *cause* of democracy. Still, Sartori's analysis provides us with a framework for our discussing specific conditions in the Arab world.

46. See Abed, "Palestinian State," for a discussion of the specific Palestinian conditions that may prove conducive to the eventual establishment of a democratic Palestinian state.

47. Greece (10 percent), Yugoslavia (10 percent), and Portugal (17 percent), as reported in the article on illiteracy in *The World Book*, Vol. 10, 1991.

48. Polk, *The Arab World Today* (Cambridge, Mass.: Harvard University Press, 1992), pp. xxxiv–xxxv.

49. Cuba, for example, has one of the lowest illiteracy rates in the world (4 percent), as do most of the formerly communist countries in Europe, where the average rate of illiteracy matches that of Western Europe (about 1 percent).

50. Sartori, "Democracy," p. 119.

51. It can be argued that the United States's democracy has always worked best for its Caucasian population and often not at all for its black, Hispanic, Oriental, and Native American populations, which leads one to question how "genuine" a democracy this paragon of democratic principles really is.

52. Barakat, *Arab Society,* p. 9.

53. For details of the ability of Iraq's and Syria's leadership to control their respective countries through oppressive means, see Muslih and Norton, "Arab Democracy," pp. 6–8. The authors of this article classify the Ba'thist leadership of Syria and Iraq as "the leader-state" with "the most personalized style of decision making, and . . . the least prone to political reform and democratization." *Ibid.,* p. 8.

54. *Ibid.*

55. *Ibid.*

56. With its large Coptic minority, estimated at 10 percent of the population, or about five million people.

57. All societies grapple with the individual-community dialectic. Even in the most advanced democracies, individuals are required to serve in the army and often to sacrifice their lives for their country in times of war. Yet in democratic societies, the individual is accorded a great deal of respect and authority, whereas in Arab society community rights and interests tend to take preference over individual rights and interests.

58. Polk, *The Arab World Today,* p. xx. The author goes on to connect this trend of antimaterialism with the resurgence of Islam as an expression of this trend.

59. Muslih and Norton, "Arab Democracy," p. 6.

60. Robert Rothstein, "Weak Democracy and the Prospects for Peace and Prosperity in the Third World," delivered at United States Institute of Peace conference, October 1990.

61. Jon Kraus, "Building Democracy in Africa," in *Current History* (May 1991), p. 209. Somalia and Sudan are both Arab countries.

62. Kerr, "Radical Notions," pp. 24–25.

63. *Ibid.,* pp. 28–29.

64. *Ibid.,* p. 27. See also the brief description in the author's introduction to *The Republic of Fear* (New York: Pantheon Books, 1990), p. ix.

65. See Kraus, "Building Democracy," pp. 211–212.

66. What happened recently in the Philippines, where U.S. ships were asked to leave the Subic Bay Base after almost a century of U.S. military presence in the island country, is a case in point. Had it been up to former President Ferdinand Marcos, who ruled absolutely in the Philippines for two decades (1965–1986), he would most likely have agreed to the continuation of a U.S. military presence in his country because his regime, despite its undemocratic nature, was in return supported by the United States. It is only due to the Philippine Senate, which voted in favor of terminating the treaty, that the Americans will be leaving the naval base they held for so many decades.

67. In fact, with the exception of the Sudan, those Arab countries that opposed the coalition activities during the Gulf War have one thing in common: They all have been through democratic awakenings of various kinds. The rulers of these countries (Algeria, Tunisia, Morocco, Jordan, Yemen, and the PLO) have realized that they are somehow *accountable* for their actions and decisions.

68. Adeed Dawisha, "The United States in the Middle East: The Gulf War and its Aftermath," *Current History* (January 1992), Vol. 91, No. 561, p. 4.

69. Sartori, "Democracy," p. 120.

9

Democratization Among West Bank Palestinians and Palestinian-Israeli Relations

Moshe Ma'oz

"Democracies do not fight other democracies." This Kantian notion has attracted the attention of scholars and has thus produced many studies on the relation between democracy and peace in various parts of the world. Political leaders in the West, most recently President George Bush, have frequently hailed democracy as a prerequisite for peace and stability; and against the background of the current peace process in the Middle East, it is important to find out whether this linkage between democracy and peace could also apply to Arab-Israeli relations, and more specifically to the Palestinian-Israeli case.

This chapter is a preliminary attempt to trace the development of a democratic process in the Palestinian Arab community in the West Bank and to examine the relevance of this process to Palestinian attitudes toward the state of Israel. Such an investigation could appear farfetched, if not futile. For while Israel has been since its birth a Western-type democracy, most Arab nations, with the exception of Lebanon and Tunisia, have not experienced any form of democratic life for several decades (even according to a public statement by Arab writers and scholars in 1983).[1] The standard explanations for this lack of Arab democracy are, inter alia, the absence of Western-like political culture, tradition, and institutions; the semifeudal Arab social structure; and the long domination of European imperialism in the Arab world.

Palestinian Arabs share the same nondemocratic background as other Arabs. Worse than that, they are the only Arab nation that has not been able to create its own state and institutions; has been dispersed since 1948 in various parts of the region; and, since 1967, has been under Israeli occupation in the core of their homeland—the West Bank and East Jerusalem (plus Gaza). Could the Palestinian Arabs have developed a democratic process under such severe conditions? Even more crucial, could the Palestinian Arabs have developed any peaceful tendencies toward the Israeli Jews, with whom they have been in bitter conflict for about a century (much longer than any other Arab nation)? From the Palestinian Arabs' point of view, Israel is indeed the archenemy, the enemy who defeated them in 1948, who has usurped their land and suppressed their basic national aspirations since 1967.

Nevertheless, despite these powerful odds, both external and internal, the Palestinian Arabs have gradually developed a democratic process, starting in a superficial-elitist form under the British Mandate and becoming a grassroots movement under the intifada.

Similarly with respect to the Palestinian attitudes toward Israel, alongside the deep-rooted ideological antagonism there have developed among various Palestinian groups positive-pragmatic attitudes toward the Jewish Yishuv and the state of Israel aimed at reaching a political settlement to the conflict. These peaceful tendencies have been recently reflected in the Palestinian positions at the [Madrid] Middle East peace conference.

But what is the nature of the Palestinians' peaceful positions and the motives and forces behind them? Are they genuine or tactical? What kind of democratic process have the Palestinian Arabs undergone? Is it a Western type of stable democracy resting on wide political participation, freedom of choice and expression, and socioeconomic modernization? Or is it a kind of unstable Third World democracy based on populism and abuses of basic human rights? And finally, have there been any significant linkages or interrelations between the Palestinians' democratization process and their pragmatic-peaceful tendencies toward Zionism and Israel?

In this chapter an attempt will be made to address most of these queries through a historical inquiry starting at the first phase of the Arab-Jewish conflict in Palestine (1908–1948) and ending with the recent phase, the intifada.

1908–1948: The Era of Arab and Jewish Nationalism

The Pre-Mandatory Period: Anti-Zionism as a Popular Sentiment

The 1908 Young Turk rebellion gave rise to new ideas and aspirations of political freedom among some Arabs in Palestine, mostly young intellectuals who joined the small, newly emerging Arab nationalist and reformist associations in the Ottoman Empire. These intellectuals, Muslims and Christians alike, as well as Arab members of the Turkish Parliament and the newly appearing Arabic newspapers in Palestine, were engaged for more than a decade in a prolonged debate regarding the political and cultural rights of the Arabs and their representation in the Ottoman Empire. The common denominator among these various personalities, groups, and newspapers was a strong opposition to the new Jewish-Zionist venture in Palestine, which had started in the early 1880s and gained momentum in subsequent years. Reflecting Arab popular sentiments, this opposition derived from sociocultural, religious, political, and economic motives. The Zionists were an alien European group, nationally oriented, mostly secular and socialist, assertive if not aggressive. Their presence and behavior threatened traditional Arab cultural and religious norms, and the movement's growth and land purchases endangered the political and economic interests of large sections of the indigenous population.

Thus, for example, Sa'id al-Husayni and Ruhi al-Khalidi, two of the three Arab members of the Turkish Parliament and representatives of the district of Jerusalem during the years 1908–1918, "used the Parliament platform in order to expound the dangerous nature of Zionism and the need to prevent its implementation in Palestine." (Al-Husayni later told certain Jewish functionaries that "his anti-Zionist position derived only from his wish to be popular and in consideration of the Arab public opinion.") Similarly, Raghib al-Nashashibi, a Jerusalemite candidate for parliament (who became during the British Mandatory period an ally of the Jewish-Zionist Yishuv) declared in 1914, on the eve of parliamentary elections: "If elected as a delegate I shall do all in my power day and night, to get rid of the damage and danger which we can expect from the Zionists and Zionism."[2]

The British Mandatory Period:
The Development of Quasidemocracy and Arab-Jewish Relations

The end of Turkish rule and the establishment of the British Mandate in Palestine facilitated the expansion of various public associations, political organizations and parties, social and municipal bodies, and newspapers and journals within the Arab community. Among the political organizations and parties there were the Muslim-Christian Association; the Arab Executive (succeeded by the Higher Arab Committee); several Palestinian congresses; the Supreme Muslim Council; the Muslim National Association (which was succeeded by the Arab Nationalist Party); the Islamic National Congress (which was succeeded by the National Defense Party); as well as the Palestinian Arab Party, the Reformist Party, and so on.[3] All these parties and organizations, as well as most other political and public bodies, were democratic superficially, but not in their essence: They did not reflect a democratic society in Western European–North American terms. Rather they represented a different kind of sociopolitical regime, one characteristic of a traditional society evolving from a feudal oligarchical and authoritarian system into a more modern political community. The Arabs had growing popular participation and a multiparty electoral system patterned after Western norms and under the direction of European rule. This type of limited democracy developed among the Arab population in Palestine during the British Mandatory period. The various political parties and organizations established during this period formally experienced democratic elections, reflecting a variety of political agendas and mobilizing a growing number of members and followers. Young people and intellectuals established new parties as well as other political, social, and professional associations.

This emerging pluralism in public life posed a potential threat to the traditional hegemony of the old aristocracy and theoretically could have advanced the democratization of the Arab community in Palestine. In fact, however, most of the parties and associations were controlled by members of the traditional elite (and by some big village shaikhs). This oligarchy of notable and wealthy families derived its authority from traditional elements of prestige—e.g., senior religious and government positions, possession of many lands—and did not require popular democratic sanction for its status. According to Porath, "even if the common people were asked then who represented them, they would undoubtedly grant full authorization to the representatives of this social elite whose leadership they accepted without any question."[4]

Even the young political activists and intellectuals, with the possible exception of members of the new Istiqlal (Independence) Party, did not advocate the adoption of Western-style democracy for their community. On the contrary, many of them, notably the followers of Hajj Amin al-Husayni, the chief Palestinian nationalist leader, strongly professed fascist ideas, particularly during the 1930s. Apparently those activists and many other Arab nationalists believed that through the adoption of a fascist political system they could eliminate the British Mandate and especially the Zionist-Jewish national community.

Democracy and the Palestinian-Zionist Struggle

The ultimate objective of the Palestinian Arab nationalist movement and its principal ethos continued unabated during the Mandatory period: to fight the Zionist venture and to prevent the creation of a Jewish national home in Palestine. Upon this ideology and political agenda Palestinian writers, educators, and other intellectuals were mobilized. They committed themselves to indoctrinating and educating the public and the young generations in books, articles, and the school system. There is no record of any Palestinian writer or educator advocating peaceful coexistence with the Jewish national community.[5]

Very few Palestinian writers dealt with the issues of reform in the sociopolitical system and the attitude toward Western democracy, although many Palestinian intellectuals received their education in Europe. Significantly, those few who advocated the democratic system were also anti-Zionists. In his book *Arab Cultural Nationalism in Palestine During the British Mandate,* Adnan Abu-Ghazaleh mentions only two contemporary Palestinian writers who vaguely referred to the need for "reform unity and democracy" in the Palestinian community.[6] Both of them, Izzat Darwaza and Qadri Tuqan, were committed to the struggle against the Zionists in Palestine. Another Arab writer, Khalil Baydas (also an anti-Zionist), advocated the adoption of an "authocratic rule as a forerunner of unity and democracy" because he felt the Arabs were not yet ready for democracy.[7] Most Palestinian writers, in fact, were concerned in their writings with finding ways to unify the Arabs and strengthen them in order to effectively combat Zionism.[8] Most of them favored an authoritarian regime, and during the 1930s they were inclined to adopt the fascist system of Germany.[9] A great many Palestinian nationalists during that era admired the Nazi regime in Germany, partly because of its vitality and strength, partly because of its persecution of Jews, and partly in anticipation of its help in ousting the British and the Zionists from Palestine. Already in 1933, following the Nazi victory in the German national elections, Hajj Amin al-Husayni publicly stated to the German consul in Jerusalem that "Muslims in and out of Palestine welcome the new regime in Germany and long for the expansion of the fascist antidemocratic governmental system in other countries, too."[10]

Yet notwithstanding their favorable attitudes toward fascism, in their deliberations with the British Mandatory government Palestinian nationalist leaders and delegations frequently used arguments derived from the Western democratic system to combat the Jewish Zionist community. Claiming that they constituted the majority population, the Palestinians insisted that an Arab government should be established and be responsible before a legislative council or parliament elected only by the Arab inhabitants of Palestine.[11] On certain occasions, the Palestinian nationalist leaders would describe the future Arab government as democratic and agree that Jews could participate alongside Arabs in the parliamentary elections, although only in accordance with their proportion in the population and not exceeding a third of the total population.[12] The Palestinian nationalists insisted that such arrangements could be implemented only on the condition that the Balfour Declaration regarding the creation of a Jewish homeland in Palestine was abrogated and Jewish immigration and land acquisitions stopped.

It would thus appear that the Palestinian Arab nationalist movement, under the leadership of al-Husayni, was ready to employ any method or policy in its struggle against the Zionist-Jewish community, from illegal violent measures to legitimate political argumentation. Essentially nondemocratic if not antidemocratic, the nationalists used, inter alia, Western democratic notions and arguments in an attempt to eliminate or contain the Zionist enterprise in Palestine.

Apart from these anti-Zionist nationalists, however, there were substantial numbers of Palestinian moderates, pragmatic nationalists, and apolitical people who adopted positive attitudes toward the Jewish community and even periodically expressed pro-Zionist views. Certain moderate Palestinian groups advocated cooperation with the Zionist Jews, welcomed Jewish economic assistance, and even fully accepted the Balfour Declaration of 1917. Other parties would accept only a partial implementation of the Balfour Declaration—namely, limited Jewish immigration and the creation of a small Jewish canton within a big Arab state.[13] These positive attitudes toward the Zionists by no means stemmed from any democratic notions or practices on the part of moderate Palestinian parties. Like the radical groups, these parties—such as the Arab Nationalist Party, the National Defense Party, and several rural parties—were undemocratic in their structures and operations. They were centered around urban aristocratic notables or wealthy village shaikhs, who by and large conducted traditional autocratic politics but claimed to represent large urban and rural populations.

It is worthwhile to note that many of the moderate parties essentially shared with the radical nationalist groups an anti-Zionist ideology, but in practice they periodically deviated from this principle and conducted policies toward the Jewish Yishuv based on real politics, pragmatic or opportunistic considerations, financial incentives, or their rivalries with the radical nationalist parties. Most of those moderate organs belonged to or were affiliated with the opposition (*mu'aridun*) within the Palestinian nationalist movement, which was led primarily by the Nashashibi family. This opposition competed with the Husayni-led *majlisiyun* headed by the Jerusalem mufti Hajj Amin al-Husayni, head of the Supreme Muslim Council (*majlis*) and leader of the Palestinian nationalist movement.

As big landowners and businessmen, the Nashashibis and similar families had vested interests in political stability and economic activity and thus were more inclined than their ideologically motivated rivals to accept the British Mandate and the Zionist presence. In addition to occasional Jewish political backing, such as in the election of Raghib Nashashibi to the mayoralty of Jerusalem in 1927, they would greatly benefit from profitable land sales to the Zionist movement and/or enjoy secret Zionist payments aimed at promoting pro-Jewish positions among the various *mu'aridun* factions.[14] Yet various moderate or pragmatic factions would at times reverse their political positions and adopt strong anti-Zionist attitudes under the changing circumstances. Although certain political groups ceased to operate when Zionist payments stopped, others became anti-Zionist and even anti-Jewish under pressure from radical nationalist parties or while competing with the radical nationalists for public support, particularly during periods of popular anti-Jewish sentiment. Palestinians felt a growing Zionist menace to the future of their country, its Islamic holy places, and its Arab character; for instance, in the summer of 1928 right-wing Jewish groups

allegedly encroached on the *Haram al-sharif* (the Ten
ducting a religious service at the Western Wall.

But it was particularly following the Nazi ascend:
1933, when large waves of Jewish immigrants from Cei
in Palestine, that many Palestinian Arabs feared that th
overrun by Jews and reacted with great fury and viol
were obviously used by the Husaynis not only to incite
the Zionist Yishuv but also to discredit the pro-Zionist
latter, deeply worried about their public image and popular support and
truly concerned about the fast expansion of the Zionist Yishuv, competed
with the Husaynis by demonstrating Arab nationalistic and anti-Zionist
positions. For example, in 1934 the Nashashibi-led National Defense Party
issued severe anti-Zionist and anti-Jewish statements,[15] and in April 1936,
following the eruption of the Arab rebellion, this party and other moderate
parties joined together with the nationalist movement in forming the Higher
Arab Committee, headed by Hajj Amin al-Husayni. The committee promptly adopted extreme anti-Zionist resolutions prohibiting, inter alia, Jewish
immigration to Palestine.[16]

Later, during the 1938 Palestinian-British negotiations in London, the
Higher Arab Committee agreed to allow limited Jewish immigration into
Palestine, but only on the condition that the total Jewish population did not
exceed a third of the entire population and that an independent Arab state
was established in Palestine. The Jewish-Zionist Yishuv not only rejected
these Arab demands but on previous occasions had turned down Palestinian
suggestions to establish a small Jewish canton from Tel Aviv to Atlit, as
well as British suggestions to establish a legislative council with equal representation of Arabs and Jews. The Zionist organizations insisted that
Jewish immigration must continue and that the Jewish national home
should be established according to the Balfour Declaration as the homeland
for all Jews in the world, not merely those living in Palestine. These Jewish
positions, coupled with the systematic and dynamic creation of an
autonomous Jewish community in Palestine furnished with solid political,
social, economic, and military institutions—all these factors caused great
concern, even alarm, among the Palestinian Arab community, thus
strengthening its militant-radical elements and pushing the moderate pragmatic groups to adopt extreme anti-Zionist positions.

Consequently, by the mid-1930s the Arab-Jewish dispute in Palestine
became in many respects a zero-sum struggle, and each community mobilized its manpower and resources to advance its cause. Under such circumstances, democratic tendencies on either side could hardly help bring about
Arab-Jewish accommodation, particularly in the case of the Palestinian
Arab community, which was still far from being truly democratic.
Paradoxically, the existence of democratic structures among Palestinian

cal groups and organs enabled the militant anti-Zionist groups and wspapers to freely express their views and positions and mobilize growing support from the population to intimidate their moderate rivals.

In a similar vein, the younger and more educated Palestinians with modern political and social ideas were no more inclined than the veteran politicians to seek a political solution to the conflict with the Jews. On the contrary, most of them were highly militant and urged the Palestinian national leadership to use violence and terror against the Jewish Yishuv.[17] During the early 1930s, educated young men and women established several movements and groups aimed at fighting the Zionists by terror and armed struggle. Many of these youngsters provided guidance and organization for the 1936–1939 Arab revolt,[18] which was directed essentially against the Zionists and British but also involved armed violence by the Husayni-led radical nationalists against the Nashashibi opposition. Under such bleak conditions, the British Royal Commission's recommendations of 1937—to divide Palestine into a small Jewish state and a larger Arab state—were rejected by most Palestinians, including the Nashashibis, who were forced to oppose such a plan under the pressure of the radicals.[19] The threat of the nationalist militants was indeed so paramount that they were able to force the Higher Arab Committee to reject in 1939 the British White Paper, despite the fact that it realized the bulk of the Palestinian nationalist objectives or demands.[20]

This uncompromising line of the Higher Arab Committee reemerged after the end of World War II. In late 1947 the newly established committee rejected the UN partition resolution, which provided for the establishment of an Arab state and a Jewish state in Palestine. This rejection was one of the main factors leading to the 1948 Arab-Israeli war and its severe repercussions for the Palestinians. Badly defeated by the new Jewish state and deprived of an opportunity to realize their aspirations in part of Palestine, the Palestinian Arab community disintegrated and largely dispersed. Many became refugees in Lebanon and Syria, as well as in Jordan on the West Bank and in the Egyptian-held Gaza Strip.

1948–1967:
Democratic Experience and Antagonism to Israel

The 1948 defeat had far-reaching effects on the Palestinian people and on their relations with the newly born state of Israel. Most Palestinians were not prone to make peace with the Israelis who caused this *nakba* (disaster), nor were they in a position to form their own democratic regime, as they were dispersed in several countries and lacked the resources to establish a national entity. Under such circumstances, it is not surprising that during the 1950s and early 1960s many Palestinians were attracted by ideas of pan-Arabism rather than Palestinian nationalism. They were influenced by the Egyptian leader, Gamal Abdul Nasser, the Syrian-based Ba'th Party, and other contemporary pan-Arab groups. Although most of these parties professed to support democracy for the future Arab union, in practice they established totalitarian regimes. They were also emphatically anti-Zionist and aimed at the elimination of Israel by force of arms. Many young Palestinians were active in these pan-Arab movements, particularly in Lebanon and Jordan's West Bank. They believed that Palestine could be redeemed from the Zionists only by a united Arab state and army. When, during the early and mid-1960s, many Palestinians became disenchanted with pan-Arabism and established their own nationalist organizations, notably Fath, their only aim remained unchanged: to destroy Israel by force and liberate Palestine from Zionism.

Other important developments affected Palestinians in the West Bank prior to the 1967 Israeli occupation. They had become Jordanian citizens in 1949, and for certain periods of time they actively participated in a quaside-mocratic Jordanian parliamentary regime with a multiparty system. Many young, educated Palestinian professionals and intellectuals formed or joined Arab radical parties such as the Socialist National Party, the Ba'th Party, the Arab Nationalists ("al Qawmiyyun al-Arab"), and the like. These parties were democratic in structure and function, emphatically demanded to promote the democratization of the political system, and advanced the parliamentary regime in Jordan (although the Ba'th Party, for example, established strong autocratic regimes in Syria and Iraq).[21] Even though these parties, which largely functioned in the West Bank, were periodically outlawed by the Hashemite government, they nevertheless succeeded in significantly enhancing the process of democratization in Jordan. Yet with respect to Israel, all these modern, democratically oriented parties called for the destruction of the Zionist state (although certain parties in their agendas would permit Jews to continue living as a minority in an Arab state).[22] Two Islamic parties that were neither modern nor democratic, the Muslim Brothers and the Liberation (Tahrir) Party, were anti-Israeli and anti-Jewish.[23]

Other organizations that were wholly Palestinian, operated mostly in the West Bank, and aimed solely at Israel's annihilation were the PLO and Fath. These military-political organizations commenced their activities in the mid-1960s and gradually gained popularity among the youth and the modern intelligentsia. Initially they were not concerned with the question of democracy in their own bodies or in the future Palestinian state. Only later did the PLO raise the notion of creating a secular democratic state in Palestine, but this state was to be established not side by side with Israel but on Israel's demise.

The only modern political party that continued to recognize the legitimacy of Israel according to the 1947 partition lines was the Jordanian

Communist Party (JCP), which was composed of mostly students and workers.[24] Interestingly, the JCP was for many years the only political party that advocated the establishment of a Palestinian state alongside Israel; most parties and groups, including the PLO, did not raise at all or rejected the idea of a separate Palestinian entity or state. The Communists' position regarding the existence of (a small) Israel did not derive from their adherence to the ideas of Western democracy but rather from their obedience to the Soviet policy, which for many years supported Israel's existence. On the other end of the political spectrum, there were pro-Hashemite conservative Palestinian groups that did not profess Western democracy but, like their master, the king, held pragmatic positions vis-à-vis Israel. Although publicly making anti-Israel statements, they were ready to accept Israel's existence owing to a variety of political and economic considerations, notably Israel's military might and good political relations with the United States, as well as its common interest with Jordan in countering the radical forces in the region.

It can thus be concluded that during the period of Jordanian rule over the West Bank and of the British Mandate in Palestine, there was no linkage whatsoever between democratic or quasidemocratic trends among Palestinian political organizations and any manifestation of peaceful attitudes within the Palestinian community toward Israel or the Zionist-Jewish Yishuv. On the contrary, it would appear that while many conservative, traditional, nondemocratic Palestinian political groups or parties were inclined out of self-interest to accept Israel, modern-radical and quasidemocratic organs were consistently and intensely anti-Zionist and anti-Israel. Many would adopt any method or regime, including democracy, in order to facilitate their national struggle, while a few who genuinely professed democratic views believed that only by embracing a Western democratic regime would the Palestinians be able to successfully fight Israel. Such an approach, for example, can be seen in some writings of Musa Alami, a prominent Palestinian leader and progressive intellectual who was educated in England and held a rather moderate line regarding the Zionist Yishuv and Israel. Analyzing the Arab and Palestinian defeat in the 1948 war, he asserted, inter alia, that in order to effectively struggle against Israel the Arabs must unite, adopt a genuine constitutional regime (either monarchistic or republican), and grant democratic rights to the population.[25] If this was the position of a British-educated Palestinian intellectual, a democrat and a pragmatist, after the 1948 Arab defeat, what can expected to be the attitudes of most Palestinians toward Israel and democratic governance after the 1967 defeat (*naksa*), when a major portion of the Palestinian people were defeated and placed under Israeli military occupation?

On the face of it, neither an authentic process of democratization nor a genuine inclination for peace with Israel was likely to develop among the Palestinians after they were put under military occupation by their archenemy, suppressing their national aspirations and prohibiting the formation of political parties among them.

1967–1977: Democratic and Pragmatic Trends Among the Palestinians in the West Bank

Democratic trends and institutions have in fact developed among the Palestinians in the West Bank since 1967 through the formation of many social, professional, and municipal bodies, most of which were elected and operated democratically. They conducted de facto political activities and through a variety of newspapers and journals freely expressed political opinions and views, including severe anti-Israeli expressions. Simultaneously, alongside a prolonged and vigorous struggle against the Israeli occupation, there have appeared among the West Bank population since 1967 significant tendencies toward accommodation and coexistence with Israel.

With these general observations in mind, and against the background of pre-1967 developments, it is important to examine the factors that brought about the development of democratic organs and pragmatic attitudes toward Israel among the West Bank Palestinians. Furthermore, an attempt should also be made to find out whether or not, and to what extent, there has been any correlation or linkage between these two developments—i.e., whether the process of democratization contributed to improving Palestinian-Israeli relations or, conversely, to aggravating them. Or perhaps there has been no linkage between these two important phenomena.

Continuity and Change: 1967–1977

During the first several years of Israeli occupation, the Palestinian political community in the West Bank continued, in certain respects, to experience conditions and behave in a pattern similar to the pre-1967 period. The Israeli military authorities, while prohibiting the formation of new political parties, maintained part of the previous quasidemocratic political system on the West Bank. They permitted, indeed encouraged, the functioning of town municipalities and village councils in accordance with the 1955 Jordanian law that allowed only men beyond age twenty-one who paid property taxes—primarily members of the wealthy classes—to vote. Indeed, most of the town councillors (and certainly the village shaikhs) who operated in the West Bank following the 1967 war and those elected in 1972 municipal elections belonged to traditional, conservative, rich families.[26] Most of those conservative Palestinian mayors and councillors were pro-Jordan and politically pragmatic and thus advocated the return of the West Bank to Jordan as part of a political agreement with Israel. Yet a few conservative personalities, notably the mayor of Hebron, Shaykh Muhammad Ali al Ja'bari, and a small group of more progressive intellectuals such as lawyer Aziz Shihada and Dr. al-Taji al-Faruqi, suggested the establishment of a Palestinian entity or state that would peacefully coexist with Israel.[27] Some of these progressive personalities called for the convening of a popular Palestinian congress to discuss these issues and a constituent assembly to elect a new leadership to initiate direct negotiations with Israel.[28] To be sure, this new Palestinian approach, although partly derived from genuine democratic values professed by some West Bank intellectuals, was mainly motivated—as in the case of the conservative Palestinians—by pragmatic considerations. Indeed, the 1967 war clearly manifested the pan-Arab failure to defeat Israel and prompted realistic Palestinians, both conservative and progressive, to seek a political settlement with the powerful Jewish state: Israel would withdraw from the West Bank and let the Palestinians choose their own government. Unfortunately, the Israeli government did not encourage these pragmatic tendencies, partly because it disregarded Palestinian nationalism and wished to strike a deal with Jordan over the West Bank and partly because it feared that an autonomous Palestinian entity in the West Bank was likely to be controlled by the PLO and thus constitute a grave danger to Israel's security.

Evidently, the PLO itself vehemently opposed both the return of the West Bank to Jordan or the creation of an independent state in the framework of a political agreement with Israel. This organization was fully committed, at that period, to the total destruction of Israel through an armed struggle. Not only did the PLO threaten the lives of Palestinians who supported the establishment of a Palestinian state in the West Bank, but the idea was "still premature and heretical"[29] among most Palestinians in the West Bank, notably the modern urban intelligentsia and followers of the various radical groups (including the various guerrilla organizations, the Arab Nationalist movement, the Ba'th Party, and a militant wing of the Communist Party).

Indeed, most members and followers of radical parties in the West Bank vigorously opposed Israel's existence, although some of them held democratic notions of some sort. The adherence of those Palestinians to ideas of democracy, socialism, or secularism, either nominally or genuinely, by no means implied that they were more prone than their conservative fellow West Bankers to accept Israel and peacefully coexist with it. The PLO, for example, advanced during the late 1960s and early 1970s the idea of establishing a "secular democratic state" in all of Palestine[30]—that is, not side by side with Israel, but on Israel's ruins. Yet even though this notion was acceptable for several years by many Palestinian intellectuals in the West Bank and elsewhere, the attitude of Palestinian nationalists and politicians toward Israel's existence gradually changed during the 1970s and became more sober. Although most if not all of them were still ideologically committed to Israel's destruction, a growing number of Palestinians also realized that Israel was a strong and viable national polity that could not be easily eliminated; therefore, they accepted its existence, at least for the time being, and dedicated their efforts to the struggle against Israel's occupation of the West Bank and Gaza while consolidating Palestinian national identity in these territories.

The PNF and the PCP

This new position apparently developed and was articulated by the Palestine National Front (PNF), which was established in 1973 by the outlawed Palestinian communist party (PCP), some followers of Fath, the Democratic Front for the Liberation of Palestine (DFLP), and representatives from labor unions, professional associations, student councils, and other groups. According to Sahliyeh, the PNF reflected "the prevailing mood in the occupied territories following the 1973 war"—namely, that Jordan must not return to rule the West Bank and that an independent Palestinian state should be created in the Occupied Territories alongside Israel. The PNF regarded the PLO's objective of liberating all of Palestine unrealistic, as well as unacceptable to the world community, and argued that such an extreme position would only help perpetuate Israel's occupation of the West Bank and Gaza. It also suggested employing diplomatic means to liberate the Occupied Territories and sought a political settlement for the Palestinian-Israeli dispute.[31] Significantly, the PNF's bold new position preceded that of the PLO, which only much later endorsed the policy of creating a Palestinian state side by side with Israel.

But until this happened, the PLO endeavored to control the activities of the communist-led PNF. Failing to realize this objective, the PLO regarded the PNF as a rival and thus intensively worked to dismantle it from within. The final collapse of the PNF, however, was effected forcibly by Israel, which regarded it a "security risk" even though its program did not call for Israel's destruction, or for military struggle against the Jewish state.

It would be difficult to measure the amount of support the PNF agenda obtained from the newly emerging Palestinian political community or to what extent this support stemmed from, or was related to, a process of democratization among the Palestinians in the West Bank. According to Sahliyeh: "The Front enjoyed widespread popularity and political legitimacy in the occupied territories. It encompassed varying political opinions and social forces, and its agenda reflected the political needs and wishes of the West Bank Palestinians." By contrast, however, Fath activists inside the PNF alleged that "because of communist control, the PNF did not represent the prevailing social and political forces in the West Bank and Gaza."[32]

It stands to reason that in addition to Palestinian Communists, modern intellectuals and professionals such as lawyer Aziz Shihada, Dr. al-Taji al-Faruqi, and journalists Jamil Hamad and Muhammad Abu Shilbaya favored a peaceful coexistence with Israel on the basis of a two-state solution. The Communist Party in the West Bank was in itself well-organized and influential among labor unions, professional associations, women, and youth and student organizations.[33] It thus represented a substantial number of Palestinians, although not the majority. The Palestinian Communists were the first Arab party to prescribe peaceful coexistence between a Palestinian state and Israel (although in accordance with the 1947 UN partition resolution), and they continued to support this idea in conformity with Soviet policy and their own ideological tenets. They expected that following an era of mutual cooperation and understanding between Palestinians and Israelis, a secular democratic state could be peacefully created in Palestine for both Arabs and Jews. To achieve this end, they believed in a partnership with progressive, democratic, and socialist forces in Israel, notably the Israeli Communist Party, with which the PCP developed strong ties.

In conclusion, the PCP agenda of a two-state solution to the Palestinian-Israeli dispute, to be achieved by political means, won over significant sections of the Palestinian urban intelligentsia and workers in the West Bank. And unlike the PLO's notion of a secular democratic state, which was a false propaganda ploy,[34] the communist ideas were genuine and certainly more pragmatic than those of the PLO. When the PLO, which enjoyed majority support in the West Bank, eventually came to favor a two-state solution in the framework of a political settlement, it did so because of pressure by its mainstream followers. Such pressure was expressed, for example, by a group of mayors elected in the 1976 free democratic elections in the West Bank. Fahd Qawasmah of Hebron, Elias Freij of Bethlehem, and Rashad al-Shawwa of Gaza were among those advocating a peaceful coexistence between Israel and a Palestinian state in the West Bank and Gaza and trying to convince the PLO to adopt this position. Certain West Bank leaders criticized the "unrealistic" and "uncompromising" positions of the PLO toward Israel's existence. Others, including militant mayors Bassam Shak'a of Nablus and Karim Khalaf of Ramallah, initially argued that the PLO idea of establishing a secular democratic state in Palestine was a farfetched dream that could not be realized for many generations.[35] Freij also urged the PLO to modify the Palestine National Charter by omitting articles that called for the destruction of Israel.[36]

Freij and several nationalist mayors welcomed U.S. President Jimmy Carter's speech of March 1977 calling for the establishment of a Palestinian homeland in the West Bank and Gaza and initially praised Sadat's historical visit to Jerusalem in November 1977.[37] With these developments in mind, we will now examine to what extent the moderate attitudes of these democratically elected Palestinian leaders toward a political settlement with Israel were linked to the process of democratization among Palestinians in the West Bank and look at the main causes for and the major manifestations of that democratic process.

It would be both premature and presumptuous at this stage to trace the various factors underlining the democratic process among the West Bank Palestinians, such as the impact of Western concepts, regimes, and educational systems on the new Palestinian intelligentsia. It would also be beyond the scope of this preliminary work to detect possible imprints of certain neighboring Arab nations, such as Lebanon, Jordan, and Kuwait, on the West Bank Palestinians. As for the possible impact of PLO institutions, notably the PNC, on the democratization process among the West Bankers, it would appear that, as with the trend of pragmatism toward Israel, the West Bankers preceded their comrades in the PLO establishment and possibly also influenced them to adopt democratic procedures.

The Impact of Israel and its Occupation

It appears that the major political-institutional changes among the Palestinian people during the last generations, notably the democratization process, have occurred on the West Bank since the late 1960s and have been closely interwoven with socioeconomic developments. And these developments and changes have in turn been largely influenced by the West Bankers' multichannel relations with Israel (such as with Israeli leftist and liberal groups), the Israeli Arab community, and certain Israeli norms and institutions. In particular, the policies of the various Israeli governments regarding the West Bank have had profound effects on the socioeconomic, educational, and political changes among the Palestinians, including the trends of democratization and coexistence with Israel.

The Israeli Labor governments (1967–1977) should have enhanced the development of democratic and peaceful tendencies among the West Bank Palestinians considering the party's politically pragmatic socialist-democratic platform, which advocated the return of the Occupied Territories for the sake of peace. In fact, however, during the first several years of the occupation, the Israeli Labor government cultivated alliances with traditional-conservative leaders in the West Bank, who were neither democratic nor socialist. This government was also inclined to trade the West Bank for peace with Jordan[38] but not with the Palestinians, whom Prime Minister Golda Meir, for example, would not consider a nation. And although it acknowledged for the first time in 1974 the existence of a Palestinian problem, the Labor government continued until 1977 to seek a Jordanian solution for the West Bank-Palestinian problem.

In the long run, though, the Labor governments' policies greatly contributed both directly and indirectly to diminishing the political and socioeconomic power of the traditional conservative elite in the West Bank and to enhancing social change, political participation, and democratization among the lower classes of the West Bank Palestinians. For example, the opening of the Israeli labor market to many thousands of young Palestinians, who now draw higher wages than they could in the West Bank, sharply reduced their economic and political dependency on the conservative, pro-Jordan landowners and businessmen. The growth of the Palestinian working class, accompanied by an improved standard of living, resulted in the expansion of labor unions and enabled many Palestinian workers and peasants to give their children higher education at the newly established universities in the West Bank. These developments further contributed to an erosion of the traditional social stratification and the influence of the old elite while widening the scope of participatory politics in the West Bank among the various sections of the population. The latter process occurred through a rising number of professional associations (for lawyers, engineers, doctors, journalists, and so forth), student and women organizations, social and cultural clubs, and the like.

Although the Israeli military government prohibited the formation of political parties and PLO-related organizations, it did not curtail the creation and functioning of professional organizations. Most of these bodies did in fact conduct political activities, including discussions, publications, demonstrations, and protests relating primarily to Palestinian national issues and to the struggle against Israeli occupation. As it happened, many of these West Bank groups were largely inspired, influenced, and even organized by the PLO-Fa'th, the radical Marxist fronts, or Muslim fundamentalist movements.[39]

Significantly, most of those associations functioned democratically in electing councils and committees, as well as in decisionmaking processes, without much interference by the Israeli authorities. The Israeli government also did not normally hinder the publication of Palestinian newspapers in East Jerusalem (which became officially part of Israel), subjecting them to the same regulations that were applied to the Israeli press—namely, military (but not political) censorship. The fairly free Palestinian press published in East Jerusalem expressed a variety of political views and reflected yet another dimension of the democratization process among the West Bank Palestinians. Other democratic norms and institutions of the Israeli state and society also inspired or were emulated by the Palestinians, notably the democratic political organization and activities of the Israeli Arabs, the liberal and empathic positions of the Israeli leftist parties and peace movements, and the highly impartial rulings of the Supreme Court of Justice in cases related to Palestinian grievances.

The Israeli Labor government itself encouraged democratic procedures among Palestinians in 1976 by initiating free democratic elections for the town municipalities in the West Bank. The Israelis amended the 1955 Jordanian election law, for the first time extending the franchise to all adults above the age of twenty-one, including women. (Said one Palestinian woman leader: "The vote was our first lesson in democracy.")[40] Apart from intending to demonstrate to the world community its benign and liberal rule in the West Bank, the Israeli Labor government, particularly Minister of Defense Shimon Peres, genuinely wished to introduce among the Palestinians the norms of Western democracy, partly per se but largely in order to make the newly and democratically elected town councils a basis for a new Palestinian self-administration in the West Bank. Mr. Peres apparently assumed that those democratic elections would demonstrate that many Palestinians, notably women, favored the local conservative-pragmatic candidates, who would be willing to accept his self-administration plan for the West Bank as a basis for an Israeli-Palestinian-Jordanian settlement. But Peres was wrong on his assumptions: The free democratic elections resulted in a great victory for the pro-PLO nationalist candidates, and they were not prepared to accept his self-administration plan and/or renewed Jordanian control in the West Bank. Most of them supported the creation of a Palestinian state in the West Bank and Gaza, existing alongside Israel under PLO leadership.

Yet the Labor government, until it was replaced by a Likud government in 1977, did not encourage the pragmatic nationalist mayors such as Qawasmah, Freij, and al-Shawwa to negotiate a political settlement with Israel, either in the form of Palestinian self-rule in the West Bank or a Jordanian-Palestinian federation. But even if the Labor government had attempted to negotiate either of those settlements with the new West Bank leaders, it is highly doubtful, if not impossible, that these leaders would have struck a deal with Israel without the PLO's sanction. And the PLO itself not only strongly objected at that juncture to both those solutions but also severely warned the West Bank leaders against concluding any agreements with Israel.

1977–1987: Growing Democratization and National Struggle Among West Bank Palestinians Under the Likud Governments

The Likud Policies

Given the state of affairs under the liberal socialist Labor regime, it could be expected that, with the ascendancy of the right-wing Likud bloc in 1977, the new Israeli government would try to weaken both the democratic and nationalist trends among the West Bank Palestinians. This policy accorded the Likud platform the incorporation of the West Bank and Gaza into Israel while denying Palestinians full political rights.

In fact, however, for the first three years of its rule—with the pragmatic leaders Ezer Weizman and Moshe Dayan serving as defense and foreign ministers, respectively—the Likud government did not interfere with the processes of socioeconomic change, political participation, democratization, or institution building among the West Bank Palestinians. It even permitted, inter alia, the establishment of the National Guidance Committee (NGC) in 1978, which included six elected mayors and was regarded as a representative leadership by the Palestinians in the West Bank and Gaza. Several of the NGC members were inclined to reach an agreement with Israel provided it would bring about Palestinian self-determination and statehood, but they opposed the Likud's model of the Camp David autonomy plan, regarding it as perpetuating Israel's domination over the Occupied Territories. The radical leftist members of the NGC—mayors Shaka and Khalaf, as well as followers of the Communists and the two popular fronts—strongly rejected the Camp David accords also because of U.S. involvement. Ignoring Mr. Weizman's suggestions, the Likud government under Menachem Begin's leadership neither cultivated nor negotiated with the pragmatic faction of the NGC, which was composed of pro–Fath-PLO and pro-Jordanian members. On the contrary, Prime Minister Begin, backed by his hard-line comrades, notably Ariel Sharon, adopted an uncompromising policy regarding the Camp David talks, further alienating the NGC while prompting Dayan and Weizman to resign in 1980 from the Israeli cabinet. With Ariel Sharon as defense minister after 1981, a series of harsh measures were taken by Israel aimed at the elimination of the Palestinian representatives and/or democratically elected institutions and organs. Several elected mayors were dismissed, the NGC was outlawed, universities were periodically closed, and newspapers became subject to heavy political censorship.[41] More Arab lands were confiscated while new Jewish settlements were established in the West Bank, and various aggressive and illegal activities of the Gush Emunim settlers were tolerated by the Israeli government.

In place of the authentic and representative Palestinian leaders, the Israeli government endeavored to promote an alternative Palestinian leadership, the "Village Leagues," which were neither elected by nor representative of the West Bank Palestinians but were composed of conservative-traditional rural families who collaborated with the Israeli military administration.

Palestinian Democratization Process

The hard-line Likud government failed to install the Village Leagues in leadership positions. Moreover, the removal of the representative, partly democratically elected West Bank leaders did not stop the democratization process among the West Bank Palestinians. On the contrary, it enhanced the process. Indeed, partly in reaction to the elimination of the top elected leaders and national institutions, partly as a defense mechanism vis-à-vis Israeli repression, the democratization process further expanded among the grassroots of the Palestinian community through the growing number of and membership in trade unions, professional associations; women, student and youth movements; and the like. An increasing number of Palestinians regarded their participation in these organizations as a major way to combat Israeli occupation and establish democratic institutions. Thus, for the first time the notion of democracy became, alongside the ideas of national solidarity and struggle against occupation, a major ethos among the West Bank Palestinians.

In many articles in various Palestinian journals, as well as in public meetings, democracy was hailed throughout the 1980s as the basis of Palestinian solidarity, popular mobilization, and steadfastness. (For example: "The Palestinian people are proud of the democracy that prevails amongst them and long to preserve and cultivate it in order to gain [more] achievements and keep the existent ones.")[42] Special attention was given to the democratic practices within the PLO, notably in the PNC,[43] while on several occasions the absence of democracy in the Arab world was harshly criticized.[44] Along with the discussions regarding the merits of democracy and the dangers it encountered, there appeared during that period in Arabic newspapers and journals numerous reports and analyses regarding elections and other democratic practices in various West Bank–Gaza Palestinian organizations and associations.[45] Special attention was given to the national elections in Israel and among the Israeli Arabs.[46]

As it happened, Israel continued during the 1980s to indirectly enhance the Palestinian democratic process, not only by remaining a model for a successful democratic system but also by allowing Palestinian democratization to proceed on the level of trade unions, professional associations, and popular organizations. This democratic process developed significantly during the 1980s, gaining momentum on its own not only as a political reaction to Israeli suppression of national rights but also largely as a result of socioeconomic changes, the expansion of education, and the growing political awareness among the lower classes of Palestinians, rural and urban alike.

The Labor Unions

The largest group of West Bankers who have undergone these important changes are the Palestinian workers. Reportedly, of about 160,000 workers in 1968, only 6 percent were organized in labor unions. The number of Palestinian workers in the Occupied Territories and Israel swelled to about 230,000 in the late 1970s, with 20 percent of them registered as members of trade unions. The 100 or so labor unions, with some 40,000 members, have been organized since the early 1980s in three major federations, respectively affiliated to Fatah-PLO, the DFLP, and the PCP.[47] The great majority of these unions, although prone to occasional irregularities and subject to certain Israeli legal restrictions, conduct their affairs in a democratic manner, notably in the election and supervision of their various officers and organs.[48]

The Student Movement

Unlike the labor unions, which have kept a low profile in their political activities, the fast-growing West Bank Palestinian student movement has been highly politicized and has assumed a leading role in nationalist thinking and anti-occupation activities. Composed in the late 1980s of some 15,000 students in six universities, most of which were founded under Israeli occupation, the student movement in the West Bank and Gaza has been divided into three main rival blocs: Communist-Marxists, Nationalists (Fatah-PLO), and Islamists (Hamas).[49] In addition, there are several thousand Palestinian students in nine colleges and seminaries and some 50,000 high school students (including those in the Gaza Strip), most of them organized or affiliated to the above-mentioned three main political blocs. It could be expected that, more than any other section of the West Bank population, the Palestinian student body should be highly democratic in its structure, activities, and notions owing to its great exposure to modern higher education and Western political concepts.

Yet although elections for the student unions and councils have been conducted in a progressively democratic fashion with a very high participation of students, periodically there have occurred many irregularities and other "negative phenomena."[50] In theory one of the main objectives of the Palestinian universities is to immerse students in the democratic way, both intellectually and practically, for the sake of the Palestinian nation and revolution.[51] In fact, however, certain student blocs define democracy in a way that suits their political agendas while discrediting their rivals' views. In other words, certain student groups are intolerant of rivals having a politically pragmatic approach to the conflict with Israel. Thus, for example, in 1983 two Marxist student organizations, the Student Union Bloc and the Student Action Front, both followers of Syria, attacked Arafat's style of leadership, depicting it as "authoritarian and antidemocratic" and calling for the "democratization of the PLO's policymaking apparatus." To be sure, the main motive behind this "democratic" position was an opposition to Arafat's tendency at that juncture to seek a political settlement for the Palestinian issue in league with Egypt and Jordan despite Syrian and Soviet opposition.

In the same vein, the Student Action Front, affiliated with the Popular Front for the Liberation of Palestine (PFLP), objected to Arafat's meeting with representatives of Israeli peace groups and demanded that such contacts be confined to "progressive and democratic non-Zionist Jewish forces."[52] Such an attitude and similar positions of the PFLP did imply that this student bloc was fighting not only against Israeli occupation of the West Bank and Gaza but also against the very existence of the state of Israel. The Islamic student bloc emerging in the late 1970s openly called for Israel's destruction,[53] regardless of the fact that the bloc actively participated in the students' elections and by 1981 even dominated a majority of student councils, to the chagrin of both the pro-PLO and Marxist student blocs. As it happened, although the various student organizations were elected and functioned upon democratic procedures, they would periodically fight one another not in a civilized democratic manner but with makeshift weapons such as chains, iron bars, clubs, and Molotov cocktails.[54] Occasionally the conduct of university professors was also undemocratic, as in the case of the Bir Zeit University employees union, which demanded in April 1987 that university authorities dismiss Dr. Sari Nusseibeh because of his meeting with Simon Peres, the Israeli prime minister. This request came after Dr. Nusseibeh was physically attacked by militant students at Bir Zeit University. According to the Arabic newspaper *al-Sinara,* the union request was not only contrary to its own constitution but also undemocratic. "How can we expect from the students a democratic conduct when their teachers do not behave so?" asked writer Daoud Kuttab. "Where have been the endeavors of the professors and the university authorities to imprint among the students a democratic spirit and respect for somebody else's opinion?"[55]

In addition to thousands of university and college students and tens of thousands of high school pupils, mostly organized democratically and active politically for many years, a new youth movement called *shabiba* was established in the early 1980s by the Fatah-PLO. Consisting of thousands of youngsters, including high school pupils, the *shabiba* has not been organized or functioned in a full democratic manner. Instead it operates through regional and local committees in towns and villages throughout the West Bank. Initially this movement was created by the PLO as an instrument of youth mobilization and influence. It was assigned to help the lower classes of the population in small towns and villages to carry out maintenance works such as paving roads, gardening, cleaning, and so forth. In the course of time, the *shabiba* has become greatly involved in anti-occupation activities such as demonstrations, strikes, and stone throwing, particularly during the intifada.[56]

The Women Movements and Other Organizations

In addition to the youth movement, other new social forces emerged in the early 1980s in the West Bank, reflecting the growing social changes and widening of participatory politics in the Palestinian community. The women's movement has been a significant example. Prior to the 1980s, small groups of Palestinian women, mostly from the middle classes, had been active in various welfare associations, which were by and large apolitical. The new women's movement, however, consisted of some 10,000 members, many of them from the lower classes and from villages. It was subdivided into four federations, affiliated respectively to the Fatah-PLO, PCP, PFLP, and DFLP. These federations periodically conducted democratic elections and became highly active in social, vocational, cultural, and medical work as well as in national political activities against the Israeli occupation.[57] Despite these activities, Palestinian women in the West Bank are still far from becoming fully liberated and equal partners in their society, largely because of the traditional, conservative positions of many Palestinians, particularly Muslim fundamentalists.

Other West Bank political organizations were established or expanded during the 1980s, increasing their political activities and democratic characteristics. These included associations of merchants, artisans, engineers, physicians, lawyers, writers, and journalists.[58] And although the big organizations of workers, students, and women provided the frameworks for mass political participation, national struggle, and democratic experience for the growing number of Palestinians, the small professional associations, notably of the journalists, lawyers, and writers, rendered the intellectual guidance and conceptual articulation for these new developments. Both types of organizations reflected the structural social change and mass political mobilization that occurred among the West Bank Palestinians under the impact of Israeli occupation.

The Intifada:
The Democratic Process and Attitudes Toward Israel

Most, if not all, of these sociopolitical organizations provided the solid infrastructure for the intifada, which erupted in December 1987. The intifada, in turn, has for the last four years significantly accelerated social change and political participation among the Palestinians in the West Bank and Gaza. Indeed, the intifada, despite its brutal aspects, has represented not only a popular nationalist uprising against Israeli occupation but also a social-political upheaval in the Palestinian community. The wider sectors of the population—workers, women, and youth, along with intellectuals and professionals—have been mobilized. The small, traditional Palestinian upper class of notables and wealthy families that had controlled political, economic, and social life for generations has been eliminated.

Without dwelling on the causes for or course of the intifada, which are outside the scope of this work,[59] it is worth making several observations with respect to the two major aspects of the intifada that are the objects of our discussion—namely, the democratic process among West Bank Palestinians and its possible bearing on their attitude toward Israel.

Significantly, one of the major objectives of the intifada, according to the mainstream leadership (the Unified National Command of the Uprising, or UNCU) was the establishment of an independent Palestinian state alongside Israel in accordance with UN Resolution 181 of November 29, 1947, which reads:

> The nature of the independent Palestinian State will be a [democratic] republic—elected president, ministerial council made up of elected parties. The state will allow multiple political parties and religions, and the freedom of all believers to worship. It will guarantee the citizen to live in freedom, dignity and the pursuit of happiness. It will guarantee to him all the rights stated in the UN Declaration of Human Rights, including the freedoms of expression, education and ownership.[60]

Similarly, the first manifesto of the UNCU of January 14, 1988, included a demand for free democratic elections in the territories, while subsequent documents requested not only free elections but also political negotiations with Israel (with the PLO representing the Palestinians).[61] In addition to these "official" statements, various Palestinian organs, leaders, and common people in the West Bank would from time to time hail democracy and the democratic experience as an essential condition for the intifada's success.[62]

Indeed, the intifada by and large has been structured and conducted fairly democratically. The UNCU has been organized with some fifteen rotating members, three each from Fatah, PFLP, DFLP, PCP, and occasionally the Islamic Jihad. UNCU decisions have been made unanimously after consultation with local committees (and with the PLO in Tunis), which operated at the grassroots level in most towns and villages and represented various sections of the Palestinian population.[63] Furthermore the UNCU has in one way or another been affiliated with the numerous labor unions and professional associations and particularly to the student and women's movements in the West Bank. During the intifada some of these organizations continued to conduct their elections and other functions democratically, notably the commerce chambers and the journalists association, both of which have become important vehicles of the intifada.[64]

As it happened, most of the elections in the West Bank (although not in Gaza) resulted, as in previous years, in victories for candidates affiliated with the PLO-Fatah, i.e., the core group of the UNCU.[65] These observations lead us to the other aspects of our discussion—namely, Palestinian attitudes toward Israel and the possible linkage between these attitudes and the democratic process. As is well known, unlike the Islamic fundamentalist group Hamas, which has been very influencial in Gaza and has aimed at Israel's destruction, the main PLO-affiliated organizations, embodied in the

UNCU and dominant in the West Bank, have sought coexistence with Israel. This mainstream position gradually developed under Israeli occupation, notably since the mid-1970s and has not changed, even during the intifada. Intifada leaflets have called for coexistence with Israel, and intifada leaders have apparently pressured PLO-Tunis to recognize Israel and declare a Palestinian state alongside Israel.[66] This pressure started in the early 1980s and possibly contributed to statements and decisions made by the PLO during the second half of 1988 (i.e., Bassam Abu Sharif's document of June 7, 1988, the PNC Algiers declaration of November 15, 1988, and Arafat's Stockholm statement of December 8, 1988, as well as his statement to the UN Special Assembly in Geneva on December 13, 1988).[67] These documents and statements accepted Israel's existence on the basis of UN Resolutions 181 (November 1947), 242 (November 1967), and 338 (October 1973) and called for the establishment of a Palestinian state in coexistence with Israel.

To be sure, the development of an agenda favoring coexistence with Israel by the mainstream Palestinian leadership in the West Bank and the PLO-Tunis establishment does not reflect a major change in the Palestinian ideology toward Israel—namely, acceptance of Israel's right to exist as a Jewish-Zionist state. The Palestinian National Charter, which denies this right, has not been officially abrogated or changed, although recent PNC decisions have practically nullified some critical anti-Israeli clauses of the charter. Other claims, such as the notion of the Palestinians' collective right of return to their homes in Israel proper, remain unaffected. In addition to the Hamas, which calls for Israel's destruction, other Palestinian groups, notably the PFLP, still refuse to recognize Israel's right to exist. A public opinion poll conducted in the Occupied Territories in 1986 by *al-Fajr-AB'* and *Newsday* indicated that a considerable segment of the population sample (in which "professionals, white-collar, college-educated persons are clearly overrepresented") expressed radical views.

43.2% reject the "two state" solution even as an interim solution (49.7% support it), 72.9% view the Palestinian state in the whole of Palestine as a permanent solution to the Palestine problem (compared to 16.9% who are ready to accept a state in the West Bank and Gaza). Diplomatic initiative is perceived as an ineffective means for solving the Palestinian problem. 7.3% support it, compared to 60.7% who support armed struggle. Violence is perceived as justified, legitimate and effective, both on the strategic and on the tactical level. It is part of the "struggle for the right to self-determination" (83.0%). . . . Acts of terrorism against civilians enjoy widespread support, including the notorious attack on an (Israeli) . . . bus (87.6%) and planting a bomb in an El-Al plane (60.5%). The overwhelming majority does not trust either a Labor government or a Likud government as likely to bring about a solution to the Palestinian problem.[68]

This hostile attitude toward Israel, expressed mostly by Palestinian intellectuals, has possibly not changed and also may have influenced the new young generations of Palestinians. For example, numerous Palestinian children's books published in recent years in the Occupied Territories dehumanize Israeli Jews, whereas only a few books include references to peaceful coexistence with Israel.[69] Notwithstanding the deep causes for Palestinian hostility toward Israel and denial of its right to exist, many Palestinians in the West Bank, Gaza, and among the PLO establishment have sought to accept Israel and coexist with it on the condition that Israel withdraws from the Occupied Territories and lets the Palestinians determine their own political future.

This constructive attitude has not stemmed from feelings of sympathy or empathy toward Israel but rather from the growing realism among West Bank (and PLO) leaders. This Palestinian strategy has gradually developed since the mid-1970s not only because of the realization that Israel is a powerful state that cannot be easily eliminated but also because of several other crucial factors. Israel's continued military occupation and economic integration of the West Bank and Gaza and the fast expansion of Jewish settlements since the early 1980s have been leading toward de facto annexation of these territorities, a process that could be irreversible and could eliminate the prospects for creating a Palestinian state. And because this process has not been halted or reversed by the international community, the superpowers, the Arab countries, even the PLO, the Palestinians in the Occupied Territories have had essentially to rely on themselves and mold their own strategy. The major components of this strategy have been not only steadfastness (*sumud*) and popular uprising but also realpolitik—namely, a readiness to accept Israel as a state and peacefully coexist with it. Such a future Palestinian state, according to many Palestinians, should be a democratic republic based on the notions of Western democracy.

Tentative Conclusions

The Palestinians' new objective of creating a democratic state leads us finally to the difficult but important question of whether or not there has been linkage between the democratic trends among the Palestinians in the West Bank and the development of pragmatic attitudes toward Israel among them. In other words: Has democratization created or enhanced peaceful coexistence between Palestinian Arabs and Israeli Jews?

In many respects, such a linkage has not existed; by and large, the democratic developments among the Palestinians have not lessened their hostile attitudes toward the Jewish Yishuv and Israel. If anything, Palestinian political groups who were more modernized and experienced various forms of democracy have been more hostile and militant toward Israel than the conservative nondemocratic Palestinian groups. For example, Arab members of the Turkish Parliament representing Jerusalem and various nationalist and quasidemocratic Palestinian parties during the British Mandatory period (notably the Husaynis) were strongly anti-Zionist/anti-Jewish, employing democratic institutions and motions in their uncompromising struggle against the Jewish Yishuv. By contrast, the more moderate or pragmatic Palestinians who coexisted and cooperated with the Jewish Yishuv during those periods were affiliated to the conservative, nondemocratic parties and groups, notably the Nashashibis. Similarly, during the Jordanian occupation of the West Bank (1948–1967) and particularly under Israeli occupation, most Palestinian groups, leaders, or organs who for practical reasons were inclined to accept Israel and cooperate with it were conservative and nondemocratic, such as Muhammad Ali al-Ja'bari, the veteran mayor of Hebron in the early 1970s and the Village Leagues under Mustafa Dudin in the early 1980s.

The modern Palestinian groups that practiced various forms of democracy have tended to be sworn enemies of Israel and have struggled for its destruction. These were the veteran groups of Arab nationalists (al-Qawmiyyun al-Arab), which later split into the PFLP and DFLP; the Ba'thists; the Fatah and PLO; and the recently established Hamas Islamic movement. It is true that the Fatah-PLO since the mid-1970s has gradually and conditionally accepted Israel because of various military and political constraints and pragmatic considerations; but Palestinian followers of the PFLP, the Ba'th, and the Hamas have continued to vehemently reject Israel's existence, although they have advocated and/or experienced various democratic procedures. For example, two Marxist Palestinian student organizations in the West Bank that were democratically elected and affiliated to Syria and the PFLP harshly attacked Arafat's attempts to join the Middle East peace process with Israel in 1983, labeling him antidemocratic.[70] Similarly, the aforementioned public opinion poll of *Al-Fajr-ABC-Newsday* conducted in the Occupied Territories in 1986 among professionals and college-educated persons indicated that the majority of Palestinians rejected Israel's existence but simultaneously demanded free elections for city councils and municipalities in the Occupied Territories.[71] Finally, the Hamas movement has fully participated in the democratic process in the Occupied Territories through various professional and student associations but has openly called for Israel's annihilation.

The major Palestinian groups or organs that both practiced democratic procedures and advocated coexistence with Israel were the PCP (for long periods of time although not consistently); several of the 1970-elected West Bank mayors; part of the NGC (1978–1981); and, during recent years, perhaps also the hard core of the UNCU, possibly representing large sections of the Palestinians in the Occupied Territories.

Yet it could be argued that the Palestinian Communists' position toward coexistence with Israel has stemmed not from notions of Western democracy but rather from the communist concept of popular democracy and particularly from the Soviets, who long advocated peaceful coexistence between Israel and a Palestinian state along the 1947 UN partition lines. As for the NGC and the UNCU, they very likely have reflected the pragmatic approach of many Palestinians who have painfully realized that the only way to get rid of Israeli occupation and creeping annexation of the West Bank and Gaza is to accept Israel's existence and negotiate a political agreement based on a two-state solution. Thus, the important democratization process among the Palestinians in the West Bank, which largely occurred under the Israeli occupation, has, it would seem, no direct bearing on the West Bankers' tendency to coexist with Israel. Most Palestinians view their relations with Israel not through the prism of Western democracy (and certainly the Israeli occupation is far from democratic) but from a standpoint of their own vital national survival.

Nevertheless, it is possible that the democratic process and democratic notions have had a certain indirect impact on the recent development by certain Palestinian groups and intellectuals of peaceful attitudes toward Israel. Some Western-educated Palestinian intellectuals and professionals have been impressed with Israeli democratic institutions and norms and developed good working relations and personal ties with democratic-liberal Israeli groups and individuals. These Palestinians may also consider democracy one of Israel's major assets, a feature that makes it a strong entity that could not be easily eliminated—that, conversely, could be a reliable and useful neighbor to the future Palestinian state. It is also possible that various Palestinian political leaders and intellectuals have tended to stress the democratic process and practices in their society in order to convince the international community, particularly the Israelis, of Palestinians' political maturity and peaceful tendencies.

Indeed, the democratic-pluralistic development of Palestinian politics under the impact of Israeli occupation during the last decade has increasingly enabled certain groups and individuals to publicly express moderate and peaceful views regarding Israel without being assassinated. In November several Palestinian politicians in the West Bank signed a peace document that, inter alia, urged the PLO to publicly recognize Israel's right to exist, to accept UN Resolutions 242 and 338, and to renounce the use of violence.[72] A central figure among those Palestinians is Elias Freij, who for many years has fearlessly called for a peaceful coexistence between Israel and a Palestinian state. Similar positions were publicly taken by other Palestinian politicians and intellectuals such as Rashad al-Shawwa (former mayor of Gaza), Hanna Siniora, Sari Nusseibeh, Faysal Husayni, Ziad Abu Zayad, and others.

Moreover, peaceful tendencies, which are linked to democratic norms, have not been limited only to Western-educated intellectuals and pragmatic politicians in the West Bank. A new Palestinian party that started to organize clandestinely in 1989 was publicly established in the West Bank in

1991. It consisted mostly of young Palestinian activists released from Israeli jails after serving various sentences for allegedly committing terrorist actions. This new group, the Palestinian Nationalist Union Party, defined itself as democratic and progressive and openly called for peaceful negotiations with Israel toward a two-state solution on the basis of the pre-1967 borders. Asked why this party was needed and why it should not be part of the PLO, Kamil Tabanja, one of its founders, answered: "We wish to introduce democratic ways of life. Within the PLO and among the Palestinians there are various currents, and we wish to establish a new one." And although the East Jerusalem Palestinian papers would not publish the announcements of the new party, suspecting it to be an Israeli stooge, one Palestinian journalist significantly remarked: "It is not so bad that this person [Tabanja] and that party should try to operate. If we believe in democracy, they should also be given an opportunity."[73]

The party did not last long, mainly because it was not approved by the PLO and was apparently too small and poor to maintain itself. Yet the phenomenon of several hundred young former Palestinian activists in the popular committees, trade unions, student groups, and the like publicly advocating peaceful coexistence with Israel and depicting their new party as democratic—this phenomenon possibly points to an emergence of a new linkage between democracy and peace among the Palestinians in the Occupied Territories. The development of democratic-pluralistic trends and organs among the Palestinians during the last decade has enabled, even encouraged, various groups to express peaceful tendencies toward Israel. Furthermore, it can be suggested that the new democratic-pluralistic process has not only reflected certain positive changes in the attitudes of the Palestinians toward Israel but also has served to divert the violent activities of anti-Israel Palestinian groups into legitimate democratic channels.

Such phenomena could be observed, for example, in the free democratic elections of several professional associations in the Gaza Strip, which had been for years controlled by representatives of the anti-Israeli Hamas. In the elections for the Gaza physicians association in January 1990 and the Gaza lawyers association in March 1990, the PLO candidates gained great victories over their Hamas (and Marxist) opponents (although in the elections for the engineers association in January 1990, the Hamas candidates obtained better results).[74] More significantly, following the peace talks in Madrid and while Palestinian children were handing olive branches to Israeli soldiers in the Occupied Territories, the results for the Gaza Chamber of Commerce polling "suggested that Palestinians have begun to swing away from hard-line Islamic fundamentalists to favor relative moderates who support the Middle East peace process." As it happened, the PLO candidates won thirteen of the sixteen seats in the chamber council, and this outcome was widely seen as a "pro-peace message from the streets." The

Hamas, offering no alternative to the peace process, received only two seats (an independent candidate won the remaining one).[75] These trends have partly been borne out by the democratic elections in the West Bank and Gaza.

It should be stressed that the democratic process in the West Bank and Gaza, however remarkable its development, is still in its first stages and does not necessarily take the shape of a Western democracy (perhaps it looks more like a populist democracy). This democratic process will not sustain directly or indirectly the Palestinians' peaceful trends—which are themselves limited and fragile—unless there occurs a major change in Israeli-Palestinian relations—namely, the end of Israeli occupation and the establishment of a Palestinian homeland in the West Bank and Gaza. The continuing Israeli occupation of these territories is likely to eliminate the Palestinians' peaceful and pragmatic tendencies and encourage militant nationalists and Islamic fundamentalists to step up a violent struggle against Israel. It could also shatter the significant Palestinian democratic process, which is likely to provide a solid basis for a future peaceful coexistence between Israelis and Palestinians. Israel, which has had a significant impact on the development of democratic life among the West Bank–Gaza Palestinians, also has a moral and political obligation to grant them freedom and peace—for their sake, and for its own interest.

Notes

I am grateful to Yossi Torfstein for his research assistance.

1. *Al-Bayadir al-Siyasi*, No. 46 (April 23, 1983), p. 45, reporting on an Arab cultural meeting in Tunis; cf. Bassam Tibi, "Political Freedom in the Arab Societies," *Arab Studies Quarterly*, Vol. 6, No. 3 (1984), p. 222.

2. Y. Porath, *The Emergence of the Palestinian Arab National Movement 1918–1929* (Tel Aviv: 'Am Oved, 1970) p. 19, in Hebrew.

3. Compare A. Moseley Lesch, "The Palestinian Arab Nationalist Movement Under the Mandate," in W. B. Quandt, F. Jabber, and A. M. Lesch, eds., *The Politics of Palestinian Nationalism* (Berkeley: University of California, Press, 1973).

4. Porath, *Emergence*, pp. 233, 230.

5. Compare A. L. Tibawi, *Arab Education in Mandatory Palestine* (London, Luzac 1956), for example, p. 194.

6. Beirut, 1973, pp. 54–55. See also pp. 69–72, 86–87, 91–94, 97, 100–101.

7. *Ibid.*, pp. 54–55. See also S. Moreh, "The Image of the Israeli in Arab Literature," *The Arab-Israeli Conflict in the Mirror of Arab Literature* (Jerusalem: Van Leer Institute, n.d.) pp. 35–36, in Hebrew.

8. Abu-Ghazaleh, p. 87.

9. *Ibid.*, pp. 72, 86.

10. Quoted in Y. Porath, *From Riots to Rebellion: The Palestinian Arab National Movement 1929–1939* (Tel Aviv: Am Oved, 1978), p. 101, in Hebrew. See also p. 148.

11. Porath, *Emergence*, pp. 232–233; Lesch, "Nationalist Movement," p. 20.

12. Porath, *Emergence*, p. 89; Porath, *Riots*, pp. 36, 37, 175, 321.

13. Porath, *Emergence*, pp. 72–73, 173, 182, 186; Porath, *Riots*, pp. 41, 93–94.

14. Porath, *Emergence*, pp. 178ff.

15. Porath, *Riots*, pp. 69, 94.

16. Abu Ghazaleh, p. 45.

17. Lesch, "Nationalist Movement," pp. 30–31, 214.

18. Porath, *Riots*, pp. 147–152, 161ff.

19. *Ibid.*, pp. 272–273; Lesch, "Nationalist Movement," p. 37.

20. Lesch, "Nationalist Movement," pp. 39–40.

21. Ammon Cohen, *Political Parties in the West Bank Under Jordanian Rule* (Jerusalem: Magnes Press, 1980), pp. 53, 81, 255, in Hebrew; cf. Emile Sahliyeh, *In Search of Leadership West Bank Politics Since 1967* (Washington, D.C.: Brookings, 1988), pp. 13–14, 17, 19.

22. Cohen, *Political Parties*, pp. 88, 266–267.

23. *Ibid.*, pp. 207, 242, 244, 247, 267.

24. *Ibid.*, p. 256; cf. Sahliyeh, *Leadership*, p. 18.

25. *Arab Lessons from the 1948 War* (IDF: 1955), pp. 50–51, 56, in Hebrew.

26. On Jordan's 1955 Municipalities Law and its application to 1972 elections, see: Moshe Ma'oz, *Palestinian Leadership on the West Bank* (London, 1984), pp. 28–29, 103; cf. Sahliyeh, *Leadership*, pp. 39–40.

27. Sahliyeh, *Leadership*, pp. 27–30; Ma'oz, *West Bank*, pp. 94ff; *Al-Fikr-ah-Dimugrati*, No. 2, Spring 1988, article by Saji Khalil.

28. Sahliyeh, *Leadership*, p. 27.

29. Ann M. Lesch, *Political Perceptions of the Palestinians on the West Bank and the Gaza Strip* (Washington, D.C.: 1980), p. 41.

30. Ma'oz, *West Bank*, p. 115; Sahliyeh, *Leadership*, p. 29.

31. Sahliyeh, *Leadership*, pp. 52, 56–57.

32. Sahliyeh, *Leadership*, pp. 62 and 60, respectively.

33. For details see Sahliyeh, *Leadership*, pp. 100ff.

34. For a thorough analysis see Y. Harkabi, "The Meaning of a Democratic Palestinian State," in W. Laqueur and B. Rubin, *The Israel Arab Reader* (Penguin, 1984), pp. 531–544.

35. *Al-Quds*, November 28, 1976; *Washington Post*, September 15, 1976.

36. *Middle East News Agency*, Cairo, March 18, 1977; cf. Ma'oz, *West Bank*, p. 148; Sahliyeh, *Leadership*, p. 108.

37. Sahliyeh, *Leadership*, p. 70; Ma'oz, *West Bank*, pp. 177–178.

38. Ma'oz, *West Bank*, pp. 106–109, 122ff.

39. *Ibid.*, p. 129; Sahliyeh, *Leadership*, p. 46.

40. For more details see Ma'oz, *West Bank*, pp. 133ff. See A. Zycher, "Exercise in Democracy," *Jerusalem Post* weekly, May 4, 1976.

41. For details see Ma'oz, *West Bank*, pp. 162ff; Sahliyeh, *Leadership*, pp. 71ff.

42. *Al-Bayadir al-Siyasi*, No. 44 (April 3, 1983), article by Nada Hazmu; cf. *Al-Bayadir al-Siyasi*, No. 2 (May 1981), article by Alias Zananiri; No. 31 (December 1, 1982), articles by Jack Khazmo and Ismail Ajwa; *Al fikr al-dimuqrati*, No. 2 (Spring 1988), article by Jamil Hilal.

43. *Al-Bayadir al-Siyasi*, No. 127 (November 17, 1984), pp. 5, 10–11, 13, 70; *Al-Sinara*, No. 237 (September 25, 1987), p. 2.

44. *Al-Bayadir al-Siyasi*, No. 46 (April 23, 1983), p. 45.

45. See, for example, *Al-Bayadir al-Siyasi* (June 3, 1981), p. 45; No. 11 (February 1, 1982), p. 17; No. 48 (May 7, 1983), p. 40; No. 92 (March 10, 1984), p. 29; No. 150 (April 27, 1985), p. 32.

46. *Idem.* no. 111 (July 24, 1984), p. 33; No. 112 (July 28, 1984).

47. For more details see *Al-Fikr al-Dimuqrati,* No. 2 (Spring 1988), article by Saji Khalil; cf. Sahliyeh, *Leadership,* pp. 103–106.

48. See, for example, "The Organic Regulation of the General Federation of the Labor Unions in the West Bank" (Nablus, n.d.), in Arabic; "A statement by the Central Bureau of the Workers Unified Bloc" in the West Bank and the Gaza Strip, September 10, 1985; *Al-Bayadir,* No. 11 (February 1, 1982), pp. 4–5, 17, 22; No. 48 (May 7, 1983), p. 40.

49. Sahliyeh, *Leadership,* p. 115; cf. Khalil, *Al-Fikr.*

50. Khalil, *Al-Fikr.*

51. Abd al-Jawad Salih, "The Mission of High Learning and the Objectives its Institutions in the (West) Bank and (Gaza) Strip" (Nicosiah: M. I. Publishing, n.d.), p. 42.

52. Sahliyeh, *Leadership,* pp. 129–131.

53. Sahliyeh, *Leadership,* pp. 148–150.

54. Don Peretz, *Intifada* (Boulder: Westview Press, 1990), p. 101; Sahliyeh, *Leadership,* p. 126; Ismail Ajwa, in *Al-Bayadir,* No. 10–11 (February 1, 1982), p. 22.

55. *Al-Sinarah* (April 10, 1987), p. 4, and September 1987, p. 2.

56. For example, *Al-Bayadir,* No. 30 (November 15, 1982), pp. 61–63; No. 40 (March 12, 1983), p. 37; No. 115 (August 18, 1984), p. 36.

57. Khalil, *Al-Fikr*; Peretz, *Intifada,* p. 77; *Ha'aretz,* article by Ori Nir, January 26, 1990; *Abir* [Women's Journal], No. 20 (October 1988), pp. 23–33; No. 14 (September 1987), p. 38; *Al-Bayadir,* No. 5 (August 1981), p. 60.

58. Khalil, *Al-Fikr*; *Al-Bayadir,* No. 111 (July 24, 1984), p. 20.

59. For accounts of the intifada see: Peretz, *Intifada*; Z. Lockman & J. Beinin, eds., *Intifada* (Boston, 1989); Z. Schiff and E. Ya'ari, *Intifada* (Tel Aviv: Schocken, 1990), in Hebrew; and R. Brynen, ed., *Echoes of the Intifada* (Boulder: Westview Press, 1991).

60. "The Palestinian Independence Document Prepared by Faisal Husseini," in Peretz, *Intifada,* pp. 204ff. and p. 110.

61. Schiff and Ya'ari, *Intifada,* pp. 174, 176, 194; Emile A. Nakhleh, "The Palestinian Intifada and Israel," in A. Z. Rubinstein, ed., *The Arab-Israeli Conflict,* 2nd edition (Harper Collins, 1991), pp. 177–178.

62. Jamil Hilal, al-Fikr dimuqrati p. 13; *Ha'aretz,* February 19, 1990, and March 1991, quoting George Hizbun and Ghassan al-Khatib, two Communist leaders.

63. Peretz, *Intifada,* pp. 89–90; Nakhleh, "Palestinian Intifada," p. 175; Schiff and Ya'ari, *Intifada,* pp. 171, 254, 256–257.

64. *Ha'aretz,* March 7, June 18 and 19, 1991; August 2 and 8, 1991; *New York Times,* November 6, 1991; for other elections see *Al-Bayadir al-Siyasi,* August 2, 1991.

65. See, for example, the election to the journalists association, *Ha'aretz,* August 2 and 13, 1991, and *Ha'aretz,* March 21, 1991. See also the election results for the labor unions, *Ha'aretz,* March 4, 1990.

66. Peretz, *Intifada,* p. 110; cf. Nakhleh, "Palestinian Intifada," pp. 169–170, 176.

67. For texts of those documents (except for the last) see Peretz, *Intifada,* pp. 208ff. See also A. Udovitch, "Making Peace," *The Village Voice* (December 27, 1988).

68. *Al-Fajr,* Arabic edition, September 8, 1986; *Al-Fajr,* English edition, September 12, 1986; an analysis by Meron Benvenisti, head of the West Bank Data

Base project; cf. Daoud Kuttab, "Poll Shows Palestinian Political Reality," *Ibid;* also *Ha'aretz*, September 12, 1986.

69. *Ha'aretz*, June 15, 1990, article by Nili Mandler reporting on research by Khawla Abu-Bakr of Haifa University.

70. Sahliyeh, *Leadership*, pp. 129–130.

71. *Al-Fajr*, September 12, 1986.

72. Sahliyeh, *Leadership*, p. 168.

73. *Ha'aretz*, June 12, 14, and 26, 1991, articles by D. Rubinstein and E. Rabin.

74. *Ha'aretz*, January 21, and March 2, 1990.

75. *New York Times*, November 6, 1991.

10

Palestinian Islamists, Pluralism, and Democracy

Ziad Abu-Amr

In this chapter I try to identify the positions of Palestinian Islamists in the West Bank and Gaza toward the issues of pluralism and democracy. The chapter focuses on organized political groups committed to Islamic doctrine and programs. Therefore, the term "Palestinian Islamists" in this context refers to, and is used interchangeably with, the Islamic resistance movement (Hamas) and the Islamic jihad movement. The views of individuals with Islamic leanings who are not part of these two groups fall outside the scope of this discussion.

The stunning December 1991, victory of the Islamic Salvation Front in Algeria's first multiparty parliamentary elections since the country's independence, along with the rise of the Islamic movement in Jordan, makes the Palestinian Islamic groups' stand on pluralism and democracy particularly interesting. As the Palestinian Islamists of the Occupied Territories have no experience of their own in political participation, pluralism, democracy, and political rule, it is expected that both the Algerian and the Jordanian experiences will provide the Palestinian Islamists with a source of inspiration. Like the outcome of the parliamentary elections in Jordan in 1990, the outcome of the balloting in Algeria may give the Palestinian Islamists more confidence to try a pluralistic and democratic system. But the suspension of democratic values in Algeria created a sense of fear and anxiety among Palestinian Islamists and raised the gloomy prospect of losing outside support and having a confrontation with the nationalists in the Occupied Territories.

The Algerian example may be of special significance to the Palestinian Islamists, for the two situations are analogous. While the Algerian Islamists are contesting the incumbent National Liberation Front, the Palestinian Islamists are contesting the Palestine Liberation Organization, which is incumbent in terms of formal representation of the Palestinian people. But perhaps of equal importance are the experiences of the Islamic Republic in

Iran and the Islamic Front in Sudan, led by Hasan al-Turabi. The examples of Iran and Sudan are revealing because in both cases Islam is actually in power, not simply striving for it.

In the Occupied Territories, there has not been so far a reliable criterion to assess the strength of the Islamists vis-à-vis the nationalists. None of the assessments made are done on empirical bases. Therefore, in light of the volatility of the political situation and changing modes of support, free elections could produce surprising results similar to the results of the Algerian parliamentary elections. Although elections in professional associations, trade unions, student councils, and chambers of commerce in the West Bank and Gaza are only partially representative and cannot be used as a decisive evidence, some of these indicate a possible Islamic sweep, at least in some areas.

Aspects of pluralism and democracy that are relevant to Islamic movements in Arab countries are not exactly applicable to the Islamic groups in the Occupied Territories. Major Islamic movements in Arab countries have become concerned with the question of Islamic rule; the Islamic groups in the Occupied Territories function in a different context, that of struggle for national liberation. The primary concern of these groups is to rid themselves and Palestinian society of the Israeli occupation and to seize power. Furthermore, while the Islamists in the Arab world believe political power will enable them to build an Islamic society, their Palestinian counterparts see Islamization primarily as the way to put an end to Israeli occupation and only secondarily as the way to establish an Islamic polity in Palestine.

Palestinian Islamists are only marginally preoccupied with the issues of pluralism and democracy. These issues are discussed in a limited way, particularly pluralism's effect on inter-Palestinian relations. Mutual tolerance is preached, but in the absence of a single political frame of reference and in an atmosphere of rivalry and competition, there is not complete agreement on a specific set of rules to guide inter-Palestinian relations. The various groups pay lip service to democratic values because of the appeal these values have to the Palestinian people as the best means to ensure national unity.

But certain self-serving positions are also advocated by one group or another. Palestinian Islamists, for example, view local political elections favorably even in the context of Israeli occupation. Elections are bound to reveal the strength of the Islamists vis-à-vis the secular nationalist following of the Palestine Liberation Organization. For this reason, Palestinian Islamists have participated in elections conducted in trade unions, professional associations, and student councils in Palestinian universities in the West Bank and Gaza. Yet at the same time, Palestinian Islamists argue that the concept of democracy has no origins in the Islamic tradition. Although certain institutions in the Western tradition are entrusted to the people to legislate, the source of legislation in Islam is the Quran. It is the constitution of the Muslim *ummah,* and it cannot be altered or amended. The *sunna* and *ijtihad* provide detailed and specific interpretations.

An Islamic legislative authority can resort to *ijtihad* to rule on certain issues. There exists in this regard the concept of "legislative policy," which includes the rulings that are bound to serve the interest of the *ummah.* These rulings should be derived from and consistent with the *Shari'ah.* Instead of "the rule of the people by the people," which Western democracy prescribes, Islam prescribes "the rule of God over the people."[1]

Palestinian Islamists argue that while the sources of legislation in Islamic and Western traditions are totally different, there is some similarity in terms of the executive powers in both traditions. However, in Islam, the mass of the people is not entrusted with the task of selecting the ruler. Because this mass is not sufficiently educated, it can only, and according to certain specifications, select an elite of extremely well-informed Muslims, *Ahlal-hall Wa-'l-'aqd* (those who bind and loosen). *Ahlal-hall Wa-'l-'aqd* in turn undertake the selection of the ruler. The ruler has to fulfill certain requirements in order to be accorded the trust of this informed group of Muslims. In this sense, Islamic politics can be described by Western criteria as elite politics rather than democratic politics.

In Western democracy, members of parliament are chosen through elections. These members in turn select a prime minister. Members of parliament can also legislate. But unlike Islamic leaders, Western rulers are sometimes selected directly by the mass of the people. In modern times, however, the notion of elections has become accepted by the Muslims. In the Islamic Republic of Iran, Western-style elections are conducted to select members of a consultative council (*majlis*), which can be viewed as an Islamic adaptation of the Western parliament. But in substance and function, it may be closer to the institution of *ahl al-hal Wa-'l'aqd al-'aqd.* According to Sheikh Bassam Jarrar, an Islamic leader in the West Bank, elections are the "variable" used as a mechanism to verify the "invariable": the consent of the *umma.*[2]

The bottom line from the viewpoint of Islamic groups in the Occupied Territories is that democracy is a Western concept. It is therefore alien to Islam. Palestinian Islamists reject it on doctrinal basis and argue that, whatever democracy signifies, the Islamic doctrine is more encompassing because it provides principles that are more just and comprehensive. Therefore, they conclude, the Western concept of democracy has no place and cannot be applied in a Muslim society.

According to Dr. Mahmoud al-Zahhar, a prominent Hamas supporter, the Islamic movement in the Occupied Territories rejects democracy because it does not provide a just system that fits all societies. Al-Zahhar points out that democracy means the rule of the majority and that the majority often can be a slim one: The views of 51 percent of the population can be imposed on 49 percent. And when there is a tie, one single vote can determine a country's choice and direction.[3] The conclusion: democracy is not just because it subjects a sizable minority (49 percent) to the will of a slim majority (51 percent). In contrast, Islam is supposed to ensure the consent of everyone. But if the case of Iran is to be taken again as a model, total consent is not always realized. On a number of occasions, there has been opposition to majority rulings. Such contradictions will always arise in examining Islam and democracy.

As for non-Muslim minorities, the place of these groups in society is prescribed in the Quran. But under existing circumstances, Palestinian Islamists deal with *ahl al-kitab* (the people of the Book) as equals both in terms of rights and duties. Notably, two of the major PLO factions—the Popular Front for the Liberation of Palestine (PFLP) and the Democratic Front for the Liberation of Palestine (DFLP)—are headed by Palestinian Christians. Until Islamic society and rule are established, Islamists believe, they have to coexist and deal with the existing non-Islamic order. According to the Hamas movement in the Occupied Territories, participation in a non-Islamic government by Islamic groups is not acceptable if the purpose is to implement a program that is in contradiction with Islam. These Islamic groups cannot commit themselves to decisions that contradict Islam and the *shari'ah,* even if they are taken by a majority.

The cases of the Islamic movements in the Occupied Territories and Jordan vis-à-vis the PLO and the Jordanian government, respectively, are different. While the PLO offers Islamists participation in the organization and its institutions, it does not commit itself to altering its secular orientation and program. This alteration is considered a precondition for Islamic participation. As for participation in elections, to which the Islamic movement in the Occupied Territories subscribes in principle, the objective is to obtain a majority of votes in order to institute the law of God.

In the case of Jordan, the Muslim Brotherhood established that it would not commit itself to decisions or legislation that contradict the Islamic *shari'ah.* For this specific reason, the Brotherhood in Jordan declined participation in the government of Taher al-Masri and later in the government of Zeid bin Shaker, the reason being the commitment of both governments to participate in the peace process, which the Brotherhood opposes on the basis that it violates Islamic principles. While withholding their support of certain government policies, the Islamic groups in Jordan still abide by decisions and rulings made by non-Islamic governments. They also see law and order as defined by the ruling regime.

According to Dr. al-Zahhar, once Islamic society and Islamic rule are established, no political parties with non-Islamic ideologies will be tolerated. Only Islamic groups that take Islam as their frame of reference and the Quran as their constitution will be allowed to voice their opinion, in the form of interpretations of Islamic principles or teachings.[4] Sheikh Bassam Jarrar states that any party that functions under Islamic rule according to the constitution is a legitimate party. But he also adds that the Islamic rulers will have to decide whether the spread of Islam is helped by circulation of different ideas or whether these ideas should be banned.[5]

Until Islamic rule is established, the attitude of Palestinian Islamists toward democracy will be colored and influenced by a number of considerations. The first are the peculiar conditions of the Palestinian society being subjected to foreign rule, where opinions differ about the nature of the struggle against the occupation and about the role of Muslims in it. The second consideration is the fact that the Islamic movement in the Occupied Territories is a nascent one in terms of defining its positions on serious issues such as pluralism and democracy. The third consideration is that in defining their practical positions on political issues, the Palestinian Islamists have to rely on the advice of other Islamists and on the experience and tradition of other Muslim groups.

Rather than democracy, the more pressing theme for the Palestinian Islamists at this point is the issue of pluralism, which affects the relationships among the various Palestinian groups. According to Dr. Mahmoud al-Zahhar, the Islamists, in the absence of an Islamic rule, accept the notion of pluralism because it is imposed on them. But the Islamic movement does not seek the establishment of a multiparty system, especially if the parties are non-Islamic. Al-Zahhar also argues that the Islamists accept the notion of democracy in a non-Islamic order because Islam can thrive under democracy more than under dictatorship.[6] Sheik Bassam Jarrar argues that Islam differentiates between "those who differ with you in the ideas they carry, and those who are hostile to you. Alliance between Islamic and non-Islamic forces is permissible as long as it is done according to Islamic principles."[7]

An alliance with the PLO does not, however, meet this criterion. But there is no room for coordination on specific issues that do not contradict Islam. The Palestinian Islamists and the PLO do not, in this case, have to abandon their differing political or ideological commitments. Hamas itself does not object to the notion of coordinating with other Palestinian political groups. In the aftermath of the peace conference in Madrid, Hamas actually took the initiative in advocating such coordination[8] to forge broad opposition to the conference. But because of its tactical nature and the fact that it was not predicated on shared ideological or doctrinal bases, this cooperation between Islamic and non-Islamic groups was not genuine or permanent. The same can be said about the shifting alliances among these groups. Although there may be agreement on certain positions at specific points in time, conflict may arise over other issues and at different times. For example, Hamas coordinated a comprehensive strike with the secular and leftist PFLP to protest the Palestinian participation in the conference, but at a later stage the PFLP's supporters in the West Bank clashed with Hamas activists over a different issue.

A number of Hamas leaders have on different occasions made reference to what can be described as "democratic measures." Shaikh Ahmad Yasin, the founder and leader of Hamas, has indicated that he supports a democratic Palestinian state with a multiparty system: "Whoever wins will be entitled to assuming authority. Even if the communists win, I will respect the will of the Palestinian people."9 It is not clear, however, how Yasin can reconcile this prodemocracy position with his determined stand on the necessity of establishing an Islamic state in Palestine. There is no doubt that Yasin's talk about a multiparty system is tactical, because Islam forbids political parties.

When Shaikh Yasin was asked if his movement presents an alternative to the PLO, his reply reflected a willingness to respect free choice: "We have an idea, and the PLO has an idea, and the sole arbiter is the people. What the people decide is acceptable to us."10 Implicit in Yasin's answer is the idea of elections. On a different occasion, Yasin has indicated that he would respect the opinion of the majority, though he would not agree with it.11

According to another Hamas leader, Dr. Abdel-Aziz al-Rantisi, reaching agreement with a group that does not embrace an Islamic ideology (the reference in this case being to the Fatah movement) is justified if the purpose is "to avert internal conflict which would have destroyed everything." An agreement of this sort "blocks the enemies of our people from seizing the opportunity to exploit the differences between us." Al-Rantisi also stated that difference in political points of view have many positive aspects.12

The fact of the matter is that the Islamists in the Occupied Territories have no choice but to support pluralism and political tolerance. Because the Islamists do not constitute the major force in society, advocating pluralism serves their case and provides them with protection. During the Madrid peace conference in October 1991, Hamas refrained from clashing with nationalist supporters of the conference who violated the protest strike Hamas organized. The nationalists stormed a number of mosques, wrote anti-Hamas slogans on walls, and even clashed physically with some Hamas supporters. The mitigated reaction of Hamas was motivated by a realization that the balance of forces on the ground was not in its favor. In previous cases and under different circumstances, the Islamic movement demonstrated more resolve and aggressiveness and openly challenged the nationalists.

Hamas's charter is considered the ultimate definition of the movement's attitude toward and relationship with other Islamic and non-Islamic Palestinian groups. Regarding other Islamic groups, the charter states: "The Islamic Resistance Movement looks at other Islamic movements with respect and esteem. If it differs with them in a given aspect or idea, it agrees with them in general aspects and ideas. It looks at those movements as being covered by the principle of *ijtihad,* as long as they are well-intended and sincere, and as long as their actions remain within the bounds of the Islamic framework. . . . The Islamic Resistance Movement considers those movements an asset. . . . Hamas will continue to raise the banner of unity and try hard to achieve it on the basis of the Quran and the *sunna.*"[13]

As for nationalist factions, the charter states that Hamas "exchanges respect with them and appreciates their circumstances, the factors surrounding them, and the impact of these factors. Hamas presses on their hands, so long as they do not give their allegiance to the communist East or the crusader West." Hamas "assures all nationalist trends active in Palestine that they have its support and assistance for the purpose of liberating Palestine. Hamas will do nothing other than that, in word and in deed, with the understanding that it has the right to self-defense."[14]

As far as the PLO is concerned, the charter says that Hamas considers it "the closest to the Islamic Resistance Movement and regards it as a father or brother, or a relative or friend. Can the Muslim be alienated from his father or brother or relative or friend?"[15] But the charter also states, in a rather apparent contradiction, that the PLO endorses secular ideas and that "secular thought is incompatible with religious thought, completely incompatible. . . . Accordingly, and with our esteem for the PLO . . . and what it may evolve into . . . we cannot abandon the present and future Islamism of Palestine." But the day the PLO adopts Islam as its way of life, "we will be its troops and the fuel for its fire that burns the enemy."[16]

After the publication of the Hamas charter and in response to a call for Hamas to join the PLO, Hamas demanded that it be given 40 percent of the seats in the Palestine National Council (PNC). Hamas argued that this percentage reflected its actual weight among the Palestinian people, especially in the Occupied Territories. It was not clear, however, whether the Hamas demand was real or tactical. Working under the PLO umbrella would mean accepting a non-Islamic framework for cooperation, something that runs counter to the Hamas charter.

A different, but daring, perspective toward the concept of pluralism is articulated by Dr. Bashir Nafi', a prominent Palestinian Islamic thinker whose ideas are usually inspired by the Islamic jihad movement in Palestine. Dr. Nafi' advocates the concept of *al-jama'a al-wataniyya* (the national group). This concept advocates the representation of all political forces, regardless of their commitment to Islam, in a single coalition. According to Nafi', the Islamic movement cannot realize its goal of establishing an Islamic order (and cannot lead the liberation project in the case of Palestine) without being representative of the national group.[17]

Commitment to the idea of comprehensive Islamic rule, or the Islamic caliphate, cannot alone achieve this kind of representation. For an Islamic movement to embody *al-jama'a al-wataniyya,* it must ensure the acceptance and inclusion of all factions and groups, including non-Islamic and even Westernized communities.[18] Nafi' criticizes the tendency of dominant

Islamic forces to exclude non-Islamic elements from economic and cultural institutions. Such an attitude, according to Nafi', isolates Islamic groups in society, creates division and friction among Muslim and Christian communities, and alienates the socially and culturally Westernized segments.[19] He argues that the Islamic movement cannot represent the national group unless it adopts a plan that enjoys the support of society at large and achieves national consensus. This plan has to address the most critical concerns of the national group. For example, an Islamic trend in Palestine that ignores the struggle with the Zionists cannot claim to represent the national group.[20]

Nafi' also states that the contemporary Islamic movement is in dire need of an extensive and far-reaching process of *ijtihad*. This process cannot be achieved by one single theologian; rather, it requires the endeavor of dozens of institutions and groups across the nation. But this does not mean, according to Nafi', that the Islamic forces should become only preoccupied by the narrow concerns of each national group and abandon their commitment to the Muslim *ummah*. The central objective should always remain the achievement of the rise of the Muslim *ummah*.[21]

Nafi' concludes that the concept of *al-jama'a al-wataniyya*, which emerged after the failure to actualize the concept of the Muslim *ummah*, has become essential to the attainment of national independence from foreign occupation on the level of the nation-state. Yet this concept is different from the concept of the nation-state, for whereas the first carries within it "all the attributes of Islamic belonging, and seeks unity versus partition, the second is bound by definition to consolidate separate entities."[22] The national group represents a middle way between the framework of the Muslim *ummha* and the split of this *ummah* into nation-states. The orientation of the national group toward Islamic solidarity manifested itself in support for the Algerian struggle for independence and for the mujahidin in Afghanistan. Now it manifests itself in the case of Palestine.[23]

The views of Nafi' are eclectic and may not be consistent with Islamic doctrine. It is obvious that he, like all other Islamists, strives for the establishment of an Islamic order. In this sense, *al-jama'a al-wataniyya* is only a transitional phase that, it is hoped, will lead to consolidation of the Islamic order. And if this order is not feasible now on the caliphate level, the next logical step is to establish it on the nation-state level. Because of its Islamic nature, Nafi' implies, this nation-state is different both in character and function from the existing non-Islamic nation-states.

Although the concept of *al-jama'a al-wataniyya* accounts for the political participation of all citizens, it presupposes that the Islamic movement will be entrusted with the leadership of society. Nafi' does not clearly explain through what means (democratic or nondemocratic) the Islamists will assume power in society. Nor does he establish the Islamic doctrinal basis for the concept of *al-jama'a al-wataniyya*. Failure to do so would undermine the concept among Islamists who may view the innovation or *ijtihad* of Dr. Nafi' as heretical.

Conclusion

Palestinian Islamists have no authentic positions or articulations of their own regarding theological, doctrinal, or theoretical issues, including the issue of Islam and democracy. Positions on such issues are usually defined or articulated by theologians or theoreticians of Islamic groups that have a tradition in the areas of *fiqh* or *ijtihad*. Even Shaikh Ahmad Yasin, the most prominent Islamic leader in the Occupied Territories, has made no significant theological or doctrinal contributions. Yasin is not a Khomeini, a Fadlullah, or a Shari'ati; he is neither a Banna nor a Qutb. Yasin's prominence as an Islamic leader is derived primarily from political considerations, as he and his movement have emerged as a serious rival to the PLO.

Perhaps it is still premature to make final conclusions about Palestinian Islamists and the issues of pluralism and democracy. These groups have not yet been forced to deal with such issues. They lack a tradition in this regard, and their positions may still be evolving. This lack of tradition may account for the incoherent and sometimes ambiguous positions of the Palestinian Islamic groups. For example, Hamas, less fundamentalist and more reform-oriented than the Islamic jihad, is more orthodox about its insistence on the incompatibility of Islam and democracy. On the other hand, the Islamic jihad, more militant than Hamas in terms of its attitude on the Palestinian nationalist question, is willing to entertain pluralistic notions that may not be consistent with Islamic doctrine. Such peculiarities may be attributed to the fact that these groups are still nascent and involved in a nationalist struggle.

As the political positions of the Palestinian Islamic groups are still evolving, their final attitudes and articulations regarding pluralism and democracy are likely to evolve, too. The direction of this evolution will be subject to intervening events; other Islamic groups had to accommodate themselves to the prevailing circumstances in their respective societies. The case of the Islamists in Jordan may be instructive here (although one can argue that their acceptance of the principles of pluralism and democracy may be only tactical and temporary). Circumstances may induce Palestinian Islamists to be more amenable to pluralism or democratic conduct. For instance, an increase in popular support for the PLO in the Occupied Territories may force Palestinian Islamists to become more sensitive to the nationalists' agenda and to the rules of conduct set by the PLO. Conversely, the weakening of the PLO as a result of its failure to deliver to its constituency may encourage the Islamists to challenge the old rules and try to establish new ones that are more favorable to them.

The performance of the PLO nationalists in the peace process initiated by the United States in the aftermath of the Gulf War, along with the immediate and final outcome of this process, will play a major role in defining the equation between the Islamists and the nationalists. A political settlement that enjoys the support of a majority of the Palestinians in the Occupied Territories may deprive the Islamists of opportunities to capitalize on the failure of the nationalists.

If the Islamists become the dominant political force in the Occupied Territories, they will be required, just like the PLO, to deliver to the Palestinian people. It is not likely that the Islamists will be, in the foreseeable future, in a better position than the PLO to pursue Palestinian national objectives. The task of the Islamists is even more complicated because they embrace maximalist demands such as the establishment of an Islamic state in the entire area of Palestine.

The Islamists' awareness of Israeli power and harsh measures may force them to mitigate their rigid views and seek closer coordination and cooperation with other Palestinian groups, whose solidarity may be needed to ensure a measure of national unity and steadfastness. But the future of Palestinian Islamists in the Occupied Territories lies equally in the hands of the Israeli authorities, who regardless of what the Islamists do are likely to stick to Israel's agenda in dealing with Islamists and nationalists alike.

The discussion of pluralism and democracy by Palestinian Islamists remains academic. The dilemma they and all other Islamic groups confront lies in reconciling the Western concepts of pluralism and democracy to the Islamic doctrine. Even if they become genuinely susceptible to these notions, they will remain at odds with Islamic doctrine as given in the Quran and the *sunna*. Abandoning the text and drawing on Islam as a methodology is seen by orthodox Islamists as a deviation. In this sense, the issue of Islam and democracy remains unresolved. The contradiction seems to lie in the fundamentals, in the attempt to coercively reconcile to sources of thought that are epistemologically diametrically opposed. The first is religious and Islamic, while the second is secular and Western.

Notes

1. Personal interview with Sheikh Bassam Jarrar, an Islamic leader in the West Bank, Ramallah, December 22, 1991.
2. *Ibid.*
3. Personal interview with Dr. Mahmoud Al-Zahhar, an Islamic leader in the Gaza Strip, Gaza, December 24, 1991.
4. Al-Zahhar, *ibid.*
5. Jarrar, interview.
6. Al-Zahhar, interview.
7. Jarrar, interview.

8. The Islamic Resistance Movement (Hamas), leaflet No. 82, January 2, 1992.

9. Interview with Sheikh Ahmad Yasin, *Al-Nahar*, April 30, 1989.

10. *Al-Sha'b*, September 11, 1988.

11. *Al-Islam wa-Filastin*, December 30, 1988, p. 10.

12. *Al-Fajr*, September 24, 1990, p. 16.

13. *Mithaq Harakat al-Muqawama al-Islamiyya—Hamas* [Charter of the Islamic Resistance Movement—Hamas], August 1988, p. 26.

14. *Ibid.*, p. 28

15. *Ibid.*, pp. 29–30.

16. *Ibid.*

17. *Al-Islam wa-Filastin*, October 5, 1989, p. 7.

18. *Ibid.*

19. *Ibid.*

20. *Ibid.*

21. *Ibid.*

22. *Ibid.*

23. *Ibid.*

11

The Democratization Process in the PLO: Ideology, Structure, and Strategy

Manuel Hassassian

The quest for democracy is emerging as a global phenomenon. In the post–World War II era, democracy has developed into a universal political norm.[1] In fact, the philosophical aspects of democracy that led to the rise of nationalism are a prelude to independence and a prime factor for "the democratization of the peripheralized society."[2] For democracy to be entrenched in a society, it must be strengthened not only on the institutional level but also in sociopolitical structures and processes.[3] World recognition of the principle of national self-determination has culminated in the globalization of democracy, a principle that most Third World societies are struggling to achieve.

The Palestinians are no exception. The Palestine Liberation Organization, as an actor in world politics could not evade the new global trends of democratization even if it wished to. Hence it has incorporated these trends in its ideology, structure, and strategy. The PLO's political thinking has of late been characterized by political realism and pragmatism.

Like any other Third World movement, the PLO defines its political and military struggle according to the four elements of national liberation that S. Neil MacFarlane enumerates: 1) political independence, 2) freedom from external economic control; 3) social revolution, and 4) cultural regeneration.[4] However, for democracy to succeed, it must be institutionalized in a way that mediates the multiple and conflicting interests that emerge once statehood is declared. This process of transition is difficult for developing societies because they lack experience in dealing with methods that often hamper their legitimacy and performance.[5]

Pluralism in Palestinian politics must be analyzed in the context of the erosion evident in Arab politics, resulting from fragmentation, repressive conditions, economic disparities, and lack of legitimacy and credibility. It is no wonder that the basic tenets of democracy—political participation, power sharing, and public accountability—are nonexistent in the present

Arab states. Furthermore, the lack of self-sustaining institutions embedded in consolidated communities is a serious impediment to the emergence of democracy.[6] Consequently, the Arab Middle East suffers from inadequate industrial growth and a heavily militarized, bureaucratized, and centralized government.[7] Nonetheless, its people are striving to achieve political freedom, justice, and decent lives, and thus it is important to look at the human element, which transcends geopolitical boundaries, when analyzing the Middle East.

An offshoot of pan-Arabism, Palestinian nationalism over the years developed a secular ideology. Based largely on territorial determination, it sought to encompass members of different faiths, Christians as well as Muslims. The history of Mandatory Palestine attests to the secular tendencies in the Palestinian national movement. Its first political organization, in the early 1920s, was the Muslim-Christian Association. The sociopolitical and religious tolerance of Palestinian politics stood in clear contrast to the norms of Arab politics. In the ensuing years, when the PLO was founded, a senior political organization, Fatah, emphasized the nonreligious and pluralistic character of Palestinian nationalism.

The Palestinian national movement has committed itself to democracy, and great numbers of Palestinians embrace this objective. The process of democratization has been facilitated by the high level of education achieved by Palestinians and the existence of their institutions and professional societies. An umbrella organization, the PLO has portrayed itself as "the institutional expression of Palestinian nationalism."[8] It is the organizational framework within which all Palestinian cultural, social, educational, political, and military activities are integrated.[9] By providing complex services to the Palestinians, it gains legitimacy. An added burden for a democratic PLO is the integration of the various attitudes and positions of Palestinians—refugees living in camps, intellectuals, middle-class merchants, and resistance fighters. The high degree of political consciousness and participation is an additional feature of Palestinian politics. All these factors contribute to the fact that the political institutions and processes of Palestinians are substantially more secular than those of most Arab people.[10] They provide the basis for democratic behavior and the characterization of the PLO as a quasigovernmental agency. In recent years the PLO has managed to emphasize certain trends toward democratization and pragmatism in its political program, and undoubtedly the intifada has been a catalyst in changing certain perceptions, attitudes, and even political strategies to lay the groundwork for negotiations for political settlement and accommodation.

This study analyzes the nature of democratic behavior and trends in PLO politics and infrastructure. The Palestine National Council (PNC) resolutions reflect certain democratic trends and the pluralistic thinking among Palestinian decisionmakers. An emphasis on the PLO's political institutions and its shift from consensus to majority politics, along with its extensive civilian institutional infrastructure, sets the basis for a democratic Palestinian state.

The Absence of Democracy in the Arab Regimes

The pluralistic thinking in Palestinian politics should be evaluated in the context of a wider Arab politics that has failed for decades to institute any sort of meaningful, workable democratic system. While the constitutions of most Arab states boast of democratic ideals, the situation on the ground has remained the same: no separation of powers, no checks and balances, and no genuinely representative governments. The nation-state in the Arab world is at the mercy of its chief executive, who manipulates both the legislature and the judiciary. Students of the Middle East constantly attempt to rationalize the factors that have led to the failure of democracy. Socioeconomic, political, historical, and cultural factors all lie at the heart of this state of affairs.

Though pan-Arabism is proclaimed as a value among the ruling classes and widely shared as a sentiment by the masses, Arab society is highly heterogeneous in its structure and plagued by factionalism, parochialism, tribalism, and regionalism. Furthermore, it suffers from foreign control, economic subservience, the power of traditional loyalties (religious, kinship, and ethnic), and repressive socioeconomic and political conditions. Above all, it is fragmented because it lacks genuine links between the political power base and civil society. The consequence is a crisis in the legitimacy of a leadership that only survives through oppression and authoritarianism. No wonder, then, that the central problem of Arab governments today is the absence of political accountability. This lack of legitimacy explains the unstable, autocratic, and volatile behavior of Arab regimes.

One of the explanations that has been advanced for the shortcomings of Middle Eastern democracies is the suffering of the Arab world and the installment of ruling classes as proxy regimes. Dominating powers have attempted to create economically and socially dependent entities that would best serve their interests in the region.[11] It must be acknowledged, though, that not all of the impediments to Arab progress have been created by external forces. The prevalence of traditional loyalties and value orientations, as well as high illiteracy rates, has been a significant factor in slowing the pace of democratization in the Arab world. Moreover, the discord between Arab heritage and Western values has made it difficult for Arab societies to absorb democratic ideas that were the culmination of a long process of development in the West. The lack of an Arab substructural system to respond to the Westernization and modernization processes created a gap between reality and dream.[12]

The absence of democracy in the Arab world is an outcome of successive failures by the nationalists to transform the fundamental social structures that perpetuate tribalism and traditional loyalties. Consequently, the opposition to the ruling political system is oppressed, and the imposition of policies by the ruling elite is common in the Arab world. Unfortunately, the crisis of Arab intellectuals has also exacerbated the status quo and hindered efforts to bridge the gaps in society. Most intellectuals are being co-opted by the political systems in the Arab world, and those who refuse suffer from alienation and emigrate to the West. This scenario partially explains why there is a brain drain in the Middle East.[13] The region simply lacks the structural institutional framework for democratic participation.[14]

In a brilliant analysis of the economic and social foundations of democracy in the Middle East, a distinguished Arab scholar, Charles Issawi, pointed out that democracy does not thrive in the contemporary Middle East "because the economic and social basis which it requires is as yet non-existent."[15] He emphasized the importance of socioeconomic transformation in Arab societies in bringing about the capability to respond to the modern state and lay down the principles of democracy.[16] Issawi, in fact, criticized constitutional and administrative reforms because they are not reflective of the true nature of democracy.[17] Bassam Tibi, a Middle Eastern scholar, bolsters Issawi's arguments with the observation that "Arabs have witnessed numerous changes of governments and changes of political personnel carrying an abundance of different labels."[18] But, he adds, "Arabs continue to experience one and the same pattern of political culture, i.e., political oppression and the lack of political freedom."[19] Arab states dominate all aspects of life and society in the Middle East, and respect for the individual citizen in the Arab polity is nonexistent.

Arab liberal thought failed to define democracy as a structure or system of social transformation. It simply portrayed democracy as a panacea for the Arab sociopolitical malaise. One of the major pitfalls of Arab liberal thought was its taking an idea from the West without understanding the need to build an economic infrastructure that could generate a social system responsive to democratic change. Value systems cannot be implemented without viable corresponding structural roots.[20] The concepts of democracy were not solidified by the ruling elites, despite the slogans of secularism, nationalism, and freedom they espoused in their defiance of colonialism. Once the Arab world was independent of the vestiges of colonialism, the ruling elites jockeyed to establish societies dependent on the West. This dependence is the crux of the problem that faces Arab societies today. How can a society be democratic when an integral part of democracy— freedom—is nonexistent? The political systems in the Arab world use liberal and democratic terminology such as "pluralism as instruments aimed at containing the street, rather than unleashing it."[21] According to Mohamed

Sid-Ahmed, a noted Arab scholar and Islamist, "People must be ready and equipped to actively take part in public life. Outbursts of popular participation due to frustration, alienation, and repression need not necessarily lead to genuine democratic conduct but can, on the contrary, breed populism, demagoguery, and fascism."[22]

Sid-Ahmed adds that "democracy needs a certain level of social maturity to be genuinely implemented. Democracy always comes through conquest, it is not given. It is implemented through a process."[23] The populist socialists who came after the liberals emphasized the freedom of the state in shaping society and denied political freedom to individual citizens. Thus, democracy was short-lived and doomed to failure—just as the liberals were.

Among the vibrant actors on the political scene are the proponents of political Islam, who categorically oppose the notion of freedom and democracy as *hulul mustaurada* (imported solutions).[24] For the Muslim fundamentalists, Islam is the only viable option for the resolution of Arab problems on the socioeconomic and political levels. In Islam there is *shura* (consultation) and *ijma'* (consensus) but no democracy. Democracy is viewed as an alien concept; it has been stigmatized by association with the Western hegemonies and their imperialist motives in recolonizing the Arab Muslim world. Furthermore, the fundamentalists accuse present Arab regimes of being stooges of the West that should be ousted. Muslim fundamentalists in the Arab world have never succeeded in controlling any Arab political system—their popularity in recent Algerian parliamentary elections merely reflects the mood of despair among the Arabs, particularly after the Gulf War. This ebb and flow of Islamic resurgence in the Middle East is related to the degree of success or failure on the part of secular Arab regimes in responding to the aspirations of the Arab masses. Arab nationalists try to put pressure on the Arab regimes to modernize, industrialize, build institutions, and above all protect basic human rights.

Democracy is not an absolute concept. In its ideal state it is intertwined organically with freedom. It strives to create parity between the individual and society through representative government. Unfortunately, the Arab world suffers from divisiveness, fractionalizaton, social incohesiveness, parochialism, patriarchal relations, authoritarianism, and glaring inequities of income and opportunity. Moreover, democracy in the Arab world is almost seen as a fantasy objective because it is not an organic development. This perception results in demoralization and dependency among the people. The Arab world today is sitting on a powder keg. If Arab secularists fail to change the status quo, the strong fundamentalist tide that emerges will be hard to contain. Therefore, Arab society is at a crossroads. The global transformation taking place makes it imperative for the Arab leaders to initiate radical changes in their respective countries. The required changes must be substantive and instrumental, aiming at the grassroots level and leading to economic parity, political participation, and representative government.

Origins of Palestinian Nationalism and the Evolution of the PLO

The PLO is an organizational framework that comprises commando groups, trade unions, and professional associations, as well as leading national figures that meet to work for the achievement of Palestinian aspirations and goals.[25] Its military aim is to demonstrate its international presence, mobilize the scattered Palestinian people, and actively wear down the Israelis.[26] It is important to shed light on the evolution of Palestinian nationalism in order to come to a better understanding of trends toward democratization.

The awakening of Arab consciousness in modern times and the consequent rise of Arab nationalism can be attributed, inter alia, to the activities of the Zionists, the rise of Turkish nationalism, and the impact of World War I. The Palestinians are part of the Arab world, sharing with it many of its internal developments and external influences. Zionism has been particularly influential in shaping their current politics and in determining their political destiny.

Historically, the Palestinian question can be related to Western cultural penetration in the form of nationalism and political penetration in the form of colonial rule. While Jewish nationalism—political Zionism—originated in the intellectual and emotional responses to the pogroms of Eastern Europe and Russia, the nationalism of the Arabs was a direct reaction to Ottoman oppression and European colonialism. The two nationalisms appeared around the same time, toward the end of the nineteenth century, and reached the peak of their political strength later in the twentieth century. In the meantime, although their aspirations centered on Palestine, their fortunes and misfortunes depended heavily on European politics, particularly those of the big powers.

The awakening interest of Arabs in their cultural heritage and traditions gave birth to Arab nationalism in the key cities of the Fertile Crescent. The political organization and strength of the nascent Arab national movement was in Syria, particularly in Damascus. However, Western colonial rule and the threat of Zionism caused Arab nationalism to splinter, propelling the political elites of Syria, Iraq, and Palestine toward local priorities and concerns. In particular, the Palestinian *a'yan* (notables) were disenchanted with the fragmentation of the Arab nationalist movement, which contradicted their aspiration of national self-determination and political independence. Mohammad Muslih, a noted historian on the origins of Palestinian nationalism, comments on early manifestations of pluralism in the area:

> There were three threads in the Palestinian opposition to Zionism in Ottoman times: Ottoman loyalism, Palestinian patriotism, and Arab nationalism. Ottoman loyalism dictated the rejection of Zionism because it was bent upon separating Palestine from the Ottoman State; Palestinian patriotism dictated its rejection on the ground that it was a deadly threat to the Palestinians; and Arab nationalism called for its rejection because it would wrest Palestine from Arab hands and thwart the cherished goal of Arab unity.[27]

Palestinian nationalism developed its own ideology and institutional framework because of two important developments after the war. According to Muslih: "One, internal, pertained to the fragmentation of the Arab nationalist movement, and the other, external, pertained to the dismemberment of Syria at the hands of Britain and France."[28] Zionism, then, was a catalyst in developing Palestinian nationalism but never contributed to its creation. Zionism provided the Palestinians with a centralized focus for their national struggle.[29] Regardless of its unique characteristics, Palestinian nationalism incorporated the ideals of pan-Arabism revolving around Arab unity and independence.

It is impossible to understand the Palestinian national movement without keeping in mind the profound influence of its long and difficult struggle with Zionism. One would expect the ferocity of the struggle between the Palestinian Arabs on the one hand and the Zionists and their British ally on the other to unite the Palestinian Arab movement and consolidate its forces. Unfortunately, the Palestinians could not escape their own traditional rivalries, and their national movement fell victim to internal divisions and political fragmentation. At times, Arabs fought against Arabs, while their Zionist enemy confronted them with unusual stubbornness and determination to reach their ultimate goal—creating a Jewish state in Palestine.

The British policy of "divide and rule" succeeded, and the rivalry between the two leading Palestinian families, the Husaynis and Nashashibis (the *a'yan* class of Jerusalem), took a sharp turn during the first decade of British mandate. These families manipulated all the ties of kin, class, and patronage to win over new supporters. Unfortunately, the traditional leadership did not realize in the 1930s that their factionalism would help lead to the loss of part of Palestine in 1948. A Jewish state would be established in most of the country, and the rest would be placed under Jordanian and Egyptian rule. The future was even gloomier: The whole of Palestine would fall to Jewish rule, with no assurances that stability or peace might one day prevail in the region.[30]

With a new leadership in the early sixties, the Palestinian national movement took up the challenge of pursuing an independent Palestinian state. This heavy burden was shouldered by the PLO, officially created in 1964 by the Arab League. Nasser's Egypt backed the idea in order to co-opt the new organization and control it.[31] Egypt used its influence to preclude any Palestinian action against Israel that might draw Egypt into a confrontation with it.[32] The PLO was headed by Ahmad al-Shuqayri, known for his affiliation with Nasser, and the Palestinian Liberation Army was directly under the Arab unified command and headed by an Egyptian. At the inaugural conference of the PLO in May 1964, al-Shuqayri immediately started agitating for material and public support from the various Arab capitals, in particular the Arab Gulf states.

From its inception, the PLO was embroiled in factional bickering. Its existence and decisionmaking processes were affected by inter-Arab rivalries, especially those between Syria and Egypt, and to a certain degree Jordan. Fatah, a leading organization within the PLO, emphasized military action against Israel and removed itself from the inter-Arab feud. According to Helena Cobban, "It was in the collapse of the previously existing system of inter-state relations in the Arab World, its checks, balances and interrelated ideologies, that Fatah's most explosively dynamic chance for growth arose, the chance that was to catapult Fatah into the leadership of the PLO."[33]

Irrespective of Fatah's predominance in the PLO, the June 1967 war was a disaster for the Arab states and the Palestinians. Some of the latter suffered another exodus to Jordan, Syria, and Lebanon and were denied return to their homes, while others were destined to stay on their native soil under Israeli occupation. In spite of this cataclysmic event that exacerbated the plight of the Palestinians, new orientations to Palestinian nationalism were brought to the fore by the political organizations. Arab military might was shattered and the leadership disoriented and disarrayed, and the international community became more sympathetic with Israel than with Arab "intransigent regimes," as they were portrayed in the international press and world public opinion. Consequently, Palestinian leaders became disenchanted with the Arab regimes despite their support and began to call for the establishment of Palestinian organizations independent of outside Arab control. Here, again, Palestinians were diverted from the cause of pan-Arabism and Arab unity in favor of Palestinian nationalism and the struggle for independence.

After the 1967 *naksa* (disaster), there appeared a crushing need for the reconstruction of Palestinian life. Ideology, armed struggle, and diplomatic posturing became secondary to the building of an organization that could advocate and take action on behalf of all Palestinians. The Palestinian leadership made a concrete effort to gain legitimacy and credibility, not only from Palestinians but also from the international community. The task entailed mundane activities such as purchasing arms, raising funds, and developing a territorial base that could facilitate closer ties to the Palestinians on the West Bank and Gaza, as well as launching military activities against Israel. Building such an organization was difficult and required strenuous efforts. In 1967–1968 the mainstream Palestinian organizations, struggling to consolidate their power, could not afford open confrontations with the small organizations that proliferated at the time. Instead, the larger commando groups contrived, not by sheer force but by persuasion, to co-opt those small groups. Tolerance of division and diversity characterized the Palestinian nationalist movement, and the sense of pluralism became almost a tradition. However, despite the effort invested in building a unified movement, the Palestinians could not overcome the social divisions and fragmented authority in their society. It was only in February 1969 that Fatah succeeded in controlling the PLO and gradually uniting the fragmented commando movements.[34]

The Institutional Infrastructure of the PLO

The PLO succeeded in reconstituting a shattered Palestinian society under difficult conditions and in a difficult environment. It managed to make operational a remarkable infrastructure against high odds, thus addressing the political and material needs of the dispersed Palestinians.[35] According to Cheryl Rubenberg:

> The PLO's role goes beyond the traditional roles of national liberation movements, for it not only struggles for the attainment of the national political rights of the Palestinian people, but is the only instrument for the reconstitution of Palestinian shattered society. . . . The PLO has to rehabilitate a nation as well as to struggle for its liberation.[36]

Despite the militant elements in its organizational structure, the PLO succeeded in building a civilian-institutional infrastructure that catered to the needs of the Palestinian nation in exile. The political implications of building a myriad of social institutions were crucial to the development of a framework in which to deal with the internal political process and strategy formulations.[37] The viability of this infrastructure gave the PLO the means and mechanisms to contain factionalism and divisiveness among the resistance groups, to represent the Palestinians abroad, and to provide medical and social care to the refugee communities in Lebanon and elsewhere.[38] It is important to note that although Fatah, being the largest group within the PLO, is the wealthiest and the most influential, it cannot arbitrarily set PLO policies without coordination with the smaller groups. Because it fears fragmentation, it cannot afford to lose its representative and democratic image. Above all, it is the influence of Arab states that prompts Fatah to accommodate to the smaller groups and permit them political leverage far beyond their proportion and capabilities.[39] The PLO leadership has always struggled to portray a democratic image at the expense of managing conflicting interests and factions in the Palestinian community. In spite of an occasionally abrasive relationship with the smaller groups in the PLO, Fatah has buttressed national unity within the organization, an imperative for building democratic relations. In terms of tactics, the smaller groups differ from the mainstream, but Fatah always contrives to find commonalities.[40] The pluralism of the PLO transcends the traditional concept of a national liberation movement. In the eyes of many experts, the PLO's institutionalization process reflects the political maturity of the Palestinian people and their historic leadership, thus legitimizing their quest for nationhood and ultimately for statehood.[41]

The Political Institutions of the PLO

The most important democratic political institutions of the PLO are the Palestine National Council (PNC), the Central Committee (CC), and the Executive Committee (EC). The PLO has the infrastructure of a state, with three branches of government: legislative, executive, and judiciary.[42]

The National Council

The PNC is the equivalent of a parliament. It is the supreme authority formulating the PLO's policies and programs. Its members' term of office is two years. It meets regularly upon the request of the Executive Committee or one-fourth of its members. Between 1964 and 1967 it met annually, but the fourth session, in July 1968, resolved that the council should convene twice a year.[43] The council is run by a chairman, two vice-chairmen, and a secretary, all elected by the PNC. Its membership is nominated by a committee of the EC and CC and general organizations of the Palestinian communities. The objective is to secure fair representation of Palestinians from all walks of life. Ideally, the members of the PNC would be elected directly by the Palestinian people; however, direct elections have not been possible.[44] During its regular sessions the PNC considers the report of the Executive Committee on the accomplishments of various organs of the PLO, the report of the Palestine National Fund, the budget of the PLO, the recommendations of various council committees, and other issues submitted for consideration. Two-thirds of its membership constitutes a quorum, and decisions are taken by a simple majority.

The Central Council

In its eleventh session, in January 1973, the PNC created a Central Council from within its own membership to follow up and implement its resolutions.[45] The CC serves in a consultative role to the PLO leadership. It is an intermediary between the Executive Committee and the PNC, and ensures the various factions within the PLO of continued effective participation in PLO affairs and among the PLO's constituency.[46] Its membership is made up of the Executive Committee along with at least an equivalent number of other members directly elected from the PNC.[47] The CC meets at least once every three months and executes a combined legislative-executive function.[48]

The Executive Committee

The second most important organization within the PLO is the Executive Committee, or "Cabinet," which functions as the executive branch of the organization. The PNC selects its members, who in turn elect the chairman. The EC is in permanent session, and its members work on a fulltime basis.[49] They are responsible to the PNC collectively and individually for the execution of the policies, plans, and programs the PNC has drawn up. The number of EC members was set by the Fundamental Law at a maximum of fifteen (including the chairman).[50]

The Executive Committee carries out four major functions: 1) It officially represents the Palestinian people; 2) it supervises the various organs of the PLO; 3) it draws up programs, issues directives, and makes decisions on the organization of the PLO, provided that these do not contradict the National Charter; and 4) it executes the financial policy set by PLO and prepares its budget.[51] In short, the Executive Committee directs all the activities of the PLO in accordance with the general plan and resolutions passed by the National Council. Within the EC, two-thirds of the members form a quorum, and decisions are made by simple majority.[52] Since the EC is elected by the PNC and its members come from within it, it is usually fairly representative of the power structure of the various commando organizations in the National Council.[53]

The Palestine National Fund

Another major institution of the PLO stipulated in the Fundamental Law is the Palestine National Fund. Revenues were to come from the following sources: 1) a fixed tax on all Palestinians of 5 to 7 percent of wages earned, collected by the Arab governments of the states in which they reside; 2) financial contributions by Arab governments and people; 3) loans and contributions from Arab governments and friendly nations; and 4) any additional sources approved by the PNC.[54] The chairman of the fund's board of directors is elected by the National Council and automatically becomes a member of the Executive Committee. The other eleven members of the board are appointed by the Executive Committee for three-year terms. One of the fund's major functions is to supervise the expenditures of the PLO and its various institutions.[55]

The Political Department

The PLO's diplomatic activities are carried out through the political department. The head of the department has the status of a foreign minister, representing the PLO at Arab summits and conferences and at special UN sessions and performing other diplomatic duties. The department oversees the activities and operations of the PLO offices in foreign countries.[56]

The Information Bureau

The PLO Information Bureau performs both informational and public relations functions. It deals with news people and has its own newspaper, *Filastine al-Thawra* (Palestine Revolution), its own news agency, WAFA, and a bimonthly journal published in French and English entitled *Palestine*.[57]

Other Functions of PLO Institutions

In addition to its political bodies, the PLO was able to develop its own regular army and an active military police in Lebanon. However, with the Israeli invasion of that country in 1982, the military and civilian infrastructures of the Palestinians were almost shattered. A closer look at the formal structure of the major political organs of the PLO permits several inferences to be made about the nature of the political process in the PLO and the extent of power sharing and collective decisionmaking. Throughout the years the PLO has established a quasistate that functions in a democratic way; it could not have practiced authoritarianism, as there is no territorial state and Palestinians are dispersed. It is valid to say, then, that the legitimacy of the PLO is derived from the Palestinian people; "the PLO as an umbrella organization subsumes all the various elements of the Palestinian nationalist movement, [which] makes authoritarianism an unlikely *modus operandi*."[58] Furthermore, as noted earlier, the PLO has succeeded in maintaining its legitimacy by integrating the diverse and complex positions and attitudes of the various Palestinian social strata. The high level of literacy among Palestinians and the depth of their political consciousness due to dispersion, occupation, and repression by Israel and the authoritarian Arab regimes give the Palestinians a unique character not exhibited in any of the Arab states.

Although the PLO strives for consensus decisionmaking according to its terms of constitution, a simple majority suffices. Unlike rulers of the Arab states, the chief executive of the PLO cannot make unilateral or arbitrary decisions; he may only use the tools of persuasion and bargaining in order to arrive at a balance among the diverse political factions in the PLO. Authoritarianism could exacerbate factionalism and divisiveness, a trend that could dismantle the PLO and deprive it of its legitimacy. However, the decentralization of PLO authority in a finite territorial state would tend to inhibit the development of an authoritarian regime that could crush the opposition. Because the PLO leadership has always used functional pragmatism to accommodate the various factions, negotiations and bargaining along with persuasion have been considered desirable not only for tactical reasons but for ideological reasons as well. Since Fatah is the predominant faction, it can call the shots without deep confrontation and outright hostility. Chairman Yassir Arafat has been a master of diplomacy in containing Palestinian factionalism and has successfully contrived to use the PLO's political structure to promote his ideas and achieve his objectives. Certainly he could not have survived all the debacles within Fatah, especially when a group of commando leaders joined forces with the Syrians in 1983, without popular support, particularly from the Palestinians living in the Occupied Territories. It is fair to infer that, regardless of factionalism within the PLO, democratic practices are embedded in its pragmatic politics, which will make it hard to sustain authoritarianism once an independent Palestinian state is established. The pragmatic trends in the PLO are evident in PNC resolutions, in particular those of the nineteenth PNC and the Declaration of Independence. Thus, according to Rubenberg, "The efforts at institution-building (or 'state-building') have served the dual purpose of pragmatic functionalism and political nation-building."[59] Equally important in bolstering Palestinian nationalism is the Palestinian civil infrastructure, which ranges from the areas of culture, education, welfare, and health to a system of information, communication, socioeconomic development, and mass organizations at the grassroots level. To illustrate this point, a quick look at the civilian infrastructure that sought to tie the PLO to the Palestinian people and their daily life is imperative. For the purpose of this study, it is sufficient to mention the following institutions in Lebanon:[60] 1) The Palestinian Red Crescent Society; 2) SAMED—the Sons of Martyrs Society; 3) the PLO's Planning Center, which sponsors social research; 4) the Palestinian Research Center, which sponsors political and historical research on Palestine; 5) the Social Welfare Organization, which manages a network of social welfare schemes; and 6) the Department of Mass Organizations, which encompasses all Palestinian unions.

These Palestinian social institutions emphasize the PLO's strong commitment to meeting the functional needs of the Palestinian people. They have instilled in the Palestinians a sense of self-reliance and national identity, not to mention an appreciation of the value of education. Above all, the PLO institutions reflect the urgently felt need for international recognition and acceptance. The PLO has represented itself as expressing the national will of the Palestinians, and the degree of sophistication displayed by PLO political institutions, along with its policy of consensus building based on bargaining and negotiations, provide the basis of democratic government and statehood.[61]

Indeed, the PLO's accommodation to a wide range of exigencies has placed military activities at a subservient level and prompted the PLO to behave responsibly as a non-state actor in international and regional politics as well as in its conflict with Israel.[62] All the factions are well integrated in its political structure, thus obviating fragmentation and authoritarian rule. This feature of the PLO, which has operated outside the sphere of direct Arab influence at least since 1969, has equipped it with a sense of fortitude in representing the Palestinian nation and its quest for national and political rights.

The pragmatic line of thought incorporated by the PLO in recent years has enhanced its image as a flexible organization making choices within the context of constraints.[63] According to Khalid al-Hasan, a PLO senior official, "Political struggle cannot be seen in terms of black and white. . . . Without a proper understanding of a political reality, it is impossible to understand the implications of any decision and to attain the proper picture."[64] He further adds:

> From the intellectual standpoint, the Palestinians realize that, given the present balance of forces, the attainment of this goal (i.e., Palestinian armed might) is not possible for now: the international situation does not offer any favorable conditions, while the Arab World is in a state of collapse and lacks any real strength or determination to press onward; thus the intellect of the Palestinian indicates that the only real option is to formulate a step-by-step program.[65]

The practical approach initiated by the PLO is designed to win over the United States and hence Israel for a negotiated settlement to the Palestinian-Israeli conflict. In past years this strategy has had a visible impact on the formulation of PNC resolutions. Therefore, pragmatism and making choices within constraints have been the principal elements in Palestinian politics, with the military option ruled out and perceptions for interim objectives spelled out clearly. Diplomacy has been, at least since the intifada, the course by which Palestinians have pursued their national aspirations. Again to quote Khalid al-Hasan: "Pragmatism, which is an effort to adjust to changing realities without surrendering one's principles, is a product not of altered value systems but rather the recognition that a wide gap exists between sacred values and the options available for their realization."[66]

A survey of the decisions made by the PNC throughout the years makes evident the concrete changes in Palestinian political attitudes, especially since the twelfth PNC in 1974. The stages of Palestinian politics, as assessed through PNC meetings, shed more light on the deliberations on the substantive issues and illustrate the evolution of the political strategy that ultimately led to the PLO's official endorsement of a two-state solution (in November 1988 at the nineteenth PNC). Since then the PLO has been hammering on the theme of a peaceful solution to the conflict through a negotiated settlement and political accommodation. The United States has played a crucial role in bridging the gap between the Arabs and Israel on the one hand and between Israel and the Palestinians on the other, particularly after the Gulf War. Secretary of State James Baker has been instrumental in bringing the conflicting parties to the table of negotiation. The process of negotiation is likely to be hard, frustrating, and slow. Yet with growing democratization, certain convictions have developed within the mainstream of the PLO, and a sizable majority of Palestinians who support the peace process realize that a permanent solution to the enigma of the Middle East is just a matter of time. Patience, endurance, and stamina are required to avoid being pushed and provoked toward unilateral concessions without achieving the optimum goal, one defined within the parameters of a defined set of principles that have always been the Palestinian frame of national reference.

In order for the PLO to arrive at a decision through its political process, it has to overcome the constraints imposed by the dispersal of the Palestinian people and the absence of a territorially based national authority. This state of affairs leaves no alternative to the PNC, through which the "politics of consensus on a pluralistic basis prevail."[67]

Toward Pragmatism and Peaceful Coexistence: An Analysis of the Resolutions of the PNC

An examination of the PNC's resolutions, in particular those from the twelfth PNC onward, sheds light on Palestinian democratic trends and pluralistic thinking. Since 1974 the Palestinians moved steadily toward accommodation and compromise. By the eighteenth PNC, convened in Algiers in April 1987, most of the elements for an embrace of a peaceful strategy and the acceptance of a two-state solution based on UN resolutions were in place. As mentioned earlier, PNC resolutions are considered the culmination of the PLO's dialogue and an "important barometer of the actual thinking of the Palestinian movement."[68] Thus, once adopted they become "a legitimizing instrument for politics pursued by the PLO leadership."[69] This role is best illustrated by Arafat's reference to the nineteenth PNC as the basis for his statement in Geneva in December 1988.[70]

The PNC sessions since the inception of the PLO can be divided into three distinct phases in order to highlight the major turning points in the Palestinian decisionmaking process.

First Phase:
Liberation and Return (1964–1968)

After the destruction of Palestine in 1948, Palestinians suffered homelessness and exile and therefore sought to redress these injustices through the liberation of their occupied homeland and the repatriation of their community.[71] The Palestinian National Charter of 1964 and the amended National Charter of 1968, drawn up during the fourth PNC using the resolutions of the second and third PNCs, emphasized the total liberation of Palestine.[72] The fourth PNC exhibited a dramatic shift, for it centered not only on total liberation through armed struggle but moved the agent of liberation from the Arab political scene to that of the Palestinians.[73] Self-reliance and armed struggle were stipulated in Article 9 of the 1968 National Charter. Moreover, the concept of national unity was reiterated to coordinate the different commando groups within the PLO infrastructure. The PLO emerging from the fourth PNC vigorously stressed the building of sociopolitical and economic institutions that could cater to the needs of a shattered society.[74]

Second Phase:
The Secular Democratic State (1969–1974)

During this phase, Palestinians addressed the problem of how to reconcile their legitimate national political rights with the political and demographic realities created after the destruction of Palestine and subsequent events.[75] This phase was characterized by a marked revision in Palestinian objectives, from total liberation to a democratic secular state in which Christians, Muslims, and Jews could live together harmoniously. One important concession was demanded of the Israelis: They must renounce Zionism and the messianic vision of Eretz Israel. Thus, the fifth PNC, in 1969, introduced the idea of establishing a "free democratic society in Palestine." In the sixth PNC the same concept was reiterated with a stipulation changing the word "society" to "state."[76] By the eleventh PNC, the establishment of a "democratic society where all citizens can live in equality, justice and fraternity" and "opposed to all forms of prejudice on the basis of race, creed and color" was emphasized. This proposal represented a dramatic and historic compromise in which a framework for peace was presented and zero-sum claims were renounced by the Palestinians. This official policy remained the PLO's basic objective until 1974, when the organization made the first gesture toward a two-state solution at the twelfth PNC.[77]

Third Phase:
The Two-State Solution (1974–1988)

It was in July 1974, after the October War, that new realities evolved in the Middle East. Hopes for a comprehensive settlement were high, which induced the PLO to embark on a pragmatic course culminating in the declaration of a Palestinian state in the Occupied Territories and the ultimate acceptance of a two-state solution in 1988. Of course, this historic decision was not made in a vacuum; it was rather a response to successive important events such as the Lebanese civil war, the Camp David accords, the Egyptian-Israeli peace treaty, Sadat's visit to Jerusalem, the 1982 Israeli invasion of Lebanon, and the intifada in the Occupied Territories. All these events led to the bold decision of peaceful coexistence with Israel. Moreover, during these crucial years the PLO witnessed internal changes and dramatic events such as the temporary withdrawal of the Popular Front for the Liberation of Palestine (PFLP) from the PLO's Executive Committee, the dissension of the Abu Mousa faction from Fatah in 1983, and the controversial trip of Arafat to Cairo after the PLO's ouster from Lebanon. These incidents were crucial to the development and existence of the Palestinian national movement. Not only did the Palestinians survive them, the PLO also managed to stabilize its objectives and profound commitment to the concept of the two-state solution. The twelfth PNC was the turning point in Palestinian political decisionmaking, a prelude to peaceful coexistence and political accommodation. It was in this council that the "Ten Point" program was drafted, calling for the establishment of the "peoples' national, independent, and fighting authority on every part of liberated Palestinian land."[78] This program was the first official indication that a nonmilitary option could be accepted and that Israel would be accepted within its 1967 borders. After the twelfth PNC, the concept of armed struggle became subservient to political diplomacy but was never ruled out as an option. The strategy adopted favored a peaceful resolution to the conflict through mediation, conciliation, mutual reciprocity, and parity.

The thirteenth, fourteenth, and fifteenth PNCs emphasized methodically and systematically the rights of the Palestinians to establish an independent state under the leadership of the PLO in any part of Palestine.[79] During the fifteenth PNC, the Brezhnev initiative was welcomed, the dialogue with Jordan was resumed, the European initiative proposing UN Resolutions 248 and 338 as the basis for settlement was considered, and much attention was paid to the organizational structure of the PLO.[80] During this period, a broad-based international consensus emerged in favor of the creation of an independent Palestinian state in parts of Palestine as the basis for resolving the Arab-Israeli conflict. It is worth mentioning here that the PLO endorsed the resolutions of the Fez conference convened in Morocco in 1982, which laid down a practical vision for the resolution of the Arab-Israeli conflict.[81]

The sixteenth PNC indicated another shift in PLO policy, toward accommodation and open dialogue with Jordan and the formation of a confederation. The confederation plan was reiterated in subsequent PNCs despite the abrogation of the February accords in 1986.[82]

In the seventeenth PNC (the Amman conference of 1984) consensus in PLO politics shifted to majority politics, a good indication for the democratization process (especially because the Damascus-based opposition to the mainstream within the PLO had a small base). The Amman PNC explicitly espoused the primacy of the Palestinian aspirations and wishes in the

Occupied Territories. Rashid Khalidi sums up the Palestinian desiderata in the following five points:

1. There is a Palestinian people living on its historic land.
2. It has the right to self-determination.
3. It is represented by the PLO.
4. It has the right to an independent state.
5. Negotiations (should take place) in the context of an international conference.[83]

While the Palestinian national movement was transforming from a liberation movement into a national independence movement, accepting UN Resolutions 242 and 338 and later the Baker Plan of 1989–1990 in accordance with a well-defined peaceful strategy culminating in consensus on coexistence with Israel, there was a shift toward the extreme by Israel's Likud government, which espoused maximalist policies.[84]

The eighteenth PNC, convened in Algiers from April 20–25, 1987, symbolizes a major PLO triumph over any threat to its unity, national cohesion, and legitimacy. According to an analysis presented by Muhammad Hallaj, a noted Palestinian scholar:

> The return of the opposition [to the mainstream Fatah] to the parliamentary and constitutional structures of the PLO was an admission of the failure of extra-constitutional confrontation and the triumph of democratic dissent within the Palestinian political process. The importance of the reinforcement of the PLO's democratic traditions by the PNC cannot be overestimated.[85]

He adds:

> The re-election of Yassir Arafat to the chairmanship of the Executive Committee happened with the consent of the formerly rebellious opposition, which enhanced the importance of legality and constitutionalism and the principle of the consent of the governed as the basis for legitimacy.[86]

The strategy of the Palestinian leadership during this third phase comprised three substantial elements: mobilizing and politicizing the Palestinian people behind an organization representing them; maintaining the unity of the Palestinian movement through very difficult times; and achieving a political program based on consensus.[87]

In November 1988 the nineteenth PNC met in Algiers to adopt a Declaration of Independence and a political statement. In these documents a clear and concise peace strategy was laid down, along with explicit acceptance of UN Security Council Resolutions 242 and 338, as well as the recognition of Israel. Couched in unambiguous language, the document states the most explicit formulation of the Palestinian objectives toward a comprehensive, peaceful two-state solution of the Palestinian-Israeli conflict.[88] The nineteenth PNC irrevocably changed the course of the PLO; claims for a state in all of Palestine gave way to claims for a limited state on the West Bank and Gaza. The PFLP and the Democratic Front for the Liberation of Palestine (DFLP) opposed the mainstream Fatah in the PLO, but George Habash, general-secretary of the PFLP, reiterated: "The PFLP and I will remain in the PLO and in all its institutions for ever."[89]

Current Palestinian thinking rests on a clear and unequivocal need to develop a flexible strategy that rejects tendencies to adopt the familiar all-or-nothing position. As we have seen, the "no" option, which the Palestinians have been known to choose with regard to negotiations with Israel and the restoration of their rights in Palestine, has been affected by two important developments: 1) the PLO's acceptance of a two-state solution and the relevant UN resolutions, and 2) the willingness of the Palestinians in the Occupied Territories to be part of a negotiating team whose eventual task it would be to implement a two-state solution.[90]

The Declaration of Independence grounds Palestinian independence in international law and sets forth the guidelines of the constitution of the new state. It also explicitly spells out principles of equality, mutuality, and social justice in the Declaration:

> The State of Palestine is the state of Palestinians wherever they may be. In it they shall develop their national and cultural identity and enjoy full equality in rights. Their religious and political beliefs and their human dignity shall be safeguarded under a democratic parliamentary system of government built on the freedom of opinion; and on the freedom to form parties; and on the protection of the rights of the minority by the majority and respect of the decisions of the majority by the minority; and on social justice and equal rights, free of ethnic, religious, racial or sexual discrimination; and on a constitution that guarantees the rule of law and the independence of the Judiciary.[91]

Furthermore, there was absolute clarity about a peaceful settlement to the conflict; concepts such as "armed struggle" never appeared in the text. The Declaration emphasizes:

> The State of Palestine, declaring itself a peace-loving state committed to the principles of peaceful coexistence, shall strive with all states and peoples to attain a permanent peace built on justice and respect of rights.[92]

Moreover, the Declaration emphasizes settling disputes by peaceful means in accordance with the UN charter and resolutions and rejects the use of force and violence in conflict settlement unless attacked. The rejection of terrorism, as spelled out in the Declaration, makes an emphatic distinction between resistance to occupation and indiscriminate violence meant to terrorize civilians. In sum, there is ample evidence of the willingness of the Palestinians for direct peace negotiations.[93]

Some Palestinian groups continue to call for unswerving commitment to the 1964 National Charter, but these groups are peripheral to the locus of power and decisionmaking. It is common knowledge that no political community, least of all Israel, is without political discrepancies and rejectionism within its ranks. Palestinian democracy is not ideal because it is not directly practiced within a centralized polity. However, with the Palestinian intifada, the ball game for the Palestinians has changed, and the PLO's concentration and efforts have been diverted toward the bolstering of the civil infrastructure and institution building in the Occupied Territories. This process generated the "quota system" to represent the various factions competing to achieve their interests. Basically, the political drawback of the PLO's bureaucratic infrastructure outside had permeated the socioinstitutional fabric in the Occupied Territories. Hence, voices among "independent" Palestinians have been vociferous in insisting on democratic procedures.[94]

The PLO, The Intifada, and Democratic Reforms

A microcosm of Palestinian politics in exile has always been manifested in the Occupied Territories. Continuous debate takes place among Palestinians regarding their national interests. As we have seen, Palestinian national identity and the process of nation building have become a concrete reality. Between 1982 and 1987 the Palestinians in the Occupied Territories started building an infrastructure that challenged Israeli occupation. The intifada played a crucial role in sparking a synchronized effort by the Palestinian diaspora to discover the potential of its new empowerment.[95]

According to Salim Tamari, a noted Palestinian sociologist, on the eve of the uprising, the public debate within the Palestinian national movement focused on two trends of political thinking. "The first stressed steadfastness, a development strategy of survival and communal preservation until political conditions allowed for an external intervention," he writes, and "the second, seeing the conditions of transformation to be irreversible, concluded the search for sovereignty had to be traded for equality within the Israeli polity."[96] One could simply assert that the concept of steadfastness had been buttressed by *sumud* funds from the PLO, which exacerbated the reinforcement of *a'yan* political hierarchies characterized by traditionalism and a facade of moderation. Urban notables were often manipulated by the Israeli civil administration to defuse potential threats emanating from populist reactions. This populist trend posed a direct challenge to the traditional leadership inside and outside the Occupied Territories.[97] However, the main traits of this radical populism were manifested at the institutional level. The traditional mode of thinking was rejected, be it in women's associations, charitable societies, or student movements criticizing the formal university curriculum.[98] Furthermore, this populist trend had concentrated on the role of the labor force as a genuine component of the labor and trade unions in the Occupied Territories. Ideologically, the intifada could not avoid the factionalism of Palestinian politics.[99] Nevertheless, the already existing institutional infrastructure was the determining power in boosting the uprising and sustaining it to a point of no return. The mass organizations and the grassroots networks, along with the popular committees, formed the organizational nucleus to the uprising.[100]

At the same time, the intifada has managed to create a national debate among the various political groups within the PLO, between the "interior" and the "exterior," and between the "nationalist" and "religious" camps. This debate reflects the democratic trend within the Palestinian national movement. There are differences in the national camp over how to pursue the strategy of peace, but its detractors are not disruptive and could yet be categorized as "loyal opposition." However, the religious groups spearheaded by the Islamic resistance movement, Hamas, reject the Palestinian state and the convening of an international conference. They espouse the establishment of an Islamic state in the entire area of Palestine.[101] One should not underestimate the power and influence of Hamas on the Palestinian street, for since 1982 it has developed the potential to challenge the PLO in the Occupied Territories. The two camps are irreconcilable.

With the peace process going on, the nationalist camp has been divided between two polarized positions. One, introduced by Fatah, advocates a political initiative that starts with a transitional period of self-government and concludes with a Palestinian state. The other, introduced by the PFLP and, to a certain degree, by hard-liners in Fatah and independents, unaffiliated with any Palestinian political faction, advocates the end of Israeli occupation and the immediate establishment of a state. The second view encourages the escalation of the uprising, believing that neither the United States nor Israel will change its position vis-à-vis the Palestinian issue. They believe the peace process would diffuse the inner potential of the uprising and induce the Palestinians to make unilateral concessions that ultimately would lead them to accept an "autonomy plan" and not receive the land.[102]

Several Palestinian leaders have never stopped criticizing the stringent bureaucratic red tape in the PLO's infrastructure and have openly challenged the PLO leadership to introduce administrative reforms. There is ample evidence of inconsistencies between PNC resolutions and the PLO leadership's political ploys in promoting one factional interest at the expense of another. Critics of the PLO characterize administrative reforms as a prelude to political reform and democratization. One dominant feature of Palestinian politics is factionalism that exacerbates individualism and parochialism in the PNC debates. However, self-criticism and genuine democratic reform are lacking not only at the formal level but at the substantive level as well.[103] According to PFLP leader George Habash, PLO institutions and procedures should be democratically reformed using the principle of proportional representation. He openly requests that the Executive Committee and the Central Committee reorganize the various PLO organs and bureaus based on this principle and calls for 1) a commitment by Palestinian parties to PNC resolutions enhancing the democratic spirit in the institution-building process; 2) respect for pluralism (i.e., political participation in the decisionmaking process); and 3) the involvement of all Palestinian forces in the institutional infrastructure and transitional government.[104]

On the other hand, Nayef Hawatmeh, leader of the DFLP, thinks the organizational corruption and lack of democratization in the PLO is caused by the subversive actions of the national bourgeois elements and the immediate impact of those actions on the PLO decisionmaking process.[105] In contrast to the PLO's hierarchical leadership, Hawatmeh commends the Unified Leadership of the Uprising (UNLU) and its democratic representation at the grassroots level. He further believes in the initiation of democratic reforms in the PLO as a precondition for the building of the state infrastructure.[106]

The late Salah Khalaf, a prominent Fatah leader, asserted on several occasions that "real democracy should be based on dialogue prior to decision-making."[107] Furthermore, he believed that "democracy is full participation in the decision-making process and total compliance to its resolutions."[108] Khalaf was known as a caustic critic of the PLO and on many occasions promoted self-criticism as an essential tool for democratic reform. He lobbied for pluralism and democratic reforms in the PLO and encouraged democratic relations between the interior and the exterior.

Israeli Perceptions of Democratization Within the PLO

The Israeli political literature that deals with the PLO is divided mainly into three categories: 1) academic political books; 2) published articles by Israeli strategic and research centers; and 3) newspaper articles. It is rare to find a book or an article dealing with the democratization process in the PLO or its electoral behavior. Israeli journalists and, to a certain degree, scholars attempt to distort the PLO's image by emphasizing its terrorist actions and portraying its autocratic rule over the Palestinians. The writing in all genres reveals the Israelis' lack of understanding of the civilian and institutional services rendered by the PLO. Most of the Israeli literature on the PLO deals with its historic origins, old slogans, and policies and categorically denies the dramatic changes that have been taking place in the PLO. Much of the journalistic and academic work published about the PLO uses as its sources the Israeli intelligence (Shin Bet, the Shabak, and the Civil Administration Authority).

Justifications and rationales for not dealing with the democratic trends in the PLO revolve around 1) total ignorance of the changes that have been taking place in the PLO; 2) reluctance to accept the bitter fact that the PLO, unlike the rest of the Arab world, is practicing certain forms of democracy, as reflected in its institutional and civilian infrastructure; and 3) the negative impact of the Israeli right wing on Israeli press and research centers, leading to the portrayal of the PLO as a terrorist organization that seeks the destruction of Israel.[109] Such stereotyped attitudes impede the peace process and build psychological and political barriers between Israelis and Palestinians.

Palestinian scholars are trying hard to change these images by addressing the Israeli public and revealing the democratization process in the Occupied Territories and the diaspora. Although Palestinian democratic trends cannot be compared with the Western style of democracy, they are a considerable accomplishment. Israelis must realize that the process cannot be concrete as long as Palestinians are suffering from lack of basic human rights under Israeli occupation, above all the right for national elections. Palestinians still have a long way to go to achieve democracy; however, they contrive against all odds to lay down the principles and do the groundwork. It is not surprising, then, to see Palestinians fighting each other, even to the point of physical elimination; such conflict occurs in every national liberation movement.

The Assessment of the Intifada and Concluding Remarks

Since its eruption on December 9, 1987, the intifada in the Occupied Territories has defied the status quo and opened new avenues for both peace and conflict in the region. In fact, it has emerged as the most urgent and complex repurcussion of the Arab-Israeli conflict, contriving to score a pyrrhic victory by influencing international and, to a lesser degree, Israeli public opinion. The dramatic impact of the intifada has created universal awareness that the Israeli occupation cannot be sustained. However, neither this awareness nor the intifada's remarkable persistence could have been accomplished without the translation of political consciousness into political action through a mobilization of Palestinians of every age, sex, place of residence, and social background. Grassroots action, self-reliance, communal solidarity, and a sense of responsibility have been important factors in inspiring the Palestinians and giving the leadership of the PLO the self-confidence to consider what was once political suicide: negotiating a peace agreement with Israel. This change of political mood can be attributed to the intifada, which portrays itself as an authentic manifestation of creative power and a legitimate expression of Palestinian nationalism, embedded in the culture, community, and power of resistance. Yet Israeli reaction to the uprising has consistently been characterized by an unprecedented degree of brutality and confusion. Further, Israel has failed to counteract the Palestinian diplomatic offensive.

The intifada has been remarkable in pushing Israel toward political accommodation with the Palestinians in spite of Israel's resistance to negotiations that will pressure it to give up control over the West Bank and Gaza. The Likud government was willing to afford the Palestinians only limited autonomy. Palestinian moderates reject this plan, but they are ready to negotiate peace with Israel on the West Bank and Gaza; accept an interim period with UN supervision; accept a form of confederation with Jordan, and even with Israel, in the future; and accept U.S. mediation (as was already done) for a negotiated, peaceful settlement.[110]

In sum, this study has portrayed the basic trends toward democratic behavior by the PLO in its political and institutional infrastructure. Elections, which are a cornerstone of democratic behavior, have been held by the Palestinians in their mass organization, in universities, and at the grassroots level. The ideological commitment of the Palestinian national movement to democracy was spelled out in the Declaration of Independence.

The high level of education and political consciousness and the existence of numerous independent Palestinian institutions and professional societies work in support of a democratic government. In fact, the Palestinian society has significant experience with democratic forms on the local level; some of its most respected leaders are the elected mayors of Palestinian villages and cities who were deposed by the Israelis.[111] The Palestinian emphasis on majority rule in decisionmaking and the diffusion of power is a precondition for pluralist thinking and collective behavior.[112]

All these factors are good indicators of Palestinian readiness to establish a genuine democratic government and hence a state on 22 percent of its historic land. So far, the PLO's decision to recognize Israel represents a partial victory for the pragmatic wing of the organization, but if the PLO and the moderates fail to reap the benefits of their positions, they will be condemned and ostracized, and the radicals may gain strength, especially the Islamic bloc. Such a situation would stall the peace process and deepen the contradictions, which could lead to a renewed vicious cycle of extremism between the Palestinians and Israelis. The reality is that Palestinians and Israelis have been coexisting as neighbors and will continue to exist as such. Making peace with the Palestinians seems very low on Israel's list of priorities, yet it is in the interest of all actors in the region, including Israel, that the Palestinians be freed through a process of mediation, negotiation, and conciliation before they are freed through confrontation. There is no doubt that sooner or later the Palestinians and Israelis must make peace with each other. Peace, however, is not a nonbelligerency agreement or military disengagement; it is a resolution of conflict on the basis of coexistence and cooperation between two peoples.

Notes

1. Yashikazou Sakamato, "Introduction: The Global Context of Democratization," *Alternatives* 16 (1991), p. 119.

2. *Ibid.*, p. 125.

3. *Ibid.*, p. 121.

4. S. Neil MacFarlane, *Superpower Rivalry and Third World Radicalism: The Idea of National Liberation* (Baltimore: Johns Hopkins University Press, 1985), p. 5.

5. Giuseppe Di Palma, "Transition in Eastern Europe," *Journal of Democracy* (1991), as cited in *Dialogue* 4 (1991), p. 25.

6. M. Muslih and August R. Norton, "The Need for Arab Democracy," *Foreign Policy*, No. 83 (Summer 1991), p. 5.

7. *Ibid.*

8. Cheryl A. Rubenberg, "The Civilian Infrastructure of the Palestinian Liberation Organization: An Analysis of the PLO in Lebanon Until June 1982," *Journal of Palestine Studies*, Vol. 12, No. 3 (Spring 1983), p. 54.

9. *Ibid.*

10. *Ibid.*, p. 78.

11. Khalid Al-Naser, *The Crisis of Democracy in the Arab World* (Azmat Dimuqratiyyah fi Al-'Alam Al-'Arabi) (Beirut: Centre of the Arab Unity Studies, 1989), pp. 47–48.

12. *Ibid.*

13. *Ibid.*, pp. 50–53. See also Abdallah Laroui, *The Crisis of the Arab Intellectual: Traditionalism or Historicism?* (Berkeley: University of California Press, 1976), pp. 153–174; and Bassam Tibi, "Political Freedom in Arab Societies," *Arab Studies Quarterly*, Vol. 6, No. 3 (1984), p. 222.

14. Tibi, "Political Freedom," pp. 225–226.

15. Charles Issawi, "Economic and Social Foundations of Democracy in the Middle East," *International Affairs* 32 (January 1956), p. 28.

16. *Ibid.*, p. 41.

17. *Ibid.*, p. 40.

18. Tibi, "Political Freedom," p. 224.

19. *Ibid.*, pp. 224–225.

20. *Ibid.*, p. 226.

21. Mohammed Sid-Ahmed, "Initiatives for Deepening Democracy in the Middle East," *Alternatives* 15 (1990), p. 352.

22. *Ibid.*, p. 347.

23. *Ibid.*

24. See Yussuf Al-Qurdawi, *Al-Hulul Al-Mustawradah Wa Kaif Janat 'Ala Ummatina* (Beirut: Dar El-Arabi, 1980). For further information on Islamic fundamentalism, doctrines, beliefs, ideals, see Hussein Marwah, Mahmoud Amin Al-'Alem, Mohammaed Dakroub, and Samir' Sa'd, *Dirasat fi'l-Islam* (Beirut: Dar El-Arabi, 1980); Mohammed 'Amarah, *Al 'Uruba fi'l-'asr Al-Hadith* (Beirut: Dar El-Wihdah, 1981); Sayyid Qutb, *Al-'Adalah Al-Ijtima'iyyah fi'l-Islam* (Beirut: Dar

El-Shuruq, 1954); Muhomed 'Amarah and *Al-Islam Wa Mushkilat Al-Hadara* (Beirut: Dar El-Shuruq, no date); and *Khasais Al-Tasawor Al-Islami Wa Muqawamatuha,* 7th edition (Beirut: Dar el-Shuruq, 1980). On the Islamic movement on the West Bank and Gaza see Ziad Abu 'Amr, *The Islamic Movement in the West Bank and Gaza* (Acre: Dar El-Aswar, 1989); on the same topic see Jean-Francois Legrain, "The Islamic Movement and the Intifada," in Jamal R. Nassar and Roger Heacock, eds., *Intifada: Palestine at the Crossroads* (New York: Praeger, 1990). See also R. Hrair Dekmejian, *Islam in Revolution: Fundamentalism in the Arab World* (Syracuse: Syracuse University Press, 1985).

25. Rashid Hamid, "What is the PLO?" *Journal of Palestine Studies,* Vol. 4, No. 4 (Summer 1975), p. 90.

26. Yezid Sayegh, "The Politics of Palestinian Exile," *Third World Quarterly,* Vol. 9, No. 1 (January 1987), p. 56.

27. Mohammad Muslih, *The Origins of Palestinian Nationalism,* The Institute for Palestine Studies Series (New York: Columbia University Press, 1988), pp. 215–216.

28. *Ibid.,* p. 216.

29. *Ibid.,* p. 217.

30. See Manuel Hassassian, *Palestine: Factionalism in the National Movement (1919–1939)* (Jerusalem: Palestinian Academic Society for the Study of International Affairs [PASSIA], 1990).

31. Charles D. Smith, *Palestine and the Arab-Israeli Conflict* (New York: St. Martin's Press, 1988), pp. 188–189.

32. *Ibid.*

33. Helena Cobban, *The Palestine Liberation Organization: People, Power and Politics* (London: Cambridge University Press, 1984), p. 35.

34. For the historic evolution of the PLO see Jaber Quandt and Ann Lesch, *The Politics of Palestinian Nationalism* (Berkeley: University of California Press, 1973).

35. Sayegh, "Palestinian Exile," p. 57.

36. Cheryl Rubenberg, *The PLO: Its Institutional Infrastructure* (Cambridge, Mass.: The Institute of Arab Studies, Inc., 1983), p.1.

37. Sayegh, "Palestinan Exile," p. 59.

38. Aaron David Miller, "The PLO and the Politics of Survival," *The Washington Papers* 99 (1983), p. 56.

39. *Ibid.,* p. 57.

40. *Ibid.,* p. 59.

41. "A Discussion with Yasser Arafat," *Journal of Palestine Studies,* Vol. 9. No. 4 (1981), pp. 4–5.

42. Sami Musslam, "Al Bunya Al-Tahtiya Wa Al-Haikal Al-Mouassassati Li Munathamat Al-Tahrir Al-Filastiniyya," *Shu'un Filastiniyya,* No. 166–167, (December–January 1987), p. 18.

43. Rashid Hamid, "What is the PLO?" *Journal of Palestine Studies,* Vol. 4, No. 4 (Summer 1975), p. 103.

44. Cobban, *The Palestine Liberation Organization,* p. 11.

45. Rubenberg, *The PLO,* p. 8; see also Hamid, "What is the PLO?" p. 103, and *Palestine Diary* (London: The Palestinian Liberation Organization, 1982), p. 14.

46. Cobban, *The Palestine Liberation Organization,* p. 12.

47. *Ibid.*

48. Hamid, *Palestine Diary,* p. 14.

49. Rubenberg, *The PLO,* p. 10.

50. Hamid, "What is the PLO?" p. 103.
51. Hamid, *Palestine Diary*, pp. 14–15.
52. Hamid, "What is the PLO?" p. 103.
53. Hamid, *Palestine Diary*, p. 15.
54. *Ibid.*
55. *Ibid.*
56. Rubenberg, *The PLO*, p. 14.
57. *Ibid.*
58. *Ibid.*
59. *Ibid.*, p. 17.
60. See Rubenberg, "Civilian Infrastructure," pp. 54–78.
61. *Ibid.*, p. 78.
62. Muhammad Muslih, "Towards Coexistence: An Analysis of the Resolutions of the Palestine National Council (PNC)," *Journal of Palestine Studies,* Vol. 20, No. 2 (Spring 1990), p. 4.
63. Matti Steinberg, "The Pragmatic Stream of Thought Within the PLO: According to Khalid Al-Hasan," *The Jerusalem Journal of International Relations,* Vol. 11, No. 1 (1989), p. 40.
64. *Ibid.*
65. *Ibid.*, p. 41.
66. *Ibid.*, p. 54.
67. Muslih, "Towards Coexistence," p. 6.
68. *Ibid.*
69. *Ibid.*
70. *Ibid.*
71. Muhammad Hallaj, "The Arab-Israeli Conflict: A Palestinian View," *Vierteljahresberichte* (Problems of International Cooperation), No. 99 (March 1985), p. 32.
72. Muslih, "Towards Coexistence," p. 8; see also Rashid Hamid, "Munazzamat Al-Tahrir Al-Filastiniyya Fi 'Ashr Sanawat," *Shu'un Filastiniyya,* No. 41–42 (January–February 1975), pp. 515–519; see also Sai'd Hammoud, "Al-Majalis Al-Wataniyya Al-Filastiniyya Wa Al-Wihda Al-Wataniyya," *Shu'un Filastiniyya,* No. 18 (February 1973), pp. 78–82.
73. Muslih, "Towards Coexistence," p. 80.
74. Hammoud, "Al-Majalis Al-Wataniyya," p. 80.
75. Hallaj, "The Arab-Israeli Conflict," p. 32.
76. For the historical background and the PLO deliberations on the concept of a democratic secular state see Alain Gresh, "Shi'ar Al-Dawla Al Dimocratia Fi Al-Thawra Al-Filastiniyya, 1968–1971," *Shu'un Filastiniyya,* No. 122–123 (February 1982), pp. 142, 167. See also Hamid, *Palestine Diary*, pp. 521–522, and Hammoud, "Al-Majalis Al-Wataniyya," pp.78–82.
77. Hamid, *Palestine Diary*, pp. 525–526, and Hammoud, "Al-Majalis Al-Wataniyya, p. 82.
78. Faysal Hourani, "Munazzamat Al-Tahrir Al-Filastiniyya Wa Al-Itijah Nahwa Al-Taswiya," *Shu'un Filastiniyya,* No. 99 (February 1980), pp. 52–66.
79. Bilal Al-Hasan, "Al-Dawra Al-Khamisa 'Ashar Lil Majlis Al-Watani Al-Filastini: Dawrat Al-Tadqiq Fi Al-Qarar Al-Siyasi," *Shu'un Filastiniyya,* No. 115 (June 1981), pp. 5–13.
80. *Ibid.* See also Al-Hasan, "Min Mawathiq Al-Dawra Al-Sabi'a Ashar Li-l-Majlis Al-Watani Al-Filastini," Amman, November 22–29, 1984, *Shu'un Filastiniyya.*
81. Hallaj, "The Arab-Israeli Conflict," p. 33; see also "Al-Hiwar Al-Watani

Qabl Wa Ba'd Al-Dawra Al-Sabi'a 'Ashra Lil-Majlis Al-Watani Al-Filastini,"
Shu'un Filastiniyya, Nos. 142–143 (January–February 1985), pp. 127–141.

82. Rashid Khalidi, "The Palestinian Dilemma: PLO Policy After Lebanon,"
Journal of Palestine Studies XV:1 (Autumn 1985), pp. 88–91; see also Faisal
Hourani, "Majlis Al-Aghlabiya Wa Al-Tariq Al-Jadid," *Shu'un Filastiniyya*, Nos.
140–141 (November–December 1984), pp. 3–8.

83. *Ibid.*, p. 101.

84. Edward W. Said, "Reflections on Twenty Years of Palestinian History,"
Journal of Palestinian Studies, Vol. 20, No. 4 (Summer 1991), p. 9.

85. Mohammad Hallaj, "PNC 18th," *American-Arab Affairs*, No. 21 (Summer
1987), p. 44.

86. *Ibid.* For further assessment on the eighteenth PNC see Farouq Al-
Qaddumi, "Assessing the 18th PNC," *Journal of Palestine Studies* XVII:2 (Winter
1988).

87. Nadia Hijab, "The Strategy of the Powerless," *Middle East International*,
May 12, 1989, pp. 17–18.

88. Rashid Khalidi, "The Resolutions of the 19th Palestine National Council,"
Journal of Palestine Studies XIX:3 (Spring 1990), pp. 29–32. See also Matti
Steinberg, "Change Despite Duality," *New Outlook*, Vol. 32, No. 1 (1989), pp.
15–17.

89. Maxim Ghilan, "The Palestinians: What Has Changed in PLO," *Israel-
Palestine* (November 1988), pp. 2–3.

90. Fouad Moughrabi, Elia Zureik, Manuel Hassassian, and Aziz Haidar,
"Palestinians on the Peace Process," *Journal of Palestine Studies*, Vol. 12 No. 81
(Autumn 1991), p. 37. The questionnaire to this study was done by the author in the
month of May 1991 in the West Bank and Gaza.

91. As quoted from the original Declaration of Independence document.

92. *Ibid.*

93. Edward W. Said, "From Intifada to Independence," *Middle East Report*
(May–June 1989), p. 14.

94. See Manuel Hassassian and Tahir Nammari, "An Independent Perspective
of the Palestinian National Movement in the Occupied Territories." Unpublished
paper delivered for the national Palestinian representative forces in Jerusalem in
January 1992, pp. 1–21. See also a symposium sponsored by the Center for
Research and Development in Jerusalem, September 1991, The Ideological Choices
for the Palestinian Society and the Question of Democracy. However, for a critique
of the PLO's bureaucratic approach see Jamil Hilal, "Al-Islah Al-Democrati Wa
Mihan Al-Marhala," *Sawt Al-Watan*, No. 21 (May 1991), pp. 30–32; As'ad Abdul
Rahman, "Al-Islah Fi Munazzamat Al-Tahrir Al-Filastiniyya: Ishamat Fi Al-
Hiwar," *Sawt Al-Watan*, No. 21 (May 1991), pp. 21–22; Tawfic Abu Baker,
"Munazzamat Al-Tahrir Wa Qadaya Al-Islah Al-Dimoqrati," *Sawt Al-Watan*, No.
21 (May 1991), pp. 29–30; Ghassan Al-Khatib, "Likai Takoun Dimuqratiytouna
Jadira Haqan Bifakhrina," *Sawt Al-Watan*, No. 21 (May 1991), p. 32; and Zakaria
Mohammad, "Al-Intifada Wa Al-Islah Al-Tanzimi Fi Munazzamat Al-Tahrir Al-
Filastiniyya," *Al-Fikr Al-Dimuqrati*, No. 5 (Winter 1989), pp. 23–25.

95. Helena Cobban, "The PLO and the Intifada," *Middle East Journal*, Vol. 44,
No. 2 (Spring 1990), p. 229.

96. Salim Tamari, "The Palestinian Movement in Transition: Historical
Reversals and the Uprising," *Journal of Palestine Studies*, Vol. 20 No. 2 (Winter
1991), p. 60.

97. *Ibid.*, p. 64.

98. *Ibid.*, p. 65.

99. *Ibid.*, p. 66.

100. *Ibid.*

101. Ziad Abu 'Amr, "The Debate Within the Palestinian Camp," *American/Arab Affairs*, No. 26 (Fall 1988), p. 43. See also by the same author, "Notes On Palestinian Political Leadership," *Middle East Report*, September–October 1988, p. 23.

102. On the issue of how to escalate the intifada, see George Habash, "Al-Istratijiyya Al-Filastiniyyah Fi Zaman Al-Intifada: A Dialogue with Habash," *Al-Fikr Al-Dimuqrati*, No. 7 (Summer 1989), pp. 12–13; see also Nayef Hawatmeh, "Al-Istratijiyah Al-Filastiniyyah Fi Zaman Al-Intifada: A Dialogue with Hawatmeh," *Al-Fikr Al-Dimoqrati*, No. 7 (Summer 1989), pp. 72–74.

103. Interview with Habash published in *Al-Fikr Al-Dimoqrati*, No. 7 (Summer 1989), p. 13.

104. *Ibid.*

105. Interview with Hawatmeh published in *Al-Fikr Al-Dimuqrati*, No. 7 (Summer 1989), p. 42.

106. *Ibid.* p. 45.

107. Interview with Salah Khalaf published in *Al-Fikr Al-Dimuqrati*, No. 7 (Summer 1989), p. 72.

108. *Ibid.*

109. Anbari, Benjas, *The Palestinian Choice* (Jerusalem: Carmel, 1989), in Hebrew; *PLO After the War in Lebanon* (Tel Aviv: Kibbutz HaMeuhad, 1985) [in Hebrew]; Ehud Yaari, *PLO* (Levin Evishtein, 1970), in Hebrew; Ehud Ya'ari, *Strike Terror* (New York: Sabra Books, 1970); Hillel Frisch, *The Establishment of Palestinian Institutions in the Territories 1967–1985*, doctoral thesis, Hebrew University, Jerusalem, 1989, in Hebrew; Yuval Arnon-Ohanna and Aryeh Yodfat, *PLO: A Tale of Organization* (Tel Aviv: Ma'ariv Press, 1985) (a similar book by the same authors has been published); Aryeh Yodfat and Yuval Arnon-Ohanna, *PLO: Strategy and Politics* (London: Croom Helm, 1981); Moshe Shemesh, *The Palestinian Entity: 1959–1974* (London: Frank Cass, 1988); Aaron David Miller, *The PLO and the Politics of Survival* (New York: Praeger, 1983); Ministry of Foreign Affairs, *The Threat of PLO Terrorism* (Jerusalem: Ministry of Foreign Affairs, 1985); Joseph Olmert, "Dissension in PLO: The Background, Path and Results of the Role of Syria," *Skrah Hodshit*, Vol. 30, No. 9 (September 1983), pp. 3–12, in Hebrew; Matti Steinberg and Yehoshua Porath, "The Meaning of Change in the PLO," *Skirah Hodshit*, Vol. 36, No. 8 (October 1989), pp. 3–12, in Hebrew; David Hakham and Yehoshua' Tiger, "The Crisis in PLO: From Exodus from Beirut to the Conference in Amman," *Skirah Hodshit*, Vol. 31, No. 11 (November 1984), pp. 3–12; Yuval Arnon-Ohanna, "The Attitude of the PLO Towards Israel: An Ideology Under Test," *Skirah Hodshit*, Vol. 27, No. 27 (October 1980), pp. 19–26, in Hebrew; Asher Sussar, "PLO: Intifada and Political Strategy," *Skirah Hodshit*, Vol. 37, No. 1 (December 1990), pp. 11–18, in Hebrew; Emmanuel Sivan, "The Dilemma of the PLO," *Migvan*, No. 61 (July 1981), pp. 27–29; and Matti Steinberg, "PLO: Changes After the Lebanese War," *Migvan*, No. 74–75 (October–November 1982), pp. 19–22.

110. Emile A. Nakhleh, "The West Bank and Gaza: Towards the Making of a Palestinian State," American Enterprise Institute for Public Policy Research, Washington, D.C., 1979.

111. Jerome M. Segal, *Creating the Palestinian State: A Strategy for Peace* (Chicago: Lawrence Hills, 1989), pp. 132–133.

112. Shukri Abed and Edy Kaufman, "The Relevancy of Democracy to the Resolution of the Israeli-Palestinian Conflict," unpublished paper.

CONCLUSION

12

Cooperation Across the Lines: Constraints and Opportunities

Robert L. Rothstein

I am neither an Israeli, nor a Palestinian, nor an expert on the Middle East. I am an American of Jewish extraction and a professor of international relations at Colgate University. How, then, did I become involved in this unusual collaborative venture among Israeli, Israeli Arab, and Palestinian scholars?

My involvement from a relatively early stage of this enterprise was in part accidental. I happened to be visiting Israel a few years ago, when one of the first meetings of the group was scheduled. Professors Ma'oz and Kaufman, feeling the need for some more general contribution on the problems of democratization and knowing that I was working on a book on the topic, asked whether I would participate in the project. I agreed because I think the project is potentially valuable, both practically and conceptually, and because I hoped I could make a useful contribution to this joint enterprise. My involvement has increased over time: I have participated in a variety of meetings, commented on the original draft of the papers, and agreed to add this conclusion to my original contribution of a piece on democracy and conflict. Still, my presence is something of an anomaly in the midst of an effort to generate cooperative work between Israelis and Palestinians. But, perhaps ironically, given the current and future involvement of the United States in the peace process (and, one hopes, in its aftermath), involvement by an American may be at least symbolically appropriate.

It does seem to me necessary, however, to clarify some aspects of my participation. In the first place, I share with the collaborators a desire to see established a democratic and potentially prosperous Palestinian state. But I am less optimistic than my colleagues that the mere creation of an entity, even if democratic, will resolve the conflict between Israel and the Palestinians or the rest of the Arab world. There are simply too many uncertainties and too many other factors at play: patterns of hatred and distrust that will not easily be dissipated; significant questions about economic viability and the availability of sufficient resources; worries about the possibility that the Palestinians will not be satisfied with the West Bank and Gaza and will begin demanding concessions in Israel itself; the likelihood that Islamic fundamentalists and various other groups opposed to the peace process will use any or all means to undermine a settlement; the continuation of regional rivalries; the tendency to use the conflict with Israel as a smoke screen behind which to pursue other goals; the list could go on. In such difficult circumstances, I would hope that, in exchange for an Israeli commitment to the phased creation of a demilitarized Palestinian state, the Palestinians would relinquish all claims to any other territorial changes and that the United States and perhaps the international community would provide security guarantees for Israel and promises of substantial financial aid for both Israel and the Palestinian entity-state.[1] It is in this context that I also think the extension of democracy to the Palestinians and, if possible, the rest of the region might make an important contribution, both psychologically and practically, to regional peace. I shall say more about this issue later.

Another introductory point is of some importance. This is a collection of essays that is meant to work at several levels. On one level—the level that I, as an outsider, find most congenial—all of the contributors have hoped to make an analytical or scholarly contribution to the debate about democratization in the Middle East or, more generally, the Third World. On another level, however, the participants have sought to send a signal both within and across the boundaries of conflict, a signal that meaningful intellectual cooperation is possible and that there are at least some shared interests and perspectives that could be useful in establishing a genuine peace between ancient antagonists. In this sense, this collection is one small step toward de-demonizing the image of the enemy. It is not the first such venture, although it is among the largest and most varied in terms of participants and subject matter, and we can only hope it will not be the last. Finally, at yet another level all the participants hope that some useful practical prescriptions for facilitating the democratization process will emerge from their joint efforts.[2]

At the same time, the intermingling of academic, symbolic, and political ideas has costs and dangers of its own. Balancing scholarly concerns (conceptual clarification, nuanced analysis, openness about premises, etc.) with symbolic and political concerns is never easy, and it certainly has not been in this instance. In the first place, there is inevitably some restraint about criticisms within the group, in part because easy and open criticism is difficult to establish across the lines of conflict (even between individuals who share many perspectives on that conflict) and in part because the very need to make political and symbolic points can undermine a completely evenhanded approach. One result has been some oversimplification and some bias in analysis. For example, two chapters sharply criticizing the decline in Israeli democracy are surely justified, but it would have been useful (and fair) to include a more balanced analysis of the benefits of Israeli democracy to its own citizens and to the region. After all, whatever the deficiencies of Israeli democracy, it is democratic, and all rights are not violated. One might ask in what Arab country this book itself could even be contemplated? Conversely, the Palestinian participants obviously have also been constrained in the expression of self-criticism, which is hardly surprising in the context of a protracted conflict and a felt need to maintain a unified public front.[3] Are the costs of these biases and constraints worth paying? The reader must judge for himself or herself, but I think the answer is yes: The symbolism of cooperation is important, there have been some joint learning efforts in the group's private and public meetings, and the chapters, despite the above comments, still contain much that is useful and informative.

Finally, there are some important missing links in the analysis of the potential impact of democratization on the Arab-Israeli conflict that we have not been able to cover. It would have been useful to have a chapter discussing the meaning of democracy in a Middle Eastern context—how we are defining the term and how its meaning may or may not differ from its meaning in the developed world. It would also have been useful to have a chapter discussing the relationship between democracy and socioeconomic performance because, however difficult it is to establish a clear relationship conceptually, the fate of democracy in poor countries is likely to rest on how well it meets citizens' material needs. In addition, it would have been useful to have a chapter discussing the kinds of political and economic strategies that might facilitate the survival of new and weak democracies. Perhaps more on regional trends toward (and away from) democratization might have provided a wider framework for the discussion of the Israeli-Palestinian relationship.[4] In any case, while I can barely touch the complexities of these issues and thus risk adding some oversimplications of my own, I shall in the next sections add a few brief comments on each.

Some Missing Analytical Links

Any discussions of democracy in the Arab world must be speculative. Any number of plausible arguments can be made about whether democracy will emerge, whether it will survive, and what effects it may or may not have. In such circumstances, one must be very careful to specify what this book is meant to be about and what meaning is being attributed to the idea of democracy in a Middle Eastern context. The first question has been largely answered: We have sought to describe and analyze various trends toward (and away from) democratization in the area and to suggest some reasons why these trends may or may not persist. Analysis has also prefaced some prescriptions about actions that might advance either democratization or the peace process. The second question, however, has not received the attention it deserves. To even begin to answer it, one needs to understand the conventional, Western interpretation of democracy and how well or badly that interpretation fits the circumstances of the Middle East.

Democracy is a classic instance of an "essentially contested concept." There is much disagreement about the appropriate theoretical framework, how to measure and evaluate democratic behavior, and the impact of various background conditions. Seeking a common meaning is probably futile because the disagreements cannot by resolved either by intellectual debate or by prolonged investigation of the real world.[5] As Connolly argues, the best we can do is to be precise about how we are using the term "democracy."[6] There is in the Western world one dominant usage that we have extrapolated to our analyses of Third World democracy.

Huntington has argued that a political system is democratic to the extent that its most powerful collective decisionmakers are selected through periodic elections in which candidates freely compete for votes and in which virtually all adults are eligible to vote.[7] As Dahl has noted, this definition implies that the key characteristic of democracy is the continuing responsiveness of government to the preferences of its citizens, who are considered political equals. The dimensions that measure the degree to which this ideal is approximated are the competitiveness of the political system and the amount and kind of political participation it permits.[8] One of the primary purposes of democracy is to dampen and resolve group conflict. Power is shared and dispersed (with much power outside the government in autonomous groups or associations), compromise agreements are reached through negotiations between shifting coalitions of groups, cleavages are moderate and not rigid, and there is much consensus on values. A culture of accommodation and moderation exists, especially among elites and political activists. The permanent tension between the government's need to govern and its need to be responsive to the preferences of its citizens is managed or moderated not only through various procedural devices (elections, parties, strong legislatures, etc.) but also by citizen attitudes that balance involvement and apathy (which presumably permits the government to govern). Note that this essentially procedural definition of democracy excludes any defined connection to socioeconomic conditions or to the results generated by the procedures.

This model of pluralist democracy, which probably seems reasonable to most citizens of Western countries, must be qualified by a number of familiar considerations. Differences in economic and social power, the growing influence of large bureaucracies, differences in access to information, and excessive apathy among large groups of citizens have given great power to the elites, leading indeed to the assertion that contemporary Western democracy can be best described as a kind of "legitimate oligarchy." Still, the political system remains at least relatively democratic to the extent that the elites are committed to maintaining a pluralist system and sharing power. On the part of the masses, high levels of affluence and expectations that the prospects for economic advancement will continue to grow (or, these days, that the prospects are better than in other systems) presumably generate continued support for, or inhibit active opposition to, a form of democracy that falls well short of the democratic ideal.

Criticisms of the pluralist model of democratic politics must be even more strongly stated in reference to the Third World. Inequalities in power, wealth, and information are vast and in many cases seem to be growing. The power and influence of the state and central bureaucracies are great in determining policies, if not in effectively implementing them. Societies are more rigidly factionalized, cultures and habits of mind seem less supportive of democracy, elite dominance is strong and pervasive—the list could go on. Nevertheless, given the fact that democracy always falls short of the ideal and is consequently a matter of degree of movement along a spectrum, not an either/or choice, are Third World countries too far away from that ideal to be considered genuine democracies? The great majority of Third World countries that we so designate achieve forms of democracy before they achieve a culture of democracy, which makes the forms weak. They represent some degree of political liberalization but not real democracy. Still, it seems pointless to invent another term for these hybrid regimes as long as we remember the qualifications, the distance from the ideal, and the limitations on what we can reasonably expect from such regimes.[9]

The differences between democracy in the Western world and democracy in the Third World are especially pronounced with regard to the Middle East. Middle Eastern experts tend to be divided into optimists, pessimists, and agnostics about the likelihood of a transition to democracy in the region. The optimists, it seems to me, take too seriously various grudging measures of political liberalization (elections, opposition parties, etc.) by reluctant democrats. Designed to relieve internal and external pressures, these steps could easily be reversed if the pressures dissipate or if the measures themselves begin to seem threatening to regime stability. Moreover, the absence of a democratic culture to support the forms and procedures of democracy with underlying predispositions toward compromise and toleration implies that commitment to democracy at least initially will be instrumental, especially among the public at large. The latter will surely greatly value the freedom from oppression that democracy provides, but unless democracy, after a honeymoon period, also begins to provide material benefits, its popularity will erode.[10] And it will be very difficult to provide these benefits in the context of rising expectations, an unstable world economy, and declining revenues from the sale of oil. Elections, parties, and formal commitments to civil liberties can be "exported," but democracy in its broader sense of a system of values cannot be exported. Nor, as we shall shortly see, can we safely assume that democracy will guarantee prosperity, which accounts for a major part of democracy's attractiveness in the Third World.

The pessimists, conversely, have very strong arguments vis-à-vis the short run but may be too downbeat about the long run. If democracy cannot be exported (especially to countries without experience of democracy) and if it is unlikely to be able to survive a prolonged period of declining economic performance, we should also emphasize that political liberalization can be built upon, that learning can take place, and that economic decline can be arrested. Tensions between rulers and ruled have increased, economic performance has declined, awareness of what is transpiring elsewhere has grown, and repression of demands for change may be less effective, especially if the reformers cannot be bought off.[11] All these things will take time to have some effect, perhaps longer than the time available if the peace process breaks down and conflict escalates. (Put differently, if we cannot safely assume that democracy in the short run will lead to peace, perhaps we ought to ask whether only a period of peace will allow democratic trends to deepen and intensify?) Nevertheless, the obstacles to democratization are formidable, and they might well be increased by adverse external developments and by self-fulfilling negative prophecies about how antithetical the Middle East is to democracy.

Some of the obstacles to democracy have already been noted. The power and brutality of the authoritarian states of the region repress any effective dissent and inhibit the development of autonomous civic groups and associations that effectively nurture a democratic spirit. The unity of the small group of ruling elites, their willingness to use any means to survive, and their close ties to other powerful groups make protest seem dangerous and futile. State-dominated economies make any movement toward the market problematic and indeed may make favored groups or individuals reluctant to challenge the authority of the state. In some states of the region, poverty, inequality, and low levels of development suggest that democracy may be "premature" (at least according to analysts who insist that stable democracy must rest on fulfillment of certain prerequisites), and in other, much richer states, the fear that democracy may threaten prosperity and the perquisites of the rich diminishes support for political change. These are important obstacles but they are not, according to the experts, as profound as two others: the prevailing social structure in Middle Eastern societies and, of course, the pervasive influence of Islam. As an outsider I am hardly expert enough about these matters to offer detailed comment, but I do want to say a brief word about how we ought to think about the *political* significance of social and religious issues.

One problem with much of the analysis of the impact of Islam and Islamic fundamentalism on democracy is that competing experts tend to pick through doctrine to find statements that support whatever position they are espousing and then come to an overly clear conclusion: Democracy and Islam are either totally incompatible (usually because of the absence of a clear separation between religion and the state) or easily compatible (because Islam supports justice, toleration, and other democratic values, or because Islamists in power will learn the need to play the democratic game). This kind of analysis may be useful and interesting, and perhaps one or the other point of view will in fact turn out to be generally correct. But it is also too narrow a framework, because the relationship between democracy and Islam or Islamic fundamentalism will not be determined by doctrine alone but rather by the interaction between doctrine and other matters, such as memories of the recent past, socioeconomic performance, internal polarization, and the state of the world economy. Moreover, looking closely at the experience of a few countries that have experienced Islamic rule (Iran, Sudan) or an Islamic fundamentalist challenge (Algeria, Jordan, Pakistan) is eminently useful, indeed indispensable, but also is not likely to provide the kind of broad framework necessary to put the democracy-Islam relationship in context.

Suppose we begin by asking: Why has Islamic fundamentalism become an important political problem at this time? Note that there have always been fundamentalists around—that is, "true believers"—who are impervious to compromise, indifferent to the values of others (such as development, equity, human rights), and intent on creating a society governed only by their own beliefs.[12] In some places, because of a degree of situational power, fundamentalists have managed to achieve more political influence than mere numbers might suggest. What analysts obviously fear is that Islamic fundamentalism will totally dominate some important Islamic countries (as in Iran), that they will use democratic rules and procedures to overthrow democracy, and that they will pursue policies that are dangerously destabilizing—terrorism, jihads, the acquisition of deadly weapons. The possibilities are surely there. The empirical record in Iran and the Sudan is hardly encouraging, and judgments about how to think about the fundamentalist threat or how to respond to it seem largely responses to passing events or personal predispositions. As a result, governments confronting the threat tend to respond inconsistently, alternating between ineffective repression and ineffective socioeconomic policies, thus losing even more legitimacy. The United States and its allies respond inconsistently, alternating support for authoritarians whose only "virtue" is their ability to repress effectively (such as the various anticommunist thugs the United States has backed) with a rather desperate quest to generate influence with the "moderates" in the fundamentalist camp.

Perhaps some progress can be made in clarifying the issue if we ask why fundamentalism has become so dangerous and so much of a political problem. In the past, most citizens were not greatly attracted to fundamentalism and were more concerned with their own material progress. But

deteriorating economic conditions and a loss of faith in the idea that better-
ment would soon be possible have generated massive frustration and discontent. Given the level of effective repression, which is the only thing
most governments were good at, the major (sometimes the only) arena for
the expression of that discontent was the mosque, especially mosques not
under heavy government control.[13] In the rich Gulf states, the availability
of massive financial resources allowed governments to buy off much discontent, lowering the demand for "goods" such as democracy and the free
expression of views. However, excessive corruption, unfair treatment of
minorities, or "guest workers," and increased educational levels (and
awareness of experience elsewhere) have also generated discontent in the
Gulf. In some places the discontent has manifested itself as a demand for
fundamentalism (which implies a shift from material to nonmaterial goals),
in other places as a demand for democracy, and in yet others as some mixture of the two. The discontent was galvanized by the Gulf War, Saddam's
spurious promises to share the wealth of the region more equitably, and his
military humiliation, all of which increased discontent because of another
Arab defeat and another Western (and Israeli) victory. Mass support for
fundamentalism thus results from repeated failures and disappointments
transformed into demands for an entirely different kind of society and an
entirely different set of goals.

The surge of fundamentalism is not likely to be turned back, at least as
a mass movement, unless there is an improvement in material conditions
for the majority of the population. Such gains can only be accomplished by
a development strategy that seeks both growth and equity, that reduces corruption and biased allocation of resources, that diverts some military
spending into development spending, and that receives some support from
abroad via foreign aid and private investment. Existing governments are
not likely to be willing or able to carry out such a strategy. A democratic
government also may not be capable of implementing the necessary
changes, especially if the economic and security environment remains
problematic, but it has a greater chance of doing so than a nondemocratic
one because it will be relatively more disposed to respond to mass needs, it
will have a honeymoon period in which to carry out necessary reforms, and
the other potential benefits of democracy—protection of human rights,
chances for personal self-fulfillment—may provide some counterweight
vis-à-vis economic sacrifices. Nevertheless, democracy is not a panacea. It
will be imperfect and supported instrumentally until it proves itself, and it
may very well fall victim to the forces of reaction and repression. Thus, the
next decade is likely to see a confused and confusing mixture of diverse
trends, with both democracy and radical Islam waxing and waning, but
without clear victory or defeat for either. Sharply improved material
prospects might make a democratic victory more likely in some countries;
conversely, sharply declining material prospects might make the revival of

oppression and militarism, with or without a theocratic rationale, more likely.

This argument is reinforced if we consider more generally the effects of religion on politics. In any cultural or religious movement there are likely to be a small number of strongly committed true believers. For them, the connection between religion and politics is direct and unmediated, unaffected by more worldly conditions. For followers, however, the effect is indirect and mediated by the circumstances of their lives. Without mass support, the movement is likely to remain peripheral and relatively unimportant politically. At a minimum, the degree and kind of support provided by most followers is contingent and dependent on changes in their social and political environments. Thus, considering a religious movement or any other movement as a monolithic challenge is usually misleading.[14] It misses not only important differences in national and local religious patterns of belief but also the distinctions between those who are impervious to change and those who are much more responsive to it. Put differently, if we want to understand the fundamentalist challenge, we must look beyond doctrinal disputes to such issues as the socioeconomic and political performance of various governments, the alternatives available to improve the quality of life for individuals and governments, and the demonstration effect from abroad. This perspective does not make fundamentalism any easier to deal with, and it surely does not imply that it will diminish in force in the near future, but it does at least clarify where we ought to be looking for solutions. It also implies that the solutions are long-term but the threats are immediate and that if the only alternatives left seem to be democracy or theocracy we have even stronger reasons to support the continued liberalization of Middle Eastern political systems.

A number of analysts have argued that the social structure of most Middle Eastern countries is also antithetical to democracy. Family and clan-based loyalties, patriarchal and hierarchical authority patterns, and strong patron-client relationships obviously make it difficult to develop a democratic civic culture, not to mention great trust or loyalty toward any central government. Apart from the fact that there are many variations in this pattern, I would only re-emphasize the point made about the effects of religion. Social structures cannot easily be changed, but they *can* be changed. Such structures are not immune to the pressures arising from urbanization, industrialization, improved standards of living, changes in labor mobility and family size, and so on. After all, very similar arguments were once made about the presumed inability of ethnic groups in the United States to adapt to a democratic political culture—they had, so the argument went, no experience with democracy and no affinity for it. But they quickly learned the benefits of democracy and how to play by its rules. In any case, initial support for democracy will almost always be instrumental; if democracy proves its worth, support will gradually become more powerful.

I do not mean by these arguments to imply that the obstacles to democracy in the Middle East are trivial or that the path to democratization will be easy. Brutally effective repression, money to buy off dissent, religious extremism, a difficult social structure—these are powerful disincentives. Nevertheless, they are not insurmountable. Middle Eastern nations cannot wholly isolate themselves from the inevitable effects of socioeconomic development or from the growing desires of their citizens to enjoy some of the same freedoms that exist elsewhere. The obstacles will delay democratization and perhaps make its arrival more costly and its consolidation more difficult, but they will not prevent a gradual movement toward political liberalization and ultimately genuine democracy. Perhaps, as in Eastern Europe, the supposed power of the central authorities will prove surprisingly brittle and the movement away from authoritarianism will accelerate.

The Benefits of Democracy in the Middle East

The arguments in the preceding section suggest that I am a restrained pessimist in the short run and a moderate optimist in the long run. Democracy will not come easily to the Middle East, and the process of transition will be long, difficult, and erratic. There will be some spectacular failures, I expect, but I doubt that even the formidable obstacles—powerful national security states, a difficult social structure, the reluctance to risk prosperity, and Islamic fundamentalism—will be able to overcome a long-term trend toward democratization. Democracy may also make some problems more difficult to resolve, if largely because its political logic is not always commensurate with economic logic. Given these limitations, one very important point must be kept in mind: The new and weak democracies that may emerge in the Middle East will not immediately achieve all the benefits of democracy, and their performance must be assessed not against abstract standards or the performance of developed democracies but against the record of the regimes they have replaced.

I have already noted in Chapter 2 that the argument that democracies do not fight other democracies is not immediately relevant in a Middle Eastern context. Moreover, the possibility that democracy might actually increase the likelihood of internal conflict cannot be dismissed, especially in the period before democracy becomes consolidated. What this argument implies is that, although the spread of democracy may indeed increase the likelihood of peace over the long run, we need to look elsewhere in the short run for arguments to justify strong support for democracy. One argument, of course, is that democracy is the only form of government with a high degree of moral legitimacy and with some possibility of earning the principled support of its constituents.[15] There is also a strong negative case for democracy: Other forms of government have failed dismally, and democracy is all that is left. Some democratic theorists have argued that democracy is not merely an instrumental value (say, as a superior means of resolving internal conflicts) but is also an end in itself because it permits and facilitates individual self-fulfillment. I generally agree with this argument but do not believe it is immediately relevant in a Third World context. Rather, given profound dissatisfaction with the status quo and a strong desire for change, support for democracy is likely to be sustained only if democracy promises better material results—effectively and fairly—than do available alternatives. The idea of democracy is widely popular now not only because of the desire to be free of oppression but also because it is, in the Third World, closely associated with the idea of prosperity. We shall ask if this association is justified.[16]

Questions about the relationship between democracy and economic development have been extraordinarily difficult to resolve. Does democracy impede or facilitate the achievement of high rates of economic growth? Or are its effects inconsequential? Are high levels of economic development a prerequisite for stable democracy? Do democracies or authoritarian regimes have better records in dealing with economic crisis? Which kind of regime is better at improving the distribution of income and providing all its citizens with a better standard of living? These and many other questions about the relationship between democracy and economic performance have been answered inconclusively. Huntington has thus argued that "apart from politics, the meaning of democracy is modest."[17]

The indictment against democracy is quite clear. Put simply and briefly, democracy politicizes the process of making economic decisions, thus sacrificing economic growth for consumption, generating runaway inflation, and imposing a short-run bias—the next election. Although some recent studies argue that democracy has a beneficial impact on economic growth, much of the empirical record tends to show the opposite. One recent review of thirteen empirical studies of the relationship between democracy and economic growth found three that showed a negative effect, six that found no relationship at all, and four that found mixed results.[18] The findings were similarly inconclusive or negative in terms of the effects of democracy on distribution of income, if largely because most Third World democracies are too poor to invest heavily in welfare policies.[19] Finally, although the new democracies have rather surprisingly survived the economic crises of the 1980s in reasonably good shape, they have not consistently done a better job than have authoritarian regimes at implementing either stabilization or reform packages.[20] Huntington's assertion that the economic meaning of democracy is modest seems justified as long as we ask only conventional questions about the effects of democracy on growth and equity. The inconclusive results are important because they warn against simple judgments about the economic consequences of democracy, but they are also unsurprising because economic outcomes are affected by many variables apart from the nature of the regime itself.

In a general way, these conclusions are sobering, if not disappointing. One would like conclusive results, especially results assuring us that democracy is able, or more able than the alternatives, to achieve desirable economic results and earn the trust and loyalty of the great majority of its citizens. But we do not have such results, and we are unlikely to get them soon because the performance of new democracies is likely to be erratic and inconsistent. Severe economic pressures may overwhelm any regime, and the time period has probably been too short to reach any strong conclusions about the effects of different regime types. Still, perhaps we can advance the argument a bit if we ask not whether democracies achieve outcomes that are better or worse than the outcomes of authoritarian regimes, but rather whether they have different strategies and different intentions than other regimes. And to answer this question, even in a very cursory fashion, we must draw on the experience of the few Third World countries that have been stable democracies since independence, despite decades of internal and external turbulence.[21]

The Third World and Eastern Europe are under immense pressure to undertake two liberalizations simultaneously—toward democracy and toward the market. Whatever their long-run compatibilities, democracy and economic liberalization obviously can be incompatible in the short run, the first reflecting some bias toward equality and the second some bias toward inequality. Many analysts of the problems of consolidating new democracies have advocated a conservative strategy of accommodation as a way to avoid or diminish these conflicts: Do not threaten rich or powerful interests, do not allow participation to "get out of hand," progress slowly so that political and technical skills can be developed effectively. One understands full well that a strategy of accommodation may seem necessary in the extraordinarily difficult internal and external circumstances confronting new democracies. But it is also a strategy that may fail because the temporary need for accommodation often becomes a permanent need to retain privilege and restrict participation. It seems to me not without interest that countries like Costa Rica have managed to maintain stability with a different kind of formula, one that may not satisfy either the International Monetary Fund or the staunchest supporters of democracy but has managed to allow them to muddle through a great many crises that have destroyed other regimes. Moreover, it is important to emphasize another point that we cannot pursue in detail at this time. Although it has not been possible to establish clear relationships between democracy and either economic growth or the raw distribution of income, all of the stable, long-term Third World democracies score much higher on various quality of life or human development indexes that could be anticipated from per capita GNP levels.

This implies that their governments have used an important share of their revenues to reduce some of the effects of poverty and to indicate an intention to create a more equitable society. In short, if we look only at Third World democracies that have survived for at least twenty years, and not the wider number of sometime-democracies, the "modest meaning" of democracy in socioeconomic terms may not be quite so modest.

There is a standard cliche in the development literature: Economic performance must be both fair and effective. Difficulties arise when it is not possible to get both at once, and cruel choices become necessary. But difficulties also arise if economic trade-offs are made too narrowly, if economic choices are made entirely in economic terms, or if political choices ignore questions of economic efficiency. Some economic inefficiencies can be politically necessary: for example, a large bureaucracy that provides jobs or welfare spending that buffers the poor. At some point, such inefficiencies may generate more problems than they resolve, but that calculation must be carefully made and not imposed by ideology or by the tacit assumption, so congenial to many economists, that politics is an evil to be avoided. Consolidating democratic government, while inextricably linked to economic performance, is in itself a higher goal than the achievement of any particular economic outcome.

Democracy will not survive if it offers only elections, competitive parties, and relief from oppression. Only democracy can restore faith in the civic community and generate increased possibilities for individual self-fulfillment. It will be able to provide all of these benefits only if its economic performance is relatively effective (so as not to revive the appeal of discredited alternatives) and, above all, if it establishes among the citizenry a perception of both increasing capacity to meet citizens' needs and benign intent. There must be a clear intent to increase opportunities for all, to share the pain of adjustment and the benefits of success, and to provide some special help for the disadvantaged. Providing evidence of these intentions generates some political space to take other painful but necessary actions. The state has a large role in this strategy, but only where the market functions badly and where social needs must prevail over economic rationality. In effect, a gradualist approach that rests on initial accommodation with the rich and powerful may be necessary, but it is not sufficient. Only a balanced strategy that worries as much about equity as growth and as much about political consolidation as economic rationality can lead to stable democracy and the management of rising expectations.[22]

This balanced strategy is hardly a cure-all. Mistakes can be made in calculating trade-offs, unanticipated events can undermine even sensible policy choices, and the experiences of the past may make the compromises of the present difficult to accept. Much depends on the wisdom and unity of the elites, because they must understand the need to sustain the democratic system itself and to sacrifice some benefits in exchange for social peace and regime stability. Elite unity and cooperation will not everywhere be present, perhaps because of ethnic conflict or intense resource shortages, which implies that stable democracy will fail in some instances.

I have the strong impression that stable democracies in the Third World—countries such as Costa Rica, Jamaica, India, and even Israel (as part of a Third World region)—have attempted at least an approximation of the major themes of this strategy. Details vary greatly and degrees of success and failure are different. No single blueprint will work everywhere or guarantee success in the midst of profound internal and external problems. Still, if some Middle Eastern countries begin to democratize in the current policy environment, and if they need to develop a strategy to consolidate both political and economic liberalization in the midst of rising demands and insufficient resources (barring the rich Gulf States), perhaps they can learn some useful lessons from the experiences of other democracies that have survived internal conflicts, high levels of poverty, cultures that are not entirely compatible with democracy, and a dangerous international environment. A strategy of accommodation with the rich and powerful and the gradual implementation of structural reforms may be imperative in the short run, but it will not lead to a genuine democratic regime unless the new government displays a clear intention to seek a more equitable society. The government must be more than the guardian of the market, and the elites must be committed to democracy and shared prosperity. If not, is there much point in calling an inequitable oligarchy democratic because it holds elections?

Conclusions

Democracy will come slowly to the Middle East, the forms and procedures appearing well before the beliefs and values that support them. Initial support is thus likely to be instrumental—what is democracy doing for me now?—which implies that new and weak governments will be under tremendous pressure to respond quickly to the demands of citizens whose hopes and expectations have been smashed by brutal authoritarian regimes. In such circumstances, democratic forms and procedures may themselves be misused or appropriated by the forces of repression. People may rapidly become disenchanted, especially if they compare their new democracy to an ideal picture (government of, by, and for the people) and not to the previous regime. They may even welcome back or tolerate the return of authoritarianism. The stability and predictability of the latter may even come to seem preferable to the messiness of democratic politics and the uncertainty that is implicit in democratic policymaking—in effect, a psychological "escape from freedom."

We need to be very cautious about any inferences that we draw from the analysis of developed-country democracies. We call various countries in the Third World "democratic," but they are at best a rough approximation of anyone's definition of democracy. Most of these regimes, and especially the new democracies, are hybrids, mixing persisting elements of authoritarianism and newer elements of democracy. We cannot simply take it on faith that such regimes will behave as more established democracies have behaved in the past. We cannot even safely assume that the democratic elements will inevitably triumph over the authoritarian elements. What we need at the moment are not expressions of faith about democracy but rather hard analysis of the strategies that might deepen democracy and resist the forces opposed to it.

I have already noted the many factors that may serve as obstacles to democratization.[23] But it would be wrong to be completely pessimistic, because democracy can be deepened. The social changes attendant on economic development will continue to generate pressures for liberalization, international pressures to democratize are likely to continue, and existing regimes—no matter how opposed they are to any relaxation of controls—may have no choice but to accept some opening if citizens are asked once again to bear the costs of economic adjustment.[24] It is also not entirely irrelevant to note that most of the stable Third World democracies (and Israel) did not have a democratic culture before acquiring democratic forms and procedures. Nor did they have a very high level of development when the latter were established. Yet they were able to instill some aspects of a democratic culture, achieve enough prosperity to survive, and earn enough trust and legitimacy to ride out some very tough times. Both masses and elites have thus seemed to internalize the values of democracy in these countries, at least to some important degree.

The potential effects of democratization on the peace process are unclear. The peace process may well have come to an end, good or bad, before democracy has any effect at all. If the peace process continues and if democratization also begins to accelerate—a big if—the *long-run* effects could be very beneficial. As Mark Tessler has noted, democracy may provide legitimate channels for public protest about something other than Israel, thus lowering the centrality of Israel in Arab political debates. There also may be less need to use Israel as a scapegoat to deflect attention from governmental failures.[25] Perhaps most significantly, the presence of democracy in a Palestinian entity-state and perhaps in other parts of the Arab world may increase shared interests in preserving domestic regimes by avoiding war and preserving the shared values and norms that make the absence of war possible.[26] There will also be less need to fear that any agreement made with one dictator will be broken by his successor. Finally, democracy could well be subverted by Islamic fundamentalists, but in the long run democracy is also probably the only form of government that may serve as an effective bulwark against religious or other forms of extremism.[27]

We do at least have one small empirical illustration of the benefits of democracy. In Chapter 7, Rouhana and Ghanem show how socioeconomic development has altered family structures in the Israeli Arab community. Such things as increased education, the movement away from agriculture, and the entrance of women into the labor force have begun to create patterns of authority and changes in thinking that facilitate modernization and the acceptance of democratic values. Perhaps more important, Rouhana and Ghanem argue that the experience of living in a democratic society has inculcated some elements of a culture of democracy (the need for compromise, the rights of the opposition, etc.) and "taken out a fuse of violence." In short, even if this Palestinian community supports the intifada, it has resisted using violence (with some exceptions) in pursuit of its goals. One hardly needs to note that the costs of using violence, in terms of Israeli retaliation, were also consequential here. Nevertheless, the modernization, secularization, and relative moderation of this community send an important signal that Islamic beliefs are not necessarily antithetical to democratization and that democratization, in turn, may foster attitudes and beliefs conducive to peaceful settlement of ancient conflicts.

The values of Western democracy are nearly everywhere accepted, and the discussion of democracy is usually carried on in the framework of liberal democracy. Of course, support for the rhetoric and support for the reality of democracy are widely divergent. Many Third World intellectuals genuinely support democracy, and many of the masses support it because it signifies to them change and prosperity, but the ruling elites and the upper classes are at best reluctant converts. As a result, the democracy that we shall see emerging will be weak, fragile, and incomplete. It must be said, however, that even this kind of democracy is preferable to the governments most Third World and Middle Eastern citizens have had to endure. In any case, only by supporting weak democracy can we prepare the ground for strong democracy. The procedural definition of democracy is inadequate in the Third World because we cannot presume the existence of the culture of accommodation that makes democracy work. And that cultural foundation and the local associations and groups that provide a training ground for democracy are unlikely to emerge or prosper in an environment of fear. Democracy may not succeed in the Third World or in the Middle East, but the risks of failure are well worth taking.

Notes

1. For my views on the peace process, see "Getting to Maybe: Large Steps to End a Large Stalemate in the Arab-Israeli Peace Process," *The Jerusalem*

Quarterly, No. 52 (Fall 1989), pp. 79–107, and "The Middle East After the War: Change and Continuity," *Washington Quarterly,* Vol. 14, No. 3 (Summer 1991), pp. 139–160.

2. I think we as a group have been less successful in this regard because much of the focus is on what has and has not been done in the past. Thus, too little attention has been paid to the issue of how to consolidate a new democracy in a difficult environment.

3. One would have liked, for example, more open comment on the problem of Palestinians killing other Palestinians who may be cooperating with Israel, on the reasons for supporting Saddam's brutal aggression against Kuwait (which undermined PLO assertions that oppose territorial acquisitions by force), and on the nature of other Arab political regimes. The absence of comment weakens the strong moral case that the Palestinians have for fairer treatment of their needs.

4. There are other studies underway that may diminish the significance of the absence of wider coverage of regional trends.

5. As Jack Lively notes in *Democracy* (New York: St. Martin's Press, 1975), p. 146, "No definition of democracy can be found by gazing at the real world, no matter how meticulous the inspection."

6. William E. Connolly, *The Terms of Political Discourse* (Lexington, Mass.: D. C. Heath, 1974), pp. 22–32.

7. Samuel P. Huntington, "Will More Countries Become Democratic?" *Political Science Quarterly,* Vol. 99, No. 2 (Summer 1984), p. 195. Some would add other characteristics, such as the rule of law and the protection of civil and political rights.

8. Robert A. Dahl, *Polyarchy Participation and Opposition* (New Haven: Yale University Press, 1971), pp. 2ff.

9. There is an important school of analysis that focuses on the prerequisites for democracy. For sophisticated treatment see Huntington, "Will More Countries?" and Dahl, *Polyarchy.* I shall not comment further on these matters because they do not change the thrust of the argument.

10. Recent abortive coups in Venezuela and Trinidad and Tobago and an apparently successful coup in Haiti are instructive in this regard.

11. Various socioeconomic trends, such as increased literacy, wider availability of communications technology, and the expansion of the middle class will also increase pressures for liberalization.

12. The true believers shift the grounds for evaluation from conventional indices (economic performance, etc.) to the implementation of God's will, which only they can interpret. One should note that this phenomenon has also appeared in Israeli society, although not yet to quite the same effect.

13. The governments of the region, fearful of their own citizens, also tend to appoint to key security positions only those whose fate depends on regime survival: Alawites in Syria, Tikritis in Iraq, members of various royal families.

14. On the ambiguous and frequently indeterminate effect of sets on belief on political behavior, note earlier judgments about the effects of Confucianism in East Asia. The same characteristics (hard work, willingness to save, hierarchical patterns of authority, etc.) that were once used to explain why these countries could never develop a market economy or a free society are now used to explain why they have succeeded to some important degree in doing so.

15. Note also that democracy may now provide the major practical and moral grounds for receiving foreign aid.

16. I have not discussed all the advantages, or indeed the disadvantages, of democracy because of space constraints.

17. Samuel P. Huntington, "The Modest Meaning of Democracy," in Robert A. Pastor, ed., *Democracy in the Americas: Stopping the Pendulum* (New York: Holmes and Meier, 1989), p. 25.

18. See Larry Sirowy and Alex Inkeles, "The Effects of Democracy on Economic Growth and Inequality: A Review," in Alex Inkeles, ed., *On Measuring Democracy* (New Brunswick, N.J.: Transaction Publishers, 1991), pp. 132ff. For a study arguing the economic benefits of democracy, see Gerald W. Scully, "The Institutional Framework of Economic Development," *Journal of Political Economy,* Vol. 96, No. 3 (1988), pp. 657–658.

19. See Sikowy and Inkeles, "The Effects of Democracy," pp. 135–136.

20. For a good introduction to this debate, see Karen L. Remmer, "The Politics of Economic Stabilization—IMF Standby Programs in Latin America, 1954–1984," *Comparative Politics,* Vol. 36, No. 3 (October 1986), pp. 20ff.

21. The comments that follow draw on a longer work-in-progress that I do not wish to cite at this time.

22. One important point here is that, even if democracies do not consistently outperform some or many nondemocratic regimes, the display of benign intentions may affect citizen support and regime legitimacy. This is, of course, not to deny the other attractions of democracy in terms of freedom from oppression, which may give new democracies a more extended honeymoon period than new authoritarian regimes.

23. See Chapter 8 by Shukri Abed in this volume for other comments on this issue. The obstacles include the role of the state, ethnic conflicts, high degrees of inequality, a weak educational system, and, of course, Islam and a tribalized social structure.

24. There are also some signs, as yet not very deep, of the emergence of a stronger civil society in some Arab countries, but the experts disagree about how important these signs are.

25. See Mark Tessler, "Some Propositions about Democracy in the Arab World and Its Relationship to the Israeli-Palestinian Conflict," paper prepared for the American Academy, April 1991. One should also note that over time, democracies tend to spend less on the military and to confront less costly civic violence.

26. See Chapter 2 for more detailed comment. On the downside of this argument, the protracted Arab-Israeli conflict may go on for a long time whatever the governing regime, because both sides really want *all* the territory in conflict and it is not clear that any compromise agreement will alter this. In addition, it is also a conflict between different cultures and *weltanschaungs,* and these are notoriously difficult to resolve. The slow development of a common democratic culture may help in this context.

27. Perhaps only governments that are legitimate can take the risks of peace in the Middle East, but how true this is likely to be will depend on how bellicose the mass public really is—or, perhaps, whether the achievement of democracy will diminish the frustrations generating the demand for a jihad against Israel. Note that the notion that only a legitimate or popular government (presumably democratic) can impose unpopular policies conflicts with the old notion that only authoritarian governments can impose unpopular policies.

Index

The Contributors

Shukri B. Abed is a senior fellow at the Center for International Development and Conflict Management (CIDCM) at the University of Maryland-College Park. Between 1986 and 1991 he was affiliated with the Harry S Truman Institute for the Advancement of Peace at the Hebrew University of Jerusalem. The focus of his research and teaching is Islamic and Arabic culture, and he has published several books and articles on the subject.

Edy Kaufman, who served as the executive director of the Harry S Truman Institute for the Advancement of Peace, is currently on leave from the Hebrew University of Jerusalem and director of CIDCM at the University of Maryland-College Park. A political scientist, he specializes in human rights and international relations topics with regional focus on Latin America and the Middle East. His special interest in promoting Israeli-Palestinian academic cooperation contributed to the development of this study, which he coordinated as project director.

Ziad Abu-Amr is a professor in the Department of Political Science at Bir Zeit University. He is author of a book (published in Arabic) on Islamic movements in the West Bank and Gaza Strip.

As'ad Ghanem is a Ph.D. candidate in the department of political science at Haifa University, where he is coordinator of the Arab Jewish Center.

Manuel Hassassian is associate professor of international politics and relations and dean of the Faculty of Arts at Bethlehem University on the West Bank. Specializing in comparative politics, with an emphasis on the Middle East, his latest book is *Palestine: Factionalism in the National Movement, 1919–1939.*

Charles S. Liebman is professor of political science and director of the Argov Center for the Study of Israel and the Jewish people at Bar-Ilan University. In addition to his research interests in the sociology of American Jews, he has published numerous books and articles concerning religion and politics in Israel. His most recent book, coauthored with Steven Cohen, is *Two Worlds of Judaism: The Israeli and American Experiences.*

Moshe Ma'oz is professor of Islamic and Middle East Studies and chairperson of the Harry S Truman Institute for Advancement of Peace at the Hebrew University of Jerusalem. He is the author of several books and many articles on Middle East-related topics, including *Palestinian Leadership on the West Bank* and the political biography *Asad: The Sphinx of Damascus.*

Alon Pinkas is currently the Policy Adviser to Foreign Minister Shimon Peres. Formerly an assistant military attaché at the Israeli Embassy in Washington, Mr. Pinkas was later the military correspondent of the *Jerusalem Post* and a columnist of U.S. affairs for *Davar*. He is completing his doctoral dissertation on the US-Israeli strategic relationship.

Robert L. Rothstein is Harvey Picker Distinguished Professor of International Relations at Colgate University. He has written five books and edited or coedited two others and is currently working on a book about the domestic and international implications of Third World democratization.

Nadim Rouhana cochairs a seminar on international conflict analysis and resolution at the Center for International Affairs, Harvard University.

About the Book

This important book tests the relevance for resolving the Arab-Israeli conflict on the assumption that democratic countries do not wage war against one another. In the process, the authors address two fundamental questions: Can Israel remain democratic while facing recurrent wars and exercising military rule over a large disenfranchised population? And can the Palestinians become a democratic polity, given the historical, religious, and cultural obstacles they confront?

The themes shared by the authors—Palestinian, Israeli, and U.S. scholars—allow the expectation that the broad ideas and specific arguments found in the book will be instrumental to the peace process.